The International Companion to Nineteenth-Century Scottish Literature

INTERNATIONAL COMPANIONS TO SCOTTISH LITERATURE

Series Editors: Ian Brown and Thomas Owen Clancy

Titles in the series include:

International Companion to Lewis Grassic Gibbon
Edited by Scott Lyall
ISBN 978-1-908980-13-7

International Companion to Edwin Morgan
Edited by Alan Riach
ISBN 978-1-908980-14-4

International Companion to Scottish Poetry
Edited by Carla Sassi
ISBN 978-1-908980-15-1

International Companion to James Macpherson and The Poems of Ossian
Edited by Dafydd Moore
ISBN 978-1-908980-19-9

International Companion to John Galt
Edited by Gerard Carruthers and Colin Kidd
ISBN 978-1-908980-27-4

International Companion to Scottish Literature 1400–1650
Edited by Nicola Royan
ISBN 978-1-908980-23-6

International Companion to Scottish Literature of the Long Eighteenth Century
Edited by Leith Davis and Janet Sorensen
ISBN 978-1-908980-31-1

International Companion to Nineteenth-Century Scottish Literature
Edited by Sheila M. Kidd, Caroline McCracken-Flesher, and Kenneth McNeil
ISBN 978-1-908980-35-9

The International Companion to Nineteenth-Century Scottish Literature

Edited by Sheila M. Kidd,
Caroline McCracken-Flesher,
and Kenneth McNeil

Scottish Literature International

Published by
Scottish Literature International
Scottish Literature
7 University Gardens
University of Glasgow
Glasgow G12 8QH

Scottish Literature International is an imprint of
the Association for Scottish Literature

www.asls.org.uk

ASL is a registered charity no. SC006535

First published 2022

Text © ASL and the individual contributors

All rights reserved. No part of this book may be
reproduced, stored in a retrieval system, or
transmitted in any form or means, electronic,
mechanical, photocopying, recording or otherwise,
without the prior permission of the
Association for Scottish Literature.

A CIP catalogue for this title
is available from the British Library

ISBN 978-1-908980-35-9

Contents

Series Editors' Preface vii
Acknowledgements ix

Introduction: The Strangeness of Centuries 1
Sheila M. Kidd, Caroline McCracken-Flesher, and Kenneth McNeil

PART 1: EXPERIMENTS 5
Sheila M. Kidd, Caroline McCracken-Flesher, and Kenneth McNeil

1. Gaelic Poets and New Patterns of Patronage 9
   Ruairidh Maciver
2. Inspiring Songs: The Rise of Ballad Culture 18
   Valentina Bold
3. The Novel: Romance and History 26
   Pam Perkins
4. Slavery, Kinship, and Capital 33
   Michael Morris
5. Private Thoughts and Public Display: Gender,
   Genre, and Lives 42
   Susan Oliver
6. The Gothic, Supernatural and Religious 50
   Samuel Baker
7. Drama and Adaptation 58
   Barbara Bell
8. The Short Story to 1832 64
   Thomas C. Richardson

PART 2: CONSOLIDATIONS 72
Sheila M. Kidd, Caroline McCracken-Flesher, and Kenneth McNeil

9. Diaries and Letters 77
   Paul Barnaby
10. Public Education, Science, and Metaphor 85
    Cairns Craig
11. Religion and Popular Literature in Scotland: The Literary
    Imagination as Inspiration 93
    Alison Jack
12. Social Comment 100
    Regina Hewitt

Contents (continued)

13. 'Urban Folk': Scottish Victorian Adaptations and Transmutations of Earlier Verse Traditions. 108
    C. M. Jackson-Houlston
14. Gaelic Literature of the Diaspora 115
    Sheila M. Kidd
15. David Pae, the Newspaper Novel, and the Imagined Community of North Britain 125
    Graham Law
16. Industrial-Strength Fiction: Margaret Oliphant and James Grant 132
    Joanne Wilkes
17. Scottish Travel Writing 140
    Jennifer Hayward
18. Travel Writing about the Highlands in the Nineteenth Century. 148
    Nigel Leask

PART 3: EXPANSIONS 156
Sheila M. Kidd, Caroline McCracken-Flesher, and Kenneth McNeil

19. City Songs 161
    Kirstie Blair
20. Gaelic Political Poetry 1870–1900 170
    Priscilla Scott
21. The Kailyard Novelists 180
    Andrew Nash
22. The International Author: Robert Louis Stevenson 188
    Lesley Graham
23. Celticists and Anthropologists. 194
    Michael Shaw
24. Science and Speculation. 203
    Julia Reid
25. Scotland's New Women. 210
    Juliet Shields

Endnotes 217
Further Reading 267
Notes on Contributors 269
Index 275

Series Editors' Preface

There was a time when the period this *Companion* deals with was considered as relatively barren in terms of Scottish literatures – despite its brilliant opening with such writers as Walter Scott, Ailean Dall, and James Hogg, and concluding with figures of such importance as Robert Louis Stevenson, Màiri Mhòr nan Òran, and J. M. Barrie. Yet, if there is one thing that the study of those literatures over the last twenty years has demonstrated, it is that such a perception is misguided. We are grateful to the distinguished contributors to the volume who make clear the positive contribution of nineteenth-century authors to the literatures of Scotland. Above all, we are grateful to Sheila M. Kidd, Caroline McCracken-Flesher, and Kenneth McNeil for their energetic collaboration on this volume. Their attentive and meticulous editorship has not only drawn on recent scholarship but has helped extend its depth and range.

The editors' decision to organise the chapters under the headings 'Experiments', 'Consolidations', and 'Expansions' is a constructive means of emphasising the dynamic ways in which literature in Scotland's languages developed, interacted, and changed throughout the nineteenth century. The very decision to use plurals in each heading highlights the fact that there can be no simple narrative in discussing that century's Scottish literature. This *Companion* draws fruitful attention to the varieties and complexities of that literature as it developed and does so with fluency and scholarship accessibly expressed.

The International Companion to Nineteenth-Century Scottish Literature provides a fascinating and fresh continuation of the revelations to be found in *The International Companion to Scottish Literature of the Long Eighteenth Century* and feeds into the earlier explorations of *The Edinburgh Companion to Twentieth-Century Scottish Literature*. In doing so it joins a series of period *Companions* covering Scottish literature since 1400.

This sequence will be completed when, in due course, a planned volume on the period before 1400 emerges.

Ian Brown
Thomas Owen Clancy

Acknowledgements

Companion volumes seek to accompany their audience in exploration of territory sometimes unfamiliar. In this book, the editors seek to remap a landscape we often think we know. Readers may find new ways of getting pleasurably lost, make unexpected discoveries, develop new understandings. As editors we have been immeasurably lucky to have as our companions not just one another, but our colleagues at the ASL: our commissioning editors Ian Brown and Thomas Owen Clancy, and Director Duncan Jones, who has been our constant support. We are grateful to our contributors for their expertise and the excitement they have brought to this project, indicating significant and often neglected materials, and challenging us with today's questions.

We are grateful, too, for the work of predecessors in important volumes like *The History of Scottish Literature, Volume 3*, edited by Douglas Gifford (1988), *Scotland's Books*, by Robert Crawford (2007), *The Edinburgh History of the Book in Scotland, Volume 3: Ambition and Industry 1800–1880*, edited by Bill Bell (2007), *Scotland and the Nineteenth-Century World*, edited by Gerard Carruthers et al. (2012), *Caran an t-Saoghail (The Wiles of the World): An Anthology of Nineteenth-Century Scottish Gaelic Verse*, edited by Donald E. Meek (2003), *Popular Literature in Victorian Scotland*, by William Donaldson (1986), and *The Edinburgh History of Scottish Literature, Volume 2: Enlightenment, Britain and Empire (1707–1918)*, edited by Susan Manning (2007), to name but a few. Colleagues like Penny Fielding and Alan Riach have been generous advisers throughout.

At our home institutions, we thank supportive department chairs and deans, and of course our essential colleagues in libraries and interlibrary loan at the universities of Glasgow, Eastern Connecticut State, and Wyoming.

And thanks, as always, to our families, who by now are probably experts in the Scottish nineteenth century in their own right.

Introduction: The Strangeness of Centuries

Sheila M. Kidd, Caroline McCracken-Flesher, and Kenneth McNeil

The nineteenth century is the great undiscovered country for Scottish literary studies. Or at least, it has been mapped by twentieth-century criticism and politics to the extent that it is difficult to see the territory. This book aims to remap the century to showcase the complexity of a period and place. It hopes to lay open to today's readers, to future scholars, and to students, new horizons for knowledge and understanding.

From a twentieth-century perspective the prior century's literature was deadened by the lack of a national polity and the consequence: lost opportunities for progress. What was there to say any more that was worth saying? Worse, modernists thought, their predecessors had focused on the market – considered as British or, eventually, imperial – and either forgot or sold for profit the distinctive Scottishness that should have built a national discourse to rival that of England. For Edwin Muir, working to establish a 'Scottish Renaissance', nineteenth-century authors were to be abjured as agents that had subsumed Scottish literature into a wholly English paradigm of 'progress' in which it would always be deemed behind the times.[1] Twentieth-century Gaelic critics were equally disparaging of what Donald Meek has more recently described as 'this much-misunderstood century'.[2] Sorley MacLean dismissed much of the century's Gaelic poetry as 'flabby and anaemic' with its literary output failing to measure up to either of the centuries which flanked it.[3] Characteristic of this critical approach was an unwillingness to embrace the diversity and international nature of poets and writers, or to engage meaningfully with the falteringly emergent periodical press. A more confident Scotland, in this twenty-first century, increasingly sees a more interesting and vibrant story – a multiplicity of more interesting stories – to be told of a time when Scots stood to the fore (for better and also for worse) in fields from literature to geology to thermodynamics to emigration and workers' and women's opportunities.

No longer anxious about English influence in part because that influence seems less worthy of emulation, today's critics can pursue those challenges previously obscured by an undue concern with traditions and canons (whether pro or con). As Cairns Craig recognised, a crucial 'feature of our ordinary lives is one which is almost impossible to recreate in narrative, and that is simultaneity'.[4] Critical narratives in thrall to power tell only one tale; but as master- and counter- narratives stumble over their necessary parameters, Scotland's many stories, with their imprecise, jumbled and contesting boundaries, stand out – amplified, multiplied, exciting.

Expressing the complexity of nineteenth-century Scottish writing surely begins with the problem of centuries. What sets one century off from another, and why? The answer is ... nothing really. Culture is various, challenging, uneven all the time. Thus, this book stands in context of the *Companions* that precede and follow it, and interrelate with it. It owns its debt to Enlightenment ballad collectors; it hears the silence that resounds from cleared landscapes; it anticipates the turn to a globalised literary politics.

Scholars increasingly have recognised the richness of the Scottish nineteenth century. Recent critics have seen in the period the genesis of a 'green' Scotland; they have tracked down Scots, their influences, and their responsibility in the Caribbean; ploughed over the Kailyard and found beneath it fertile ground for Scots in an international context; heard Gaelic voices resounding in distant places; and sensed the alternate dimensions of a nation both Scottish and advanced in science.[5]

This volume aims to honour the many modes, contexts, and languages of Scottish literary expression through the nineteenth century. Knowing that periodisation has its problems, yet recognising that moments matter, it organises its materials in three sections that acknowledge pressures at once social, literary, and industrial.

Part 1: Experiments, sees gentleman collectors yield to Romantic poets; new systems of patronage evolve for Gaelic poets; novels burgeon and theatre embrace their plots; transatlantic traffic include cleared Gaels, ambitious colonists, and enslaved peoples; celebrity comes in conflict with the personal and private; and the steam press rattle everything into print. And that is all before 1832. Walter Scott's death offers a convenient, longstanding but insufficient marker between moments.

Here, as with the strangeness of centuries, a division may operate on one level, but not another. Scott was gone, but the novel went from strength to strength; the Gaels were on the move, but so were the colonists. And all were borne along on tides of print.

Part 2: Consolidations, reflects how changes in society and the speed of publishing together instantiated a period of literary expression that was both public in direction and popular in reception. The private emerged into print as letters and journals found wide readership; magazine, newspaper, and novel publishing surged to industrial strength; markets opened and diversified with an increasingly literate public. Famed for its journals, Scotland added to the *Edinburgh Review* and *Blackwood's* specialist journals like *Chambers*, that advanced the cause of science and technology for working people, and *Tait's* that, under the editorship of Christian Isobel Johnstone, pursued radical causes – including proto-feminism. Songs expressed a labouring public and novels anthropologised a shifting society; Gaelic literature gained a distinctively international dimension. Scotland, like the rest of the world, was on the move, gathering pace and range in publishing and in person.

Part 3: Expansions, suggests how far that movement could go, physically and intellectually. Scots had long looked outward, and international tourism looked toward Scotland. Now that two-way traffic, assisted by steamships and early telecommunications, united and problematised a Scottish world from the Highlands to Cape Breton; from the parochial 'Drumtochty' to the cities of America and the foothills of Samoa. At the same time, the social implications of developing sciences shaped new sensibilities that surface in proto-science fiction, social problem novels, challenges to gender norms, and the imagination of better pasts and futures. On the cusp of the twentieth century, Scottish literature remained on the move.

Readers of this book will find that it both assists and resists the mapping we take for granted when we survey literary landscapes. The immediate and the very precisely local stand close up against the global; the songs of labour echo the ballads of a past perhaps romantic yet real; subaltern stories intrude upon master tales; the far away voice echoes at home. To read it, then, we hope will prove both a pleasure and a challenge. Those seeking to track a theme or a genre can do so, from period to period; those pursuing a language, be it Gaelic, Scots, or English also can do so – always remembering that those languages joined in conversation with a wider world through the opportunities and problems of emigration, enterprise, and empire. At the same time, those who choose to dwell in a moment may be astounded by its variety of voice, genre, challenge, and interest.

What the editors hope, most of all, is that encountering the many literatures and languages of nineteenth-century Scotland, readers will set aside assumptions, and see with new eyes what is actually there.

PART 1: EXPERIMENTS

Sheila M. Kidd, Caroline McCracken-Flesher, and Kenneth McNeil

Historians of our century have looked back on the period from 1800 to 1832 as an age of innovation and expansion in Scottish publishing, a golden age of print when Scottish cities, particularly Edinburgh, came to rival and sometimes surpass London as the centre of the British book trade. Even those living through the age could perceive its unprecedented nature. Henry Cockburn (1779–1854), admittedly in retrospect, described the 'instant and universal impression' that the 1814 publication of Walter Scott's (1771–1832) *Waverley* made in Scotland's capital, which came as an 'electric shock of delight' at the 'unexpected newness of the thing'.[1] Innovative, impressive, unprecedented – these are the terms associated with the period, but even so, as is the case for all historical periods, the foundations of Scotland's golden age of print were built upon trends of the previous era. After all, Walter Scott, the Wizard of the North, had begun his literary career working in the antiquarian-inflected genre of ballad collecting that had commenced in the eighteenth century, appropriating in book form for a high-brow readership traditional Scottish Border ballads, many he had heard from childhood. As James Macpherson (1736–1796) had done with his Ossian 'manuscripts' in the later eighteenth century, Scott also silently reshaped his material as he committed it to paper, but unlike Macpherson's, Scott's reworkings inspired no great controversy as to their authenticity. Though spoken-word balladeering and poetry lived on and adapted, as they circulated and were disseminated in a matrix of formal and informal print and public performance, antiquarian writers, particularly in English, sought to preserve in print the material of a traditional world they felt was in danger of becoming lost forever. For Gaelic literature, the collecting of Gaelic song and poetry, galvanised by the Ossianic controversy, and the subsequent emergence of this in printed collections, continued apace in the first three decades of the nineteenth century. Among the most notable of these was Patrick Turner's collection published in 1813, its subtitle emphasising the transition from oral to print form in noting that these songs had not been published before but had been collected 'o mheodhair' ('from memory').[2] His volume also underlines the changing nature of Gaelic literary patronage with his collection, on the one hand, opening with a dedication to Alexander Wentworth Macdonald, chief of the MacDonalds of Sleat, while on the other concluding the volume with the names of its 1725 subscribers and providing a wealth of detail on a growing book-buying, Gaelic audience. A sense of the unprecedentedness of the times – Cockburn's electric shock of the new – provides the impetus for continuing in Scotland the investigation in print of what is gained and what is lost in modernity.

This golden age was signalled by the appearance of the *Edinburgh Review* in 1802, founded by four men, three of them Edinburgh Whig lawyers who, having been blocked from the usual avenues of advancement during the Pitt-Dundas regime, found themselves with much free time and undirected energy.[3] This time and energy inspired a new, innovative, and ultimately immensely successful approach to the review genre. Their periodical was issued quarterly, rather than monthly, and comprised long essays ('dissertations', one later critic complained) for which they paid their contributors, and their editor, handsomely: Francis Jeffrey's editorship fees began at two hundred pounds, which were not far behind his entire 1804 professional income of two hundred and forty pounds.[4] The success of the *Edinburgh Review* inspired imitators. The Tory *Quarterly Review*, launched in 1809 over a dispute about British policy in the Peninsular war against Napoleon, would be published in London, but through John Murray, of Scottish descent. The *Edinburgh Review*'s greatest rival was the Tory Blackwood's *Edinburgh Monthly Magazine*, which eventually, as *Blackwood's Edinburgh Magazine*, would devote many of its pages to serialising fiction that subsequently appeared in book form, a practice that became standard in the nineteenth century. The magazine was launched in 1817 and saw anaemic sales at first, but rebranded as *Blackwood's* after its first editors contentiously departed it went on to become as successful and influential as the *Edinburgh Review*. Behind the success of the periodicals was a new breed of youngish and ambitious entrepreneur publishers, willing to take chances and invest handsomely to ensure the success of their literary concerns. Archibald Constable underwrote the *Edinburgh Review* but gave its editors a free hand, while William Blackwood served as a hands-on publisher.

Edinburgh had been very prominent in Gaelic publishing in the later eighteenth century, but it was in Glasgow that the first, tentative attempts at a Gaelic periodical press were made in the early decades of the nineteenth century, although these were certainly not a financially profitable endeavour for anyone involved. Rather, they aimed to provide suitable reading material for those being educated in the recently established Gaelic schools and to make accessible information that was 'glaiste o Ghaedheil ann an leabhraichibh beurla' ('locked from Gaels in English books').[5] This period was framed by the first Gaelic journal, the very short-lived *An Rosroine* (*The Rose of the Field*) in 1803, and by the more successful *An Teachdaire Gae'lach* (*The Highland Messenger*), running to twenty-four issues between 1829 and 1831. With the editors and many contributors to these early periodicals drawn from the ranks of the clergy – the most influential of these being the Rev. Dr Norman MacLeod – spiritual texts are prominent. However, these early journals also mark new directions for the form and subject matter of secular writing and a strong sense of the journal format as a means of linking an increasingly dispersed, and indeed international, Gaelic readership through the printed word. These journals confirmed the importance of the Lowlands for the production of Gaelic literature, with ready access to printing presses, and Glasgow in particular, with its rapidly improving transport links to the west Highland seaboard and beyond, a position which would be strengthened in the course of the century.

In the middle of the frenzied and conspicuous activity of English-language publishing in Edinburgh, or more like sitting atop it, was, indeed, Walter Scott, who became a phenomenon as the world's first great literary star. Scott had moved beyond ballad collecting to fully-fledged imitation of traditional material and then imaginative evocation of the times in which they were produced, in quasi-medieval verse romances. Success in poetry – Constable paid Scott a thousand pound advance for *Marmion* in 1808 – eventually began to wane, but some time probably around 1810, Scott looked at the market and decided to capitalise on the popularity of regional novels, largely up to that point written by women such as Jane Porter (1776–1850), Elizabeth Hamilton (1756–1816), and Maria Edgeworth (1768–1849).[6] Switching to prose, and dropping his name from the title page, Scott commenced the series of novels by the Author of *Waverley* which would eventually outsell the novels of everybody else put together. In the process, Scott facilitated the careers of other Scottish writers like James Hogg (1770–1835) and John Galt (1779–1839), who, though they recognised that Scott had provided the hothouse climate for their success, chafed at having to write under his enormous shadow. For a market that seemed limitless, Scott's publishers struggled to get each new Waverley Novel into the hands of everyone who wanted it; their London agents had men waiting for the boat from Leith to arrive to get the sheets of the latest novel to the binders as quickly as possible. Though Scottish publishing suffered a downturn in the mid-1820s – Scott himself went bankrupt – the publication of the Waverley Novels during this period singlehandedly catalysed the growth of publishing networks as far away as the United States.

1832 saw the year of the first Reform Bill, the death of Scott, and the ascendancy of Whig government in London, all of which altered the publishing and literary landscape in Scotland. Cockburn's 'shock of the new' epoch had come to an end, and from the perspective of mid-century, he would survey a contemporary landscape that seemed not nearly so sublime. But if 1800 to 1832 was a period of dramatic change, there were also notable continuities, to which the history of the reviews provides a window. Though readership was less narrow than it had been in the eighteenth century, Jeffrey could still imagine the ideal reader of the *Edinburgh Review* to be someone among 'fashionable or public life' and earning more than eight hundred pounds per year.[7] And, at one guinea, the price of *Waverley* amounted to several weeks' wages for a labourer of the time. The tradition of spoken-word balladeering and poetry, which antiquarians were so keen to preserve in pristine form, lived on and adapted, despite its high-brow appropriation in print. What else did not change amid all the changes? Although Blackwood paid Susan Ferrier one thousand pounds for *The Inheritance* in 1824, periodicals remained bastions of male dominance; the *Edinburgh Review* generally shut its doors to women as contributors and editors.[8] And while 1832 saw light at the end of the dark tunnel that was the history of British enslavement, *Blackwood's*, as a foil to the generally abolitionist stance of the *Edinburgh Review,* continued to devote much space to pro-slavery arguments. In its pages, Scots made wealthy through the colonies and their advocates, like John Galt, insisted on limited or gradual emancipation and compensation for enslavers, seeking to secure the interests of Glasgow-based planters. Many things had indeed changed in the period, but many things had not.

CHAPTER ONE

Gaelic Poets and New Patterns of Patronage

Ruairidh Maciver

The nineteenth century, as the eighteenth century had been before it, was a period of fundamental change for the Gaelic-speaking people of Scotland. In the half-century following the cataclysmic events of *Bliadhna Theàrlaich* ('the year of Charles', i.e. the year of the Jacobite rebellion, 1745–46), the weakened bonds of clanship fell apart and the transition from chiefs to landlords, and clansmen to tenants, became complete.[1] Large-scale clearance and emigration from the late eighteenth century onwards was the end result of this shift in the balance of power and land ownership in the region. The fiscal-military state filled the power vacuum after Culloden, leading to mass militarisation of the region from 1756 onwards, which continued into the nineteenth century.[2]

But this period also – and perhaps counterintuitively – coincided with the flowering of Gaelic vernacular poetry. The post-1745 period was one in which a group of six major Gaelic poets created a body of work perhaps unprecedented in range and innovation in Gaelic verse. This group consisted of Alasdair mac Mhaighstir Alasdair (Alexander MacDonald, c. 1695–c. 1770), Donnchadh Bàn Mac an t-Saoir (Duncan Ban Macintyre, 1724–1812), Rob Donn MacAoidh (Rob Donn MacKay, 1714–1778), Uilleam Ros (William Ross, 1762–c. 1791), Dùghall Bochanan (Dugald Buchanan, 1716–1768), and Iain mac Fhearchair (John MacCodrum, 1693–1779). Transition was fundamental to these poets' verse.[3] A major innovation came in poets' adaption of the panegyric code, so that they praised, for example, the natural world, the Gaelic language, and officers in the Highland regiments, rather than the chiefs and clan gentry who had previously been the preserve of such poetry.[4]

The decline of the old order of clan society was therefore reflected in the subject matter of Gaelic poetry, but it also played a major part in shaping modes of production. Networks of Gaelic literary production were realigned in the second half of the eighteenth century as direct forms of poetic allegiance to clan chiefs were replaced with more varied systems of support. Highland gentry continued to exert some influence as patrons in new-found positions of authority, for instance as officers in the British army, and there were even late instances of (supposed) clan chiefs hiring official poets to compose panegyrics, as will be considered in more detail below. But the dominance of the Highland aristocracy as patrons had eroded, and poets increasingly turned towards different channels of support. Increased access to the printing press allowed for Gaelic poetry to be circulated to wider audiences and, importantly, facilitated access to money, often through the gathering of subscriptions. The first book of secular Gaelic poetry, Alasdair mac Mhaighstir Alasdair's *Ais-Eiridh na Sean Chánoin Albannaich*, was published in 1751, heralding a new era for the publication of Gaelic verse.[5] The book was followed by a steady stream of collections from individual poets, as well as anthologies of verse, which tapped into and flowed from the new networks of patronage that emerged in the post-Culloden period.[6] This chapter will examine these networks through the works of three Gaelic poets who operated within this emerging nexus of patronage. It will be argued that this was a pivotal moment in the history of Gaelic poetry, when the structures which underpinned Gaelic poetic production were fundamentally altered.

Donnchadh Bàn Mac an t-Saoir

The editions and pamphlets of Donnchadh Bàn Mac an t-Saoir's poetry published between 1768 and 1804 are indicative of the varied forms of support harnessed by Gaelic poets in the late eighteenth and nineteenth centuries. Mac an t-Saoir's first collection of 1768 contained a number of pieces in praise of Clan Campbell aristocracy who, as his employers when he was a forester and gamekeeper in Argyll from c. 1746 to 1766, had effectively been his patrons. As Derick Thomson has said, 'Although it was as a forester or a gamekeeper he was employed by members of the Campbell aristocracy, he thought it proper that he should use his poetic gifts to praise them in the traditional way.'[7] Songs such as 'Oran do Mhormhair Ghlinn Urchaidh' (*'Song to Lord Glenorchy'*) and 'Òran do Iain Caimbeul a' Bhanca' (*'Song to John Campbell, Banker'*) display his loyalty to his Clan Campbell employers, as does his 'Òran do Chaiptean Donnchadh Caimbeul an Geàrd Dhùn Èideann' (*'Song to Captain Duncan Campbell, Edinburgh Town Guard'*), composed after his move to Edinburgh and change of profession c. 1766. When his first edition was published two years later, Mac an t-Saoir relied on a different kind of patronage, in the form of the services of two men from a profession to which so many of the Gaelic literati of the period belonged: the ministry. The Rev. Dr John Stuart of Luss (1743–1821) and the Rev. Joseph Macintyre (1735–1823), minister of Glenorchy and Inishail, were instrumental in having his edition published.[8] Ministers often operated as mediators in Gaelic literature of the period, through roles such as transcribing poets' work, preparing it for publication, and gathering material from the oral record.[9]

Five pamphlets of Mac an t-Saoir's work were published between this first edition and his second in 1790, and these were probably sold directly by the poet.[10] These included two pieces composed for competitions, a panegyric to the Earl of Breadalbane, a song on Highland dress, and a praise poem for the Black Watch. Mac an t-Saoir was a regular competitor for, and winner of, a prize offered by the Highland Society of London for a poem on Gaelic and the bagpipe.[11] He was also in the running to become official bard to the Highland Society of Scotland in 1789.[12] In the first two decades of his poetic career, Mac an t-Saoir evidently relied on various forms of support and patronage, which ranged from traditional appeals to artistocracy, to more innovative direct engagement with the reading (and paying) public.

When it came to trying to gain support for his second edition of 1790, Mac an t-Saoir turned to another relatively recent innovation in Gaelic poetry: the gathering of subscriptions. Ronald Black has shown that six Gaelic books that included a subscription list were published between 1778 and 1798.[13] This practice continued into the nineteenth century, as Michel Byrne and Sheila M. Kidd have recently outlined.[14] Byrne and Kidd have pointed out that eight books with subscribers' lists were published between 1800 and 1836, but have also noted that some books that were gathered through subscription did not include a list.[15] The precise number of books which relied on subscriptions is impossible to ascertain, but it is clear that this form of what would today be called crowdfunding had become a major impetus in getting Gaelic books published by the early decades of the nineteenth century.

Black has noted that due to the subscription system 'authors had little choice but to go out and meet their potential readers', and this is what Mac an t-Saoir did when he toured the Highlands seeking subscriptions for the second (1790) and third (1804) editions of his *Orain Ghaidhealach*.[16] Anja Gunderloch's study of Mac an t-Saoir's subscribers has provided a detailed analysis of these subscription lists.[17] The list published in the

1790 edition contains 1478 names, including people from all classes of Highland society, with information supplied about their place of residence, trade or profession, title, and the number of copies they took.[18] Military subscribers feature prominently in the list and indicate the extent to which the British fiscal-military state had become a site of patronage for Gaelic poets during the period.[19] Evidently, though, Mac an t-Saoir's support was not limited to any particular profession or social group.[20]

Mac an t-Saoir's late period of service with the Breadalbane Fencibles from 1793 to 1799 saw him again receiving a form of patronage from Campbell aristocracy, by now firmly part of the officer class of the British army. He composed five pieces about his service with the Fencibles, raised by John Campbell (1782–1834), the fourth Earl of Breadalbane, in which he praised its leaders and lauded the financial security that the soldier's lifestyle afforded him. These poems appeared in the last collection of Mac an t-Saoir's poetry (1804) to be published in his own lifetime, also brought to the press through the gathering of subscriptions. This list includes 673 subscribers, and ninety-seven of these have a military rank. It is worth noting too that military figures are listed before other professions under each surname in the subscribers' list (preceded only by the aristocracy and gentry). Both the 1790 and 1804 editions are dedicated to John Campbell, and the later edition includes a panegyric addressed directly to the Earl. As well as being effectively his military employer, Campbell purchased eight copies of Mac an t-Saoir's second and third editions and, as Gunderloch has noted, there was 'clearly a patronage relationship operating between our poet and the nobleman'.[21] It appears that the poet continued to receive some form of support from the Earl of Breadalbane after his service with the Fencibles had come to an end, for a note in this 1804 edition states that he 'now lives a retired life, rendered not uncomfortable by the beneficence of that Noble-man'.[22]

Ailean Dùghallach

Where Campbell aristocracy gave indirect patronage to Mac an t-Saoir through other forms of employment, the Glencoe-born poet Ailean Dùghallach (Allan MacDougall, c. 1750–1829), or Ailean Dall (*Blind Allan*), relied on more direct support. Dùghallach, who had trained and worked as a tailor in his youth, was hired c. 1798 as a poet to the Glengarry chief Alexander Ranaldson Macdonell (1773–1828).[23] A close friend of Walter Scott (1771–1832) and the subject of an iconic portrait by Henry

Raeburn (1756–1823), Glengarry was in reality a ruthless landlord and an utter fraud in his self-promoted image as the 'Last of the Chiefs'.[24] He hired Dùghallach shortly after the appearance of his first collection, *Orain Ghaidhealacha* (1798), and it seems likely that the success of this volume was what motivated Glengarry's approach.[25] The tradition of hiring an official poet had all but died out by the second half of the eighteenth century, but having a bard to sing his praises was in line with the romantic image that Glengarry sought to convey.[26] As part of the payment for his services, Dùghallach was given a cottage and croft by Loch Oich, close to Macdonell's own residence in Invergarry.[27] In characteristically florid terms, John Mackenzie (Iain MacCoinnich, 1806–1848), the editor of the highly influential nineteenth-century anthology of Gaelic poetry, *Sar-Obair nam Bard Gaelach* (1841), describes the transformation that this change in material circumstances brought about for the poet:

> And now might the palmy days of our minstrel be said to have commenced – he occupied the proud and enviable position of family-bard to the most famed *Ceann-taighe* in the Highlands. He laid aside his blue, home-made great-coat, and *hat*, and was equipped in habiliments suited to his newly acquired rank. Never was there a more marvellous transition outwardly; and we venture to presume that the buoyancy of his feelings kept pace with his improved exterior [...] His minstrelsy tended to enliven the scene and to inspire the party with the almost dormant chivalric spirit of their country.[28]

Dùghallach would henceforth be seen accompanying Glengarry to public engagements in the Highlands, such as the annual gymnastic games in Fort William. Mackenzie informs us that he

> previously composed appropriate songs for these exhibitions, and sung them at the games, as if they had been strung together on the spur of the moment – always making sure of having his lyre tuned by two or three copious draughts, not of *Helicon*, but of *Benevis!*[29]

Glengarry raised the Glengarry Highlanders in 1794 and became colonel of the regiment, and a number of Dùghallach's panegyrics are addressed to the clan-chief as officer.[30] This includes his 'Òran do 'n aon Cheudna; 's e sin ri ràdh – an Coirneal Domhnullach, do 'n Goirear "Tighearna

Ghlinne Garradh"' ('*Song to the Same; that is to say – Colonel MacDonald, styled "The Laird of Glengarry"'*), where he draws deeply on the panegyric code in his praise of Glengarry:

> Lean do chruadal, 's do ghaisgeadh,
> 'S am fasan bu dual
> A bhi colgarra, cosanta
> M prosnuchadh sluaigh;
> Gu h-airmealteach, treubhach,
> Gu geur lannach cruaidh;
> 'S tu shliochd nam fear treuna,
> Nach geilleadh 's an ruaig.[31]

Keep up your courage and heroism / In the expected manner, / To be fierce and vigorous, / Encouraging an army; / Valorously, gallantly, / Armed with a sharp sword and formidable; / You are the descendant of the brave men, / Who would not yield in the rout.

It is difficult to view the bulk of Dùghallach's panegyrics for Glengarry and other associated gentry as amounting to much more than the necessary results of his employment and the need to have it continued, but he was by no means a poet incapable of expressing independence of thought. His 'Òran do na Cìobairibh Gallda' ('*Song to the Lowland Shepherds*'), composed c. 1798, expresses a desire that the French will come over and cut the heads off the hated shepherds, whose influence Dùghallach derides in the piece.[32] His later elegy for John Cameron of Fassiefern (1771–1815), after the Battle of Waterloo in 1815, laments the price paid by the Gàidhealtachd in losing so many men in the wars against France, and hints at criticism of the war office in London over their handling of the conflict.[33]

Glengarry's patronage did not extend to supporting the publication of another edition of the poet's work; indeed, it was only after the chief's death that Dùghallach's second book appeared, in 1829. This second collection, too, was raised through the gathering of subscriptions. Unlike Donnchadh Bàn's second and third volumes, neither book includes the subscriber list, so we are in the dark about the exact sources of support, though Mackenzie does inform us that the poet travelled through Argyll, Inverness-shire and Ross seeking subscriptions for the 'new and enlarged edition of his works'.[34] Despite the absence of subscriber lists, we do have an illustration of the arduous process of gathering subscribers in

'Comhradh an Ughdair 's a Charaid mu thimchioll an leabhair so' (*'The Author's Conversation with his Friend about this Book'*). The friend in question is Dùghallach's collaborator, the Lochaber-born poet and scholar, Eòghann MacLachlainn (Ewen MacLachlan, 1775–1822).[35] In a section in his own voice, Dùghallach says:

> 'S nach smuainich thu, 'Dhuin' uasail!
> A liuthad fuachd a's allaban,
> Trioblaid, agus cruadal,
> A fhuair mi 'n tir aineolaich,
> Le sneachd agus gaoth tuatha,
> 'Toirt dhiom nan cluas bho 'n ailleagan,
> Gun duine 'ghabhadh truas dhiom,
> No dh'fhuasgladh air m' an-shochdair?[36]

And won't you consider, noble Man! / How much cold and wandering, / Difficulty and hardship, / I endured in unfamiliar places, / With snow and north wind, / That would take my ear off, / With nobody who would take pity on me / Or resolve my distress?

Dùghallach was a poet who ran the gamut of patronage in the period, ranging from the hardship of the itinerant subscription-seeker to the relative pampering of Glengarry's backing.

Iain MacGilleain

Like Mac an t-Saoir and Dùghallach before him, Iain MacGilleain (John MacLean, 1787–1848) straddled the old order of traditional patronage and the new forms of support that emerged in the later eighteenth and nineteenth centuries. A native of Caolas, Tiree, MacGilleain emigrated to Nova Scotia in 1819. There he would become known as Am Bàrd MacGilleain (The Bard MacLean), while in Scotland he was referred to by his patronymic, Iain mac Ailein, and Bàrd Thighearna Chola (The Laird of Coll's Poet).[37] It is by this last title that MacLean was, and remains, best known outside of his native island. It is unclear when this title was given to MacGilleain or whether it was bestowed by Alexander Maclean (1753–1835), the 15th Laird of Coll, himself.[38] As Eric Cregeen and Donald W. Mackenzie have said: 'It may be that the title [...] was largely honorific, but it is interesting as being the latest example of the use of a traditional style of this kind in the Highlands.'[39]

MacGilleain started composing poetry for the Laird of Coll early in his poetic career, during the first decade of the nineteenth century.[40] This poetry is highly traditional and exalts Alexander Maclean through the conventions of the panegyric code. Unlike Dùghallach, it does not seem that MacGilleain received material patronage in the form of land or housing. Indeed, the poet lived in Caolas, Tiree, not on the Coll estate, and would have been a tenant of the Duke of Argyll.[41] There do seem, however, to have been instances when support of various forms was provided to MacGilleain by the Laird of Coll directly. One such instance appears to have occurred when the latter intervened to secure the poet's release from the Argyll Militia in 1811, into which the poet had been drafted against his will. MacGilleain appears to celebrate this in his 'Òran do dh'Alasdair MacGilleain' ('*Song to Alexander Maclean*'), where he says that the Laird placed a letter 'ann am phochda, / Dh'ionnsuidh Chòirneil 'bh' os mo cheann' ('*in my pocket / To the colonel who was in charge*').[42]

The years between MacGilleain's discharge from the military and his emigration to Canada in 1819 proved a period of significant output and were when the bulk of his poetry composed in Scotland was created.[43] MacGilleain was also a collector of Gaelic poetry, and the fruits of this work, along with his own verse, were collected in a substantial manuscript, running to about fifteen thousand lines. He was unusual, though not unique, in having been a collector and a poet.[44] This manuscript was the basis for the poet's first collection, *Orain Nuadh Ghaedhlach*, published in 1818. As has been seen previously, the business of bringing a book to publication was seldom a simple one for Gaelic poets. It usually required various appeals to individuals or groups and the undertaking of extensive travel. In his 'Do Thighearna Chola' ('*To the Laird of Coll*') MacGilleain explains how he went to Edinburgh in an unsuccessful attempt to secure support for the book from the city's Highland Society:

> 'S nach robh fear-dàimh no carraid ann
> A ghabh mo phàirt, na shealladh orm,
> Cha tug iad mòran gealladh dhomh,
> 'S e th'uirt iad rinneadh mearachd òirn
> Gar mealladh ann sa'n t-seòl sin.[45]

> *And there was no relation or friend there / To take my part, or look at me, / They did not give me much of a promise. / They said, 'we were mistaken / To be enticed in that direction'*.[46]

The poet implies in the song that had his patron been present the Society would not have turned him down. He was finally able to make a deal with an Edinburgh printer, Robert Menzies, to publish a book, and a run of four hundred copies seems to have been made.[47]

Where a substantial proportion of his poetry in Scotland (twelve of twenty-six poems) was clan panegyric, just three of the eighteen poems composed in Canada fall into this category. The poet's new allegiances and concerns on the other side of the Atlantic come to the fore in his Nova Scotian verse. It might be said that he became a community, rather than a clan, poet, addressing subjects such as an election, a wedding, and a Highland Ball in his songs. He formed a lasting friendship in Canada with a local Catholic priest, Father Colin Grant (1784–1839), who seems to have provided him with material support during a period of hardship. As Dunbar has noted, the poet composed three poems for Grant, each in a highly traditional style, as if addressing a clan chief.[48] His sources of patronage had changed in Nova Scotia, but he continued to respond in a traditional manner.

Conclusion

Each of these poets' work is representative of the changing nature of patronage in Gaelic poetry in the late eighteenth and early nineteenth centuries. Looking to multiple sources of patronage was a matter of necessity for Gaelic poets of this period. Greater access to the printing press brought their poetry to wider audiences, while the gathering of subscriptions led to the creation of a new relationship between poets and these audiences. Highland societies became important centres of patronage, and military networks filled the spaces left by the breakdown of clan structures. Mac an t-Saoir, Dùghallach, and MacGilleain were, in many respects, highly traditional poets, but they operated within a new and multifarious system of patronage that would continue to shape Gaelic poetic production throughout the nineteenth century.

CHAPTER TWO

Inspiring Songs: The Rise of Ballad Culture

Valentina Bold

When these good old Bards *wrote, we had not yet made Use of imported Trimmings* [...] *Their* Images *are native, and their* Landskips *domestick* [...] *We are not carried to* Greece *or* Italy *for a Shade, a Stream or a Breeze* [...] *I find not Fault with those Things, as they are in* Greece *or* Italy: *But with a* Northern Poet *for fetching his Materials from these Places, in a Poem, of which his own Country is the Scene.*
—Allan Ramsay, The Ever Green[1]

The music and poetry of each country must keep pace with their usual tone of mind [...] the reader must not expect to find, in the border ballads, refined sentiment, and, far less, elegant expression, although the stile of such composition has, in modern hands, been found highly susceptible of both. But passages might be pointed out, in which the rude minstrel has melted in natural pathos, or risen into rude energy [...] the stories themselves, and the curious picture of manners, which they frequently present, authorize them to claim some respect.
—Walter Scott, *Minstrelsy of the Scottish Border*[2]

This chapter explores the rise of ballad culture in early nineteenth-century Scotland and, in particular, the dominant role of Walter Scott's (1771–1832) *Minstrelsy of the Scottish Border* (1802–03) in understanding, and defining, the ballad form in literary contexts. It considers both the impulse to collect and publish ballads, and the rise of ballad as a form which could (and would) inspire new poetry, building on eighteenth-century notions of a nation defined by songs. In terms of inspiring collecting, affecting collection practices, and encouraging the composition of ballad-style songs and poetry, the *Minstrelsy* would play a dominant role in Scotland's ballad culture – both positive and negative – from the nineteenth century onwards. The early nineteenth century, significantly, saw a shift of interest from lyric – the predominant form in James Johnson's *Scots Musical Museum* (1787–1803), for instance – to that of narrative ballads. This was largely the result of the publication of the first and subsequent volumes of Scott's *Minstrelsy*. This chapter considers the impact of the *Minstrelsy* on ballad collectors in manuscript as well as print. These range from the semi-anonymised Mrs Creighton to Charles Kirkpatrick Sharpe; those who were ballad imitators, as well as collecting ballads from oral traditions, print collections and broadsides, like John Leyden (1775–1811), Allan Cunningham (1784–1842), and James Hogg (1770–1835) (and Scott himself).

Defining the Ballad: foregrounding Scotland's song culture

The growing interest in ballad, as a characteristically Scottish genre, was not solely inspired by Scott's work, but was built on several precedents, particularly the work of Allan Ramsay (1684–1758), James Macpherson (1736–1796), and David Herd (1732–1810). Ramsay's *The Ever Green* (1724), referenced at the outset of this chapter, played a key role, both in identifying types of Scottish song, and in mixing traditional songs with authored work. Drawing together oral tradition, manuscript, and printed material, Ramsay's work began a nation-defining exercise through song, initially valuing the lyric (and epic) over what became identified as 'ballad'.

So too, the (disputed) methodology of Macpherson's 1760 *Fragments of Ancient Poetry* was vital. Just as Macpherson sought to create Scotland's lost and perfect epic by re-assembling fragments, Scott would later edit his sources to create, as near as possible, national *ur*-texts: stand-alone episodes of song. After Johann Gottfried Herder's *Von Deutschen Art und Kunst* (1773), which consolidated notions of national eloquence being expressed through song, the stage was set for a pervasive interest in ballad as the ultimate song genre, an equivalent to the epic which Macpherson eulogised through the notion of the lost Ossianic texts.

David Herd's *Ancient and Modern Songs* (1769, expanded in 1776 and 1791) was arguably the most important precursor to Scott's work in fostering the notion that, as William Donaldson stated, 'Scottish tradition ran truer than the English, featuring songs and ballads that were older, better, and more "authentic"'.[3] Herd's insistence on Scotland's status as a pre-eminent song location, evidenced by what he presented as song survivals, was hugely influential to those who came next. His manuscript collection for the volumes was equally important: Scott used these in his compilation of the *Minstrelsy*, Robert Burns (1759–1796) had access to

Herd's materials too, and later collectors, like Joseph Ritson, would also acknowledge their debt to Herd.

Most significantly, Herd arranged his collection in three parts. The category of heroic ballads or epic tales (in effect, narrative songs) included Jacobite songs alongside ballads such as 'Gil Morrice', 'Edom o' Gordon', 'Johnie Armstrang', and 'Young Waters'. The second and third groupings included sentimental pastoral and love songs and, lastly, comic songs. These categorisations would mark a profound and influential shift in the way scholars approached Scottish songs. Ballad, in this context, was a form of 'high' folk art, composed by the most skilled 'anonymous' 'folk' poets.

An increasing interest in ballad was linked to broader trends. The rise of antiquarianism in Britain in the first quarter of the nineteenth century – in which Scott played an active part – encouraged the notion of seeking the past in the present, as remnant or as residue. In this context, ballad could be hailed as the Lowland contribution to the national story and, through the reception of the *Minstrelsy*, would be.

Defining the Ballad: Scott's Border *Minstrelsy*

Scott's conception, or representation, of ballad was as a Border genre of national significance: a lost but recreatable form. The *Minstrelsy* dedication draws attention to 'these tales which in elder times have celebrated the prowess and cheered the halls of his [the Duke of Buccleuch's] Gallant Ancestors', in an act of spatial and historical mapping based on Scott's fondness for his Borders lineage. In the process, Scott established the idea of a shared 'Southern Counties' song heritage – a notion which can be disputed. As David Buchan, much later, observed: 'despite the romantic accounts of his "raids into Liddesdale" [...] many of his ballad correspondents came from the Northeast'.[4] The notion of the border ballad, then, is wholly linked to Scott's creative agenda of regional and national definition, part of a deeply subjective construction of (initially) his personal repertoire and, later, those of selected collaborators.

Scott's *Minstrelsy* mapped out the song landscape of the 'Southern Counties' through ballad, with a regionally and nationally definitive 'character', exemplified by the marchmen. Scott writes: 'their morality was of a singular kind [...] National animosity usually gave an additional stimulus [...] the music and songs of the borders were of a military nature, and celebrated the valour and success of their predatory expeditions'.[5]

The 'military nature' and 'valour' of the Borders is of prime importance to the selective picture the *Minstrelsy* presents of a homogenous song culture.[6]

Scott's Scottish 'Border' is centred on Selkirkshire, Roxburghshire, and some of the Debateable Lands – the area from the Solway Firth to Langholm, bounded by the Liddel and Esk at its eastern extremity, and the Sark at its western: Liddesdale and Eskdale. This is the historical Middle Marches, including Hawick, Kelso, and Jedburgh and the areas around, like Smailholm and Melrose – the lands of 'Thomas the Rhymer' and the reivers.[7] To a large extent – and this is not coincidental – it equates with Buccleuch estates of Scott's period, especially the Bowhill estate and around Langholm. The Queensberry estate, which includes swathes of the Western marches, was not Buccleuch territory until 1810, when the third Duke, Sir Henry Montagu Scott, inherited it. Scott is part of what I have called the 'Collection as Colonization' process, in an internalised way, identifying songs he likes about places he knows, and from people he likes (the Hogg family, the Laidlaws, and John Leyden, for instance), mapping a territory around them to the neglect of other areas around the Border – this, despite using materials from, for instance, the South West.[8] While Scott's construction of Highland-based identities has been questioned, the Border notions implicit in his work have been left unexplored, although they richly merit further examination.

Equally, Scott's active role in (re)creating lost song, exemplifying his contemporaries' standards, is actually close to that of a song-maker.[9] David Buchan noted that singer, performer, and composer are all involved in the creation of texts, through 're-composition': 'the oral poet re-creates each story at each performance, during one performance'.[10] Equally, as David Atkinson has remarked, an impulse to 'conservatism' means ballad variation through performance is comparable to variation among written texts: 'the quarto and folio *Hamlets* and *King Lears* [...] the variant endings of *Great Expectations*'.[11]

There is, in short, 'a sort of equivalence between performer and author / composer [...] the concept of "type" [...] is similar to, but not identical with, the literary or musical "work"'.[12] As Atkinson observes:

> the ballad is an aesthetic artefact [...] existing both within and outside of the reactions it provokes among its readers and listeners [...] including singers [...] the ballad cannot be located in a single place, but demands instead an organizing principle.[13]

Looked at this way, nineteenth-century ballad collectors and editors like Scott can be seen, primarily, as textual organisers. Although their ideas of editorial boundaries arguably were broader than those of modern collectors, the processing and creating of ballad texts by writers in the nineteenth century is a continuum: starting with collecting, progressing through editing, and ending, for some, with imitation.

Other collections are equally important in developing an understanding of the rise in ballad culture. Although unpublished, they both reflected literary tastes and, in some cases, made an impact. The eleventh volume of Robert Riddell's twelve-volume manuscript *Collection of Scottish Antiquities,* made in the late eighteenth century, fed directly into the later *Minstrelsy*.[14] Riddell displayed a marked interest in local material from South West Scotland – seven out of sixteen pieces in the eleventh volume are specific to the region, including 'Archie of Capeld', 'Lord Maxwell's Goodnight', 'Lads of Wamphray', two versions of 'Fair Helen of Kirkconnel', and two of 'The Lochmaben Harper'; these encouraged Scott's picture of a shared Borders tradition.

The work of other collectors, who lacked Scott's German-influenced agenda of national definition, offers quite a different picture. Take, for instance, 'A Collection of Old Songs Written from the Memory of Mrs Creighton By her Daughter Agnes Thorburn Creighton January 31st 1818'.[15] There is, unfortunately, little direct information about this although it is likely that the women were from Dumfries and Galloway, probably New Abbey. Despite the fact that they must have known the *Minstrelsy*, out of 107 items in the Creighton collection only a handful are ballads, and none of these are particularly 'martial' in the way Scott identified as typical. The Creightons were more interested in songs about human experience than in songs relating to regional identity, or in historical ballads, or in definitions around place. Their ballads are about love gone wrong, or personal conflicts: 'Lord Lovel', 'Mal Boy', 'William and Margaret', 'An Old Ballad', 'Young Watters', 'Adam o Gordon', 'The Braes o Yarrow', and 'Young Douglas and Fair Margaret'.

Similarly, while Sharpe's *Ballad Book* of 1823 was inspired by the *Minstrelsy*, his repertoire tells a different story and has a different agenda: 'to preserve a few songs that afforded me much delight in my early youth' which were 'not to be found at all [...] or in the same shape, in other collections'.[16] Claiming to epitomise the traditions of 'nurses [...] dairy maids [...] and tenants-daughters', they are an amalgam of lyrics: ('Fair Janet'), the occasional 'stupid Ballad, printed as it was sung in Annandale'

('Lady Dysmal'), or more serious ones like 'Glenlogie'; items with local associations feature strongly, for instance, a 'May Collin', which locates the ballad specifically,

> Twixt Wigton and the town of Air
> Portpatrick and the cruives of Cree
> No man needs think to byde there
> Unless he court with Kennedie

and 'Fair Margaret of Craignargat', set in Luce Bay and associated with the Macdowall family.[17]

Like Creighton, Sharpe does not focus on the martial pieces Scott liked, but on ballads of human encounters, love gone wrong, and treacherous murders. Here, distinctions between ballad and lyric – which can be sometimes arbitrary – blur. Sharpe's correspondence with Scott – post *Minstrelsy*, but still useful – shows a deep understanding, too, of the interaction between oral and print traditions. He talks, for instance, of having a 'stall copy' of Captain Glen, which he remembered 'at spinning dales in Annandale' (letter of 1825), and he includes in his collection an Annandale version which he believed to be better than those he heard elsewhere.[18]

Collecting, both in service of Scott's work and for personal use, was hugely influential in the rise of ballad culture. Scott's work played a crucial role in defining the notion of the Borders as Scotland's ballad heartland. More than this, on a practical level, it inspired those involved in the collecting process, like James Hogg and John Leyden. Their involvement in the *Minstrelsy* enterprise encouraged them to place value on the ballad texts they already knew and inspired them to locate new texts – for Hogg, through the parallel genre of *Jacobite Songs* (1819–21), for instance – and to create new ballad-style compositions.

Afterword: The sincerest form of flattery (ballad imitations)

Finally, the rise of ballad culture is important in the nineteenth century for the way it fostered ballad imitations. The final volume of the *Minstrelsy* offered something of a masterclass in this, including a range of examples explicitly labelled as 'Imitations'. John Leyden's 'The Mermaid' (which was much admired, along with his 'The Cout of Keeldar'), takes as its starting point a Gaelic original, 'Macphail of Colonsay'.[19] Despite its traditional beginnings and associated tales, Leyden's style is unapologetically modern – it makes no attempt to emulate the tightness of ballad structures, the simplicity of ballad language, or the familiar formulae associated with the traditional genre.[20] Instead, it adopts romantic idioms from the outset: 'On Jura's heath how sweetly swell / The murmurs of the mountain bee', as it celebrates 'the mermaid's sweet sea-soothing lay'. The only conventions it draws on are through the storyline, giving real compositional possibilities to later imitators of the ballad. James Hogg's version of 'Lord William'[21] is more faithful to its originals: drawing on 'Earl Richard' it goes further, showing Hogg's keen understanding of conventions around dialogue in ballad and his mastery of Scots language from start to end, as a 'bodkin' pierces the heart of his protagonist. Other contributors, such as 'Mr Hamilton, Music-seller, Edinburgh', fall between these two extremes. 'Proud Lady Margaret', which he provided, employs ballad idioms – 'She looked east, and she looks west' – combined with more literary phrasing – 'on a night, an evening bright' – for instance, in the opening section of the piece.[22] Robert Jamieson's (1772–1844) 'Water Kelpie' takes a similar hybrid approach.[23] The phrasing is redolent of oral tradition – the 'mirker grey' of the 'lift', for instance – but the use of the first person, along with expressions of emotions – such as 'Gart aw my members quake' – give a more personal, literary flavour to the whole. This is ballad tribute writing, at its best.

Scott would carry his own interest of ballad into longer, narrative settings – the context for *The Lay of the Last Minstrel* (1805) for instance, or the creation of the anti-hero *Marmion* (1808). Allan Cunningham, too, explored ballad-inspired characters in his longer works, including *Sir Marmaduke Maxwell* (1822). Lady Nairne (1766–1845) drew on a sense of ballad 'atmosphere' for some of her more elegiac songs, just as Joanna Baillie (1762–1851) would in her verse dramas, most obviously in the somewhat Gothic *Orra* (1812). Ballad informs Byron's (1788–1824) poetry throughout, as in the dark humour of a work like *Don Juan*, but the culmination of this process, arguably, was James Hogg's imaginative, ballad-inspired collection, *A Queer Book* (1832). This exemplifies the ways in which the 'antient style' of ballad inspired experimentation, generating new forms and new ideas, and connecting literature and the traditional in creative and innovative ways.

Scott's pioneering collection in the *Minstrelsy*, in short, opened new doors: for those who collected, those who were collected, and those who wanted to write new songs and poetry based on ballad styles. The ballad became Scotland's 'national' genre with an imagined 'Border' area as its notional heartlands. From 1802 onwards, for writers and critics, ballad became both an identifiable and collectable form, rooted in oral tradition, and a source of inspiration, allowing for new forms and experimentation.

CHAPTER THREE

The Novel: Romance and History

Pam Perkins

Any early nineteenth-century admirer of Scottish fiction with a taste for enjoyably romanticised history would have been spoilt for choice. There was Jane Porter (1776–1850) on William Wallace; Walter Scott (1771–1832) and James Hogg (1770–1835) on the court of Mary Stuart; Scott, Hogg, and John Galt (1779–1839) on the Covenanting wars; and perhaps most famously of all, Scott (again) on Highland society and the Jacobite uprisings. Contemporary critics and reviewers did not always approve of mingling fact and fancy, but the romantic elements of historical fiction were not necessarily there simply to spice up the dry facts of history. Much of the romance in *Waverley* (1814), for example, arises from the perspective of the naïve young Englishman Edward Waverley, and the novel uses his gradual awakening from his original romantic views of the Highlands and Highlanders to suggest both individual and national maturation. More generally, romance could also be used to evoke or critique theoretical concepts of historical development. Scottish Enlightenment theories of stadial history – which held (in part) that all societies progressed through the same developmental stages but at uneven rates[1] – underlie at least some of the more romantic depictions of unfamiliar societies in these writers' works. Accounts of societies at supposedly earlier stages of development are tinged with elements of romantic nostalgia for a way of life that might have been ultimately unsustainable but that was seen as being not just simpler but also more exciting, glamorous, or swashbuckling. In this respect, romance becomes less a matter of escapism than a technique for suggesting the costs of historical change or perhaps the difficulty of achieving such change in the first place.

That could be the case even in narratives in which the 'past' culture is distanced by geography rather than by time. Jane Porter's first major success, *Thaddeus of Warsaw* (1803), only just barely qualifies as a historical novel – the opening action takes place in the lead-up to and aftermath of the Polish–Russian War of 1792 – but Porter develops her initial Polish setting using techniques similar to those she later employed in *The Scottish Chiefs* (1810) to create her influential picture of medieval Scotland. The opening scenes of the novel depict a society in which the roughness and violence of a still more distant past have given way to a world of 'comfortable villages', prosperous farms, and affectionate bonds between the peasants and their feudal leaders.[2] At the same time, Porter's late eighteenth-century Poland remains a world of chivalric valour, in which young Thaddeus demonstrates his worth by battlefield exploits and hand-to-hand conflict that would not be out of place in any medieval romance. In one particularly memorable episode, Thaddeus strikes up a battlefield friendship with a wounded soldier from the opposite side, raising him from the ground, protecting him from the attack of a fellow Polish soldier, then returning his sword with a chivalric flourish. 'I consider myself ennobled', Thaddeus proclaims, 'in restoring this sword to one, who so courageously defended it'.[3] (In a plot twist that belongs more in the world of romance than that of realist fiction, the 'Russian' soldier turns out to be not only an Englishman but also Thaddeus's half-brother.) In effect, Porter is creating interest in and inviting sympathy for what was, to her contemporary British readers, a remote and unfamiliar culture by presenting its recent and very real conflicts in the familiar terms of a romantically chivalric past. In so doing, she also quietly reinforces the central polemical point of the novel, which is to create sympathy for the Poles she had encountered in London. When Thaddeus enters the 'modern' world, he does so as a penniless exile struggling to make his way in an England that Porter presents as being indifferent at best, and hostile at worst, to refugees and émigrés. Yet by imagining his 'foreignness' in terms of the familiar tropes of historical romance, rather than those of geographic and cultural distance, she familiarises him to her British readers.

Porter's 1790s Poland functions in more or less the same way as the medieval Scotland that she created a few years later: both are idealised societies that produce romantically noble-minded and chivalric heroes, but both are, inevitably, attacked by hostile outsiders. In that respect, both novels anticipate Scott's *Waverley*, although Scott is more ambivalent in his presentation of the threatened and romanticised 'earlier' version of society. The representative of that world in *Waverley* is the anti-hero Fergus MacIvor, who is much more ambiguous than Thaddeus in his embodiment of romance. Fergus is in fact better adapted than Waverley to the complex world of mid-eighteenth-century political intrigue, but even so, by the end of the novel, the only place for him is in the sentimentalised posthumous portrait commissioned by Waverley. Fergus's death is tragic, but the novel presents it as being necessary; in this case, nostalgia for a more 'chivalric' past is a measure less of what has been lost in the move towards modernity, as it tends to be for Porter, than it is of one's success in leaving that past behind, smoothing over messy complexities with pleasurably aestheticised romance.

Yet Scott, like Porter, could use the trappings of romance to explore more recent pasts, as he does in *The Antiquary* (1816) and *St Ronan's Well* (1823). Likewise, he employs romance in his examinations of other concepts of historical development and progress. *The Pirate* (1822), set in Shetland and Orkney in the opening years of the eighteenth century, is superficially more 'historic' than either *Thaddeus of Warsaw* or even *Waverley*, in which the 'sixty years since' of the subtitle places the action at the edge of living memory. (It was, of course, closer to seventy 'years since' by the time Scott published the novel.) Yet the exact time of action is not fixed as precisely as it is in *Waverley*; in his 1831 introduction to the novel, Scott merely says that he set his tale 'a generation or two farther back'. He has done so, he explains, in order to create yet another account of an older culture being replaced by a newer one: his intention was to 'trace the features of the old Norwegian Udaller', Magnus Troil, the representative of a society that Scott implies has vanished entirely by the early nineteenth century.[4] His reviewers also picked up on this narrative of uneasy social change, with a writer for the *Quarterly* observing that in their insular hostility towards incomers, Scott's Shetlanders are akin to the 'Saxons in Ivanhoe'.[5]

What is missing from *The Pirate*, however, is the sort of narrative of improvement that one finds in *Waverley*, *Ivanhoe* (1819), or *Thaddeus of Warsaw* and that explains, even justifies, change. There is an 'improver' who has come north to try to bring modern farming techniques to the islands, but he is a comic figure with almost no influence. The romance of a vanishing culture in *The Pirate* is thus complicated by the lack of any clear exploration of what is replacing it and why. The tragic heroine Minna gestures towards what she sees as the corrupting forces of 'modern' ideas and social values and customs flowing in from the south, as she dreams of reclaiming independence from metropolitan rule. Like *Waverley*'s Flora MacIvor, she remains associated with a romantic past, living unmarried and absorbed in her memories of the larger-than-life antihero whom she had loved. The difference is that for Minna, this absorption in memory and the past is rooted as much in geography as ideology: she insists that her character is so entwined with the Shetland landscape that she can never leave. But her dashing piratical lover cannot make himself part of that world, despite what is ultimately revealed about his maternal Shetlandic heritage. If geography shapes destiny, as Minna implies when she explains to Cleveland why she will not go with him to the paradisical southern islands that he describes, the optimistic narrative of historical improvement becomes much harder to sustain. Cleveland's amusement at Minna's vision of progress – an independent Shetland that embraces its Norse heritage – arises from what he sees as the irreversible decline of the northern powers. Cleveland takes for granted that England is the future, and that the northern landscapes that Minna says are part of herself can never be 'improved' in the only way that Minna sees as being meaningful. The bleak and barren land and seascapes that Minna loves leave their inhabitants without the wealth or resources to sustain or improve their own traditional values.

Scott and Porter imply varied ideas about the past through their uses of romance, but in all the novels mentioned, romance becomes a means of establishing the appeal of a lost or distant world. One can find a very different and much more ambivalent use of romance in the historical fiction of their contemporaries Hogg and Galt. Hogg's most famous historical work, *The Private Memoirs and Confessions of a Justified Sinner* (1824), is not remotely inclined to glamourise the past. Indeed, it originates in a *Blackwood's* 'Noctes Ambrosianae' column that mocks naïve romanticism, as Hogg, in the voice of his alter ego the Ettrick Shepherd, responds to a request for descriptions of the romantic glories of the Ettrick valley with an account of the discovery of the mummified body of a century-old suicide. A more obscure work by Hogg, the novella 'The Surpassing Adventures of Allan Gordon' (1837), might initially seem closer to the world of glamorous historical adventure, but it is even more critical of romance. First published in 1837 and set in the 1750s and 1760s, it combines elements of the Robinsoniad with the early nineteenth-century obsession with polar exploration. The eponymous narrator is the sole survivor of a whaling ship trapped and destroyed by polar ice, but Hogg refuses to offer any sort of conventional romance of the north. The discovery of the holy grail of nineteenth-century polar exploration – a pathway to open water at the North Pole – occurs within a few paragraphs of the beginning of the journey, and is comically anticlimactic. Allan himself never quite realises where he has been, mocking the captain for making such a fuss about a place where there 'was nothing but a calm open sea and the sun beating on us all the four-and-twenty hours' and commenting that the only real oddity was that the compass needle 'had no power, not a grain'.[6] Nor is Allan initially much of a Crusoe figure: his first action after the shipwreck is to find a supply of spirits and to sink into a drunken stupor that lasts, by his estimate, at least a month.

Yet even if Allan opens his story as an incuriously drunken reworking of the more typical adventurer, Hogg complicates this relatively straightforward anti-romantic narrative by recalling some of the techniques used in the more serious historical fiction of Scott and Porter, as he has Allan move 'back' into what stadial theory constructs as an earlier stage of human history through encounters with unfamiliar cultures and with the 'exotic' women (or at least females) who embody aspects of those societies. Just as Waverley finds a glimpse of what he construes as a simpler and 'primitive' way of life as he journeys into the Highlands, Allan steps back into a forgotten past as his journey across the ice fields brings him into contact with a surviving remnant of the lost Greenland settlers. Like Porter's Poles or medieval Scots, these people, peacefully inhabiting an earlier stage of history, are threatened by brutally violent invaders, although in this case the invaders are literally brutes: the Greenlanders are destroyed by an army of polar bears who combine shrewd, tactical skills in battle with a remarkable degree of malevolent sadism. And like both Waverley and Mertoun, the hero of *The Pirate*, Allan is torn between love interests who embody very different cultural values. In Allan's case, however, the contrast is not a straightforward one between dark and fair women or women who look back to the past or forward to the future, but rather between the Greenland women in general (almost all of whom seduce him under the cover of darkness) and a polar bear named Nancy, whom he has raised from a cub after killing and eating her mother, and who travels with him, protects him, and who risks her own life to protect him from her polar bear kin.

Given the exuberant absurdity of some of the plot details of the 'Surpassing Adventures', it might be tempting to read the novella simply as a parody of historical romance, rather than as a contribution to the genre in its own right. Yet the casual violence of the conclusion, as Allan and Nancy listen from their hiding place as the other bears massacre the last remnants of the Greenland colony (including Allan's children by his various mistresses), implies a more darkly cynical take than those of Scott or Porter on the basic assumptions of historical process implicit in concepts of stadial history. The other two novelists use romantic nostalgia to evoke a sense of the loss that (they imply) inevitably accompanies progress, differing mainly in the degree to which they see that cost as being worth the accompanying gains, but in his anti-romantic excesses, Hogg implies doubt about the idea of progress itself. The Greenlanders are kindly innocents, living in communal harmony, but even before the climactic massacre, Allan is wearied and disheartened by the drudgery of eking out a life in the harsh arctic landscape and disillusioned about any possibility of helping his new companions progress beyond the demands of mere survival. In the world of Allan Gordon, uneven historical development results not in the (temporary) survival of a romantic past in a more or less unwelcoming present but rather leaves the inhabitants of those earlier stages forgotten, isolated, and vulnerable.

If Hogg uses his anti-romance to critique ideas of historical progress, John Galt goes a step further and avoids romanticising the past in the first place. In *Annals of the Parish* (1821), perhaps his best-known work of historical fiction, historical progress is a matter of slow accretion rather than of moments of grand, nation-shaking change. Micah Balwhidder, the rural minster who records the events taking place in his parish during his long ministry, witnesses many changes in himself, his parishioners, and the world around them in the half century following his arrival in 1760. Yet even as he regrets what has been lost or left behind, he does so without any significant gloss of romantic nostalgia. Instead, Galt offers, through Balwhidder, what Ann Rigney has called 'behind-the-scenes history', in which he avoids glamorous adventure and concentrates instead on the 'culture of everyday life'.[7] In Balwhidder's eyes, the French Revolution is worrisome mainly because it sparks rising political feeling among his parishioners, and while he sees the arrival of a recruiting party in the district in 1795 as a disturbing sign of social decline, he is scarcely less worried (if more fascinated) by a troupe of travelling actors who arrive in the parish that summer. The titular narrator of Galt's later and lesser-known *Bogle Corbet* (1831) is also touched only lightly by the large-scale political changes around him as he comes of age in the turbulent 1790s. He falls in with some radical weavers but is affected neither by their political rhetoric nor by the ensuing backlash against them. The romance of revolutionary change that drives so much historical fiction is completely absent here: Bogle is uninterested in the world-changing events that he is living through, focusing instead only on the economic impacts on himself and his household.

Yet like Hogg, Galt draws upon elements of romance to reinforce his unromantic approach to historical narrative. *Bogle Corbet* is about imperial expansion as well as about the economic forces that drive Bogle to ruin. In addition to a subplot about India and a lengthy episode set in Jamaica, the novel follows Bogle's emigrant experience in Canada and ends with a flourish of romantic melodrama, as a trio of long-lost relatives rediscover each other and are reinstated to financial and familial security. The flagrant implausibility of these happy meetings is flagged by Bogle's prosaic wife, Urseline, whose main contribution to the novel up to that point has been disapproving comments on the distracting noise of Niagara Falls. After hearing all of the concluding revelations she exclaims, 'who ever thought that I would be a heroine, and live in a midnight turret in America?'[8] and then tells Bogle to rush the narrative that he has been preparing to the press, since he now has a conclusion that will make people want to read it. This is a nod towards the preface, in which Galt explains that he has decided to illustrate what one 'has really to expect in emigrating to Canada' in the form of a novel rather than a tract in order to help 'disguise' the 'medicine'.[9] That 'medicine' is the insistence that while settling in Canada involves a return to a more 'primitive' way of life, it is a version of an earlier stage that is shorn of the romance or glamour that accompanies a step back in to the past in the work of Scott or Porter. Yet despite that insistence, by the end of the novel, Galt infuses Bogle's new life in Canada, however lightly and belatedly, with the comforting tropes of romance. The happily-ever-after restoration of fiscal and familial security to at least some of the emigrants involves stepping away from the more or less grim realism with which Galt had depicted Canadian settler experience up to that point. In this case, the nostalgic escapism of romance is associated not so much with a specific past culture as with the form of the novel itself: romance is the sweetener that helps the 'medicine' of the truth about emigration to go down.

Bogle Corbet is not, of course, a conventional historical novel despite having a large part of the action set a generation back from the time of writing, and Hogg's absurdist fantasia on polar exploration is even further removed from standard historical fiction – much less actual history. One could develop a very different reading of Scottish historical romance by looking at, for example, Porter, Scott, and Hogg's treatment of medieval and early modern Scotland or Scott, Hogg, and Galt's novels about the Covenanters. Yet bringing some of the ostensibly anti-romantic treatments of history and progress by Galt and Hogg together with the more familiar work of their best-selling contemporaries can help us to see both the complex range of ways that elements of romance are drawn into the work of these historical novelists and the resulting rich diversity of the genre in the early nineteenth-century Scottish literary world.

CHAPTER FOUR

Slavery, Kinship, and Capital

Michael Morris

Enslaved women played a crucial role in production and reproduction – labour and childbirth – in Atlantic slavery.[1] Emphasising the key relationship between gender, kinship, and capitalism, Jennifer L. Morgan notes that 'The insinuation of economic rationality into colonial intimacies is the crux of the matter'.[2] Kinship includes family and also 'affective relationships' of community. Morgan elaborates on the Slave Codes of the 1660s which legislated that the children born of a white freeman and an enslaved woman would take the condition of the mother. For slavers, then, property rights could not be

> unsettled by sexual congress. Reproduction (and thus enslavability) was tethered to enslavement in a way that foreclosed the possibility that kinship might destabilize capital. To be enslaved meant to be locked into a productive relationship whereby all that your body could do was harnessed to accumulate capital for another.[3]

Given that historians have emphasised the kin (even clannish) networks of Scots in the Atlantic world, this has implications for Scotland.[4] For slavers, legal and acknowledged kinship networks had to be carefully curated; this required the disavowal of 'outside children' who threatened to destabilise capital and inheritance. For enslaved families, the maintenance of kinship networks was a struggle given that kin could be broken up and sold separately to increase profits and reduce resistance. The competing denouncements and justifications of such kinship practices have shaped our ideas of 'race, inheritance, trade, freedom, value, and slavery'. In short, colonial intimacies 'needed to be carefully navigated because kinship posed dangers' for the emerging world-system of racial capitalism.[5]

This chapter reads two novels against two testimonies, all navigating the 'dangers of kinship' during the decade of intense emancipation debates between the founding of the 'Society for the Mitigation and Gradual Abolition of Slavery Throughout the British Dominions' (Anti-Slavery Society) in 1823 and the Slavery Abolition Act of 1833. The first section analyses the Jacobite exiled following the defeat at Culloden in 1746 and rehabilitated through Caribbean slavery in Robert Wedderburn's (1762–1835?) political pamphlet *The Horrors of Slavery* (1824) and the anonymous colonial romance *Marly; or a Planter's Life in Jamaica* (1828 – written 1826). The second section examines kinship through the figure of the nurse in two texts from 1831. *The History of Mary Prince* was edited by Thomas Pringle (1789–1834) the Berwickshire-born poet, journalist, and secretary of the Anti-Slavery Society. It was opposed in *Blackwood's* by James MacQueen (1778–1870), who was born in Crawford, Lanarkshire. The contest between Pringle and MacQueen invites an analysis of *The History* in relation to a Scottish colonial framework in which the nature of kinship and slavery was fiercely contested.[6] This is read against John Galt's (1779–1839) novel *Bogle Corbet; or The Emigrants* (1831), which re-works the figure of the nurse as part of his pro-slavery campaigning of the 1830s.

Jacobites and Jamaica: Robert Wedderburn and Marly

As a leader of Thomas Spence's (1750–1814) radical group, Robert Wedderburn was a key figure in the London 'Radical Underworld', where he looked to 'integrate the prospect of slave revolution in the West Indies with that of working-class revolution in England'.[7] Robert was the son of James Wedderburn (1739–1807), of a landed Jacobite family who had fled Scotland to Jamaica following the execution of Sir John Wedderburn. Robert observes of his paternal family line, 'My grandfather was a staunch Jacobite, and exerted himself strenuously in the cause of the Pretender, in the rebellion of the year 1745':

> When I first came to England in the year 1779, I remember seeing the remains of a rebel's skull which had been affixed over Temple Bar; but I never yet could fully ascertain if it was my dear grandfather's skull, or not. Perhaps my dear brother, A. COLVILLE, can lend me some assistance in this affair.[8]

James established himself as a wealthy sugar plantation owner around Westmoreland and would return to Inveresk near Musselburgh as a respectable man of property. His more favoured son, the above-mentioned

Andrew Wedderburn-Colville (1779–1856), inherited the family sugar estates, became the Chairman of the West India Docks in London, and governor of the Hudson Bay company.[9] *The Horrors of Slavery* was originally formed by an exchange of letters between the half-brothers which centred on the question of kinship (in the newspaper *Bell's Life in London*). Andrew denied Robert's claim to belong to his family and insinuated the loose morals of his mother Rosanna who '*could not tell who was the father*'.[10] In response, Wedderburn wrote 'to defend the memory of my unfortunate mother'.[11] The pamphlet pivots on the contrasting nature of kinship and inheritance between, on the one side, his father and half-brother; and on the other, his mother and grandmother. His testimony details his origins in Jamaica – the entrapment and rape of his mother by his father – in order to lay bare the 'horrors of slavery' and to advocate rebellion.

In relation to his father, his depiction of Jamaican planters emphasises sexuality and capitalism – or more specifically a certain 'Scotch economy'[12] – including 'intercourse with their female slaves' with the purpose of 'selling their slaves while pregnant, and making that a pretence to enhance their value'.[13]

> My father ranged through the whole of his house-hold for his own lewd purposes; for they being his personal property, cost nothing extra; and if any one proved with child – why, it was an acquisition which might one day fetch something in the market, like a horse or pig in Smithfield.

Although Robert would himself be later convicted of running a 'bawdy house', in this portrayal James Wedderburn is transformed from successful planter to a 'perfect parish bull; and his pleasure was the greater, because he at the same time increased his profits'.[14] Robert is supported by the editor of *Bell's*, who notes that under slavery economic production and sexual reproduction are combined, yet kinship is ruptured:

> Slave-Buyers, we are aware, frequently have many children born to them by this dreadful species of female *property* – when the dearest ties of consanguinity are trampled upon by a sordid thirst of interest, we had almost said *inherent* in the *Slaver*.[15]

The Horrors of Slavery links sexual predation, reproduction, and the marketplace, highlighting the grotesquely deformed kinship relations of racial capitalism.

Yet neither Rosanna nor Robert remains a passive victim. If his father refused to acknowledge his inheritance in terms of kin and finance, Robert argues that he receives instead an inheritance of character from his mother. He glories 'in her *rebellious* disposition [...] which I have inherited from her'.[16] Elizabeth Bohls notes that 'Rosanna seems to have succeeded more than once in leveraging major changes' as she was canny enough to engineer her escape from a number of [Scottish] owners and to insist on Robert's freedom.[17] The pamphlet closes by moving from Rosanna's personal resistance to a suave reference to the Haitian revolution and the destruction of the plantation economy more broadly: 'I shall give some particulars of the treatment of the blacks in the West Indies, and the prospect of a general rebellion and massacre there, from my own experience.'[18] Robert's claim of kinship threatens to undermine the standing of the recently restored Jacobite family and destabilise the substantial inheritance of Andrew Wedderburn-Colville. He uses concepts of kinship to fuel his radical working-class and anti-slavery politics of resistance as he implies that Jamaica itself is pregnant with the possibility of revolt.

Wedderburn's portrayal of lust, cruelty, avarice and rebellion is suppressed in *Marly; or a Planter's Life in Jamaica* (1828), in which production and reproduction on the island are carefully managed. Karina Williamson suggests the most likely candidate for authorship to be John Stewart, the son of an Edinburgh lawyer who was 'resident in Jamaica from 1787 to 1808, acquired property there, and wrote two books about the island'.[19] Like James Wedderburn, the original 'Old Marly' (grandfather) had landed in Trelawney Parish with 'many conjecturing that he had been out in the year forty-five'.[20] Old Marly was displeased 'when any person happened to call it a rebellion, and the Prince Charles Edward, the Pretender', preferring 'the rising, and the Pretender was always honoured with the name of the Prince'.[21] On the day of his wedding, Marly planted sugar canes in 'Marriage Field' on 'Happy Fortune' estate and before the year was out a son and heir was born.[22] 'Marriage Field' announces the novel's linked concerns with the sugar economy, generating production and reproduction, serviced by contented negro swains 'who rejoiced at whatever pleased their massa and missa'.[23] Capital is at risk from two sources in this colonial romance: broken kinship, and immediate emancipation. The Marly heir drowned at sea and the sugar estates fell into the clutches of a dishonest Scotch attorney. The orphaned Marly (grandson) sails from Leith in a 'Scotch Guineaman'[24] with John Campbell from Argyll who takes a post at an exclusively Gaelic-speaking slave plantation.[25] Marly eventually ousts the usurper to claim his inheritance, marry the daughter, and introduce improvements for a grateful enslaved workforce who 'never desired their freedom', only a good master.[26]

In *Marly*, three balls reveal the dangers of kinship in the courtship codes of white supremacy. At the 'black ball', overseers gather to dance a reel with 'black belles' and 'brown beauties', some of whom even have features resembling more 'the European than the African, and with the exception of their jet black hue they would have been accounted tolerably handsome in any country'.[27] Birling through numerous partners, the reel portrays the indiscriminate availability of black women who exhibited 'none of that prudery' associated with 'their fair sisters in this country, each lady being only eager to get into the dance, apparently equally pleased with each partner who offered'.[28] This is a stark reversal of Wedderburn's portrayal of his mother Rosanna resisting the advances of James Wedderburn. Yet for Marly, the dangers of reproduction across the racial divide are foreclosed outside the dance, as he repeatedly refuses to take a 'sable wife' although it is 'the common custom', because 'his aversion to the black colour had not yet subsided'.[29] In the second dance, an incognito Marly dances the waltz with the 'angelic' Miss McFathom, making a glamorous, cosmopolitan twosome.[30] At the third ball, Marly's dance set gives a glimpse of an alternative vector of marriage arrangements, though his dance partner seems 'only half-educated, and rather too much of the negro'.[31] Stepping surely through a reel, waltz, and country dance, Marly, with his strict sexual continence and white supremacism, can marry Mary McFathom with no troublesome 'outside children' to destabilise the picture. Marly's inheritance of the sugar estates mends the broken relationship between capital and kinship: productivity is improved, family is restored, and the slave system is secured. In this colonial romance, the skulls of the Jacobite past are laid to rest under the commercial success of Jamaica's sugar estates.

Nursing on the Eve of Emancipation: Mary Prince and Bogle Corbet

Born into slavery in Bermuda in 1788, Prince was to act, in part, as nurse for the children of the families who enslaved her. Indeed she was brought to England by the Woods family to nurse their child but was forced to seek assistance from the Anti-Slavery Society in 1828. The opening pages of *The History* portray Mary's childhood in Bermuda as a relatively happy period in which shifting and precarious colonial kinships are formed before being shattered by the market realities of the auction block.[32]

Her early days attest to a profound emotional attachment to those she repeatedly calls 'my kindred': her 'dear mother', her two sisters and two brothers, under the charge of comparatively benign slaving families.[33] As nurse to the Pruden family, *The History* suggests the possibility of forging bonds of 'affective community' even under conditions of slavery:

> All my employment at this time was nursing a sweet baby little Master Daniel; and I grew so fond of my nursling that it was my greatest delight to walk with him by the sea-shore, accompanied by his brother and sister, Miss Fanny and Master James.[34]

However, the precarity of these kinship networks is exposed when her enslaver abruptly looks to sell Mary and her two sisters to pay for a wedding to his new wife. Mary's broken family is devastated by separation, and Mary even regrets leaving her nursling: 'the dear baby who had grown so fond of me […] I kissed and hugged the baby, thinking I should never see him again'.[35] Echoing Wedderburn's reference to Smithfield market, Prince's description of the 'vendue' dramatically pitches kinship against capital at the market-place. Her mother laments over her three daughters: 'I am going to carry my little chickens to market.'[36] *The History* therefore attests to degrees of intimacy and bonds of kinship through the figure of the nurse, but shows these to be ruptured by the demands of capital. She never manages to recover those early networks with 'my kindred', though her final quest is to re-unite with her husband, a freeman on Antigua. However, the Woods family refuse to sell her manumission so that she may return as a freewoman. This refusal, alongside MacQueen's detailed attacks on Prince in *Blackwood's*, suggest that there is a great deal at stake for the West India Lobby.[37] As Pringle notes, this case reveals 'the true spirit of the slave system'. Although apologists argued that 'self-interest is a sufficient check to the indulgence of vindictive feelings in the master', yet:

> Here is a case where a man (a *respectable* and *benevolent* man as his friends aver,) prefers losing entirely the full price of the slave, for the mere satisfaction of preventing a poor black woman from returning home to her husband![38]

For the West India lobby, to concede the primacy of Prince's kinship claims over property rights would undermine the case against emancipation more broadly.

By 1830, the common rhetorical position of the West India lobby was to admit that emancipation was inevitable, even desirable, on two conditions: firstly financial compensation for loss of property; secondly a delay until enslaved people could be sufficiently 'improved' to be ready for the vicissitudes of freedom. In three letters between 1830 and 1831 to the pungently pro-slavery *Fraser's Magazine*, John Galt sings loudly from that hymn sheet. Raised in Greenock, which became known as 'Sugaropolis', Galt's father 'was the captain and owner of a ship trading to the West Indies'.[39] Galt emphasises his kinship loyalties: 'early connexions and old associations have induced me *voluntarily* to undertake' the task of countering the 'philanthropists'.[40] Galt's letters belligerently disparage abolitionists and deploy a variety of time-honoured arguments – the Biblical justification found in Leviticus,[41] and the worse condition of 'white slaves'[42] of Britain. Galt proposes his own scheme to raise one hundred million pounds to compensate slavers, without which emancipation would ruin the national economy and the enslaved would lose the protection they currently enjoy from the 'parental solicitude' of masters: 'You must treat the negro as a child.'[43]

Galt's novel *Bogle Corbet; Or the Emigrants* was written over the same period as his letters. Where Marly's inheritance of Happy Fortune estate concludes an optimistic colonial romance, this melancholic colonial novel revolves around the first person narrator's 'crisis of fortune' and abounds in orphans, illegitimate children, and troubled inheritance.[44] Like Andrew Wedderburn-Colville, Galt became a coloniser of Upper Canada, though by 1829 he was recalled and landed in debtor's prison where he drafted this novel. Kenneth McNeil usefully conceives of it as a 'circum-atlantic' novel which maps capital across merchant imperial circuits between Glasgow, London, Jamaica, and Canada.[45] Bogle was born in 1775, the year the American revolution precipitated the crash of the Glasgow tobacco firms and associated banks. His name recalls both the Scots word 'bogle' for 'ghost', and the Glasgow merchant firm of Robert Bogle of Gilmorehill, which suffered in the tobacco crash and recovered via West Indian slave-sugar. This combination of imperial and economic trauma, and gothic hauntings, shapes this novel of recessions, depressions, and repressions. McNeil notes that Galt's 'theoretical fiction' combines the empirical, the statistical, and the theoretical to provide a 'guidebook' for emigrants to Canada.[46] I argue that the Caribbean sections are similarly designed to be 'useful to social and economic improvers' as Galt's fiction mediates the arguments of the West India lobby. This links together production and reproduction through two female figures who bookend volume one: Bogle's nurse and a Maroon he encounters on his return to Jamaica as an adult.

Born on Plantagenet sugar estate in Jamaica, Bogle, like Marly, is orphaned in infancy. His fondest memories are of his nurse:

> Methinks I see her, blithe and caroling, with large good-natured eyes, and though she be black, she has such cheerful teeth, every one of them is a smile in ivory […] never was I in arms more fond and kind than in thine, my dear, my dark, but comely Baba![47]

Baba's shining teeth recall the African-American 'Mammy' stereotype which Kimberly Wallace-Sanders notes first appeared as (wet) nurses in novels of the 1820s American South: 'proslavery authors use these images of slave women with a white child as a symbol of racial harmony within the slave system'.[48] A sentimental icon of surrogate maternity, suckling and nurturing, 'singing and ever-caressing' before disappearing from view, she never articulates discernible words, only affectionate noises.[49] Baba soothes the trauma of the break in the family line caused by the death of the parents and her nurture secures the prosperity of the sugar estate on which Bogle's 'little fortune was originally mortgaged'.[50] While Prince does attest to the possibility of affective kinship between nurse and nursling, it is a brief moment which is overwhelmed by vindictive cruelty meted out even by the families for whom she acted as nurse. Where nursing in Prince's testimony reveals how slave-capital devastates kinship, the devotion of Baba and Bogle promotes the mythology of a benevolent kinship in which, Galt claims, 'the slaves are carefully tended by their proprietors'.[51] As a young man, in addition to his naïve dalliance with Jacobinism, Bogle expresses the kind of vague abolitionist sentiment that Galt lambasted in his letters.[52] However, Bogle's expectations of Caribbean slavery, shaped by 'theoretical argumentators',[53] are confounded by eye-witness experience leading him to question, with increasing force, what is said by the 'philanthropists of England?'.[54] *Bogle Corbet* was published in the same year that Mary Prince revealed her body to be 'chequered' with scars and gashes, 'the vestiges of severe floggings'.[55] Yet 'that undecaying affection with which I must ever think of Baba'[56] recurs repeatedly to an adult Bogle to confirm his new vision of a content slave system nourished by the intimate bonds between nurse and nursling.

By contrast, the second female figure is a grandmother Bogle encounters travelling along the Maroon road 'with three ebony imps around her'. Like Rosanna and James Wedderburn, she had been 'Dulcinea to a

Scottish overseer' though 'she had assisted an African lover one night to murder [him] and burn his house'. She utters no discernible words but she and the children speak a 'wild mockery of language' which Bogle finds 'to my inexpressible amusement, was Negro-Scotch'.[57] This hybrid language speaks of a kinship between Scots and enslaved Africans rendered grotesque, even absurd, by the act of rebellion. The woman appears to be a version of Nanny of the Maroons, now a national hero in Jamaica, though colonial writers described her as a 'Hagg'.[58] Galt's physical description of the naked woman depicts a 'hideous Sycorax' whom he could barely 'believe was really human'.[59] The significance of the Maroons as 'self-emancipated slaves' in this novel is that they 'afforded afflicting exhibitions to civilized man of the state that awaits the Negroes when the control of the proprietors shall have been withdrawn'.[60] This Maroon Sycorax is a gothic omen of emancipation erupting into an otherwise 'romantic' and improving Jamaican landscape.[61] On Plantagenet estate, Baba's role as surrogate mother had sustained and nourished the sugar economy. High in the Blue Mountains which 'rose like the magnificent pyramids' of Egypt, Sycorax is 'withered like a mummy'.[62] Her 'bust of womanhood [...] was as shriveled and shrunk as beggar's purses'.[63] This image combines the desiccation of maternity with the collapse of the economy as the 'poverty and affliction'[64] that Galt warned of in immediate emancipation is made flesh. At Plantagenet, Bogle finds Baba's daughter whom he regards as a 'foster-sister' at the estate's lying-in hospital replete with mothers, grandmothers, nurses and newborns all compassionately tended for by 'my kinsman', the Scottish overseer Mr Buchanan.[65]

This chapter has emphasised the contested nature of kinship in the debates leading up to emancipation. The Caribbean testimonies from Wedderburn and Prince demonstrate kinship to be shattered by slavery, while the Scottish novelists portray slavery to be rescued and nourished by compassionate kinship between slaver and enslaved. As Scotland is currently reckoning with its own inheritance from slavery, this chapter has looked to probe the concept of kinship to argue for a more critical understanding of its relation to capital, race, and family.

CHAPTER FIVE

Private Thoughts and Public Display: Gender, Genre, and Lives

Susan Oliver

Studies in literature of the late eighteenth and nineteenth centuries often associate masculinity with public lives while femininity is linked to the domestic world of marriage and families. Comparing life writing by two of Scotland's best-known male writers – Walter Scott (1771–1832) and Lord Byron (1788–1824) – with that by three women who, while popular in their lifetimes, more or less disappeared from public view for a century and a half after their deaths – Susan Ferrier (1782–1854), Mary Brunton (1778–1818), and Elizabeth Grant (1797–1885) – this chapter explores how gendered public and private thought interacts in Scottish Romanticism.[1] The term 'life writing' is extended to include narratives of communal groups as well as of individuals. Not all the works discussed were published during their authors' lifetimes, raising further questions about categories of the private and public in items such as memoirs, letters, and unfinished novels.

The celebrity author arrived dramatically in the early nineteenth century. Walter Scott's and Lord Byron's latest works sold out overnight or soon afterwards, leaving their publishers rushing to produce new print runs and editions.[2] Interest in these writers' lives increased with their literary fame, and in Byron's case was exacerbated by often outrageous behaviour that contrasted with his more serious social concerns. By the time his satirical mock-epic *Don Juan* was published between 1819 and 1824, Byron was being read as almost indistinguishable from the darkly seductive, troubled character that appeared in his own poems: the Byronic hero was a literary type, but also a flamboyant Anglo-Scottish émigré living in Europe. However, during the years in which Scott and Byron were writing their way to becoming literary giants, a more expansive circle of writers of which they formed only a part added to a vibrantly diverse Scottish literary world. Ferrier and Brunton wrote successful novels that ran to multiple print runs, along with memoirs and travelogues, while Grant would write memoirs that include one of the most informative and imaginative accounts of early nineteenth-century life in the Scottish Highlands.

Scott's sense of his own masculine style is evident in an 1826 journal entry: 'The Big Bow wow strain I can do myself like any now going but the exquisite touch which renders ordinary common-place things and characters interesting from the truth of the description and the sentiment is denied to me'.[3] His comparison is with Jane Austen (1775–1817), but he could as easily be measuring himself against Ferrier, Brunton, and Grant (although *Memoirs of a Highland Lady* was not published until after his and Grant's deaths). Indeed fourteen days later he added that, 'thoughts and sentiments' are much better done by 'the women', citing the examples of Maria Edgeworth (1768–1849), Ferrier, and Austen.[4] But while these often-quoted remarks differentiate between the display-oriented style and subject matter of writing produced by men and sentiments-based narratives by women, Scott's *Journal*, like his extensive correspondence and other life writing, is an archive of personal thoughts that reflect on his domestic as well as his public life.

1826 was one of the most significant years of Scott's life for other reasons. January brought the humiliation that came with his declaration of insolvency, then in May his wife of twenty-nine years died following a sudden illness. These catastrophes show the public exposure of financial ruin, from which there was no refuge, having an impact on the most vulnerable of private moments. The prose that records the insolvency strives for professionally detached self-control, as if Scott were his own lawyer: 'If I am hard pressed and measures used against me I must use all measures of legal defence and subscribe myself bankrupt [...] It is the course I would have advised a client to take.'[5] Two days later, he is anxious that insomnia might lead to the indignity of missing a public engagement. By contrast, his entries on the death of Lady Scott show a grieving husband and family man, a side of Scott often lost from sight behind the high points of his literary success and the low of financial ruin. Charlotte Scott died on 15 May 1826, 'at nine in the morning after being very ill for two days – easy at last'. Scott's first concern is for their exhausted daughter Anne. The ensuing account of his own grief shows him immersed in private thoughts and rejecting any form of display:

> I feel sometimes as firm as the Bass rock sometimes as weak as the wave that breaks on it [...] Lonely – aged – deprived of my family all but poor Anne [...] I am deprived of the sharer of my thoughts and counsels

> who could always talk down my sense of the calamitous apprehensions which break the heart that must bear them alone [...] But I will not blaze cambrick and crape in the publick eye like a disconsolate widower, that most affected of all characters.[6]

Anne's letters record Scott's pain at missing his wife's death because he was 'obliged to leave her, to attend his duty in Edinburgh'.[7] In June he mentions a further emotionally charged moment when his son Charles found him weeping from embarrassment at facing Edinburgh's lawmen combined with grief over the loss of his 'poor Charlotte', whose death he still found hard to accept.[8] These instances show Scott distressed by the incursion of public responsibilities on his personal life.

Byron's life writing more than blurred the boundaries between public and private experience, challenging distinctions between conventional autobiographical genres and poetic fiction. His first public collection, *Hours of Idleness* (1807), contained lyric reflections on his childhood in Scotland. *Childe Harold's Pilgrimage*, the four-canto poem based on travels in Europe and published between 1812 and 1818, was considered from its outset to be autobiographical even though the title character was ostensibly a fictional persona. *Don Juan* has already been mentioned. However, one of the most notorious acts of keeping private thoughts away from the public realm must be the burning of Byron's last memoir in the drawing room of his publisher John Murray's London home on 17 May 1824, by a group of the poet's friends and associates including Murray. The memoir would almost certainly have caused social embarrassment, probably with legal implications for those involved. The secrecy of the many people, including several women, who had read its contents is extraordinary.[9] Nevertheless, the substantial surviving body of Byron's correspondence and journals constitutes a collective, epistolary work of literature in its own right. With a style that Richard Lansdowne has aptly described as 'freshness and racy vigour', Byron dramatised his own controversial life at least as much as those of the heroes in his poetry. Whereas his poems interlace expertise in established metric forms with mischievous variation, his personal writing gives expression to Romantic feeling, sexual desire, and imagination, using a stream-of-consciousness mode that anticipates modernism.[10] The 'Ravenna journal' covering early January to late February 1821 is one of the highest points in Byron's writing about himself. An extract shows the importance of Scott to his thoughts and habits, as well as his seamless reflection on private and professional activity.[11] The entry for 15 January 1821 blends a vivacious articulacy, the dramatic punctuation that features throughout his letters and journals, evidence of Byron's business relationship with Murray, and his claim to be serially rereading his favourite author:

> Rose late – dull and drooping – the weather dripping and dense. Snow on the ground, and sirocco above in the sky [...] Roads up to the horse's belly, so that riding (at least for pleasure) is not very feasible. Added a postscript to my letter to Murray. Read the conclusion, for the fiftieth time (I have read all W. Scott's novels at least fifty times) of the third series of 'Tales of my Landlord', – grand work – Scotch Fielding, as well as great English poet – wonderful man! I long to get drunk with him.[12]

A week later, Byron declared Scott's novels to be 'a new literature in themselves'.[13] The ease with which he traverses private thoughts and public display in his letters and journals testifies to the arbitrariness of those boundaries.

Susan Ferrier understood Byron's abilities in boundary crossing, noting that she experienced much the same emotional effect from his poetry as did many Regency women: in 1816 she wrote in her *Memoir*, 'Did you ever read anything so exquisite as the new Canto of "Childe Harold"? It is enough to make a woman fly into the arms of a tiger.'[14] Writing originally to entertain her family and friends, and only later publishing anonymously, she shunned the celebrity of being a known author, writing that she 'could not bear the *fuss* of authorism!'.[15] And Scott, whom she knew, considered her 'gifted [...] full of humour, and [...] without the least affectation of the blue stocking'.[16] Recognised for her novels *Marriage* (1818), *The Inheritance* (1824), and *Destiny: or, the Chief's Daughter* (1831), Ferrier in her lively narrative style embraces plots that often warn women how emotional impetuosity can be followed by years of regret.

Ferrier has been called the Scottish Jane Austen on account of her marriage-based storylines. However, her confidential, gossipy narrative style, with humour that is earthy and direct, does not fit the exquisite touch that Scott ascribed to Austen. Her novels are informed by the experience of being a woman and, as such, are a form of sisterly life writing that addresses problems including the injustice that comes with prejudice. Ferrier's account of Highland life is a focal point in *Marriage*, but also a *tour de force* that combines Austen's comedies of manners with a Scott-like brilliance in building communities of colourful characters. Three comically depicted Highland spinsters are gradually revealed to be less ridiculous and to have more integrity than the spiteful London society wives with whom the main character yearns to associate. The landscape, castles, and houses that appear gloomy to the young bride who has come to them from London after marrying a Scot, seem so because distanced from the whirl of city life; Ferrier infuses them with conviviality, deconstructing stereotypes that Scottish rural life is remote or limited.

Ferrier's most innovative moments show her to be intensely sensitive to matters that shaped women's lives, including childlessness, infant and perinatal mortality, and poverty. Introducing these into her fiction, she demonstrates the collective women's life writing already mentioned. The tactlessness shown by *Marriage*'s Lady Juliana Douglas toward her Highland host and sister-in-law is a case in point. Mary Douglas is introduced knitting stockings for local children whose mothers cannot afford such garments. She is childless, her only child having been stillborn. Juliana's insensitivity peaks when, rejecting her own twin daughters, she exclaims: 'I am sure you are very happy in not having children […] I hope to goodness I shall never have any more'.[17] Mary responds with the silence of private thoughts.

Another episode concerns Mary Douglas's garden and collection of houseplants. Heliotrope, moss roses, and Cape Jessamine (gardenia) show her to be far from out of touch with the wider world and to respect nonhuman life. She rebukes Juliana for picking the flowers, saying they are intended only for 'the gratification of two senses – seeing and smelling'.[18] Mary's botanical interests reflect a fashion that was stimulated by global exploration along with a boom in botanical publications and collecting. Ferrier would have known Edinburgh's Botanic Garden and Scott's ambitious planting at Abbotsford. Another moment in *Marriage* blends aesthetics with an acknowledgement of Scotland's modernising fishing industry, in a vignette of 'a fleet of herring-boats, the drapery of whose black suspended nets, contrasted with picturesque effect the white sails of the larger vessels'.[19]

Mary Brunton was raised in Orkney as a committed Presbyterian and married a Church of Scotland minister with whom she eloped by boat. She is best known for what Lisa Wood has described as 'evangelical romance' fiction.[20] Like Ferrier, she is compared with Austen despite writing in a very different style. Brunton never met either Byron or Scott, although she was familiar with their writing and they knew hers.[21] Her literary privacy was compromised early when, soon after *Self-Control* (1811) was published anonymously, Scott disclosed her authorship in a letter to Lady Abercorn, adding that she was married to an Edinburgh clergyman and was well known in the city.[22] After a second novel, *Discipline* (1814), that took forward a similar moral theme, Brunton's unfinished third novel, *Emmeline*, was published in 1819 by her husband, in a volume that included his memoir of her life along with extracts from her correspondence and travel journals. She had died the previous year aged forty, following the stillbirth of their only child. A letter to a woman friend reflects on the compromised autonomy that came with literary fame:

> Since Self-Control was fixed upon me, my circle of acquaintance has widened so unmercifully, that my time, in Edinburgh, is very little at my command [...] I have gained associates among persons eminent for talents [...] while I have lost only the power of sitting at times dozing by my own fire-side, or of wandering out unnoticed among the crowd.[23]

Brunton's travel journals make innovative use of a popular genre. Reversing the commonplace of Scottish tour narratives by English and Welsh travellers, she reflects as a Scottish woman on how the rest of Britain seemed strangely foreign to her in its appearance, manners, and social structures. Her account of an 1812 performance of Handel's *Messiah* in Covent Garden describes with amusement how her party took tickets in the pit to be close to the stage, only to find themselves among drunken sailors and their female companions. The dramas on- and off-stage function as different forms of display that compete for the author's attention.[24]

Elizabeth Grant, like Byron, wrote about Scotland while an émigré in Europe. *Memoirs of a Highland Lady*, published by her niece in 1898 in the decade after her death, is recognised as one of the best first-hand accounts of life on a remotely located Highland estate. Written decades retrospectively, after her family's financial ruin led to their leaving their home in the Cairngorms, *Memoirs* covers the years from 1797 to 1827.

Grant's lawyer father bought one of the first three houses to be completed in Charlotte Square, Edinburgh. Her own childhood was spent between there, London, Hertfordshire, and the Cairngorms. She stresses that her best memories are of the Highlands, emphasising how family members regarded the Cairngorms as their place of homecoming, returning there after careers around the world: 'All who survived returned to end their days where they began them, for no change of circumstances can change the heart of a Highlander.'[25] From start to finish she refers to the Rothiemurchus estate as her family's 'Duchus' [dùthchas], a Gaelic word that refers to an ancestral family domain including the experience of home, its cultural traditions, and everything in the surrounding environment: '[it was] the spot on Earth dearest to every one of us [...] No other spot ever replaced it, no other scenery ever surpassed it'.[26]

Grant's narrative is particularly interesting for its traversal of the boundaries between the male-dominated world of land management and women's epistolary observation. She identifies, for example, forestry's potential as a developing industry in Scotland, explaining how her family had not recognised the value of the timber that surrounded them:

> black cattle were its [Rothiemurchus's] staple products; its real wealth, its timber, was unthought of. [By 1796] the timber was beginning to be marketable; three or four thousand a year could easily have been cut out of that extensive forest for ever, and hardly have been missed.[27]

Moving from that rural Highland environment to the very different context of the nineteenth-century city, she vividly depicts Edinburgh's New Town in the process of construction:

> The width of the streets, the size of the houses, the brightness and the cleanliness [...] It was then very far from being what it became a few years later, how very very far from what we see it now! The New Town was but in progress, the untidy appendages of buildings encumbered the half-finished streets, and where afterwards the innumerable gardens spread in every quarter to embellish the city of palaces, there were then only unsightly greens abandoned to the washerwomen.[28]

Of the five writers discussed in this chapter, only Elizabeth Grant makes a cultural distinction between Scotland's Highlands and Lowlands that is grounded in a Highland experiential integration of Christian theology, folklore, and geology. Scott identified a similar separation of those two parts of the nation in indirect ways, writing into his literary output an environmental history that changed the way Scotland was culturally understood. But religion was for him more a means to an end in storytelling, while geology becomes more fully alive because of its folkloric connections.[29] Ferrier and Brunton represent Scottish practical interests in botany and forestry alongside religious and moral didacticism. Byron's numerous references to Scotland's Highland environment are mostly in the elegiac mode of someone who was always in exile. But Grant's claim about the inseparability of faith, literature, and place is unequivocal:

> Our mountains were full of fairy legends, old clan tales, forebodings, prophecies, and other superstitions, quite as much believed in as the Bible. The Shorter Catechism and the fairy stories were mixed up together to form the innermost faith of the Highlander, a much gayer and less metaphysical character than his Saxon-tainted countryman.[30]

The final assignment here of a masculine gender to culture is striking, coming from a woman who challenged so many other attempts to limit the thoughts and behaviour of wives, mothers, daughters, and sisters.

An aim of this chapter has been to interrogate the validity of boundaries that appear to separate public from private lives in Scottish writing, asking whether such distinctions are meaningful or whether they perpetuate commonplace, misleading ideas about gender. Scottish nineteenth-century women authors have regained critical attention in recent years, while reassessments of Scott and Byron show how those authors are relevant to the concerns of twenty-first-century audiences. A longer study that explores gender in other than binary forms would be a next step in advancing understanding of the literary thresholds where private thoughts and public display converge to generate meaning.

CHAPTER SIX

The Gothic, Supernatural and Religious

Samuel Baker

Eighteenth-century Scotland did not witness the boom in Gothic fiction seen in England at that time. But by the early nineteenth century, Scottish authors like Robert Burns (1759–1796), Joanna Baillie (1762–1851), James Macpherson (1736–1796), and Walter Scott (1771–1832) had popularised the Gothic mode in poetry, drama, and pseudo-antiquarian prose, setting the stage for a distinctive style of 'Scottish Gothic' that would emerge, after 1815, in fiction by Scott, James Hogg (1770–1835), and fellow members of the *Blackwood's Edinburgh Magazine* circle, including John Galt (1779–1839). Such Scottish Gothic characteristically features an 'association of national and uncanny themes', as Ian Duncan has influentially argued.[1] This chapter introduces this corpus of Scottish Gothic literature, specifies some ways in which the 'uncanny' entailments of Scottish Gothic relate to religious discourse (very much including the self-conscious secularism incipient in the era), and situates Scottish Gothic literature within the international currents that conditioned its expressions of nationalism.

In the wake of William and Mary's 1688 arrival from the Netherlands, mainstream Presbyterianism had won for itself the status of national Church. Yet having a Church of Scotland hardly unified that characteristically riven body, and robust debates continued for centuries regarding the status of Reformed, nonconformist or seceding Presbyterians; Scottish Episcopalians (whose church Scott attended); the Scottish Catholic remnant and tradition; and new strains of evangelicalism.[2] As often as not, such debates turned on questions of foreign influence, or on observations of religious history and events elsewhere – whether in England or France, in the Holy Land, in America, or in the corners of the globe where missionaries might venture. This legacy of debating religious nationalism at home and abroad was formative for the Scottish Gothic, even if Scottish Gothic authors by and large disengaged from doctrinal struggle.[3]

Through the eighteenth century, 'literature', in the broad sense of cultivated writing, still named a largely religious practice, and a body of work much of which was devoted, explicitly or implicitly, to doctrinal debate. Yet this began to change in late eighteenth-century Scotland, setting the stage for the emergence of Gothic literature that could evoke religious sensibility without engaging in religious polemics, and that could even explain the supernatural, with recourse to a sceptical empiricism. While enlightened moderate Presbyterians like the Reverend William Robertson – now best remembered as a historian – were gaining control over the national church, philosophers like Hugh Blair (himself a minister), Adam Smith, and David Hume instituted belletristic norms for a new literary establishment. Across the nineteenth century, wherever the influence of Scottish culture was felt, literature in this new tradition would work to transcend sectarian and national divides, while taking nothing less than the whole world of histories and societies as its subject. Taking part in this secularisation and expansion of literature, the versions of Gothic crafted by Scott and his peers in Scotland would soon be manufactured around the globe, by writers attracted not least by the power it afforded their station. Scott, his friend and rival Hogg, and their associates at *Blackwood's* worked, each in his own way, to create a Romantic cult of the author that assumes something of the religious authority so important for literary cultures past. And what starts as Scottish Gothic in their work would become, by the end of the nineteenth century, a Modernist Gothic, a literary approach that owns superstition with shamanistic brio, as it cares for, collects, and curates supernatural practices in the name of literary culture as itself a higher tradition.[4]

Already, by the early nineteenth century, even quite provincial and minor Scottish writers could readily take recourse to a Gothic style. Witness, for example, a description of the funeral of George III, purportedly written by a visitor from Garnock, 'pleasantly situated between Irvine and Kilwinning', who happened to be in London to witness the event, and whose letter describing it was published in *Blackwood's* shortly thereafter.[5] 'I was within the walls of an ancient castle', begins this author, Andrew Pringle,[6] starting out in poetry, and then waxing lyrical in prose:

> So old as if they had for ever stood,
> So strong as if they would forever stand,

and it was almost midnight. The towers, like the vast spectres of departed ages, raised their embattled heads to the skies, monumental witnesses of the strength and antiquity of a great monarchy. A prodigious multitude filled the courts of that venerable edifice, surrounding on all sides a dark embossed structure, the sarcophagus, as it seemed to me at the moment, of the heroism of chivalry. 'A change came o'er the spirit of my dream' [...] Then an awful cadence of solemn music, that affected the heart like silence, was heard at intervals, and a numerous retinue of grave and venerable men,

> The fathers of their time,
> Those mighty master spirits, that withstood
> The fall of monarchies, and high upheld
> Their country's standard, glorious in the storm,

passed slowly before me, bearing the emblems and trophies of a king. They were as a series of great historical events, and I beheld behind them, following and followed, an awful and indistinct image, like the vision of Job.[7]

Informed readers, perhaps feeling the sublimity of this passage tip over into faint ridiculousness – or recognising the name 'Pringle' – will not be surprised to be told that this letter is from John Galt's *tour de force* of gentle satire *The Ayrshire Legatees*, a fictional, epistolary family travelogue that *Blackwood's* serialised in 1820. Eager as Galt's ambitious young barrister is to convey 'a series of great historical events', what he renders is a series of Gothic clichés. By having the Scotsman Andrew Pringle only fully indulge his Gothic imagination once he reaches England, Galt tweaks Scottish provincialism, as well as the xenophobia of the English Gothic tradition that induced authors like Horace Walpole (1717–1797), Edmund Burke (1729–1797), Ann Radcliffe (1764–1823), and Lord Byron (1788–1824; in this perhaps more an Englishman than a Scot) to set their fantasias abroad (chiefly in Italy, France, or Spain). In the heart of London, Pringle arrives at the odd mixture of conventionalism and sensationalism that characterises the Gothic genre generally.

Elsewhere in *The Ayrshire Legatees*, back in Garnock, the young clergyman minding the parish duties for Andrew's father while he journeys is shown to be an embarrassed but enthusiastic reader of Walter Scott, and in particular of *Ivanhoe*, which had been published in December 1819, less than a month before George III's demise. *Ivanhoe* was the first novel the Author of *Waverley* set in England, and his first set in the Middle Ages; in it, Scott depicts a milieu where Protestantism is nowhere to be found, and achieves a new intensity of Gothicism as he does so. In retrospect, Scott can be seen to have been building up the Gothic aspect of his fiction before deciding, with *Ivanhoe*, to go medieval. As early as *Waverley* (1814), Scott evokes Gothic themes as he juxtaposes his protagonist's romance imagination with war's bloody realities, although he forbears, throughout his debut novel, to 'pursue such a description' to a truly Gothic degree of explicitness.[8] Specifically, Scott remains reticent about the spectacular conversion to Catholicism that marriage to his inamorata, the French-schooled Jacobite temptress Flora MacIvor, would have entailed for Waverley, and about the gory spectacle that does ensnare Waverley's boon companion Fergus, Flora's brother, beheaded for his service to Bonnie Prince Charlie's rebellion. The ultimately religious stakes of love and war in the novel remain a closed book, much like the treasonous treatises of Waverley's Episcopalian Jacobite tutor, Pembroke, which go unread even as they precipitate Waverley's arrest and necessitate his rescue by the Presbyterian Reverend Morton (whose precise place in the Scottish doctrinal landscape Scott ostentatiously leaves ambiguous); more romantically, they remain a confined mystery, like that of Flora's fate within or beyond 'the convent of the Scottish Benedictine nuns in Paris' to which she retreats at the novel's end.[9]

Scott's follow up, *Guy Mannering* (1815), like *Waverley* reports, rather than depicts, what would have been its most Gothic scenes, significantly locating them on the other side of the world from Scotland – in India – during a seventeen-year gap in the narrative. Yet in his third novel, *The Antiquary* (1816), which completes Scott's initial trilogy of 'fictitious narratives, intended to illustrate the manners of Scotland at three different periods', the Author of *Waverley* confronts the Gothic, even as he moves to the modern setting of a French Revolutionary War invasion panic during which he himself would not have been much younger than the novel's hero. The plot of *The Antiquary* is notoriously lacking in dynamism – it serves as E. M. Forster's main exhibit when he arraigns Scott because 'to make one thing happen after another is his only serious aim'.[10] As Jonathan Oldbuck entertains a young English visitor at the converted Catholic monastery where he lives and obsesses over putative Roman ruins, his antiquarianism gathers the requisite Gothic material, but stifles Gothic passion. Yet from the moment when the unexpected Gothic spectacle of a Roman Catholic funeral procession (surely an inspiration for Pringle's pastiche) introduces the Glenallan family, the novel moves forcefully toward a conclusion. The patriarch of this local aristocratic Roman Catholic clan, who embodies, per William Hazlitt (1778–1830), in *The Spirit of the Age*, the echt Gothic traits of 'feudal tyranny and fiendish pride', reconciles himself to society when he discovers Oldbuck's visitor to be his own lost son, now a fully assimilated British army officer deployed to help fend off French invasion.[11] *The Antiquary* thus ultimately restates the equation, first laid out with *Waverley*, wherein modern war redeems for the nation a family that has succumbed to ancient Catholic attractions. In the process, Scott relegitimises the profound ambivalence toward religious heritage that both characterises and is characterised by the Gothic.[12]

However much Scott's initial three novels concern 'the manners of Scotland', their Gothic tensions involve Europe, and their resolution is fundamentally British. It is with his subsequent *Tales of My Landlord* in 1816 that Scott develops a more properly Scottish Gothic, exploring the uncanny elements of Scottish nationalism by anatomising the varieties of Scottish religion, often to horrific effect. This process begins with the conceit Scott devises for laying this new corpus on the table. The title page for the anonymously published, initial four-volume set of *Tales* announces them to have been 'collected and reported' by one Jedidiah Cleishbotham, 'schoolmaster and parish-clerk of Gandercleugh': a fictional town, whose supposed location on the road between Edinburgh and Glasgow makes its inn a convenient spot at which to record the stories of the nation.[13] Cleishbotham's preface, which purports to explain all this, takes a dark turn when it reveals he is 'NOT the writer, redacter, or compiler of the Tales of My Landlord', but that he has merely conveyed to a publisher papers produced by his late junior colleague, the Presbyterian minister turned schoolteacher, Peter Pattieson, who, like Cleishbotham, frequented the inn where these tales were told.[14] The tales, Cleishbotham explains, are the literary remains of this chronically ill poet, whose melancholic pastime it has been to collect them; they appear now as he arranged them for the press because, Cleishbotham avers, 'the will of the dead must be scrupulously obeyed'.[15] At the outset of the second and major work of the first series, *The Tale of Old Mortality* (1816), Pattieson – whom we thus know, as we read, to be dead – provides a second, internal frame narrative, in which he describes his habit of walking down to an overgrown cemetery near the school, where he would occasionally see the self-appointed custodian of Covenanter graves whose stories are said to give rise to the novel. The Gothic atmospherics of *The Tale of Old Mortality* thus come mediated not only by its titular aging Covenanter zealot, but also by schoolteachers trained in, but not practicing, the more moderate Presbyterianism of modern times.

Analysing those atmospherics, Fiona Robertson claims *The Tale of Old Mortality* is 'free of standard Gothic motifs and situations'. If this is true, it is only true because the religious themes that so saturate the novel can everywhere explain depictions of extreme psychological crises that would strike one as Gothic were they not so evidently spiritual.[16] From the hallucinatory quasi-apparition of the red-cloaked woman at the crossroads, who early on warns the fugitive Covenanting assassin John Balfour, aka Burley, of 'a lion in the path', turning him toward the moderate hero Henry Morton's hospitality, to the evocation of Balfour's own well-nigh Satanic power in his ultimate struggle with Morton, the most vivid scenes from *The Tale of Old Mortality*, so framed, demonstrate the authority of an emergently national and at least somewhat sceptical and secularised literary culture to process the terrors of faith. If Scott's Tales process these terrors without fully resorting to the Gothic, in so doing, they appropriate to themselves and their author figures something of the uncanny power of the spiritual warriors they depict. Subsequent Tales find Scott only raising the stakes for such cycles of unleashing and confining Gothic terrors: most famously, the *Bride of Lammermoor* (1819), from its opening funeral confrontation (no doubt another inspiration for Galt's aforementioned Gothic parody) to its tragic 'mad scene' nuptial bloodbath, and *The Heart of Mid-Lothian* (1818), which so labours to close a tale of purported child murder with a tragic parricide. Yet even here, readers have found Scott's Gothic palpable, but unrealised. Many modern critics writing before Robertson and Duncan (and some since), especially those who consider Scott's work – if not modern literary culture more generally – an exercise in the reproduction of ideological fantasy, dismiss the power of his Gothic stylings; so too, at least to some extent, did contemporaries like Hazlitt, Galt, and Hogg, each of whom in his own way evinced frustration with Scott for his moderation, closure, or compromise.

Like Cleishbotham, who comically calls Pattieson 'flimsy' and criticises him for 'following not the example of those strong poets whom I proposed to him as an example', Scott's contemporaries like Hogg and Galt discount the force of his work and try to improve upon it. Still, refusing his achievement of closure, they carry forward his openness to experience, however sensational, supernatural, spiritual, or otherwise Gothic. The example of a strong poet Cleishbotham holds up for Pattieson is the English divine John Donne, whose 'Elegy' by Thomas Carew he quotes for its well-known lines about how 'frivolous' poets (such as Pattieson, in the analogy) discard Donne's 'strict laws' for 'ballad rhyme'.[17] By rehearsing this amusingly pedantic opprobrium, Scott connects his Tales back to his early work translating supernatural ballads from the German and collecting his *Minstrelsy of the Scottish Border* (1802). It may be that those who read Scott's fiction in the light of the ascendance of law and the state see its reinforcement of social architectonics as predominant, while those who read it with a more immediate sense of chaotic violence can find, in the *Waverley* novels, the verve, raw imagery, and national sensibility associated with ballads. Ultimately, success, for Scott in this mode, may involve crafting his novels as multi-stable representations legible both ways – as ordered, and as disordered – even if such craft, for his critics, represents just more overreach, and hence more failure. From yet another angle, this perennial problem in the interpretation of Scott can be seen to restate theological problems of agency, omniscience, and soteriological humility that have been central for Calvinist sects such as Presbyterianism. Might the suspicion of Scott's magisterial authority derive from regarding him as a cultural Episcopalian, exhibiting tendencies toward a Catholicism that may be English, or even Roman, and that in any case fails to show a proper cultural deference to the spirit abroad in his proper nation?

Indubitably, Scott's representation of the Covenanters in *The Tale of Old Mortality* spurred his main peers, Galt and Hogg, to further engage that subject matter themselves, albeit to quite different effect. As Duncan notes, 'of Scott's most interesting rivals', Galt 'refused the conventions of Scottish Gothic in his most characteristic work, although this did not prevent him from lapses into it', whereas 'Hogg, a Scott protégé, reinvented Scottish Gothic as a powerful and original alternative to the model of fiction devised by Scott'.[18] Significantly, for this context, Duncan elsewhere argues that Galt's historical novel *Ringan Gilhaize, or The Covenanters* (1823) poses a 'programmatic challenge' to Scott when it 'reinvents historical fiction' by 'ventriloquizing belief as the foundation of narrative agency and interpretation, restoring its strong theological term, faith'.[19] Confounding scepticism, such religion disables the supernatural, and with it the Gothic. How to reconcile this Galt with the Galt whose contemporaneous serialised fictions such as *The Ayrshire Legatees* Duncan locates 'at the forefront of the literary innovations borne by *Blackwood's*', for their thematisation of travel and transport, and their innovations of the sketch and dispatch forms so compatible with emergent periodical formats?[20] The common denominator here is surely the imperial cultural nationalism synthesised by *Blackwood's*, which transposes the faith of Scottish forefathers in their Church, Kirk, or Covenant into a modern faith in a global dispensation whereby ordinary Britons can encounter and survive whatever terrors, or tales of terror, the world might circulate home to them.

A pastoral mission can likewise be identified at the heart of the Ettrick Shepherd's bruited anti-imperialism, if we recognise, with Crawford Gribben, that in the hands of the mature Hogg, the historical novel is both 'a work of art and a theological argument'.[21] Writing specifically of *The Private Memoirs and Confessions of a Justified Sinner*, and emphasising the radical experience afforded by the open form and contradictory structure of that novel, which so attracted modernists like André Gide, Gribben argues that 'far more than a satire of Calvinism', Hogg's masterpiece 'exploits a bastard form of Calvin's soteriology to [...] destabilise the process of reading, and insist that we read by faith, not by sight'. At the heart of Hogg's novel lies not a religion-damaged psychology sunk in antinomianism – which is actually well distanced by Hogg from any orthodox form of Scottish Calvinism – but, to the contrary, a scrupulous method of Calvinist interpretation that forbears strong claims for elect status or for historical knowledge. From the point of view of a literary method possessed of such scruples, it is, Gribben argues, 'ultimately Galt and Scott' who are 'in the same position as the demon-haunted and demon-deceived Robert Wringhim'. As Scottish literary innovations like the historical novel and the Scottish Gothic have travelled the world, Galt's style of faith has had its evangelists, but so too has Hogg's – and teachers in each tradition have been able to prove their arguments from the texts of the others. We might end, then, with the question of which of these lineages best contextualises a work specially chosen for the commemorative one thousandth issue of *Blackwood's*, in 1899: a tale of imperial travel, which is also a modernistic paean to constructive ambiguity and epistemological humility, entitled 'The Heart of Darkness'.[22]

CHAPTER SEVEN

Drama and Adaptation

Barbara Bell

At the beginning of the nineteenth century, theatrical venues were divided by law into Patent houses, the Theatres Royal, which were the only venues allowed to perform drama with prose dialogue, and the so-called Minors, the 'illegitimate' venues which were supposed to confine their performance to music, dance, and burletta, a form of comic, ballad opera. An additional constraint on innovation was the work of the Stage Censor in London, who assiduously stripped Scottish works submitted to him for licensing of any 'national' content. Advertisements for the 1810–11 season noted one hundred and fourteen different works on Scottish stages, but only nine with Scottish connections.[1] Still, agrarian and industrial revolutions swelled urban crowds with cash wages to spend, and broader cultural changes to Scotland's place within the Union prompted a growing demand in town and country for work that spoke directly to Scots language and imagery. In fact, the next twenty years saw the fortunes of the theatre in Scotland transformed by the emergence of the National Drama, based around dramatisations of Walter Scott's (1771–1832) *Waverley* novels. These would expand the breadth of audience members and offer a measure of financial security to Scottish theatres of all sizes, from country barns to large city venues. Dramatisations utilising prose dialogue taken directly from the novels skirted around the Patent legislation and became available to all. At the peak of their popularity, from 1820 to 1825, Scott adaptations, utilising his dialogue verbatim in Theatres Royal and Minor houses alike, appeared on one night in three.[2]

The first successful Scott dramatisations emerged in London after the publication of *Guy Mannering* in 1815. But it was a bold experiment in 1810 by Henry Siddons (1774–1815), manager of the Edinburgh Theatre Royal, to debut pieces in Edinburgh rather than to wait for them to arrive tried and tested from London, that demonstrated the industry's struggle to expand the Scottish repertoire. Siddons's brief reign (1809–15) began by moving the Patent which permitted his company to play the spoken word to a building at the top of Leith Walk, for which he commissioned Alexander Nasmyth to create the interior design and front cloth in the fashionable Gothic style. Siddons also darkened the auditorium to focus the light on the stage. Neither innovation found favour.[3] The critics, however, approved his decision to demonstrate the independence of the theatre by his choice of pieces[4] and his ambition to expand the legitimate Scottish repertoire influenced his choice of new texts. The first such experiment was Joanna Baillie's (1762–1851) *The Family Legend* (29 January 1810) which, coming from the most celebrated playwright and theorist of the day, carried large expectations along with it. A year later (15 January 1811) Siddons's company performed E. J. Eyre's (1767–1816) adaptation of Walter Scott's long poem, *The Lady of the Lake*. The stage history of Baillie's play demonstrates many of the practical challenges surrounding Georgian theatre productions and also the beginnings of a shift in audience expectations, which neither playwrights nor theatre professionals were wholly equipped to fulfil. Eyre's adaptation, which Siddons had commissioned from the playwright rather than approaching Scott, is a harbinger of change and its published format contrasts sharply with that of Baillie's play.

The first challenge to the success of *The Family Legend* came with the casting. The structure of the repertoire, whereby an evening consisted of two or more pieces, changing nightly, made a manager's job especially challenging. Around fifty individual pieces were required for a season and cast within a fixed group of performers engaged for their own particular 'lines of business' (such as Juvenile Tragedian or Hearty Comedy Old Man). This prompted the repetition of dramatic forms that supported the skills of the company, allowing audiences to see their favourites perform regularly in different but similarly structured pieces. In such an environment novelty might be considered an imperative, but innovation could be an altogether more unsettling challenge to professionals and audiences alike, and Joanna Baillie's text did not necessarily conform on a number of fronts; the principal 'heroic' role would automatically go to the 'first actor', whereas Baillie's plot depended on an under-written faithless husband, inevitably assigned to a performer of 'young husbands/suitors'.

Baillie's 'Highland' drama tells the story of Helen of Argyle, daughter of the Campbell Earl of Argyle, married off to the chief of the neighbouring clan Maclean to ensure peace between them. Her husband's followers regard her as an implacable enemy and persuade their vacilating leader to abandon her on a rock, to be swept away by the incoming tide. Her brother and erstwhile southern sweetheart rescue her; her traitorous husband is confronted with his villainy by her father and dies in combat with her brother; her child is recovered and she is reunited with her first love.

Correspondence between Joanna Baillie, then living in London, Walter Scott, and Henry Siddons reveals the protracted process that they went through working on text at a distance: the sole complete copy of *The Family Legend*, sent by Baillie to Scott, shuttled between Leith Walk and Scott's houses and friends, whilst Baillie initially tried to keep up with their suggestions using some crossed, draft pages as her reference. Scott later sent her the first three acts copied by Siddons with his cuts. Scott attended all the rehearsals, liaising between playwright and manager, and wrote to Baillie that he had entrusted Siddons with the manuscript as being the person whose remarks would be 'really of consequence'.[5] The Abbotsford manuscript[6] for *The Family Legend* shows comments, corrections, and cuts marked in pencil, with others in ink that internal evidence suggests may have come from Baillie before it was sent up to Edinburgh.[7] In this first review, Siddons is excising instances of repetition, in particular making exits brisker[8] and clarifying meaning, for example, the exchange between Dugald and the Piper at the beginning of Act IV, Scene I, where the pencil query 'Is this Comic Dialogue?' is at the bottom of the page.[9] An instance of an adjustment to characterisation comes early on in the play with a speech originally split between Lochtarish and Benlora, which Siddons's pencil mark through Benlora's name blends into one speech, reinforcing the observant, calculating elements of Lochtarish's character.[10]

> LOCH: […] Maclean, thou knowst,
> Is of a soft, unsteady, yielding nature;
> ~~BEN:~~ And this, too well, the crafty Campbell knew,
> When to our isle he sent this wily witch
> To mould, and govern, and besot his wits,
> As suits his crafty ends. I know the youth:
> This dame or we must hold his will in thraldom:
> Which of the two,—But softly: steps approach.
> Of this again.

The adjustment is included in the 1810 published edition. However, there is no evidence of the wholesale editing, particularly of the Cavern Scene, suggested by Scott's letters.[11] This would have happened both in rehearsal and in nightly revisions as the piece worked itself in before an audience, with changes noted in the Prompt Book.[12] Scott's changes to the clan names, Maclean becoming Duart, head of Clangillian, are well known but appear nowhere on the MS.

Accounts of the Theatre Royal production indicate that the final curtain fell as soon as De Grey appeared bearing Helen's stolen child, so that Argyle's lengthy speech articulating a vision of progress towards friendship and martial unity disappeared in performance.[13] Scott had recognised from the first that Argyle's final speech was too long, suggesting it as a possible Epilogue.[14] He and Baillie were plainly torn, for they repeatedly regretted the edits. Scott compared them to 'tearing ornaments from a balloon', the result being 'less elegant' but the piece 'rose more lightly', whilst at the same time he acknowledged the necessity of fitting the text for stage performance.[15] One of Scott's letters urged Baillie to come to Edinburgh to supervise text changes herself: 'you must come down and assist at the next play you bring forward – the amputations of a player have a very raw and unpleasant effect admitting them to be necessary on the whole.'[16]

There were also challenges in casting, within a fixed, mixed, acting company, the large number of roles vital to the plot, so that minor players faced tackling key speeches in blank verse. Even Mr Thomson, described as 'docile and anxious' by Scott,[17] and who later played Malcolm Graeme in the adaptation of *The Lady of the Lake*, here playing Maclean/Duart, seems to have struggled with his role. Scott would eventually chide Baillie for giving her minor characters speeches beyond the capabilities of some of the players.[18] In addition, the building, at first sight so suitable in terms of size, proved to have very poor acoustics which, as Scott pointed out, mattered very little with most new plays, but was 'seriously inconvenient on this occasion'.[19] Scott writes about Duart's antagonists, Benlora and Lochtarish, being 'defaced by bad action'[20] to the point that their baleful influence on Duart seems unfathomable, which suggests that Siddons may have substituted physical action for the meaning of inaudible speeches.[21] Baillie had been clear about what she had intended with Duart, but acknowledged in the Preface to the 1810 printed edition that if she worked further on Maclean/Duart to strengthen the role, in order to follow the 'lines of business', it would have to be assigned to the 'first actor', Siddons himself, rather than the role of John of Lorne, Helen's brother.[22]

If the theatre and its inhabitants demonstrated limitations, the playwright and her amateur dramaturg were also guilty of failing to catch the changing mood of audiences who were, for example, developing a taste for pictorial realism onstage.[23] On the one hand Baillie included requests for naturalistic lighting and sound effects in the manuscript,[24] whilst on the other she wrote to Scott urging him to tell Siddons not to paint scenery or provide costumes that could not be used for other pieces.[25] Whether Scott passed on her advice is unclear, but two critics mentioned deviations from a unified image of the world of the play. The playbill had advertised 'appropriate scenery, dresses and decorations'.[26] Nevertheless, one chamber appeared 'quite in the modern style, and crouded [sic] with *Corinthian* pillars', whilst Duart was criticised for not appearing in Argyle's castle wearing mourning despite there being two mentions of mourning clothes in the text.[27] Even if both mentions had been cut, the impetus remained within the plot. Commentators have regularly noted Siddons's purchase of tartans for the production; however, Thomson, as one of the principals, would have provided his own costume, and this detail was overlooked in production.

Despite its initial success, playing at the Theatre Royal for seventeen unbroken nights, *The Family Legend* proved something of a false dawn for Scottish drama: its subsequent stage career reverted to a level of respectable stagnation, played once or twice a year, often around New Year as part of a 'Scottish' programme. It was valued, admired, but not loved to the point that managers could repeat it throughout a season, confident of good houses.

E. J. Eyre's adaptation of *The Lady of the Lake* (1811),[28] another large cast production, was the first occasion on which Edinburgh's Theatre Royal played material taken from works by Scott – who had no power to stop or influence any production. Eyre claimed that he had adapted the poem in ten days, and his piece was favourably compared with others as keeping closest to the original.[29] This trait would become especially valued as dramas began to appear from Scott's novels where authenticity in plot, dialogue, and setting became key selling points.[30] Eyre's work is almost unique amongst Scott adaptations in being not only staged but also published, as a fully fledged 'melo-dramatic' entertainment.[31] J. A. Jones is credited with producing 'pantomimical' music, alongside the overture and vocal music, and there are music cues inserted into the descriptions of stage business, whereas later adaptations from *Guy Mannering* etc., contained choruses, glees, etc. but no 'pantomimical' accompaniment. The 'melo-dramatic entertainment' of *The Lady of the Lake* debuted on 15 January 1811[32] and played three times as the main piece of the evening before being compressed into an afterpiece for two more performances. Thereafter it played sporadically, as a main or afterpiece, a couple of times per year. Siddons had gone to two of Scotland's foremost literary figures for new material, but without the sustained success that the theatre needed. Baillie's text was shoe-horned into the performance structure with which the company were familiar, whilst Scott's contribution to the stage would come shortly with his invaluable prose dialogue and vibrant characterisation.

The publishing history of Baillie and Eyre's pieces would have an impact on their subsequent theatrical careers. Joanna Baillie had initially been unwilling to see *The Family Legend* published. Theoretically, playwrights could retain control over unpublished work but the theft of pieces, by bribing a stage manager to lend the prompt-book for copying or sending in shorthand writers to sit in the pit and deliver a verbatim version, was commonplace,[33] and she was persuaded to allow Scott to arrange for the publication of her original manuscript version, with some amendments and the Edinburgh cast-list.[34] In contrast, the text of Eyre's *The Lady of the Lake* was published within a few weeks of the opening, and its busy format indicates a more formal disconnect emerging between authors' printed texts – largely for private reading which might then suggest working-up for production – and the 'acting' texts – which become widely available in cheap editions, listing costume choices, props, scenery, and stage business, essentially replicating the key points of a finished prompt book.

The Edinburgh Theatre Royal under Siddons experimented with traditional forms applied to new materials, but found it difficult to provide its audiences with material that caught the public mood. Meanwhile, small touring groups and Patent houses in the west and north grasped eagerly at the new opportunities available courtesy of the Author of *Waverley*. Their experiments were safe in comparison to that of Siddons, who was in correspondence with Baillie over a proposed production of *The Beacon* when he died[35] and who took his responsibility to the so-called legitimate repertoire very seriously. It would be his brother-in-law, W. H. Murray, manager of the theatre from 1816 to 1851, who would eventually commit the Theatre Royal to performing the Scott dramatisations so beloved of the popular stage, reaping the rewards for embracing the new.

CHAPTER EIGHT

The Short Story to 1832

Thomas C. Richardson

In May 1813 James Hogg (1770–1835) wrote to the Edinburgh publisher Archibald Constable to offer a collection of his stories for publication:

> I have for many years been collecting the rural and traditionary tales of Scotland and I have of late been writing them over again and new-modelling them, and have the vanity to suppose they will form a most interesting work.[1]

Hogg had a substantial body of work, suggesting that the contents would fill 'two large vols 8vo' or '4 vols 12mo', and he proposed publishing the works under a pseudonym since his reputation 'as a bard is perhaps no commendation to a writer of prose tales'.[2] Scottish storytelling in the first decade and a half of the nineteenth century – before the publication of Walter Scott's (1771–1832) novel *Waverley* (1814) – was accomplished largely in narrative verse. Scott's poetry, such as *The Lay of the Last Minstrel* (1805), *Marmion* (1808), and *The Lady of the Lake* (1810), as well as his collection of ballads for the *Minstrelsy of the Scottish Border* (1802), dominated the market. Hogg, the Ettrick Shepherd, had also developed a reputation as a poet – with *The Mountain Bard* (1807), for example, and especially with *The Queen's Wake* (1813). However, Hogg recognised the potential for the same effective storytelling in prose that had been achieved in narrative verse, drawing on the 'rural and traditionary' sources that had such an 'undescribable' influence on Hogg's mind growing up in Ettrick.[3] As Gillian Hughes asserts, 'His lively and extensive notes to *The Mountain Bard* of 1807 had shown what he was capable of in this way, but until 1810 he seems to have regarded himself almost exclusively as a poet and song-writer'.[4] It was in his prose contributions to *The Spy* that Hogg began to see the possibilities for short fiction.

Hogg had written to Walter Scott in April 1813, prior to his letter to Constable, about his desire to publish a collection of tales, noting that Scott would be familiar with several of the works from having seen them in *The Spy*.[5] Hogg valued his stories in *The Spy* and thought that of all his works in that periodical his stories were 'best worthy of being preserved'.[6] Additionally, he told Scott, 'people' had encouraged him by telling him the stories were 'original and interesting'.[7] Apparently Scott also encouraged him, as Hogg noted in his letter to Bernard Barton:

> Many of my friends are of the same opinion with you at least with regard to the tales of the Spy. Mr Wal[r.] Scott says in a letter 'If I may judge from my own feelings and the interest I took in them the tales are superior at least in the management to any I have read: the stile of them is likewise quite new'.[8]

The early readers of Hogg's stories, and Hogg himself, understood that he was doing something innovative and significant in Scottish writing. In his *Spy* stories and his proposed collection of tales in 1813, Hogg signals his desire to shift Scottish storytelling from poetry to prose, in a genre original in form and content. The short story in Scotland developed into a distinct and influential literary form in the second and third decades of the nineteenth century from the foundation laid by Hogg. Furthermore, the long-term influence of Hogg and the Scottish short story extended well beyond Scotland, as Robert Crawford has argued: '*The Spy* is one of the places the modern short story was born'.[9]

If *The Spy* can be said to be one of the birthplaces of the short story, it is in *Blackwood's Edinburgh Magazine* where the genre developed and flourished; there, too, Hogg was a central figure. *Blackwood's* began publication as the *Edinburgh Monthly Magazine* in April 1817, but after only six issues the publisher, William Blackwood, dismissed his editors and renamed his magazine. Blackwood wanted distinctive content that would compete with two periodicals from his publishing rival Archibald Constable – the *Scots Magazine* (which Constable renamed the *Edinburgh Magazine and Literary Miscellany*) and the *Edinburgh Review*. He found that content in a broad mix of offerings: bold criticism and reviews, general interest and political essays, poetry, satirical pieces, and fiction, including serialised novels and, especially, short fiction. The early success of *Blackwood's* spurred the growth of a magazine market in Scotland and beyond that opened up a wide range of publishing outlets for short fiction in the nineteenth century. The advent of the annuals and gift-books in the early 1820s provided another option for authors of short fiction. The periodical press was ideal for the form of the short story.[10]

Blackwood's published short fiction by many writers in the period to 1832, 'these being the years', according to Robert Morrison and Chris Baldick, 'in which its short fiction made the most distinctive impact upon the world of letters'.[11] Hogg, John Wilson (1785–1854), John Galt (1779–1839), Scott, John Howison (1797–1859), Catherine Sinclair (1800–1864), Michael Scott (1789–1835), D. M. Moir (1798–1851), and Robert Macnish (1802–1837) were among the many *Blackwood's* Scottish storytellers in the period, but the magazine also published non-Scots, such as William Maginn (1794–1842), Samuel Warren (1807–1877), William Godwin the Younger (1803–1832), and William Mudford (1782–1848). Most of these writers are represented in Morrison and Baldick's edited collection, *Tales of Terror from Blackwood's Magazine* (1995). Morrison and Baldick argue that *Blackwood's* was 'notorious for the shocking power' of its stories, 'set a new standard of concentrated dread and precisely calculated alarm', and developed a 'distinctive style of hair-raising sensationalism'.[12]

Although short fiction in general, and the terror tales in particular, became a hallmark of *Blackwood's*, most of the individual writers did not achieve a lasting reputation as short story writers – even if well known for writing in other genres. John Wilson's collection of overly sentimental stories, *Lights and Shadows of Scottish Life* (1822), was popular throughout most of the nineteenth century, but it was poorly received by the reviewers for its sentimentality and is hardly read today. John Galt focused on novel writing early in his career, and although he had a facility for storytelling, he wrote few stories that were not set within the frame of a novel, or 'strung together' as a 'series of yarns', as Ian Gordon observed of *The Steam-Boat* (1822; serialised in *Blackwood's* in 1821).[13] Gordon does note, however, that Galt became more interested in the form of the short story later in his career (after 1832) and wrote several works with attention to the art of what was for him a new genre.[14] Still, even Walter Scott, the most successful novelist of this period, wrote little that can be classified as short stories. The volume of *The Shorter Fiction* in the Edinburgh Edition of the Waverley Novels includes only eight stories, and Scott's two most popular stories with modern readers are extracted from larger works: 'Wandering Willie's Tale' is part of the novel *Redgauntlet* (1824), and 'The Two Drovers' is one of three stories set within a narrative by the fictional Chrystal Croftangry in *Chronicles of the Canongate* (1827).

Morrison and Baldick chose to focus on the 'terror' stories in this 'first collection of early *Blackwood's* tales since the nineteenth century' because, they argue, these stories 'represent the most remarkable of *Blackwood's* specialities, and because the sentimental and comical fiction of that period is almost entirely unpalatable to modern readers'.[15] However, they fail to acknowledge another important kind of *Blackwood's* stories, those serious, realistic works that explore the joys, sorrows, and challenges of the human experience. These tales of realism are significant for the long-term development of the short story and are best represented by the works of James Hogg, especially in his stories written for the magazine (even if not published there) in the late 1820s and early 1830s. Hogg was among the most prolific writers of short fiction in *Blackwood's*, and he explored the greatest variety of forms and subjects. It was also after he began writing for *Blackwood's* that he finally was successful in publishing his tales in book form. The collection he first offered to Constable, although not published, 'clearly formed a bridge between *The Spy* and two important later prose collections', *The Brownie of Bodsbeck; and Other Tales* (1818), which was published by Blackwood, and *Winter Evening Tales* (1820), published by Oliver and Boyd.[16] Eleven of *The Spy* stories, most of them extensively revised, appeared in these volumes. In *The Spy*, according to Hughes, Hogg 'had effectively discovered his creative voice in prose';[17] in *Blackwood's* Hogg matured as a short story writer, and he cultivated in his works the techniques that have distinguished the genre for almost two centuries. Hogg's stories, to return to Scott's terms, were 'quite new' in both their thematic focus and boldness of expression, and their structural elements in some respects might be described as 'modern', especially in Hogg's emphasis on 'place', as well as his use of devices that would come to be known as 'magic realism' and 'metafiction'. The remainder of this chapter will focus on Hogg's contribution to the development of the short story, with attention to representative stories.

'Nancy Chisholm', which was rejected for the magazine but later published by Blackwood in Hogg's two-volume collection of tales, *The Shepherd's Calendar* (1829), is a powerful and disturbing story. It tells, in graphic details, of violent domestic abuse and, consequently, a young woman's all-too-realistic struggle to overcome her desire for murderous revenge and her general disposition 'to retaliate evil for good'.[18]

Nancy's father, with King-Lear-like pride, reacts viciously to the news that Nancy's boyfriend had revealed to her that the father is in serious financial trouble:

> he took hold of her long fair hair, wound it round his left hand in the most methodical manner, and began to beat her with his cane. She uttered a scream; [...] he beat her with such violence that he shivered the cane into pieces.

Hearing again the signal of Nancy's boyfriend to her, the father,

> seizing a heavy dog-whip that hung in the lobby, [...] returned into the parlour, and struck his daughter repeatedly in the most unmerciful manner. During the concluding part of this horrid scene, she opened not her mouth, but eyed her ferocious parent with composure, thinking she had nothing but death to expect from his hands.

Nancy is then thrown from the house 'with a curse'.[19] Although the story ends with forgiveness and reconciliation, it is nonetheless a vivid, painful portrait of the consequences of abuse and, perhaps, is a different kind of 'tale of terror'.

In 'Mary Melrose' Hogg explores other types of abuse against a woman – sexual abuse and the abuse of power and position of upper-class society over the lower classes. 'Mary Melrose' is the story of a young laird who falls in love with the daughter of a farmer, or as the narrator says, 'that is, he fell in love with her in the same way that gentlemen of fortune fall in love with very beautiful country maidens far below their rank in life'.[20] The laird pursues opportunities for a sexual encounter with Mary, but to no avail. Finally, the laird 'as a last and only resource, resolved to carry her off by stratagem or force; but at all events to have possession of her, which in the following harvest he accomplished very easily'.[21] Again Hogg turns the story to a 'happy ending', but the underlying social criticisms in many respects undermine the fairy tale conclusion. 'The Marvellous Doctor', an early science-fiction story, tells of a specialist in herbs who discovered 'a decoction from certain rare herbs' that would cause either 'beast or body' that came in contact with it to be under the spell of the person administering it.[22] This story, too, is about seduction, abuse of power, and the social and political consequences of the desire to control individuals and societies.

Hogg in his fiction was interested in representing what he referred to as 'the phenomena of nature', a term he uses frequently to define his method of portraying uncommon events or experiences as matter of fact, realistic, and 'natural' – a device that in modern terms might be called 'magic realism'. In 'A Scots Mummy', for example, by way of introducing the story of the unusual preservation of a buried body, Hogg explains that he is sending the story to *Blackwood's* at the request of 'Christopher North' (John Wilson's pen-name) for something from 'the boundless phenomena of nature'.[23] Hogg also suggests to North that if he needs rational evidence of the reality of this mysterious occurrence, he can try the experiment by hanging himself with 'a hay rope', 'be buried in a wild height', and even after being dead for ages, 'you shall set up your head at the last day as fresh as a moor-cock'.[24] Additionally, Hogg's story 'Dreams and Apparitions. Containing George Dobson's Expedition to Hell and The Souters of Selkirk' opens: 'There is no phenomenon in nature less understood, and about which greater nonsense is written, than dreaming.' The narrator argues that philosophers do not understand it, so the narrator turns to experience with dreaming rather than theory or rationality to consider the unusual place of dreaming in the natural lives of humans.[25] Dreams are part of the fabric of human experience, and their 'truth' is as acceptable as other aspects of daily life. In 'The Story of Adam Scott' Adam is saved from being hanged for a crime he did not commit because Auntie Kitty dreamed the true story of Adam's being framed for the crime, and thus Adam's friends were able to alert the authorities.[26] Hogg's depiction of magical events is usually subtle and casually natural, but in 'The Mysterious Bride' Hogg takes issue more directly with readers and writers who are dismissive of inexplicable nature as unrealistic:

> A great number of people now-a-days are beginning broadly to insinuate that there are no such things as ghosts, or spiritual beings visible to mortal sight. Even Sir Walter Scott is turned renegade, and, with his stories made up of half-and-half, like Nathaniel Gow's toddy, is trying to throw cold water on the most certain, though most impalpable, phenomena of human nature.[27]

For Hogg, the art of the short story also includes consideration of the relationship between authors and their fiction and the influences outside of the authors that shape their art. Of particular interest to Hogg is his relationship with Blackwood and the forces behind the magazine, and in several works he weaves through the stories allusions to this association that are at once central to the narrative and an invitation to explore how storytelling, printing, and publishing are intertwined in the construction of fiction. For example, in both 'The Hunt of Eildon' and 'Strange Letter of a Lunatic', Hogg uses images from the 'Chaldee Manuscript' (*Blackwood's*, October 1817), itself a fiction initiated by Hogg, to tie his persona, or his persona as the Ettrick Shepherd, to the stories' fictions. 'The Hunt of Eildon' ostensibly is an 'ancient' tale and a complex mix of history, royal intrigue, and magical events.[28] A shepherd named Croudy is mysteriously transformed into a boar and then back to a shepherd just before the boar is about to be slaughtered. Croudy, then, is associated with 'Chaldee' Hogg, the 'great wild boar from the forest of Lebanon'.[29] The story concludes by setting a context within the tale for the negative transformation of certain Edinburgh gentlemen that took place on 20 October 1817, the publication date of the new *Blackwood's Edinburgh Magazine* containing the 'Chaldee Manuscript', and the impact of the 'Chaldee' on Hogg's reputation. 'Strange Letter of a Lunatic', rejected by the magazine, employs 'Chaldee' language to account for the predicament of the character, James Beatman, who is plagued by a second self. Beatman meets an old man who gives him a pinch of snuff from a 'gold snuff box set with jewels' that seems to cast a spell on him.[30] In the 'Chaldee', Hogg describes Blackwood's snuff box as 'a gem of curious workmanship of silver, made by the hands of a cunning artificer, and overlaid within with pure gold'.[31] Hogg thus subtly holds Blackwood responsible for his difficulties with his multiple literary identities.

James Hogg, in and out of *Blackwood's Edinburgh Magazine*, more than any other author defined the genre of the short story for Scotland, and Hogg's influence in Scotland is evident in major story writers from Margaret Oliphant (1828–1897) and Robert Louis Stevenson (1850–1894) to Alasdair Gray (1934–2019) and James Kelman (b. 1946). *Blackwood's* provided an important outlet for story writers throughout the nineteenth century and had a major impact on the growth of magazine publishing, and thus short story writing, as a whole. The evidence of the commitment of *Blackwood's* to stories is in part manifest in the publication of three collections of *Tales from Blackwood*, published in thirty volumes from 1858 to 1890, but reaching back to 1817 for content. The significance of Hogg and *Blackwood's* for the development of short fiction also extended to North America. Hogg's collections of tales were published by multiple American companies and widely read,[32] and *Blackwood's*, too, was popular in America and a prominent influence on American literature, from

Edgar Allan Poe (1809–1849) and William Gilmore Simms (1806–1870) – who glowingly reviewed Hogg's works – to Nathaniel Hawthorne (1804–1864) and Mark Twain (1835–1910), and even into the twentieth century with such writers as William Faulkner (1897–1962), Eudora Welty (1909–2001), and Flannery O'Connor (1925–1964). Hogg's vision for an 'original and interesting' new form of tale gave shape to a genre that has continued to develop innovative methods of storytelling.

PART 2: CONSOLIDATIONS

Sheila M. Kidd, Caroline McCracken-Flesher, and Kenneth McNeil

In James Hogg's (1770–1835) *The Private Memoirs and Confessions of a Justified Sinner* (1824), set at the turn of the eighteenth century, the devil haunts the printing house. That was before the age of steam. In 1776, the Scottish James Watt (1736–1819) advanced the technology such that steam engines drove revolutions in agriculture, industry, transportation, and communication. Then in 1825 Walter Scott (1771–1832), a quiet partner in the steam press that cranked out his novels, imagined the press taking over the process of composition:

> [The] mechanical operation [would] only apply to those parts of the narration which are at present composed out of common-places, such as the love-speeches of the hero, the description of the heroine's person, the moral observations of all sorts, and the distribution of happiness at the conclusion of the piece.[1]

The mechanism, of course, is a joke – it is proposed by Dousterswivel, the fraudster who salts mines in *The Antiquary* (1816) and whose gambits are both suited to and resisted by the eccentric and querulous company of Scott's many personae, here gathered to ponder a 'joint stock' company for authorship. Yet the mechanism described involves

> placing the words and phrases technically employed on these subjects, in a sort of frame-work […] and changing them by such a mechanical process as that by which weavers of damask alter their patterns, many new and happy combinations cannot fail to occur.

That is, Scott imagined not just the speed of steam; he recognised the programming potential of the jacquard machine that would, in fact, provide a foundation for early computing. By the 1830s, the devil of speed and of transformation was running the printing house.

That was particularly the case in Scotland. During the early part of the nineteenth century, Scottish journals were trend-setters for the United Kingdom and beyond. As we saw in Part 1 of this book, the third *Edinburgh Review* (1802–1929), published by Archibald Constable (1774–1827), innovated by retaining – and paying – talented writers, and yielding editorial control to Francis Jeffrey (1773–1850). Trending Whig, it stimulated in opposition to *Blackwood's Edinburgh Magazine* (1817–1980), which trended Tory. Both focused on literature and culture and both, in part by their rivalry and by the authorities foregrounded in the *Edinburgh Review* and the personalities in *Blackwood's*, attracted Scottish, British, and international attention. Now, with increasing literacy and expanded markets, Scottish journals diversified their appeal, broadened their audiences, and boosted their readership. The mid-century, then, is notable for the upsurge in journals targeting widely dispersed audiences through more focused interests. Those journals often foreground the needs and desires of a working populace that is deliberately educating itself into technological and social leadership. Thus, rhetorics of engagement intersect with cultural change.

A dispersed readership was similarly characteristic of Gaelic publishing in the middle decades of the century with Glasgow's growing Highland population, alongside its ever-improving local, national, and international transport links, reinforcing its position as a centre of Gaelic publishing and facilitating the distribution of books, and particularly periodicals, to Gaelic communities abroad. A periodical's overseas readership presented its own distribution challenges, and this could impact significantly on the production process. The editor of *Cuairtear nan Gleann* (*Traveller of the Glens*, 1840–43) found himself on one occasion apologising for the many errors in the previous issue, on the grounds that the urgency of getting North American copies to their departing ship had been prioritised over proofreading.[2] A number of short-lived Gaelic journals also began to emerge from within these emigrant communities, with *Cuairtear nan Coillte* (*The Tourist of the Woods*), a bilingual publication, appearing in Kingston, Ontario between 1840 and 1842, *An Cuairtear Og Gaidhealach* (*The Young Highland Traveller*) in Antigonish, Nova Scotia in 1851, and *An Teachdaire Gaidhealach* (*The Highland Messenger*) in Hobart, Tasmania in 1857, adding to the incremental growth of an international network of Gaelic readers and writers.

What knowledge sped around the world? From 1830 to 1833 Charles Lyell (1797–1875; originally from Kirriemuir) advanced geological understanding by arguing from strata and the fossil record that geological change happened steadily, and over a much longer period than religious orthodoxy allowed.[3] In 1844 Robert Chambers (1802–1871; from Peebles) anonymously published *Vestiges of the Natural History of Creation*, in which he imagined the transmutation of species.[4] Both were published in London, but the Scottish journals of the time nonetheless steadily introduced scientific, technological, and cultural innovation to their readers – not least *Chambers's Edinburgh Journal*, founded in 1832 by Robert's brother, William (1800–1883). Magazines like *Tait's Edinburgh Magazine* (founded in 1832 by William Tait [1793–1864], then combined with *Johnstone's* in 1834) posed a challenge both artistic and radical to their predecessors – with Christian Isobel Johnstone (1781–1857) becoming the first editor of any magazine to be proto-feminist, female, and paid. Gaelic periodicals such as *Cuairtear nan Gleann* also embraced discussions of technological innovations, as *An Teachdaire Gae'lach* had done before it in the late 1820s, with an over-arching aim being to ensure that Gaelic readers had access to a similar range of informative, educative, and uplifting reading material as English readers. Much of this information was doubtless sourced, and adapted, from the English-language periodicals.

Scottish newspapers, too, met a rising and changing public, and even drove their industry nationwide. Here, the hub might be considered Dundee. In 1851 John Leng (1828–1906), a Hull native, was hired north to lead the moribund *Dundee Advertiser*. His timing was perfect, for in the next ten years major impediments to newspaper circulation were legislated away: the 'taxes on knowledge' fell one by one (1853, advertisement; 1855, newspaper stamp; 1861, paper). Taking advantage of shifts in technology (stereotyping), communications (the telegraph), and audience (a literate working population keen for news and expression), the liberal Leng, now a partner, changed the nature of newspapers and the reach of the labouring voice. He founded additional papers with national circulation. Most importantly, he founded the *Dundee People's Journal* (1858–1986), with branded editions for regions around Scotland. Appealing to working readers and writers (female and male) and featuring serialisation of long fiction, it accomplished substantial sales, and also UK syndication for its novelists.

Such innovative and widely circulated journals, magazines, and newspapers drove the period's culture industry, far beyond Scotland. Although publishing would trend toward London, for these years Scotland was famed for its Edinburgh journals and Dundee's triad of imperial industries: jute (from India), jam, and journalism. And whether the ethos be religious, military-imperial, proto-feminist, industrial, or working class, Scotland's novelists and poets had a story to tell. Indeed, readers schooled in twentieth-century assumptions about the dearth of Scotland's Victorian writing, or the lack of 'industrial' writing in general, will be surprised at the range, interest, and quality of this productivity. This was the era introduced by John Galt (1779–1839) in the 1820s, with his ear for canny businessmen and bureaucrats, and the imperial context. It became the moment of prolific writers feeding a rattling press for a voracious mass market, and thus the time of James Grant (1822–1887), and the phenomenally successful serial novelist, David Pae (1828–1884). And this moment of a burgeoning press in search of diversified markets brought opportunity, too, for working-class poets directly engaging and publicising the realities of their lives. This was, perhaps not surprisingly, the time of Margaret Oliphant (1828–1897) – struggling for income, straining against gender norms and literary romances, and ultimately retelling the tale that was *Blackwood's* as Scotland's dynastic claim on the century's market in culture.[5]

While the Gaelic press did not attempt serialised fiction in this period, one of the ways it nonetheless proved innovative was in affording poets the opportunity to access an audience far beyond their local communities. Notable among those who took advantage of this was Eòghann MacColla (Evan MacColl, 1808–1898), whose Gaelic verse first appeared in print in *An Teachdaire Ùr Gaidhealach* (*The New Highland Messenger*) in early 1836 in advance of his own volume of verse, *The Mountain Minstrel or Clàrsach nam Beann* later the same year; and similarly, Iain MacLachlainn (John MacLachlan, 1804–1874) whose 'Dan do'n Chubhaig' (Song to the Cuckoo) was published under the pen name 'Suaineardach' ('native of Sunart') in *Cuairtear nan Gleann*, although the first collection of his work would not appear until 1869. This press also fostered secular prose which allowed writers to engage with a range of subject matter, styles and genres new to Gaelic literature. And it built a network of regular writers, many of them cloaked in the anonymity of pen names although their identity often was known within contemporary literary circles, with some identifiable, such as the Rev. Alexander MacGregor (1806–1881) who continued as a prolific writer for the Gaelic press into the final quarter of the century.

Scots wrote by the ream. And they were rewriting Scotland, rewriting themselves. With Walter Scott's death in 1832, J. G. Lockhart (1794–1854,

Scott's son-in-law, erstwhile *Blackwood's* contributor, and editor of the London *Quarterly Review*) rewrote the author's life (published 1837–38).[6] The randomness of one life's experiences fell into a plot of success and failure, and proto-Victorian nobility. Thomas Carlyle (1795–1881), who sincerely disliked Lockhart's portrayal and thus Scott himself,[7] nonetheless emulated the lessons of Lockhart's seven volumes when he propounded a doctrine of 'work', of serious self-making and self-sustaining, in response to the challenges of his changing century.[8] But the variety of contemporary Scottish writing points to a more lively possibility. Under the pens of working people – many of them women, and most of them anonymous – writing and publication expanded. That writing often has been critically neglected. Yet in venues like *Whistle-binkie* or the columns of Leng's *Dundee People's Journal*, it engaged the realities of nineteenth-century life in complex, creative ways. And Scots carried a literary sensibility that was honed by their varied experience into a wider world. In Scotland and abroad, they connected home and away – from the doubled perspective allowed by both.

Alongside the big names of period publishing ran currents – often counter, always rich – that show Scotland as a place of writing, *par excellence*. That writing exceeded literary canons, and today can be valued for its very excess.

CHAPTER NINE

Diaries and Letters

Paul Barnaby

John Gibson Lockhart's (1794–1854) *Memoirs of the Life of Sir Walter Scott* (1837–38) established a new model of literary biography. It posited a dynamic unity of life and work, where the writings provide tropes to interpret the life as much as the life 'explains' the works,[1] and it celebrated a new kind of secular hero who embodied national values and humanised a collective past.[2] Lockhart's *Life* also plays a central role in the wider history of nineteenth-century self-writing. This is partly due to the prevalence of primary materials: selections from Scott's correspondence and journals from which Lockhart sought 'to extract and combine the scattered fragments of an autobiography'.[3] Just as significant as the foregrounding of Scott's voice is the resulting formal hybridity, combined with a seeming absence of thesis or unifying narrative that creates a sense of artless profusion. Refraining 'from obtruding almost anything of comment',[4] Lockhart appears to eschew emplotment and psychological synthesis. This has led to criticism that his work lacks structure, that it is a 'grave' from which the 'scattered members' of a life might be 'disentangled' (Carlyle) or a 'quarry' from which it could be dug (Hesketh Pearson).[5] In response, Francis Russell Hart has demonstrated how Lockhart fashions his raw materials into a compelling narrative of rise, fall, and redemption,[6] though sometimes exploiting techniques (excisions, compressions, relocations, contaminations) that post-Romantic scholarship has censured.[7] Still, there are valid reasons why an impression of discontinuity or formlessness may persist. Lockhart privileges vivid evocations of significant phases of activity, where association of ideas often trumps a rigorously chronological approach. An apparent excess of unfiltered primary materials sometimes serves an expressive purpose, for example the abundance of letters to Daniel Terry on the completion of Abbotsford hubristically preparing us for Scott's fall, or the insistent interpolation of third-party memoirs at the biography's close enacting

Scott's own descent into silence.[8] Elsewhere, however, the extensive quotation of texts supplied by Scott's peers may be determined by the need to forestall their appearance in rival publications.[9] The constant highlighting of Lockhart's editorial presence also adds to a sense of artlessness. While downplaying his interpretative role, Lockhart depicts himself selecting, transcribing, and authenticating illustrative documents.[10] The image of a 'compiler' sifting through sometimes-resistant materials at times suggests an enterprise teetering on the edge of chaos.

Nonetheless, the concluding volume, which portrays the ailing Scott's struggle to settle a debt of honour, follows a clear plotline that influenced Victorian fiction and life-writing: moral self-recovery, following a fall or disgrace, through stoical commitment to work and duty.[11] Victorian life-narratives also mirror Lockhart's emphasis on Scott's formative and final years, where the birth of the imagination and its defeat by brute reality are more closely portrayed than Scott's years of success. In his prime, Scott is presented as an extroverted social being, and again, the presentation of one life as a window into a wider cultural history became a staple of life-writing. Critics have regretted that, in selecting letters to illustrate Scott's social connections, Scott's son-in-law depicts his subject as the 'Laird of Abbotsford' rather than as the foremost figure of a brilliant literary generation. Gerard Carruthers argues that Lockhart's vision of Scotland as unamenable to Romanticism leads him to portray Scott as an isolated genius, instead of placing his historically charged exploration of Scottish identity within a context including Burns, Hogg, and Galt.[12] Presenting Scott as the reviver and shaper of a natural culture, Lockhart distances him from literary contemporaries, who appear, at best, grotesque doubles following superficially similar but barren paths.[13]

One might detect a self-justificatory note in the London-based Lockhart's depiction of his native Scotland as a cultural desert. Yet a society whose talents are increasingly 'devoured by hungry London' also emerges from the late-career memoirs of Henry Cockburn (1779–1854).[14] These reflect the economic, political, and technological changes that saw Edinburgh lose its preeminent status in the 1830s and London establish itself as literary capital.[15] When Cockburn depicts the post-Enlightenment Edinburgh of his prime in *Memorials of his Time* (composed 1821–30, posthumously published 1856), he portrays a literary world of unparalleled splendour, revolving around the *Edinburgh Review* of Francis Jeffrey (1773–1850), Sydney Smith (1771–1845), and Francis Horner (1778–1817).

Cockburn's *Memorials* are an innovative combination of civic and personal memory. Cockburn seeks to commemorate the 'distinguished men or important events' that have 'marked the progress of Scotland, or at least of Edinburgh, during my day',[16] convinced that he can speak with 'the knowledge of a witness, and indeed of an actor in most of its occurrences'.[17] While biographers like James Boswell (1740–1795), the Scottish journal writer and biographer of Samuel Johnson, and now Lockhart present their subject's life as a cross-section of societal history, Cockburn views his life through the heightened awareness of social change that characterises post-Enlightenment culture.

Cockburn is acutely conscious of living through a transformation, the final phase of a post-Union transition from 'ancient to modern manners', where 'enlarged intercourse with England and the world' destroys 'many picturesque peculiarities' of the national character.[18] He is concerned with charting the evolution of customs and etiquette as much as recording epochal events.[19] Like Lockhart's Scott, Cockburn is defined less by his inner life than by his friendships. Given Cockburn's historicised vision of his life, however, his friends – the young Whig lawyers marginalised by the Tory monopoly of patronage – are presented as a cohesive generation who, following the French Revolution, experience a profound dislocation from the immediate past. Indeed, the 'progress of Scotland' is synonymous with that of Cockburn's cohort, whose ascent to literary then political eminence signifies an opening of the public mind and the triumph of enlightened liberal opinion.

Still, not all change is welcome. Like Lockhart's Scott, Cockburn is often caught between nostalgia and acceptance. He celebrates the rise of the Whigs but regrets outliving 'the last purely Scotch age'.[20] The mingling of elegiac and progressive is most evident in Cockburn's evocation of Edinburgh's lost landmarks. He deplores public indifference to the destruction of 'innumerable antiquities' that 'confer interest and dignity'.[21] Yet he acknowledges the genuine 'improvement of our edifices and prospects' after the Napoleonic Wars, and laments that 'some people let their picturesque taste get so sickly that they sigh over the destruction of every old nuisance or incumbrance' while never thinking of the 'human animals who burrow there'.[22]

Cockburn's *Memorials* share something of the formal discontinuity and generic hybridity of Lockhart's *Life*. A leisurely autobiographical retrospect roaming across the people, places, and practices of Cockburn's youth gives way to an annalistic approach, recording significant events and deaths for each year. These provide the spur for pen-portraits of Edinburgh luminaries, vivified by anecdote and by Cockburn's determination to evoke his subject's physical presence. Conjuring up Sir Henry Moncrieff, for example, Cockburn urges us to 'look at him' as he walks along 'with his bands, his little cocked hat, his tall cane'.[23] It is perhaps here that Cockburn's *Memorials* most closely pre-empt another posthumous memoir, Thomas Carlyle's (1795–1881) *Reminiscences* (1881). Julian North has shown how Carlyle builds upon a tradition of verbal portraiture in Romantic memoirs, which sought to capture a 'likeness' as much as to organise a life history.[24] Thus, recollecting his father, Carlyle is driven by the memory of his 'pale, earnest face' and the desire to make it visible again.[25] Carlyle, however, extends pictorial techniques to create a complete sensory impression. Recalling Frank Dickson, Carlyle not only describes his face ('grey genially laughing eyes, something sternly serious and resolute in the squarish fine brow, nose specially aquiline, thin and rather small'), but also evokes his head-movements ('left cheek up') and 'play of point and nostrils' when he speaks.[26] Carlyle strives to reproduce intonation, which he regards as 'physiognomic of the man'.[27] The sound of Wordsworth's voice 'alone rings in [Carlyle's] ear when all else is gone'.[28]

Strikingly, Carlyle's sharpest portraits are often his most digressive. Evoking Dickson, Carlyle is deviating from his subject, Edward Irving, to record a suddenly vivid recollection. Narrative sequencing is thus dictated by the memory process, with reminiscence triggering reminiscence.[29] Carlyle often comments, in a half-exasperated, half-amused tone, on the disordered nature of his recollections. This has led to accusations – that the *Reminiscences* are shapeless, random, unprocessed – that echo Carlyle's strictures on Lockhart's *Life of Scott*. Carlyle's style is uncharacteristically conversational, evoking the 'stream of the speaking voice',[30] with a breathless spontaneity that Victorian readers would have associated with a 'feminine-coded' style and found disconcerting in a writer known for preaching the gospel of masculine silence.[31] An impression of formlessness may be reinforced by a generic hybridity that moves between biography and autobiography, public commemoration and private soliloquy, and, like Lockhart's *Life*, incorporates third-party texts (Geraldine Jewsbury's memoirs of Jane Welsh Carlyle; Grace Welsh's genealogical notes).

As the Campbell/Fielding edition reveals, Carlyle's *Reminiscences* do follow a clear chronological pattern despite Carlyle's digressivity. Both the volume as a whole and each biographical sketch move from the nurturing, organic simplicity of rural Scotland to the chaos and corruption of London.³² Throughout, Carlyle pursues the meaning and mission of his life by reference to formative friendships and influences. Like Cockburn, like Lockhart's Scott, he thus defines himself in social terms but, more than either, he views his peers as instructive doubles, whose influence must be transcended. Thus, the Messianic Edward Irving (1792–1834), the grandiloquent John Wilson (1785–1854; 'Christopher North'), and the 'shrillish', 'feminine' Robert Southey (1774–1843) personify traps into which Carlyle might have fallen.³³ Carlyle's portraits linger on his subject's decline and end with himself in the ascendant. Rather than casting himself as representative of a generation, he underlines his own stubborn integrity.

Carlyle's *Reminiscences* can nonetheless be read as a memorial of his times, illuminating the transformation that Scotland has undergone: urbanisation, mass emigration, the pull of London. While far from sentimentally nostalgic, Carlyle perceives a degeneration from the 'independent' Annandale of his youth, on which he grounds his own singularity, authority, and work ethic.³⁴ Like Lockhart's *Life*, Carlyle's *Reminiscences* skims over the years of worldly success, privileging his formative experiences and a present of penitential self-recovery following a disaster – the death of Jane Welsh Carlyle (1801–1866) – that exposes moral blindness. Reading his wife's letters, he becomes convinced that he has crushed a brilliant literary talent and seeks atonement by collecting and publishing them.

Recent critics have argued that Carlyle's guilt-stricken presentation of Jane in *Reminiscences* and *Letters and Memorials of Jane Welsh Carlyle* (1883) has skewed understanding of her work.³⁵ First, it has led readers to approach her letters as a record of domestic martyrdom, of dutiful self-sacrifice to her husband's egoism. Second, it has fostered the perception of Welsh Carlyle as a 'missing novelist', a gifted storyteller and social commentator who might have achieved literary eminence in her own right. Critics now see Welsh Carlyle as unequalled in her chosen field of personal letters, a genre of life-writing deserving of serious attention. Rather than exposing an unguarded and unmediated self, Welsh Carlyle constructs an ironic persona as a means of organising her life for consumption. Her seemingly artless and haphazard style is devised to create an air of intimacy and immediacy. Her letters are not guileless accounts that reveal suppressed pain, but controlled performances designed to contain her pain and proffer it for the sympathy – and admiration – of her correspondents. At the same time, focus on Welsh Carlyle's marital sufferings has detracted from her gift for subversive domestic comedy and for deflating Victorian masculine self-importance.

Welsh Carlyle largely shuns the confessional mode, describing the self as 'a sort of Irish-bog subject in which one is in danger of sinking overhead'.[36] Like Cockburn and Lockhart's Scott, she defines herself as a social animal, and her letters provide vivid pen-portraits of the eminent Victorians that constituted the Carlyles's social circle. She knew, moreover, that they would be read aloud or circulated among the recipients' family and acquaintances and constructed her writing self to accommodate that wider audience. Her letters are not private missives to trusted confidantes but are embedded in social networks.

Rejecting Thomas Carlyle's tragic reading of Welsh Carlyle's life and work, modern scholars argue that the letters evoke a questing self, seeking intellectual, spiritual, and artistic wholeness, or, at least, a *modus vivendi* between societal expectations and unconstricted individuality.[37] They caution against overstressing her most despondent or caustic moments. The temptation may, however, prove overpowering, particularly when Welsh Carlyle's work is encountered in an anthology.[38] It is not only that expressions of despair, self-doubt, and self-blame leave a stronger impression than displays of sparkling comedy or social satire, making the latter misleadingly resemble an attempt to put on a brave face. There is also the challenge of reading the letters as self-standing performances without imposing an overarching life-narrative. Here the difficulty is not solely that Welsh Carlyle's life may objectively appear 'a sad and dispiriting affair' dimly lit by 'gallows humour',[39] but that she sometimes suggests such a reading herself. She laments the defeat of 'beautiful illusions' nurtured in her Scottish childhood and regrets that her London years 'which might perhaps have produced something good' were 'fertile only of tares and nettles'.[40] As Norma Clarke has noted, this sense of failure is not irreconcilable with her excellence in her chosen genre. By the mid-nineteenth century, the literary status of letter writing was declining, and Welsh Carlyle fears that she has embraced a moribund tradition.[41] The implied life-narrative, then, differs radically from those of the male writers that we have examined. Welsh Carlyle's childhood leaves her unfitted for adult life. Rather than steady ascent (followed, in Carlyle and Scott's case, by fall and redemption), she portrays expulsion and exile from the Scotland of her youth (a 'land of ghosts').[42]

For another life-writer, conversely, Scotland permits the construction of a new persona following loss. Queen Victoria's (1819–1901) Highland Journals are generally evoked in a Scottish literary context only as the founding texts of the sentimental idealisation of Highland culture known as 'Balmorality'. Yet, as Kenneth McNeil has shown, they record a convincing psychological transformation – particularly in the second volume, *More Leaves from the Journal of a Life in the Highlands* (1884), covering the years after Albert's death.[43] The original *Leaves* (1868) often suggests Victoria is engaged in a 'colonizing masquerade'.[44] Here the Highlands emerge as exotic but familiar, wild yet reassuringly domesticated. The queen's impressions are filtered through reverentially cited literary and artistic references, primarily the works of Scott, which effectively serve as guidebooks. The aesthetics of the picturesque extends from the landscape to its inhabitants, whose moral excellence derives from their proximity to nature and who largely figure as nameless non-speaking players in pageants or folkloric displays organised by the local nobility. However sincere the royal couple's enthusiasm, the donning of Highland garb and adoption of Highland sports resembles cultural appropriation.[45]

In *More Leaves*, rather than objectifying and exoticising the people, Victoria inscribes herself into a minutely evoked community. She attends and describes events – sheep-clipping, christenings, funerals, kirk-services – that are intrinsic to the local calendar. While chapter-titles like 'A Highland "Kirstnin" (Christening)' or 'Highland Funeral' suggest an ethnographic perspective, their content evinces a powerful sense of belonging. Strikingly, Victoria devotes as much space to naming individuals as to describing their actions. This implies a radically changed relationship with her local subjects. If, in the first volume, she resembles 'a kindly Chatelaine' distributing alms,[46] here she styles herself as a widowed chieftainess enjoying the clan system's unmediated bond between ruler and ruled, and – particularly when two children drown – fully sharing the community's concerns and emotions.

Although she may seem culpably indifferent to the transformations sweeping the Highlands (agricultural revolution, eviction, emigration), Victoria's self-reconstruction as a Highlander has a historical dimension. She is conscious of being the first post-Union monarch to visit Northern Scotland, and she presents herself as personally uniting and reconciling the Jacobite and Hanoverian traditions. At Loch Shiel, where the Jacobite standard was raised in 1745, she remarks: 'And here was I, the descendant of the Stuarts and of the very king whom Prince Charles sought to overthrow, sitting and walking about quite privately and peaceably.'[47] Elsewhere she calls herself the Stuarts' 'representative'[48] and describes Mary Queen of Scots as her 'poor ancestress'.[49] She is neither visitor nor conqueror, but a native by history and bloodline. Clearly, Victoria is self-consciously fashioning a model of sovereignty that welcomes the hitherto marginalised Highlands into the imperial project, with clan chieftainess being a variant on the more familiar image of mother of the empire. Nonetheless, the regeneration and acculturation portrayed in *More Leaves* defies easy cynicism. The evocation of a community that lays claim to Victoria, as much as she lays claim to it, is effective and affecting.

Victoria's trajectory is thus diametrically opposed to that of earlier self-writers. Her diaries move from the metropolis to the margins, towards rather than away from a nurturing organic community. They portray a strength-giving identity forged in later life rather than childhood. Elsewhere, however, they display tropes typical of nineteenth-century memoirs: stoical recovery from personal disaster, absence of introspection, the self as social animal. Particularly in the first volume, Victoria's abrupt style and profuse narrative has the apparently spontaneous artlessness demanded of female life-writers. There is something too of the generic hybridity of her Scottish predecessors, as she moves back and forth between travelogue and portrait of a community. In these respects, and in their historically charged claiming of a Highland identity, Victoria's journals merit a place alongside Lockhart, Cockburn, Welsh Carlyle and Thomas Carlyle in a discussion of Scotland's critically-neglected genre: life-writing.

CHAPTER TEN

Public Education, Science, and Metaphor

Cairns Craig

In 1876 the *Encyclopaedia Britannica* published an article on 'The Bible' by William Robertson Smith (1846–94), appointed as Professor of Hebrew at the new Free Church College in Aberdeen in 1870 when he was only twenty-four. The article argued that the Old Testament was a historical document, challenging the notion of Scripture as uniformly and divinely authored. By 1878, Robertson Smith was on trial for 'heresy' before the Free Church General Assembly, a trial that was only resolved in 1880 when he was cleared but with admonitions about his future conduct. By the time that judgment was handed down, however, another article – on 'Hebrew Language and Literature' – had appeared in the next volume of the *Britannica* and, since it showed no change of mind on Robertson Smith's part, he was dismissed from his professorship, though he subsequently took over as editor of the encyclopaedia's ninth edition.

The Robertson Smith trial is testimony not only to the continuing commitment of many Scots to scriptural literalism but to the public importance of encyclopaedias. The ninth edition of the *Britannica* (1875–89) came to be known as 'the scholar's encyclopaedia' because so many of its entries were written by the leading thinkers of the time. Key contributions not only advanced rather than simply summarised current thinking, they also helped found new disciplines: J. G. Frazer's (1854–1941) 'Totemism' shaped the future of both anthropology and psychology, while the latter was only recognised as a separate discipline as a result of James Ward's article on the topic. The *Britannica* had been founded in 1771 – edited by the self-taught printer William Smellie (1740–1795) – but by the 1830s was in its seventh edition, each more extensive than its predecessor. Its success was driven in part by a profound desire for self-education among its readers – either up-to-date knowledge for those with some educational background or an initial access to knowledge on the part of those who had not been so fortunate. Though notable among encyclopaedias in terms of both cost and comprehensiveness, *Britannica* was by no means the only Scottish encyclopaedia of the period: Alexander Aitchison's *Encyclopaedia Perthensis* (1796–1806), when it was completed, consisted of twenty-three volumes, and *The Edinburgh Encyclopaedia* (1808–30) amounted to eighteen. The latter was edited by David Brewster (1781–1868), later Principal of both St Andrews (1837–59) and Edinburgh Universities (1859–68) and famous, among his many other innovations in optics and photography, as the inventor of the kaleidoscope. Brewster, however, was equally important for his vast range of popular writings on science, both in encyclopaedias (he contributed many articles to the later editions of the *Britannica*) and in quarterly reviews and general magazines, and he was typical of an intellectual elite which saw its role as making new knowledge available to all sections and classes of society.

Many of the encyclopaedias and major magazines were beyond the means of the ordinary working person, but experiments in the dissemination of knowledge in the period included Samuel Brown's 'Itinerating Library',[1] begun in 1817 in Haddington. Brown arranged for cases of books to be sent out for the use of people in local villages in East Lothian. By 1836 there were thirty-six libraries, spread across central Scotland, with 2380 volumes available for consultation. Brown's experiment was lauded by Henry Brougham, one of the original founders of the *Edinburgh Review*, in his *Practical Observations on the Education of the People* (1825), a tract that led, in 1826, to the formation of the Society for the Diffusion of Useful Knowledge. The SDUK set itself the task of publishing suitable materials for the self-education of working people, including its *Library of Useful Knowledge*, which produced 158 booklets on a wide range of subjects. In addition it published a monthly *Penny Cyclopedia* and a weekly *Penny Magazine*, to make 'useful knowledge' cheaply available.[2] By the 1830s, the Scottish public, already characterised by higher literacy rates than were common across Europe, had access to a wide variety of sources of information on contemporary advances in knowledge. These 'self-help' means of education – which provided the context for Samuel Smiles's (1812–1904) hugely successful promotion of *Self-Help* in 1859 – were augmented by the rise of the Mechanics Institutes, which provided lectures aimed at aspiring artisans. The first Mechanics' Institute was the Edinburgh School of Arts, founded in 1821 by Leonard Horner, an associate of Brougham and also one of the founders of the *Edinburgh Review*. Its aim was to provide skilled workmen with scientific knowledge that would allow them to exploit their practical skills. The prime example of such a combination was James Watt, the Glasgow instrument-maker whose understanding of the principles of physics, gained at the University of Glasgow, provided the basis for his improvements to the steam engine. By 1850, Scotland had fifty-five Mechanics Institutes with around 12,500 members, all committed to the extension of scientific knowledge, an extension that was enhanced by the many university professors who gave free evening courses for those either unable to attend university as paying students or, in the case of women, excluded from university by their gender.

By the mid-nineteenth century, self-education had become as firmly rooted in Scottish culture as elementary education had been in the eighteenth. Indeed, this autodidactic culture was increasingly to compensate for the failure of public education to keep up with a rapidly changing society, which meant that many of the newly urbanised parts of the country did not benefit from the parish schools that had been fundamental to education in Scotland since the Reformation. The 1851 census estimated that there were 914 Established Church schools, 719 Free Church Schools, thirty-eight supported by the Episcopal Church and thirty-two by the Roman Catholic Church. In this increasingly fragmented and sectarian system, it was reckoned by Lord Melgun, when he introduced a parliamentary bill for the reform of education in Scotland, that 180,000 children were not in any form of schooling.[3]

It was in this context that Hugh Miller's (1802–1856) *My Schools and Schoolmasters* (1854) was to become the iconic text of the autodidactic impulse of the country, for Miller insisted that books on education had much to say about 'modes of teaching others' but had nothing to offer 'on the best mode of teaching one's self'. Teaching one's self was, however, the most important issue, for 'by much the largest class of the people of this and every other civilized country' were those 'who need to learn, but have no one to teach them'.[4] The best school, Miller suggested, is one in which 'honest Labour is the teacher, – in which the ability of being useful is imparted, and the spirit of independence communicated'.[5] Miller spent seventeen years working as a journeyman mason – 'it was the necessity which made me a quarrier that taught me to be a geologist' he declared[6] – and it was as a geologist that he went on to become famous through the success of books such as *The Old Red Sandstone* (1841) and *Footprints of the Creator* (1847). He also became the editor of the *Witness* newspaper, which not only supported the evangelical cause that led to the 1843 Disruption of the Scottish Church and the formation of the Free Church of Scotland but also provided its readership with regular information on the new science of geology. The science of geology was one of the great achievements of eighteenth-century Scotland as a result of the influence of James Hutton's *Theory of the Earth* (1788), and many of its most influential proponents – such as Charles Lyell (1797–1875), whose *Principles of Geology* (1830–33) helped shape Charles Darwin's ideas on evolution – were both Scottish and self-taught in the subject. Indeed, geology was the perfect discipline for the autodidact since any amateur searcher after fossils or scrambler around rock formations could lay claim to new discoveries.

It would be easy retrospectively to interpret the Robertson Smith heresy trial as the symptom of a fundamental conflict between religion and science – sometimes described as the 'warfare of science with theology'.[7] Neither Miller nor Robertson Smith, however, were to give up their commitment to Christianity – or, indeed, to the Free Church – because of their scientific studies, and in this they were typical of their culture. Thomas Dick's (1774–1857) *The Christian Philosopher* (1823), which went through three editions by 1826 and nine by 1846, sought to show that religion and scientific investigation were approaches to the same transcendent truth: 'it becomes us to contemplate, with adoring gratitude, every ray of our Creator's glory, whether as emanating from the light of Revelation, or as reflected from the scenery of nature around us.'[8] Among Scotland's most influential scientists in the period were those engaged in the new discipline of 'thermodynamics' – William Thomson (Lord Kelvin), Peter Guthrie Tait, and James Clerk Maxwell. Moreover, despite the fact that their science predicted the 'heat death' of the universe – that time when all the energy of the universe had been dissipated into an undifferentiated state incapable of change – none of them felt such a conclusion to be in conflict with their Calvinist Christianity. Indeed, Thomson thought it entirely consistent with Calvinist eschatology and wrote regularly in popular journals such as *Good Works* to promote both his science and his religion. What, in retrospect, seems the most disruptive event of the period, the publication in 1859 of Darwin's *On the Origins of Species*, had in fact been prefigured by the enormous public response to Robert Chambers's (1802–1871) *Vestiges of the Natural History of Creation* in 1844.

Chambers, inspired by his boyhood reading of the *Encyclopaedia Britannica*, was self-taught in various aspects of contemporary science, some becoming reputable, such as geology, and some of which were later dismissed as pseudo-science, such as phrenology. With his brother William (1800–1883), he founded the publishing company of W. & R. Chambers which, from 1832, published *Chambers's Edinburgh Journal* and from 1859 to 1868 *Chambers's Encyclopaedia*, subtitled 'A Dictionary of Universal Knowledge for the People'. In the *Vestiges*, Chambers drew together elements that he had acquired from his wide reading in astronomy, geology, botany, and zoology to propound a theory of the origins of the earth and development of organic life. What Chambers proposed was that simpler forms of life developed into higher forms through very small incremental changes in their biological structure:

> the production of new forms, as shown in the pages of the geological record, has never been anything more than a new stage of progress in gestation, an event as simply natural, and attended as little by any circumstances of a wonderful or startling kind, as the silent advance of an ordinary mother from one week to another of her pregnancy.[9]

Darwin acknowledged the *Vestiges* as having prefigured his own account of evolution, and also as having identified the breeding of special characteristics in domesticated animals as an indicator of how species might change. Chambers had failed, however, to identify the mechanism which made evolutionary change possible: he had noticed the importance of selection but had not deployed the metaphor which Darwin made his own – *natural* selection. Chambers never acknowledged his authorship of the *Vestiges*, rightly fearing the antagonism of professional scientists towards an amateur and the opprobrium of the theological establishment. Throughout the *Vestiges*, however, he insisted that the laws governing geological and biological change were divinely ordained, and pointed towards a divine purpose to which humanity was central. The same intertwining of science and religion was also evident in the 'idealism' that came to dominate Scottish thought by the 1870s. The most influential of the idealists, Edward Caird (1835–1908), presented religion as itself developing through evolution towards an as-yet unreached perfection.

Insofar as there was 'warfare' between science and theology in nineteenth-century Scotland, it was the result of the resistance of scriptural literalists to the vastly increased temporal extent required for the developments of geology or of evolutionary biology. Charles Lyell had calculated, for instance, that the pace of erosion of Niagara Falls meant that it had retreated many miles over the ten thousand years since its original formation. It was a view denounced by a Scottish clergyman as a 'stab at the Christian religion', since it implied that the Falls existed before the creation of the world:

> It is on grounds such as these that the most learned and voluminous among English geologists disputes the Mosaic history of the Creation and Deluge, a strong proof that even men of argument on other subjects often reason in the most childish and ridiculous manner, and on grounds totally false, when they undertake to deny the truth of the Holy Scriptures.[10]

Hugh Miller dismissed such 'anti-geologists' not only as ignorant of science but as equally ignorant of the religion they claimed to defend. Miller presented his own reconciliation between science and religion by reading the geological record as a series of individual acts of creation of which the creation of Man was only the most recent and most important. Miller took the long tradition of reading the Old Testament as a prefiguration of the events of the New Testament – the events of the Old being 'types' of the events of the New – and applied it to the geological record. Thus each geological period was a distant prefiguration of the creation of mankind:

> the Palaeozoic, Secondary and Tertiary dispensations of creation were charged, like the patriarchal and Mosaic dispensations of grace with the 'shadows of better things to come'. The advent of Man was the great event prefigured during the old geological ages which in turn prophesied the advent of that Divine Man 'who hath abolished death, and brought life and immortality to light'.

Geology and Revelation are parts of 'one sublime scheme' in which are combined 'the geologic with the Patriarchal, the Mosaic, and the Christian ages, and all together with that new heavens and new earth, the last of many creations, in which there shall be "no more death nor curse".'[11] In effect, a symbolic way of reading the Bible became the presiding metaphor for the reading of the geological record.

Refuting Scriptural literalists could not conceal, however, that the science of geology was very different from a science which could demonstrate its truths by practical experiment or by building a better steam engine. Although Lyell's 'uniformitarianism' – the assumption that the same geological forces are at work in the contemporary world as were at work in the past – suggested we could find present evidences for past processes, no observer could be consistently present for long enough to actually witness the transformation of deposits of shells into rock. Geology was a science of the imagination as well as of empirical experiment. To illustrate the difficulty, Lyell asks his readers to envisage how much better placed than ourselves would be 'an amphibious being, who should possess our faculties', and who

> would still more easily arrive at sound theoretical opinions in geology, since he might behold, on the one hand, the decomposition of rocks in the atmosphere, and the transportation of matter by running water; and, on the other, examine the deposition of sediment in the sea, and the imbedding of animal remains in new strata.

The reader, Lyell acknowledges, 'may, perhaps, smile at the bare suggestion of such an idea' but he goes on to adumbrate the advantage to the collection of geological evidence that would accrue to such a 'gnome' or 'dusky melancholy sprite'.[12] Miller, too, invoked imaginative literature as a means of making sense of the geological past. In order to conceptualise the vast forests whose remains could be found in coal, he resorted to imagining himself as one of Swift's Liliputians in relation to modern vegetation in order to gain some sense of the scale of those earlier forests.[13]

The intrusions of such imaginary creatures into the reconstruction of the past were themselves to prefigure the most intrusive imaginary creature of nineteenth-century science, the 'creature' that Lord Kelvin described as 'Maxwell's demon'. The 'demon' was a thought experiment by which James Clerk Maxwell tried to demonstrate that the dissipation of energy, resulting in the necessary cooling of an environment, could be reversed. The demon sits between two containers of gas, one hotter than the other: being only the size of an atom, he can watch the atoms of the gases in motion and operates a trapdoor which allows atoms to pass between the two containers. When he spots one of the cooler atoms in the hotter chamber, he allows it to pass into the cooler chamber and exchanges it for one of the hotter atoms in the cooler chamber. The hotter chamber thus increases rather than decreases in its average temperature. What this demonic creature was imaginatively demonstrating was that Kelvin's 'laws' of thermodynamics were not determining features of the universe, but statistical – and, therefore, theoretically reversible – outcomes.

Maxwell's demon is often now regarded as a prefiguration of 'chaos theory', but it was to be made use of by Peter Guthrie Tait (1831–1901) and Balfour Stewart (1828–1887) in a reconciliation of science and religion that was published in 1875 as *The Unseen Universe*. Tait and Stewart used anthropological evidence – mostly gathered by William Robertson Smith – to show that human cultures had always believed that behind the visible universe there was another, invisible to us. This unseen universe, they argued, consisted of psychic matter which, like the containers and the atoms in Maxwell's thought experiment, allowed energy to be transferred from one to the other. The psychic energy expended during our lives in the material world is not dissipated, they suggested, but collected in the 'unseen' where it will reinstate our identities after our physical existence is exhausted. Modern science thus gives a new meaning to ancient beliefs and a new justification for religious belief. It was a combination with immense appeal to a culture struggling with the implications of geological and evolutionary time, and a second edition was called for in the same year as the original publication. Science itself was thus to provide the 'proof' for the religious beliefs that had been set in doubt by science. It was as though Maxwell's 'demon' had reversed the decay of religious energy and given it a new propulsion. Maxwell tells us nothing about the biography of his demon, but we might speculate that, like so many of the major figures of Scottish nineteenth-century culture, he was an autodidact raised on a diet of encyclopaedias.

CHAPTER ELEVEN

Religion and Popular Literature in Scotland: The Literary Imagination as Inspiration

Alison Jack

> The very outside of a book had a charm to me. It was a kind of sacrament – an outward and visible sign of an inward and spiritual grace; as, indeed, what on God's earth is not?
> —George MacDonald, *The Portent*

Duncan Campbell, the hero of George MacDonald's (1824–1905) novel *The Portent* (1864), finds solace and companionship among the books of his host's library, and feels compelled to bring order out of the chaos he encounters there by compiling a catalogue. He also finds much to deceive ('love poems without any love in them') and puzzling omissions (the 'perfect set of our poets – perfect' omits Chaucer and George Herbert). However, in the 'many romances of a very marvellous sort', as well as in the 'German classics', he finds both distraction and a source of 'wealth inexhaustible'. This library is the setting for an experience of a moment of supernatural insight: seated on a pile of books in the guise of 'the genius of the place', Campbell 'sees' the shifting and then vanishing face of the mysterious Lady Alice.[1] The library functions almost as a cathedral, built with human hands yet full of divine promise and presence, rewarding its devotees with meaningful interaction on multiple levels. The suggestion that the reading of fiction might have this function and potential, detached from organised religion, informs much of the work of Scottish writers as diverse as Catherine Sinclair (1800–1864), Edward Irving (1792–1834), and George MacDonald, who each had wide popular appeal.

The major event in Scottish ecclesiastical life during the period from 1832 to 1870 was, of course, the Disruption of 1843 which led to the founding of the Free Church of Scotland. Angus Calder has suggested that the Disruption proved to be 'too reasonable, too worldly' to provoke much fiction.[2] Compared to the physical bravery of the Cameronians and the poignant history of the Jacobites, in the theatre of Scottish history the Disruption generated sparse literary interest. Calder notes only Lydia Miller's (1812–1876) *Passages in the Life of an English Heiress or Recollections of Disruption Times in Scotland*, which offered a perspective on the Disruption from the Edinburgh of 1847 and ran to just one edition; and William Alexander's (1826–1894) *Johnny Gibb of Gushetneuk*, published serially in the *Aberdeen Free Press* from 1869 to 1870 and then appearing in many editions, focusing more on the influence of the Disruption on rural communities. The former was directed at an English audience, to promote the Free Church cause and emphasise its generosity and attractiveness over the temptations of other denominations, chiefly Roman Catholicism. Restrained in its expression by an evangelical anxiety about the appropriateness of fiction, nevertheless Miller's work subscribed to the view that fiction might have didactic power to be harnessed for spiritual good. Alexander's novel came from a slightly later period and is less polemical, content to outline the social criticism implicit in the Disruption while not attributing its cause or effect to the Disruption itself.

The Disruption may not have directly generated widespread or popular literary outputs but the writing of those who courted theological change often took literary form. Stewart J. Brown has noted the role that the writing of Thomas Chalmers (1780–1847), the leader of the Disruption, played in the literary imagination of those who followed him.[3] Chalmers's sermon series, *The Discourses on the Christian Revelation, Viewed in Connection with Modern Astronomy*, published in 1817, had sold nearly twenty thousand copies in the first year of its publication. Chalmers's prose tackled the grand themes of science and religion with poetic extravagance and intellectual imagination, bringing Newtonian astronomy into engagement with the revelation of God for the whole universe. Critics might attack Chalmers for his divergence from the message of scripture and his apparent shifting from the traditional understanding of the death of Christ, but his volume 'ran like wild-fire through the country'.[4] As Brown argues, the boldness and energy of Chalmers's writing appealed to readers with a strictly Evangelical view of the dangers of secular literature: it might be read as 'romantic epic, an opportunity for escape'.[5] Literature in its widest sense contributed to the energy which led to the Disruption, although the growth and development of the Free Church might not have generated a literature of its own. However, in the mid-nineteenth century, popular religion and literature forged a new relationship in the work of writers such as Edward Irving, Catherine Sinclair, and George MacDonald.

Irving and MacDonald were a generation apart but shared a vocation to ordained ministry, allied to a belief in the power of the divine to work through the literary imagination. They both gained popular appeal but were exiled physically and theologically from the orthodoxy of the established denominations of the Scottish Church (the Church of Scotland in the case of Irving, and the Congregational Church in the case of MacDonald). By some, at least, Irving and MacDonald were granted the status of writers of scripture: prophetic voices who mediated the Word of God to their readers and hearers.

Irving's extravagant use of language in his preaching, writing, and theological discourse emphasised the role of the Holy Spirit, leading him to explore new ways to interpret divine-human relationships and to read the prophecies of Daniel and the Book of Revelation. The attractive novelty of his prayer for a bereaved family to be 'thrown upon the fatherhood of God' brought him the patronage of powerful figures such as George Canning.[6] His later translating and introducing of Lacunza's millenarian *The Coming of Messiah in Glory and Majesty*, with its emphasis on the outpouring of the Spirit as evidence of the apocalyptic end-times, was less popular with the ruling classes. Nevertheless, his early morning lectures on the Apocalypse to the people of Edinburgh during the General Assembly of the Church of Scotland in 1828 brought him more popular acclaim.[7] Irving was not a lone voice in proclaiming that the Pentecostal gifts of healing and speaking in tongues were now available to all: the Scottish ministers John McLeod Campbell and A. J. Scott were also prominent in this early movement, and were deposed by the Church of Scotland for their views. However, Irving's powers of rhetoric and polemical energy in his preaching and writing brought him a high profile within Scotland and beyond.[8] Although his status within what became the Catholic Apostolic Church[9] was understood as prophetic rather than as leadership, interest in his life and work on the part of Thomas Carlyle and Margaret Oliphant meant that he remained a figure of some literary and intellectual stature through the mid-Victorian period.

George MacDonald's long life and extensive literary output gave him an even stronger claim of influence over the popular religious imagination of the period. For the eponymous hero of MacDonald's novel *Robert Falconer* (1868), church was 'weariness to every inch of flesh upon his bones'.[10] In contrast, MacDonald's aim was to release and redeem the imagination of his readers to reveal the love and purpose of God, in the belief that 'God is the God of the Beautiful, Religion is the love of the Beautiful, and Heaven the home of the Beautiful'.[11] As Dearborn has argued, 'The imagination became his ally in communicating theological ideas that had been rejected when preached directly. Novels and stories became his pulpit through which he could fulfil his call to preach the good news of Jesus Christ'.[12] By symbolic suggestion, in a variety of genres including children's fiction, MacDonald sought to reveal the eternal and divine reality he understood to be both reaching out for a response from humanity, and the object of the yearning of the inner self of the individual. While this is perhaps most fully worked out in his fantasy fiction, even in his realistic novels such as *Thomas Wingfold* (1876), there is woven a sacramental understanding of the reciprocal presence of God. There, the curate Wingfold consoles the heartbroken Leopold with the assurance that

> the same God who is in us, and upon whose tree we are the buds, if not yet the flowers, also is all about us – inside the Spirit; outside, the Word. And the two are ever trying to meet in us.[13]

As Duncan Campbell had discovered in the library in *The Portent*, the role of literature to enable the journey towards salvation, from 'bud' to 'flower', through the abandoning of the old self, is suggested clearly in MacDonald's earlier novel *Phantastes* (1858).[14] On the surface, the novel is a random and confusing sequence of journeys and experiences, as perplexing to the hero, Anodos, as it is to the reader. The outward incoherence is contrasted with the coherence and harmony which underlies the fantasy, mirroring the world of the imagination created by the literary art and guaranteed by God. After times of trial leading to new self-understanding about finding the self through serving the other, Anodos realises 'self will come to life even in the slaying of self; but there is ever something deeper and stronger than it, which will emerge at last from the unknown abysses of the soul'.[15] MacDonald's universal vision, which challenged the Calvinist Federalism of his church, found expression in the symbolic escapism of his fiction, and proved remarkably popular, whether or not its heterodoxy was noticed by all of his readers. And for him, as the prophet obediently fulfilling his calling to write as led by his imagination and informed by the Spirit, the reception was out of his hands. While his theology might provoke censure from church authorities, many critics found his 'allegorical and visionary style' to be both 'heart-reaching' in its 'setting aside the phraseology of conventional divinity', and reassuringly familiar with 'no unaccustomed words or rhymes sounding strangely [...] [to the] untutored ear'.[16] Chalmers's theological writing might have functioned as fiction for the theologically particular, but here MacDonald offers fiction with a theological function and application for those whose connection with organised religion might be less secure. For both, an appeal to the imagination offers spiritual as well as aesthetic benefits.

Imagination is a more troubled and troubling force in the work of Catherine Sinclair who, like Irving and MacDonald, appealed to the religious convictions of her readers through her literary output. In 1839, her novel *Holiday House: A Book for the Young* was published to popular acclaim. The first half of the novel offers a series of tales about two adventurous and naughty children, Laura and Harry; the second is a more serious description of the extended deathbed scenes of their older brother Frank. Some later critics have read the novel as 'an exceedingly moral tale indeed',[17] despite Sinclair's claim to 'paint that species of noisy, frolicsome, mischievous children which is now almost extinct [from a time when] there was still some individuality of character and feeling allowed to remain'.[18] Frank's approach to death from this perspective offers a thoroughly orthodox learning opportunity for his siblings, who must learn to find happiness in the eternal hope of heaven. Others have interpreted the novel as a critique of the deadening influence of technological time on the education of the young, who should, for Sinclair, exist for as long as possible in the utopic timelessness of childhood.[19] On this view, Frank's extended death is parodic, a critique of his life which has been ruled by the expectations of modernity and the demands of timekeeping from a young age, driven by the imperialistic expansion which has led to his critical wounding in a battle with slave-ships in Africa. What we might note here is that Sinclair in her introduction asserts both that reading might be a 'relaxation from study', rather than 'a study in itself'; and that she hopes her volume 'might inculcate a pleasing and permanent consciousness, that religion is the best resource in happier hours, and the only refuge in the hour of affliction'.[20] Just as her novel's binary structure seems to undermine the message of each half, so her introduction offers contradictory perspectives on the role of fiction in the formation of her readers.

This tension has been noted in her adult fiction also. In her first novel, *Modern Accomplishments* (1836),[21] the role of reading on the education of the young is discussed by the various female characters in the setting of home. '[B]ooks of practical piety and evangelical truth' are compared favourably with 'those abounding in speculation of wild enthusiasm and daring presumptions',[22] although there is no dogmatic conclusion reached. In her second novel, *Modern Society* (1837),[23] the parish minister asserts that he wishes Thomas Chalmers's 'work on Civic Economy could be rained down in thousands on the world, to show what true philanthropy means'.[24] Chalmers's writing is presented as both entertaining and a universally available indicator of 'sound morals and [...] a guide to society at large'.[25] However in Sinclair's later novel *Beatrice* (1852),[26] the relationship between literature, imagination, and right belief is more troubled. Here, imagination is associated with the dangerous dissembling which is the preserve of the 'superstition of Italy'.[27] No better actors exist than among the Jesuits, 'being able and willing to assume any part', asserts the Protestant Lady Edith to the parish minister.[28] In this novel, Chalmers appears as a marble bust in front of which a young Catholic girl recites her rosary, oblivious to his literary and spiritual wisdom: his printed words have lost their power. Nevertheless, Sinclair has chosen to use the tools of imaginative literature to make her increasingly anti-Catholic point, and her heroes are themselves revealed to be masters of disguise as they seek to escape from the clutches of the Jesuits and their false teaching. In Sinclair's later work, as Baker notes,[29] the contradictory connection between her fiction and her perception of religious responsibility which was both popular and orthodox, is stretched to breaking point.

Edward Irving, George MacDonald, and Catherine Sinclair offer very different perspectives on the relationship between literature and popular religion in the Scottish context. Irving and MacDonald pursued their ministries and literary endeavours in an uneasy exile from both their homeland and their denominations, both pushed and pulled away from their roots into a much wider readership and larger religious milieu. In the years from 1832 to 1870, while Irving's literary legacy and theological influence gradually waned, MacDonald's grew as Sinclair's shifted and uneasily reflected some of the theological and social debates within the Church in Scotland. MacDonald's image of the sacramental power of the book with which this chapter began, with the library as a place where God and the reader as worshipper might meet, is a powerful expression of an idea with popular appeal. It implies a connection between the writer and the divine which is prophetic and outwith ecclesiastical structures and theologies. MacDonald in particular was at ease with the stark contrast between what he called in *David Elginbrod* (1863) the 'ugliest forms' of Reformed worship[30] and his definition of poetry as 'truth in beauty'.[31] In their own ways, MacDonald, Irving, and Sinclair offer theological perspectives with which the popular imagination can engage, unfettered from Church control. In their literature, as MacDonald's hero Anodos discovers, there is:

> Many a wrong, and its curing song;
> Many a road, and many an inn;
> Room to roam, but only one home
> For all the world to win.[32]

CHAPTER TWELVE

Social Comment

Regina Hewitt

From Thomas Carlyle's (1795–1881) 'Signs of the Times', published in the *Edinburgh Review* in 1829, to Janet Hamilton's (1795–1873) five-lyric 'Rhymes for the Times', published in Glasgow in 1863 and 1868, mid-nineteenth-century Scottish literature teems with social comment. Several factors account for the proliferation of social commentary as the century moved forward. Periodicals founded during the Romantic era, especially the *Edinburgh Review* and *Blackwood's Edinburgh Magazine*, provided platforms for assessment of political and cultural affairs as well as for anxious speculation about their effects. Periodical platforms multiplied during the 1830s with the founding of *Chambers's Edinburgh Journal*, *Tait's Edinburgh Magazine*, and others oriented toward working-class readers and socio-political reform.[1] Educational institutions, too, heightened awareness of social relations since the relative openness of Scottish parish schools and universities across class and economic lines was celebrated by many Scots as part of their national identity and appreciated by English students who took advantage of this accessibility. Calls for extending educational opportunities echoed across Scotland and England along with calls for extending the franchise as reformers saw education as crucial for a more democratic society. Mechanics' institutes, mutual aid societies, and libraries arose to meet the demand for more opportunities for learning.[2] In such an atmosphere, the habit of remarking on social relations seems inevitable.

While social comments from this period can be easily recognised, the practice of social commentary cannot be so easily defined. In the broadest sense, social commentary might be any statement about any matter of collective relevance, but for the purpose of studying this phenomenon within Scottish literature, a narrower definition is needed. For that purpose, I define social commentary as a sustained expression of concern about the impact of some event, trend, idea, or invention on social relations. The comments may be critical, designed to point out the dangers of a trend. Such is the case with Carlyle's 'Signs of the Times', which blames industrialisation for creating a 'Mechanical Age' devoid of spiritual aspirations, personal connections, or individual initiative.[3] But social commentary may also be positive, pointing out how an invention has improved society. This type is exemplified by Samuel Smiles's (1812–1904) 'Railway Travelling', which praises railways for crossing class boundaries along with geographical ones: railways enabled workers from cities to enjoy recreation in the country and to increase their earnings by getting to distant jobs; they made communication and commerce faster and safer for residents of all ranks in all regions.[4] In the case of Gaelic literature, the còmhradh (*conversation* or *prose dialogue*) was commonly used to discuss and negotiate social change for readers.[5] Social commentary may also be exploratory, surveying an occurrence and its implications. Essays by Janet Hamilton collected under the title *Sketches of Village Life and Character* fall into this category, for they aim to document the attitudes and activities of her grandparents' generation so that they will not be lost from memory,[6] but they are not idealisations. In Florence Boos's reading, they blend Hamilton's 'respect [...] [for] her frugal ancestors' virtues' with a desire to 'distance herself from' their superstition and violence.[7] Such juxtapositions invite conjectures about how values from the past might be selectively applied to present needs.

Though all of the examples above are non-fiction prose, social commentary can occur in any genre. Novels lend themselves well to reflections on social trends, as is evident from the subgenres of the industrial novel and 'condition of England' novel developed during the nineteenth century. Earlier, the novels of John Galt (1779–1839), which often made social comments through fictional biographies, set precedents for techniques used by Samuel Smiles, whose *Life of George Stephenson* (1857), *Lives of the Engineers* (3 vols, 1862; 5 vols, 1874), and other 'industrial biographies' shape their subjects' stories into lessons on diligence, perseverance, and self-denial. Poetry can also be enlisted for social commentary. For example, Janet Hamilton's poem 'The Sunday Rail' starts with the benefits celebrated in Smiles's 'Railway Travelling', but after drawing readers into the excitement of the holiday in the country, she arrests their pleasure with her concern about the social impact of devoting the sabbath to recreation.[8]

The social comments in literary works offer more than information about technology, economics, and politics, which can be more readily gleaned from reports and other documents. Social commentary offers insights into how people interpreted technological, economic, and political developments and how they invented ways to manage their experiences. In nineteenth-century Scottish literature, this use of social commentary is notable in expressions of concern about how people can live fulfilling lives in a world that seemed increasingly determined by the machinery of industry and government. This concern runs high in the writings of Carlyle, Smiles, and Hamilton, who respond to the threatened loss of personal significance by valorising individual achievement. In the remainder of this chapter, I look more closely at their comments on self-worth, self-help, and self-education.

Having problematised the mechanisation of work, Carlyle devoted much of his career to advocating the worth of the individual. In his 1840 London lectures *Heroes, Hero-Worship, and the Heroic in History* (published 1841), and *Past and Present,* his historical study of 'the condition of England' (1843), he elaborated on a vision of society organised by 'worth-ship'[9] – the recognition by ordinary people of extraordinary leaders, who in turn prove themselves deserving of this trust through wise governance.

This social system is stratified and paternalistic, a version of earlier forms shaped by the gods, prophets, priests, poets, and kings whose heroism the lectures detail. In the nineteenth-century form, heroic spiritual guidance is furnished by Men of Letters, who, like their predecessors Robert Burns and Samuel Johnson, display greatness of soul and who preserve the 'inward sphere of things' from the threat of mechanisation.[10] Heroic governance is provided by Captains of Industry, whose role is to bring moral order to the working world. To do so, they must cultivate social relations based on love rather than money; they must prefer a 'fairer distribution' of goods over the disproportionate growth of their own wealth.[11] For their part, workers must 'subordinate' themselves to these new leaders, following in the tradition of 'reverenc[ing]' the King as 'the Ablest Man'.[12] This deference to superior character and ability is what Carlyle means by 'worth-ship'.

Carlyle's vision of society is a troublingly authoritarian one, yet Carlyle does recognise the worth of ordinary workers. In fact, Carlyle's acceptance of stratification depends on acknowledging the unique qualities of each individual: each worker has a unique ability to contribute to the 'mission' of making order in the world.[13] Every worker (at least, every male worker; Carlyle shows no interest in women workers) is 'a potential hero' insofar as the act of respecting another's ability itself is a form of heroism.[14] Carlyle's resistance against dehumanising systems extended from the workplace to the hustings. Linking Carlyle's confidence in heroic leaders to his distrust of Chartism, Chris R. Vanden Bossche argues that Carlyle objected to the Chartists' wish to extend the franchise because it limited political agency to the given political system. By approaching reform as a personal matter, Carlyle's Captains of Industry and their willing subjects act outside of the system, making systemic change follow from rather than determine human action.[15] Despite his unwillingness to examine authoritarian orders more critically, Carlyle's social commentary sheds much light on the routinisation of work and on government in his time.

A greater openness to material prosperity and upward mobility appears in the social commentary of Samuel Smiles. 'Although money ought by no means to be regarded as a chief end of a man's life', he wrote, 'neither is it a trifling matter [...] Comfort in worldly circumstances is a condition which every man is justified in striving to attain by all worthy means'.[16] The title of Smiles's most popular work, *Self-Help*, still stands for a philosophy of individual bootstrapping, though it focuses as much on character development as on economic advancement. *Self-Help* elaborates on the success stories of hundreds of individuals throughout history, advising readers to cultivate the character traits and habits that facilitated their achievements.

Smiles did not share Carlyle's fears of technology and democracy, but he did share a distrust of existing systems. His philosophy of self-help took shape early in his career: as editor of the *Leeds Times* and a frequent speaker for mechanics' institutes, mutual improvement societies, and reform associations, he advocated working-class education and the extension of the franchise. But aware that class interest drove even alternative systems of education and that violent means to political change were acceptable to some Chartists, Smiles decided that people could rely only on themselves for their advancement.[17] While not envisioning a classless society, he did envision one in which workers came closer to the middle class. Later in his career, which juggled a job in railway administration with authorship, Smiles became more open to a networked approach to social welfare, but he always maintained that individual devotion to work is the key to tangible and intangible gains.

Self-Help begins by presenting its title concept as an attitude toward making one's way in the world, taking care to distinguish it from 'selfishness' and to point out that the nation as a whole benefits from an industrious population: 'patriotism and philanthropy', Smiles maintains, are better performed by 'stimulating men to elevate and improve themselves' than by 'altering laws and modifying institutions'.[18] The following chapters explain how to practice self-help. Good practices include habits of systematic study, deferred gratification, and perseverance. Balancing physical and intellectual training is likewise important and distinguishes self-education from formal schooling. Though Smiles considered book learning important and supported the establishment of free libraries, he maintained that 'man perfects himself by work more than by reading'.[19]

Smiles's biographies of Carlyle and of Harriet Martineau underscore his sense that education should make men – and to a lesser extent, women – contributors to society. Smiles remarks that Carlyle's 'literary training' nearly 'disabled him (which it very often does) of all practical capacity for succeeding in any ordinary branch of industry' and credits him with overcoming this impediment and becoming a useful author.[20] Smiles praises Martineau for the 'manly' work ethic that drove her to be a useful and prolific author even during times of illness. But Martineau also serves him as an example of a conscientious woman who avoided being a 'burden' on her family by learning to make her own living outside of marriage; he recommends that more women follow her example in becoming 'more efficient co-operators with men in all the relations of life'.[21] While Smiles does not give any detailed attention to women in *Self-Help*, he does find the home more important than the school in forming character and habits[22] – an insight being developed almost simultaneously by Janet Hamilton.

On the whole, Smiles's commentary wavers between championing the rise of the working class and burdening them with middling class aspirations. As Hunter remarks, Smiles was oddly indifferent to the plight of people who lost their housing to railway construction, and his emphasis on character sometimes inclined him to blame poor people for lacking the discipline to improve their lot.[23] But perhaps his comments project his own fear of slipping down the rungs of the social ladder. Like Carlyle, Smiles came from a working-class background and rose partly because of educational opportunities in Scotland and partly because of his ongoing diligence. His comments may well serve to reassure himself and his readers that continuing diligence ensures continuing prosperity however many counter examples of that wishful thinking might appear outside his texts.

A working-class perspective is more directly represented by Janet Hamilton, who did not leave its rank. Fittingly, this woman who had no formal schooling won a prize for an essay on self-education from a working-class magazine.[24] While formal education for girls was available in Scotland, working-class girls often were kept at home to help their mothers.[25] Hamilton thus relied on her mother for her start at reading and on her own initiative, when she could take time from her work as a tambourer and her responsibilities as a shoemaker's wife and mother of ten children, to become familiar with a wide range of English and Scottish literature, newspapers and periodicals.[26] Consequently, she wrote from experience when she urged other workers, whom she regularly addressed as 'brothers' and 'sisters', to make gaining and sharing knowledge a priority in their lives.

Published in the same year as *Self-Help,* Hamilton's 'Social Science Essay on Self-Education' shares Smiles's individualistic and virtue-driven approach to learning. For her as for him, education depends on the willpower, 'perseverance and patience' of the self-motivated student.[27] Hamilton likewise focuses on the practical uses of knowledge, advising would-be students to adapt the resources of mechanics' institutes and mutual aid societies, along with periodicals and guidebooks, to the aim of becoming qualified for more skilful employment and thus advancing on the socio-economic scale. In an allusive generalisation that shows how she applied her reading, Hamilton quotes Shakespeare's line about the 'tide in the affairs of men' to make the point that success comes to those prepared to seize opportunities, and she continues: 'On this tide, I have seen floated out from the plough, the factory, the loom, and the forge, men who' joined the ranks of what would subsequently be called white-collar workers by means of their diligent pursuit of learning.[28] There is some irony in Hamilton's goal-oriented approach since she did not float out from her job in the textile industry to pursue a career as an author, but gender norms largely account for her position. Women remained less mobile than men. Yet Hamilton believed that self-education was no less important for women.

Hamilton's main argument in favour of women's education is that they need it to fulfil their role as mothers. To lend authority to her position, she refers to an encounter in which Germaine De Staël is alleged to have told Napoleon that 'good mothers' are the best guarantee of 'good men and good citizens'.[29] But Hamilton also argues that 'the spirit of progress now abroad' requires women 'as a class' to improve their minds.[30]

Her commentary on this demand shows a vision of society in which the separation of classes and genders is less marked than in her time. Working women, she laments, have been 'laggards in the march of mind', not keeping pace with 'females of the upper and middle classes' who are contributing more to the 'literature of their country'.[31] Hamilton advises her 'sisters' to learn to read and write well, beginning with the Bible and moving on to other texts, and to take advantage of opportunities to contribute to working-class periodicals.[32] By advocating intellectual activity for women, Hamilton expands women's roles beyond the traditional scope of 'the hearth and the heart'. But she also urges her 'brothers' to include the 'culture of the heart' in their education, keeping their ambition from making them 'selfish' and 'unamiable'.[33] Further, she asks men to share their educational resources with women and to revise their emphasis on physical and frivolous qualities when courting their future wives.[34]

Present-day readers might wish that Hamilton had been among the women speakers on the programme when the Social Science Association met at the University of Glasgow in 1860 and addressed women's education, among other topics.[35] Yet in two poems about that meeting Hamilton expressed reservations about 'speechifyin' weemen' whom she fears neglected their duty to look after their daughters' 'morals' because of their preoccupation with 'woman's quarrels'. Her comments are more positive in 'On the Meeting of the Social Science Association in Glasgow, September, 1860', which exhorts women to see their role at home as parallel to the role of those at the meeting: both should be working '[t]o teach, raise, save the underlying class'.[36]

Tension between progressive views and conservative reaction appears in Hamilton's political commentary. In 'Reminiscences of the Radical Time in 1819–20', she pronounces the radical agenda 'inimical to' both the 'Government of God' and the 'Government of Britain', and she expresses relief that the 'rebellion' was never fully launched.[37] Her closing appreciation for the 'present paternal and enlightened government' that has extended more 'privileges and [...] legitimate powers' to the general population[38] now sounds naïve, but perhaps it would be more accurately called disingenuous. Hamilton conjectures that the uprising would not have been planned at all if those earlier 'misguided brethren [...] had enjoyed the same privileges'.[39] She thus divides the responsibility for keeping order between privileged and subordinate classes and mitigates some of the blame assigned to individuals who try to enact a vision of a different system.

In sum, the social commentary of this sampling of nineteenth-century Scottish writers shows a concern with the integrity of individual persons and with finding ways to appreciate, preserve, and develop it in a world increasingly confident in the power of collective and impersonal systems. While aware that the whole of society can add up to more than the sum of its parts, these commentators nevertheless remind readers that those parts are unique persons with the ability to act for themselves in any circumstances.

CHAPTER THIRTEEN

'Urban Folk': Scottish Victorian Adaptations and Transmutations of Earlier Verse Traditions

C. M. Jackson-Houlston

Scotland's nineteenth-century urban growth was big-city growth – one in three Scots lived in one of four cities by 1900.[1] Applying the adjective 'folk' to poetry increasingly meant not the oral tradition of small rural communities, which attenuated and diversified under the influence of print.[2] The growth of densely packed towns facilitated the rise of entertainment venues – pubs, fit-up theatres, free-and-easies, and popular concert and music halls of increasing size – for both song and recitation. Repertoires crossed the boundaries implied by size and expense.[3] This chapter addresses three chronological tranches of varied forms of urban folk, each with a different social milieu and purpose. Though the evidence is equivocal, some degree of radical comment suggests the inheritance of socially critical attitudes could be linked with a familiarity with oral performance.

By the early nineteenth century Scotland was well provided with song collections, notably James Johnson's *Scots Musical Museum* (1787–1803), a mixture of old and new songs. Traditional material was often shortened and focused on lyric rather than narrative elements.[4] The word 'museum' suggests a need for preservation, but 'musical' implies continuing oral rendering. The inclusion of tunes facilitated this, but six volumes, with part settings and an assumption of piano or harpsichord accompaniment, imply a verbally and musically literate and relatively prosperous audience.

By the 1830s, the title *Whistle-binkie; or, the Piper of the Party: Being a Collection of Songs for the Social Circle* gives a clear indication of its likely audience and social function as middle-class entertainment. The title refers to a wedding gatecrasher who entertained for drink.[5] Gerard Carruthers records its reputation as 'a safely mawkish and conservative home for work in Scots', but this is unfair to its variety and inclusivity.[6]

Two of the compilers, John Donald Carrick and Alexander Rodger, are conspicuously represented, but so are the folk-song-collector poets William Motherwell and James Pinkerton, the poet James Ballantine, and several working-class writers. Rodger himself (1784–1846) had been a handloom weaver and soldier, then a radical journalist imprisoned for sedition.

Yes, some of the songs are sentimental. There is some jingoism, and the 1838 version contains poems in praise of the new Queen Victoria. The inclusion of earlier writers, however, such as Burns, as well as obscure ones like Ebenezer Ricken (c. 1765–c. 1815), roots a concern with class and the sufferings of the poor. John Robertson's 'The Toom Meal-Pock' (c. 1793) is committed to working-class protest. Its speaker offers himself to Parliament as evidence of the woes of starving weavers and explains why the Scots are 'wearied o' the chain / That hauds the state thegither'.[7]

Moreover, the sentiment is frequently hitched to a social message and/or is undermined by comedy. 'Wee Tammie Twenty', by James Ballantine, describes with comic affection a tinker couple and their hunchback son, but the tone shifts when he is transported for theft.[8] 'The Rose of the Canongate', a satire on an inconstant girl, employs the sardonic, pun-ridden metaphors popularised by Thomas Hood in the 1820s.[9] Nor is this humour always consistent with the supposedly increasing propriety of the 1830s. Carrick's 'Peter and Mary; a Kitchen Ballad' tells of a cook who hangs herself when her self-interested lover causes her to lose her place but will not marry her. It ends with the bawdy pun that when they talk about their love "Tis *pudding* that they mean';[10] though food is the vehicle, the tenor is sex.[11]

The poems employ various Englishes. Many are in the Lowland Scots that had proved a marketable vehicle for the domestic-exotic 'Scotch song' since the days of Allan Ramsay. Conventional approximations of Highland and Irish accents are also used, sometimes to satiric effect. Rodger's 'Highland Politicians' combines comic innocent-eye misunderstandings with anxieties about oppression: 'Tey'll prunt my house to *please ta laird*. / Cot! let them try't again man!'[12] His 'Shon M'Nab' is set to 'For a' that an' a' that', which would evoke Burns's radicalism even though the topic is urbanising social change.[13]

Many songs name the tune they should be sung to. Often the discrepancy between the original piece and the *Whistle-binkie* one seems intentionally comic. No music is provided. This is less a cost issue than an expectation that the audience still has the ability to import oral traditions onto a new world of middle-class domestic conviviality. Motherwell continues to use ballad formulas, as a girl urges her false lover,

> [...] think on the cauld, cauld mouls
> That file my yellow hair –
> That kiss the cheek, and kiss the chin
> Ye never sall kiss mair.[14]

Some of the older composers and singers are also cited. 'The Toom Meal-Pock' is still being sung by George Miller of Blantyre.[15] 'Glasgow Patriots' is said to be by Alex M'Donald, or 'Blind Aleck', an improvisatory street fiddler and singer, who

> was not distressed by a very delicate ear for either numbers or harmony. Whether his lines had a greater number of feet than consisted with ease and grace, or limped in their motion for want of the due proportion, these defects were amply compensated for by a rapid articulation in the one case, and in the other by a strong dash or two of the bow.[16]

Thus, oral delivery compensated for flaws in the smoother conventions of metrics acceptable to more literate audiences. Blind Aleck could get away with McGonagallesque lines like 'But I never did see a more beautifuller city, / Than that on the banks of the navigatable river, the Clyde'.[17]

A more recent mode of popular writing was the patter song, a mixture of sung and spoken elements, often with an ironic disjunction between the two. This was developing as part of the formal repertoire of the early music hall. By mid-century it was a prominent feature of words-only collections of popular songs such as *The Red, White and Blue Monster Song Book*.[18] The first song in *Whistle-binkie* is of this type. In the mildly misogynistic 'Scottish Tea-Party', guests just 'chitter-chatter, / O'er a cup of scalding water' – a hint about class pretension, as the hostess cannot afford much tea.[19]

A decade after this 1838 edition, the historical lays of the class-privileged Thomas Babington Macaulay (1800–1859) and William Edmondstoune Aytoun (1813–1865) began their enduring popularity as educational and spoken performance pieces.[20] Like Scott's narrative poems, their metrics gesture towards ballad metre, but are arranged in longer sections. Macaulay and Aytoun share the notion that ballads can both indicate and formulate the coherence of nationhood, though Aytoun's focus is more on that nation being Scotland. While Macaulay's *Lays of Ancient Rome* (1842) aims to reconstruct the lost ballads of the classical world,[21] Aytoun's *Lays of the Scottish Cavaliers* (1849) uses Scottish history. As was common in the eighteenth and nineteenth centuries, both conflate the ballad with the lay. This elevates the status of supposed minstrel composers[22] and reduces association with demotic protest in favour of nationalising histories. Aytoun follows Macaulay in characterising his narrators while the historian's voice is heard in the lengthy Scott-like paratexts. Macaulay (twice MP for Edinburgh) displays nostalgia for a society where 'the great man helped the poor, / And the poor man loved the great'.[23] Aytoun's speakers – Montrose, Claverhouse – are more directly partisan. Macaulay can be over-optimistic (and over-reticent) in his classical allusions, defining Sextus Tarquinius as he who 'wrought the deed of shame', which baffles those who do not recall the rape of Lucrece.[24] His most famous Lay, 'Horatius', created now-proverbial lines. The escape of a gallant opponent is summed up in 'even the ranks of Tuscany / Could scarce forbear to cheer'.[25] Assured use of incremental repetition consolidates the rhythmical effects in 'But those behind cried "Forward!" / And those before cried "Back!"'.[26] Beyond the *Lays*, Macaulay's 'Epitaph on a Jacobite' catches for an English exile the tone of grief that forms a sub-genre of Scottish lyric as well as a key theme in Scott and other novelists, and one more extensively dealt with by Aytoun.

Professor of Belles-Lettres at Edinburgh from 1845, Aytoun wrote criticism and comic stories for *Blackwood's*. In that year *The Book of Ballads* 'edited by Bon Gaultier' appeared, jointly written by Aytoun and Sir Theodore Martin (1816–1909). These parodies use Aytoun's knowledge of ballad tradition and his critical interest in the difficulties of imitation.[27] They both burlesque tradition and use it as a touchstone of modern poets' failings. As in Aytoun's short stories, the desire for money is a leading theme. The American ballads attack similar targets to those found in Dickens.[28]

Lays of the Scottish Cavaliers, however, are educational pastiche tales of Scottish history. From 1889–90, one set of separate pamphlet versions of individual Lays includes 'notes for Junior Classes'.[29] Aytoun's gender attitudes parallel Macaulay's. It is women's function to pray, and they are better dead than sexually assaulted.[30] Aytoun's Lays have less of the arresting narrative simplicity of Macaulay's 'Horatius', but the last four proleptic lines of Dundee's declamatory address to his troops display memorable heroic economy:

> Strike! and when the fight is over,
>   If ye look in vain for me,
> Where the dead are lying thickest,
>   Search for him that was Dundee![31]

The weaver William McGonagall (c. 1827–1902) also focused on historical events, both distant and topical, but still had roots in a rapidly attenuating working-class oral tradition. He had only a year or so of formal education.[32] In 1877 he joined the century-old procession of working-class aspirants to the status of poet.[33] He hawked his poems on the streets of Dundee as broadsides – a declining format for a semi-literate, impoverished, and now largely urban clientele – and then, from 1890, as a ninety-six page book, *Poetic Gems*.[34] McGonagall performed to local working folk, who paid a few pence to see him in a local smithy or in the circus, and occasionally to securely bourgeois organisations such as the Heather Blend Club in Inverness.[35] Some high-culture and nationalist critics have been vitriolically condemnatory, though others are amused by the irony that McGonagall runs neck and neck with Burns as Scotland's best-known poet.[36]

McGonagall is a community poet who celebrates local people and landmarks, both rural and urban. He also commemorates the powers that hold empire together: the royal family and the armed forces. This may be why his social critique has been underestimated. He often aims to evoke religiose grief over death and disaster. His factual approach resembles that of earlier news ballads, but his style seems more directly reminiscent of the conventions of hack newspaper reporting. In 'The Battle of Culloden' or 'The Execution of James Graham, Marquis of Montrose' his topic overlaps with the historical lays of Aytoun. His sociopolitical subjects include temperance, urban poverty, Irish liberation, and franchise expansion for both sexes.[37] Occasionally a moving observation lights up the verse.[38] He is capable of sympathy for foe as well as friend, noting the mourning in Delhi for the deaths of Sepoy mutineers.[39] So, ambition and range are not the problem.

McGonagall's offence is not that he is not a poet at all, but that he is a persistently bad one. The badness is partly a matter of emotional decorum and partly one of technique. In terms of content, the poems collapse from bathetic juxtapositions. He records 'The Burning of the Exeter Theatre' in 1887, which killed a hundred and fifty people:

/   x |x   / |x   / |/ x|/   x | / x | / x|/   x   / |
Human remains, beyond recognition, covered with a heap of straw;

x   / | x   / |x /| x   / |x   / | x x| /   / |
And here and there a body might be seen, and a maimed hand.

We do not need to know that

x   / |x x   / | x   /|x /| x x / |x x   / |x x /|x/|
The funerals were conducted at the expense of the local authority.[40]

His verse is not simply prose cut up, as can be seen by comparing it with news broadsides about the same event,[41] or his prose melodrama, *Jack o' the Cudgel*. As the lines above demonstrate, he frequently shifts between duple and triple and rising and falling rhythm. McGonagall's difficulties with stress are often most apparent in rhyming. He often wrenches accents, especially when dealing with unfamiliar words and names: 'distress' cannot rhyme with 'Cannes'.[42] He seems not to have recognised that polysyllabic rhymes import a comic tone. At the heart of his technical incompetence is a failure to grasp the principles of isochronicity, i.e. the adjustments of stress and syllable length by which each syllabic line takes the same time to read as its partners in the verse pattern (and which a tune helps to maintain).

Most of McGonagall's verse was for speaking but his most popular piece, 'The Rattling Boy from Dublin', was a song. Rhythmically steadier, his songs show the influence of the traditions of the Irish come-all-ye and the bucolic love song. Hamish Henderson argues that McGonagall's poems retain the infelicities oral tradition sheds: 'folk-song becomes poetry [...] when it gets rid of McGonagall'.[43] A parallel that has not gone through such a process is 'The Wreck of the "Berlin"', from the Dundee Poet's Box that also issued McGonagall's broadsides.[44]

Broadside purchasers may not have been very discriminating, but part of the McGonagall enigma is his appeal to a range of audiences. Perhaps the roughest were the circus spectators, who bombarded him with soot, rotten eggs, garbage, and a brick in the stomach that knocked him out.[45] A more genteel kind of pillory occurred in the *Weekly*

News, which sporadically published his work, but framed with negative critique.[46] Though he never achieved his fantasy of royal patronage, he did perform to well-heeled audiences, for whom his fee might include police protection.

What were their horizons of expectation? As a pre-poetic actor, he would have been a recognisable stock figure across Britain, most famously represented as Wopsle in Dickens's *Great Expectations* (1861). As street poet, he resembles the broadside vendor Silas Wegg in Dickens's *Our Mutual Friend* (1865). McGonagall's self-advertisement, 'Gentlemen waited upon at their own residences, and readings given from the British poets', matches Wegg's aspirations.[47] Wegg's nouveau-riche employer-victim, Noddy Boffin, regards as poetry Wegg's renderings of sentimental songs made comic by rhythmically disruptive interjections. Patter songs specialised in tonal disruption, as in Ned Corvan's 'The Fire on the Kee', giving a comic slant to disaster.[48]

But perhaps some listeners took McGonagall seriously, as did Shamus O. D. Wade's London ones.[49] Modern readers conditioned to giggle should listen to John Laurie reading 'The Tay Bridge Disaster', skilfully modulating the rhythm and laying weight on the earnest closing insistence of the failures in the bridge's design and construction.[50] Two testimonials from teachers and ministers in 1864 and 1865 praise McGonagall as a reciter before his career shift into writing.[51] Once he began performing his own poetry in public this was as part of a mixed set. An evening with McGonagall was not unadulterated poetry by the artist but included song and recitations from other writers.[52] Reviews in the 1890s paid tribute to his 'powerful delivery', 'strong voice and great enthusiasm', and 'dramatic force'.[53] What generated the gap between McGonagall's assessment of his talents and that of most of his audiences remains a matter for speculation. Norman Watson suggests both that he consciously exploited his 'poetic ineptitude' and that he might have been somewhere on the autism spectrum.[54] Styling himself 'Poet to her Majesty' and claiming rivalry with Kean and Shakespeare seems deluded.[55] However, the real question about McGonagall as a dogged devotee of living orality is not whether he was as good as Shakespeare, but whether he was as good as John Laurie.

Ironically, McGonagall is closer to what was left of oral tradition than *Whistle-binkie* overall. Between the two appeared verse with traditional formal influences from skilled metrists but shorn of literal musicality and adapted for recitation with an eye to historical education. What links the different artists and expanding urban audiences is an interest in continued performance.

CHAPTER FOURTEEN

Gaelic Literature of the Diaspora

Sheila M. Kidd

Gaelic literature from the middle decades of the nineteenth century frequently reflects its diasporic context, as the large-scale movement of Gaelic speakers away from the Highlands led to the production of verse and prose in the urban Lowlands, and in those areas with particular concentrations of Gaels such as North America and Australasia. The audience for the literary output of Gaelic poets and writers thus became less local and less readily identifiable, as migration and emigration created national and international networks of Gaelic writers and readers. While secular prose writing was tentatively emerging, the recognised role of the poet, as social commentator, whether on behalf of clan or community, continued and adapted in new social, cultural, and linguistic environments. Gaelic literature reflects these new experiences, juxtaposing old and new homelands, giving voice to both the individual and communal experiences of the adjustment process. This was by no means limited to those who had left the Highlands, and the voices of those who remained, surrounded by the effects of depopulation in a half-recognised homeland, are also represented.

The transformative effect of the Highland diaspora on Gaelic literature is underlined by the Gaelic periodical press which emerged in Glasgow in the third decade of the century, signalling a new phase in Gaelic writing which was to flourish – relatively speaking – in an urban environment. This, alongside a rise in the number of Lowland printers publishing secular Gaelic texts, the Glasgow firm of Islay-born Archibald Sinclair being the most prominent example, offered opportunities for Gaelic poets and emerging writers to access new audiences amid rising levels of Gaelic literacy. This press was arguably the most significant literary development of the Highland diaspora with eight periodicals published in Glasgow, three in Canada, and one in Tasmania between 1829 and 1857 (followed by a hiatus until 1871), compared with only one, single-issue attempt to publish a Gaelic periodical in the Highlands. These new vehicles for literary and cultural maintenance sought patronage not from chieftains or gentry, the traditional patrons of Gaelic poets, but from 'gach fìor-Ghàidheil, anns gach cearna do'n t-saoghal anns am faighear iad'[1] ('*every true Gael, in every corner of the world in which they are to be found*'), underlining the new directions which Gaelic literature was taking.

Published secular Gaelic prose was all but non-existent until the appearance of periodicals such as those of Tormod MacLeòid (Rev. Dr Norman MacLeod, 1783–1862, also known as Caraid nan Gàidheal – *Friend of the Gaels*), *An Teachdaire Gae'lach* (*The Highland Messenger*, 1829–31) and *Cuairtear nan Gleann* (*The Traveller of the Glens*, 1840–43). The domination of the press by the clergy in its early stages led to the moral, spiritual, and educational predominating rather than any large-scale development in the writing of fiction. The còmhradh, or prose dialogue, which proved popular throughout the century, and which aimed to both entertain and educate, was the closest genre to fiction which would appear. Its characters engaged with contemporary issues such as social change, education, emigration, and new technology, and it was to feature not only in Glasgow publications but in those produced overseas. These texts, the majority penned initially by MacLeòid himself, were often underpinned by the contrast between the urban environment experienced by many Gaels and their rural homeland. In one còmhradh, the character Eachann Tirisdeach (*Eachann, a native of Tiree*) describes the way in which his senses are bombarded by the pollution of industrial Glasgow:

> Tha do ùpraid 's do bhuaireas san àite so, 's nach 'eil mi a' tuigsinn ciamar tha daoine bochda tigh'n beò ann, air an tachdadh le toit, agus toit a' ghuail cuideachd, a' slugadh na deathcha tha 'brùchdadh a mach as na simileirean móra [...] Cha mhór nach do chaill mi sealladh nan sùl leis, agus mo chlaisdeachd, leis a' ghleadhraich.[2]

> *There is such an uproar and commotion in this place that I don't understand how poor people can live here, choked by smoke, and coal smoke too, swallowing the fumes which belch out of the tall chimneys [...] I almost lost my eyesight with it, and my hearing with the racket.*

Just as the physical urban environment draws comment, so too the transformed visual and aural landscape of the Highlands becomes a focal point. Dr Iain MacLachlainn (John MacLachlan, 1804–1874) of Rahoy in Morvern, stands out as one of the strongest voices of cianalas (*nostalgia*). His experience was not one of physical, but of sensory, dislocation, living in a barely recognisable homeland, altered by economic, social, and cultural change, all of which finds expression in his description of the natural landscape. In 'A Ghlinn ud shìos' (*'That glen down below'*) he laments the depopulated physical landscape in an image by no means unique in nineteenth-century Gaelic verse:

> Ach chi mi d'fhàrdaich air dol sìos,
> 'N an làraich', fhalamh, fhuar;
> Cha-n fhaic fear-siubhail far an stùichd
> Na smùidean 'g éiridh suas.[3]

But I see your homes reduced / To empty, cold ruins; / A traveller will not see from the hill / Smoke rising up.

It is not solely the physical landscape which pains MacLachlainn, but also the aural one. In contrast with the sounds of nature which comforted him in 'A Ghlinn ud shìos' – 'guth na cuthaig' (*'the voice of the cuckoo'*) and 'uiseag ghrinn / Ri ceilear binn 's an speur' (*'the beautiful lark / Warbling sweetly in the sky'*) – in other songs the harmony of his world is punctured by 'sgreadail bhéisdean 's a' chànain bheurla' (*'the screeching of beasts in the English language'*);[4] and the voices of incomer shepherds are jarringly out of place: 'Cha-n fhaic mi ann duine, ach cluinnidh mi 'n Gall / A' sgriachail r'a chuilein air a' mhullach ud thall' (*'I see no one, but I hear the Lowlander / Shrieking to his whelps on that yonder top'*).[5]

For many Gaelic poets, however, the dislocation was a physical one and proved a catalyst for literary creativity. Iain MacDhùghaill (John MacDougall, 1820–1891) from Ardgour used his verse as an outlet for sharing his negative experiences of (briefly) working as a policeman in Glasgow in the late 1840s, a not uncommon form of employment for Glasgow Gaels. This provides the focus for two of his songs with 'culture shock' evident in both. In 'Gun 'chuir mi uam an lanntair' (*'I gave up the policeman's lantern'*) he describes the violence he encountered in his work:

> 'Nuair 'thòisicheas an tuasaid,
> 'S a bhios an sluagh air daoraich,

> Gum buailear air a chnuaichd mi,
> 'S mo spuachdadh ann san aodann,
> A chionn a bhi le treuntas,
> Bhi ead'reiginn air béisdean,
> 'Bhi gan cuir as a chèile,
> 'S gan reiteach mar a dh'fhaodas.[6]

When the brawl begins / And the crowd is drunk / I'm hit on the forehead / And struck in the face / As a result of using strength / To intervene among the beasts / Separating them / And reconciling them as far as possible.

In describing his new surroundings, MacDhùghaill coined new epithets – not a new practice by any means – for Lowland locations such as 'Grianaig nan long' ('*Greenock of the ships*') and 'Grianaig nam mòr-long' ('*Greenock of the big ships*') in implied contrast with his description of the rural 'Sron-an-t-sithein nan geugan' ('*Strontian of the branches*').[7] He also used his verse to praise Highland societies, a feature of diaspora communities, as guardians of Gaelic language and culture:

> Bidh cànain a's cleachdainnean
> Cearta nan Gàidheal
> 'G an cumail an àirde 's bu choir dhoibh sud;
> Gu'n tearnar a' Ghàelic
> O bhàsachadh buileach,
> Ged rinneadh na h-uiread g'a fògradh uainn.[8]

The proper language and practices / Of the Gaels / Are kept up and they should be; / May Gaelic be preserved / From dying completely / Though so much was done to drive it from us.

Islay-born Uilleam MacDhunlèibhe (William Livingston, 1808–1870) also focused on Glasgow's Highland societies in his verse, including 'Rannan do Uaislean Comunn nan Gaidheal an Glaschu air Cluaidh' ('*Verses to the Gentlemen of the Glasgow Gaelic Society*') in which the urban setting is entirely ignored to celebrate Highland, and heroic, roots:

> As an d' éirich sibh riamh,
> Tìr nam breacan 's nan sgiath,
> Nan treud, nam bradan, 's nam fiadh,
> 'S nan easan steallach gu dian a' leumnaich,[9]

From which you always arose, / The land of the plaids and the shields / Of the flocks, the salmon and the deer / And of the spouting waterfalls leaping fiercely.

Such societies afforded poets a new type of patronage and the opportunity to express publicly their own cultural commitment to their homeland. Argyll-born Ontario resident, Eòghann MacColla (Evan MacColl, 1808–1898), used his 'Oran-molaidh air Comunn Gaidhealach Baile Thoronto, 1858' (*'Song in praise of Toronto Highland Society, 1858'*) as a public affirmation of his own enduring cultural commitment to a country which was 'daonnan air m' inntinn' (*'always on my mind'*), describing himself as 'eun-fuadain fad' uaip' (*'a stray bird far from it'*).[10]

Where MacDhùghaill and MacDhunlèibhe's verse found inspiration in both the Highlands and Lowlands, and MacColla's in the Highlands and Canada, Raibeart MacDhùghaill (Robert MacDougall, 1813–1887), a native of Fortingall in Perthshire, is unique in offering a Gaelic emigrant perspective on the Lowlands, Canada, and Australia. After three years in Canada's Huron Tract, he settled in Glasgow in 1839, publishing a collection of his poetry in 1840 and the first emigrant guide in Gaelic, *Ceann-Iuil an Fhir-Imrich do dh'America mu Thuath* (*The Emigrant's Guide to North America*), in 1841 while working for the Glasgow journal *Cuairtear nan Gleann*. His poetry collection *Tomas Seannsair* (*Tam o' Shanter*) contains his eponymous translation as well as translations of a further nine poems by Burns and eleven of MacDhùghaill's own compositions. His guidebook has a specific audience in mind and endeavours to describe the life which lies ahead for prospective emigrants in familiar terms: 'tha clachan an Kingston cho pailt 's a tha sglèat am Baile Chaolais'[11] (*'stones are as plentiful in Kingston [Ontario] as slate is in Ballachulish'*); 'tha am math-ghamhainn dubh dìreach mu luaths a' bhruic a tha feadh nan Gleann Gàidhealach', (*'the black bear is just about the speed of the badger which is to be found through the Highland glens'*). One poem which can be said with certainty to have been composed during his Canadian sojourn, 'Iargainn a Ghaeil an Tir Aineoil' (*'The Pain of the Gael in an Unfamiliar Land'*), has a prefatory verse explaining that it was composed during the depths of winter when he was depressed. This goes some way to explaining his harsh indictment of his surroundings '"Dhùthaich choimhich chéin fhuair, / Gun àgh gun ghrinneas, gun tuar air chòir,'[12] (*'O strange, foreign, cold land, / without joy, without beauty, without proper appearance'*) and the unfavourable comparison with the Highlands.

As with MacLachlainn, the poet is closely attuned to his acoustic environment:

> Cha be guasgail nam muc,
> (Le bruanasgail uircean òg;
> A' rùamhradh len suic',)
> Chlainnt an cluaineagean sultmhor t-fheòir,
> Ach an t-uainean geal maoth,
> 'S na minn bheaga nan sgaoth mun chrò,
> Agus fanna-gheum nan laogh,
> A co-fhreagradh do ghlaodh nam bò.'[13]

> *It wasn't the grunting of the pigs, / (With the crashing of young pigs; / Digging with their snouts,) / Which would be heard in your fertile pastures of grass, / But the tender white lamb, / And the small kids in a flock in the fold, / And the faint lowing of the calves / Answering the call of the cows.*

Having left Glasgow for Australia in 1841 MacDhùghaill sent a poem to a later Glasgow journal, *Teachdaire nan Gaidheal* (*The Messenger of the Gaels*, 1844–45). Despite the title of the poem, 'An Gàidheal air Fuadan sna Coilltean Fàs' ('*The Gael Exiled in the Desolate Woods*'), the Australian soundscape is one which seems to actively welcome him:

> Nach aoibhinn an èisteachd a' gleusadh an ciùil
> 'S gach coileach ri chaomhaig a' caogadh a shul
> 'S ag ràdh – 'Feuch am buail thu le fuaim ghlan an tràths'
> On tha an Gàidheal air fuadan sna coillteanan fàs.'[14]

> *Isn't it a joy to listen to them tuning their music / And every cock to a hen winking an eye / And saying, 'See that you strike up a clear tune now / Since the Gael is exiled in the desolate woods.'*

While MacDhùghaill's compositions were directed towards a book-buying audience, a poetic exchange between two Lochaber poets and cousins who settled in Cape Breton some eighteen years apart speaks to the enduring oral and interactive nature of Gaelic verse and encapsulates the literary accommodation of the emigration experience. Ailean MacDhòmhnaill / Ailean an Rids (Allan MacDonald / Allan the Ridge, 1794–1868) had emigrated to Cape Breton in 1816 and was well-settled by the time his cousin, Iain MacDhòmhnaill / Iain Sealgair (John MacDonald / John the Hunter, 1795–1853) arrived in 1834. The latter's composition, 'Òran do dh'America' ('*Song to America*') laments his decision to leave the Highlands, relating all that he misses, but particularly hunting deer:

> Dìreadh ghlacagan 's a' gharbhlach,
> Sealg air mac an fhéidh;
> 'S tric a leag mi e le m' luaidhe,
> Ged bu luath a cheum.

Roaming the dells on the wild moors / stalking the young deer. / Often did I fell him with my lead / though swift his stride.[15]

Ailean an Rids takes issue with his cousin's viewpoint in 'Moladh Albainn Nuaidh' ('*In Praise of Nova Scotia*'), using the same tune as his cousin, and responding to his points, for example, highlighting the restrictions placed on hunting in the Highlands:

> Thèid breith air amhaich ort gu grad
> Is gad a chur ad' mhèill,
> 'S d'fhògairt thar a' chuain air falbh
> Chiunn' thu bhith sealg an fhèidh.

They will swiftly grab you by the neck / And put a whip to your cheek, / You will be banished overseas / Since you were hunting deer.[16]

The newcomer is acutely aware of his social dislocation:

> An tìr an t-sneachda 's nam feur seachte.
> Cha b' e a chleachd mi-fhìn;
> A bhith faicinn dhaoine cairtidh,
> Grannda, glas, gun bhrìgh,
> Le triùsair fharsuinn, sgiùrsair casaig,
> 'S cha b' e 'm fasan grinn.

In the land of snows and sere grasses. / It is not what I have been accustomed to, / looking at swarthy folk, / ugly, drab, dull, / with wide trousers, the loutish long coat, / an unattractive style.[17]

His cousin, on the other hand, reassures him that he has made the right decision:

> 'S tu rinn glic 's nach deach am mearachd
> 'S cha robh do barail faoin,
> Tighinn do dhùthaich nam fear glana
> Coibhneil, tairis, caomh:
> Far am faigh thu òr a mhaireas
> Còir air fearann saor,
> Gach nì bu mhath leat bhith mu d' bhaile,
> Earras is crodh laoigh.

> *You were wise and did not err / Neither was your opinion vain, / Coming to the land of fine men / Kindly, gentle and civil: / Here you will find lasting gold / Unbounded right to land / All you would want upon your farm / Of property and cattle.*[18]

This poetic exchange speaks to both the process of adjustment and the continuing interactive and responsive nature of the Gaelic poetic tradition.

Bitterness about, rather than adjustment to, social change characterises the verse of Iain MacGillÌosa (John Gillies, 1818–1873). Originally from Skye, he settled in Glasgow where, during the 1850s, he was a printer and published a number of his own poems in pamphlet form before emigrating to New Zealand. His lengthy poetic polemic *Tuireadh airson Cruaidh-chas nan Gaidheal* (*Lament for the Adversity of the Gaels*) was prompted by evictions carried out at Greenyards, Strathcarron, in late March 1854. MacGillÌosa locates himself as a Glasgow observer to the suffering of those evicted as he opens in a form reminiscent of traditional Fenian ballads 'Latha dhomh air bruachaibh Chluaidh / Gu'm facas sluagh a' ranaich' ('*One day when I was on the banks of the Clyde / I saw a crowd crying*').[19] Acutely aware of the language barrier encountered by these Greenyard evictees facing emigration, he uses his role as a poet to advocate on their behalf:

> Cha robh cluas do ghearan cruaidh
> Aig mnathan truagh no paisdean,
> 'S am fir mar bhalbhain dol mu'n cuairt
> 'S gun ac' ga luaidh ach Gaelic.[20]

There was no one to hear the painful grievance / Of poor women or children / And their husbands like mutes going around / With no means of relating it but Gaelic.

Three years later, on his arrival in New Zealand, or shortly after, MacGillÌosa composed the poem *Litir bho Iain Mac Gil' Ios' a New Zealand* (*A Letter from John Gillies from New Zealand*). Here his continuing anger at the injustice experienced by Gaels at the hands of landlords remains palpable, as he looks back at Scotland as an evil stepmother ('muime ghraineil') who nurtures English offspring better than her own. His final verse in this text, which he sent back to Glasgow for publication and dissemination, underlines the importance of song and poetry as a means of communication and connection between people:

> Thoir soraidh uam san uair seo
> Gu Albainn thuath nam breacanan,
> Gu bràithrean 's càirdean suairce,
> Ri 'n robh e cruaidh leam dealachadh
> 'S ge mòr an t-astar cuain
> A ta ead'ruinn air an uair so,
> Mo cheangal riu' chan fhuasgail
> Gus 'm bris an uaigh na bannaibh ud.[21]

Take this greeting from me now / To northerly Scotland of the plaids / To kind brothers and friends / With whom it was hard for me to part / And though the ocean distance is great / Which is between us now / My connection to them cannot be loosened / Until the grave breaks those bonds.

MacGillÌosa's use of poetry to communicate with his acquaintances at home was not unusual. Iain MacGilleain / Bàrd Thighearna Cholla (John MacLean / The Laird of Coll's Poet, and in Canada 'the Bàrd MacLean', 1787–1848), who had emigrated to Nova Scotia in 1819, composed a panegyric in praise of the Glasgow periodical *Cuairtear nan Gleann*, sending the poem to it for publication (although it was not, in the end, printed before the journal ceased production). The poet anticipates the poem's appearance in his native Tiree as a message to his family that he is well:

> Am baile gaolach a Chaolais aillidh
> 'S an robh mi còmhnaidh na m' òige, fàg e,

> Aig cnoic Mhic-Dhùghaill mu'n dlùth mo chàirdean;
> 'S thoir fios gu'n ionnsaigh gu bheil mi 'm shlàinte.[22]

In the beloved village of beautiful Caolas / In which I lived in my youth, leave it / At Cnoc MhicDhùghaill close to my relatives; / And let them know that I'm in good health.

MacGilleain's words underline the fact that literature, and particularly song and poetry, offered a means of keeping personal and cultural connections alive for an increasingly scattered nineteenth-century Gaelic-speaking audience. This literature responded to the new physical, social, cultural, and linguistic environments in which poets and writers found themselves; on occasions this response was in a negative vein and on others, after the passage of time, more positive as acceptance and adjustment prevailed. The legacy of this diaspora is a rich and diverse range of voices from across the globe, as well as from within the Highlands, as poets and writers reflected on their experiences and their relationship with homelands old and new.

CHAPTER FIFTEEN

David Pae, the Newspaper Novel, and the Imagined Community of North Britain

Graham Law

This chapter engages with Benedict Anderson's ideas on the role of novels and newspapers in the formation of national identity. In his analysis of the origins of nationalism, Anderson views these new media as providing 'the technical means for "re-presenting" the *kind* of imagined community that is the nation',[1] situating them within developments in print-capitalism which enabled 'rapidly growing numbers of people to think about themselves [...] in profoundly new ways'.[2] However, the serial fiction encountered in the Victorian press suggests that the new identification with an imagined English national community still often had to compete with affiliations more diverse and local in character. Here, I am concerned with the role of serialists not so much in fostering a competing ideology of traditional Scottish cultural identity, but rather in creating the more modern image of a North British community. According to the *OED*, the noun form 'North Britain', referring to the northern kingdom as a political entity, emerged after the union of the crowns in 1603; however, with the Industrial Revolution such usage became archaic, and the broader meaning of 'the northern part of Great Britain' took over. In the Victorian period, in addition to scientific usage by natural historians and anthropologists, there was widespread employment of the term in this later sense in the press. Moreover, this recognition of the distinctness of the regions north of the Trent river in both geographic and ethno-linguistic terms was reinforced by growing socio-economic links between lowland Scotland and northern England. (The term 'transtrentane', meaning 'originating from beyond the Trent',[3] was often used in the nineteenth century to refer to northerners or northern phenomena.)

David Pae (1828–1884), a newspaper novelist who wrote forty-five lengthy serials between 1855 and his death, provides our focus. His construction of the reading public in both material and cultural senses is of particular interest. The material refers to his pioneering methods of self-marketing which created a circle of over forty client newspapers with local or regional readerships, centring on the Scottish Lowlands but extending outwards to cover the rest of Scotland, Ireland's northern province, and the north of England. The cultural refers to Pae's reliance on narratives shaped for particular client newspapers and embedded in specific settings both temporal and regional. Following a brief survey of newspaper fiction in Victorian Scotland, this chapter will focus on media history and then on the literary contents of Pae's stories, with particular attention to his late serial, *Grace Darling*.

Several London weekly newspapers tried publishing original instalment fiction as early as the 1840s, but the still-heavy burden of the stamp tax priced them out of the popular market. As a result, by the end of the decade, the penny weekly magazine, which contained no news and thus escaped the tax, served best to bring serial fiction to a popular audience. But things were different in the north. William Donaldson, the first scholar to study Pae's writings, proposes as a definition of popular literature in Victorian Scotland 'material which has been written specifically for publication in newspapers'.[4] Donaldson attributes the earlier prominence there of the newspaper novel to the increasing orientation of the Scottish bourgeoisie towards English metropolitan culture, and the resulting slump in book and magazine publishing.[5] With the compulsory stamp abolished at the mid-century, the newspaper press in Scotland moved quickly to fill the gap with penny weekly journals combining news summaries, political discussion, and literary material. They were distinctively Scottish in content, predominantly radical in politics, and aimed mainly at the lower classes.

Of course, Pae was not the only Scottish novelist to serialise fiction in the press. We can here distinguish two groups: first, local authors writing fiction with local settings for subscribers to specific local journals, often employing local vernacular, whose work was rarely reprinted in volume form; and second, Scottish authors writing typically in standard literary English primarily for a metropolitan audience, whose work was often broadcast initially in newspapers via syndication agencies operating nationwide, before appearing in volume from London houses. With few exceptions, the first group wrote anonymously and has been entirely forgotten, though the digitisation of provincial newspaper archives now offers opportunity to recuperate this lost chapter of literary history. Among the few whose names survive, we might note: the Perth antiquarian Robert Scott Fittis (1824–1903), whose writing divides between historical romance and narrative history proper;[6] the Aberdeen journalist

William Alexander (1826–1894), whose novelistic career reflects 'lifelong interest in the shaping power of heredity and the environment on human character';[7] and William McQueen (1841–1885), a former industrialist, whose best-known work was *Mark Main, Miner*, a tale of Glaswegian proletarian life by turns comic and brutal.[8] The metropolitan group can also be represented by three writers: George MacDonald (1824–1905), prolific in both domestic realism and historical romance, though now best known as a fantasy writer; William Black (1841–1898), whose typical novels are strong on setting and tragically juxtapose northern provincial and southern metropolitan mores, as represented by *A Daughter of Heth* (1871); and S. R. Crockett (1860–1914), whose affiliation to rustic sentimentality encouraged him to cultivate a mode of Scots vernacular accessible to an English audience. All were handled by prestigious London houses, and serialised in upmarket metropolitan weeklies like the *Graphic*. Their Scottish newspaper appearances were typically arranged by English agencies, in widely circulating middle-class papers like the *Glasgow Weekly Herald*.

The pioneer of fiction serialisation in Scottish papers, exceptional alike in quantity of output and frequency of appearance, Pae fits comfortably into neither group. Scanning through the cheap urban weeklies leaves the impression that almost half the serials are Pae's. Moreover, his popularity was not limited to Caledonia, as his readership spread like ripples on a pond. From *Jessie Melville* in 1855, Pae's early serials appeared independently in the (Edinburgh) *North Briton*, one of the first penny news miscellanies to emerge on the abolition of the stamp tax. Beginning with *Lucy, the Factory Girl* in 1858, Pae persuaded editors in Glasgow (first at the *Glasgow Times*, then the *Penny Post*) to share serials with the *North Briton*. From 1860 his work appeared in northern Irish papers, with *Norah Cushaleen* and *Biddy Macarthy* (both 1862) written with joint publication in the (Belfast) *Banner of Ulster* and *Ballymena Observer* in mind. In summer 1863, Pae arranged for *Lucy* to be reprinted in the (Dundee) *People's Journal*, thus beginning a long-term arrangement with the proprietor John Leng, whereby all Pae's forthcoming serials appeared initially in the Dundee weekly. Leng soon encouraged Pae to supply his stories, with only a brief delay, to popular weeklies in the English industrial north, beginning with the (Lancashire) *Ashton Reporter* and the *Sheffield Telegraph*, owned by his brother William Leng. By 1870, the author had perfected his self-syndication techniques, broadcasting printed publicity so that his old stories remained in circulation while new ones were issued in major weeklies all over Scotland, Ulster, and northern England.[9]

Indeed, his practice of selling the same stories either in series or in parallel to papers with complementary circulations provided the model for the professional fiction syndication agencies emerging in England. When W. F. Tillotson began to carry fiction in his *Bolton Weekly Journal* from 1871, he turned to Pae for the early stories. In 1873 he founded the 'Fiction Bureau', the most successful of the English agencies, while his biggest rival from the mid-1880s was the 'Editor's Syndicate' run by William Leng in Sheffield. By the later 1870s, the prevailing mode of instalment publication had shifted from serialisation in single metropolitan magazines to syndication in groups of provincial weekly papers, a pattern that persisted into the 1890s.[10] In the process, authors as distinguished as Wilkie Collins (1824–1889) and Margaret Oliphant (1828–1897) were attracted into the newspaper market. Yet even in such company, Pae's stories were able to hold their own.

The fine detail of the author's career as serialist is represented in a table entitled 'David Pae's Newspaper Novels'.[11] There the total of identified source newspapers is forty-two: sixteen Scottish, five Irish, and twenty-one English, with only three located south of the Trent. This demonstrates how Pae's developing methods of self-syndication served materially to construct a North British readership. If we match titles against initial newspaper venues, in addition to the two 'Irish Tales' already mentioned, we can find many examples of the principle of 'horses for courses'.[12] The table also shows several cases where a successful local newspaper appearance led to the same novel being issued in volume from a local publisher.[13] The data further illustrate how this was effected in the cultural sphere through the narrative contents of the forty-five serials which, viewed collectively, construct North Britain as an imagined community rather different from that theorised by Anderson, that is, they encouraged Pae's newspaper readers to imagine themselves as belonging to North Britain, despite that construction not having the status of a nation. Pae typically relied on historical narratives embedded in specific North British settings, so that his preference for the melodramatic style is tempered by a commitment to local realism based on extensive use of documentary materials. Many stories are thus framed around specific historical events,[14] while others feature legendary local heroes or villains.[15]

Grace Darling, the Heroine of the Longstone Lighthouse; or, The Two Wills, Pae's retelling of the 'Tale of the Wreck of the Forfarshire' in autumn 1838 en route from Hull to Dundee, provides an illustration reconstructing the young Northumbrian as a distinctively North British heroine.[16] The main setting is not the rocky Farne Islands where the 'Forfarshire' was wrecked, but the Carse of Gowrie, the low-lying fertile land on the north bank of the Tay between Perth and Dundee, where a plot concerning two wills works itself out. Grace herself only appears in nine of the forty chapters, wherein three separate shipwrecks are recounted. Instead, the principals are a Scots couple, Percy Westbrook, the true heir to Dunmore, an estate on the Carse, and Caroline, the sister of Percy's university friend Henry Travers, a prospective minister of the Kirk. The couple meet in the opening chapter, become engaged in the fifth, are married in the eighteenth, but take over the estate only in the thirty-ninth, the delay being due to the hiding of a new will, benefitting Percy, by his uncle's ward, who promotes the old will benefitting herself. The two strands of the narrative are woven together to fine dramatic effect. In the first wreck on the Farne rocks, of a sailing yacht out of Tynemouth, Percy, Caroline, and her brother are rescued and become firm friends with Grace's family. In the second wreck, of a vessel headed for Aberdeen, Percy helps to save a sailor during his and Caroline's honeymoon visit to the Longstone. The sailor reveals the whereabouts of the true will. During the third wreck, that of the 'Forfarshire' itself, a villain of the piece drowns in the disaster, while Percy's factor, one of the few survivors, brings the will safely to shore. Such is the main outline of the plot. While Percy, Caroline, and their families speak in standard literary English, there are several minor comic characters, such as the sexton of the kirk at Dunmore, or the landlord of its local inn, who employ broad Scots vernacular.

Pae's serial was of course not the first telling of Grace's famous 'deed', and comparison with potential sources helps to reveal his concerns. Jerrold Vernon's pioneering biography freely mixed reality and fantasy.[17] The rescue scenes are relatively reliable: the author cites William Darling's lighthouse journal and records events 'as they appeared in the local periodicals of the day', including the account from the *Newcastle Chronicle* of 15 September 1838.[18] Yet the volume is also inflated with extraneous description of a series of local wrecks prior to the 'Forfarshire'. The first seems entirely fictional, involving the rescue of the English occupants of a pleasure yacht caught in a storm who later befriend Grace: Caroline Dudley (daughter of the Earl of Dudley), plus her brother and his companion. However, Caroline is soon called away on family affairs, to return to the Longstone only in the final scene for a brief reunion with the now famous Darlings. Yet this does not prevent half of the intervening chapters being devoted to the unrelated meanderings of the Dudleys around continental Europe. Altogether, Vernon offers an extremely disjointed narrative, which led one reader to ask whether the affairs of Caroline and company were 'historical memorial facts' or 'mere novelty'. Grace herself confirmed she was 'quite unacquainted with the persons mentioned' who gave the narrative 'the appearance of Romance altogether'.[19]

Despite its incoherence, Vernon's text became a primary source for two later accounts of Grace's life, by Thomas Arthur (1875) and 'Eva Hope' (1876);[20] both include the saving of Caroline Dudley's party and stress the romantic elements in Vernon's version of the 'Forfarshire' rescue. Surviving family members objected to this disregard for the evidence and, during the 1880s, Grace's sister Thomasin arranged the issue of two volumes of family papers to redress the balance.[21] These provided documentation concerning both the sentimentalising of the rescue, and the 'mere novelty' of the Dudley thread.

Discerning precisely which sources were available to Pae remains conjectural, though it seems safe to assume that Thomasin's volumes appeared too late to be consulted. But his reconstruction of the character and role of Caroline and her companions proves Pae was familiar with at least one of the Vernon, Arthur, and 'Hope' lives, and perhaps all three. Following his account of the main disaster, Pae notes that details are 'gathered from the narratives of those who were deeply concerned in the catastrophe'.[22] These doubtless included the lengthy report in the *Newcastle Chronicle*, among other press accounts, and it would have been easier for Pae to consult these in Vernon than in the newspaper files. In sum, Pae may have trusted sentimentalised sources when penning the scenes where Grace herself appears, but, in profoundly transforming the fictitious events concerning Caroline, he succeeded in recreating the material both to suit his readership and to serve his own theological purposes.

The earlier biographies all pay lip service at least to the Christian faith underpinning the altruism of the Darlings in the rescue. Pae, in contrast, works specifically to associate the heroine with his own long-held commitment to the liberal evangelical creed of Arminianism, which rejects the Calvinist concept of divine election common in the presbyterian Kirk and instead preaches the universality of the Atonement. This is achieved by introducing Caroline's brother Henry as a prospective minister at Dunmore. There the incumbent is the aging Doctor Wilson, who embodies Pae's ideal of a serving minster. On moving to Dunmore Henry resides at the manse and acts as Wilson's assistant so that, at the denouement, with the recovery of the true will and the doctor's passing, Percy is able to appoint him as successor. The Arminian principle is best represented in the full forgiveness offered by the residents of the manse to the repentant ward, when her misdeeds are revealed. With the friendship between Caroline and Grace growing via regular letters as well as occasional meetings, these values are shown to be shared with the Darling family isolated on the Longstone, where, lacking both school and church, the lighthouse keeper's children regard him as teacher and minister as well as parent.

The religious theme thus underlines a community of faith linking southern Scotland and northern England. Both the route plied by the 'Forfarshire' and the losses on its destruction provide evidence of social and commercial intercourse between the two regions. The opening scene shows Percy about to board the mail coach from Newcastle to Berwick en route to Dunmore, before his intentions are changed by a chance encounter with Henry. And, among the climactic scenes, in Chapters 30 to 32 there is a lengthy account of the urgent overland journey of Percy's factor from Edinburgh to Hull, so that he can secure the true will and foil the Dunmore usurper. Despite the high drama Pae devotes considerable space to depicting the staging posts on the journey south, as well as evoking the changing landscape along the way. In sum, Pae's serial works consistently to recreate Grace Darling as an icon specifically of the imagined community of North Britain rather than as a broadly English or Scottish one; at the close of the rescue narrative, he writes that Grace's bravery made her 'one of the noblest of British heroines'.[23]

This is not to suggest that Pae's novels never evoke an affiliation to Anderson's national imagined community. Indeed, the final lines of *Grace Darling* note that the heroine's name has become familiar 'on all the continents of earth where the English language is spoken'.[24] Rather, such evocations of Union and Empire exist in tension with, but finally are subordinate to, those affirming more local commitments.

CHAPTER SIXTEEN

Industrial-Strength Fiction: Margaret Oliphant and James Grant

Joanne Wilkes

When novelist/historian James Grant (1822–1887) died at the age of sixty-four in early May 1887, one obituarist, who had been his neighbour in London, observed how 'so many people wonder at the discovery that he was so recently in the land of the living'. Such a reaction, the commentator continues, makes Grant 'an example of the fleeting character of general popularity', for he was 'once hailed as a master'. But despite his being 'a writer of very great ability', this obituarist contends, Grant's works are not memorable – unlike, say, Dickens's *David Copperfield* or George Eliot's *Romola*.[1] Not all obituaries concurred with this assessment: the Dublin *Freeman's Journal and Daily Commercial Advertiser* praised Grant's novels as 'sentimental without mawkishness, and as intelligently interesting as they were gay and rollicking'.[2] But there was general agreement that Grant had outlived his fame.

This chapter relates the still-obscure career of James Grant to that of a contemporary who is now much better-known – Margaret Oliphant (1828–1897). They each started publishing fiction before the age of twenty-five and continued writing for publication until their deaths. They both, however, enjoyed their greatest success before 1870. Both were Scottish-born, although based in England for much of their lives. While prominent as writers of fiction, they practised a variety of genres: Grant also wrote history and contributed to periodicals, while Oliphant produced biographies, literary history, travel narratives, and a vast quantity of journalism.

However much writing was for Grant and Oliphant the occupation of choice, they depended on it to support their families, which is the major reason for their extraordinary productivity. Grant had no resources other than the proceeds of his publications to support his wife and two sons; Oliphant was granted a Civil List pension of one hundred pounds a year in 1868 (a kind of recognition that Grant, by his own account, sought but failed to gain in 1874, despite his application being 'numerously signed').³ Nonetheless, within a couple of years of her own award, Oliphant had to keep afloat not only her two surviving children and one alcoholic brother, but her other brother and three of his offspring. Grant and Oliphant thus shared aspirations towards some more reliable source of income. Oliphant would have liked to edit a magazine, rather than being paid piecemeal for her contributions to several – an opportunity more open to men than to women. But Grant was equally unlucky: when in financial straits in 1879, he claimed that he had sought in vain 'a secretaryship, or some such occupation'.⁴ In addition, the two authors found their reputations undermined by the sheer amount of writing they felt compelled to publish. Finally, both had to grapple with the legacy of their great literary forebear, Walter Scott. Oliphant's engagement with Scott's influence, I propose, was ultimately less constraining than that of Grant. But for both, their Scottish background and knowledge of Scottish culture were important.

James Grant's output consisted of sixty-one novels and several narrative histories, beginning with his four-volume *The Romance of War; or the Highlanders in Spain, France and Belgium* (1845–47), which dealt with the Scottish regiments who fought in the Napoleonic Wars from the Egyptian campaign up to Waterloo, and, according to Trevor Royle, 'with its breathless style and high romance [...] presented an heroic view of battle'.⁵ As this early work foreshadows, Grant's writings had a Scottish orientation, plus a strong focus on military endeavours. Although he spent his latter decades in London, Grant lived much of his life in Edinburgh. The son of an officer in the 92nd (Gordon) Highlanders, he had had an early career as a soldier (1840–43). And while some of his fiction was set in the nineteenth century, much of it evoked notable periods of Scottish history. For example, *Bothwell* (1851) dealt with the turbulent reign of Mary, Queen of Scots, and the following year's *Jane Seton* explored the beginnings of Scottish witch-trials in the time of Mary's father, James V. Soon afterwards, *Philip Rollo; or, the Scottish Musketeers* (1855) would take Grant's military characters into Europe's Thirty Years' War (1618–48), and *The Yellow Frigate; or, The Three Sisters* (1855) is founded on legends associated with Scottish history of the late fifteenth century. Royle has judged these novels as among Grant's best.⁶ Nor did the Jacobite rebellion of 1745 escape Grant's attention, as his 1867 novel, *The White Cockade; or, Faith and Fortitude*, focused on those events, and was praised by the *Athenaeum*'s reviewer as both historically grounded and 'a dashing, high-spirited novel, extremely interesting'.⁷

It is therefore not surprising that Grant's novels were sometimes compared with those of Scott. Like Scott, Grant was genuinely fascinated by Scottish history. But, as for other writers of historical fiction, following in Scott's train was problematic, since it was difficult to have one's novels appraised as measuring up to those of the 'Wizard of the North'. Thus, in treating Grant's early novel *The Scottish Cavalier* (1850, set in the era of James VII/II), the *Literary Gazette* reviewer found an 'overabundance of descriptions in the school of Scott', without these being subordinated to the narrative, as Scott's are.[8] Meanwhile the obituarist who compared Grant's work unfavourably with that of Dickens and George Eliot characterised it as old-fashioned like Scott's, yet as lacking the touch of that 'magician'.

James Grant's rapid succession of publications meant that his output was uneven – another circumstance which told against his reputation. One of the few post-nineteenth-century discussions of Grant, Stewart M. Ellis's *Mainly Victorian* (1925), declares that although the sheer number of publications 'may be impressive as evidence of energy, ingenuity and mental power', it is 'deplorable from an artistic point of view', since 'no man has it in him to write twelve or more superlative books'.[9] That is, industriousness militated against quality.

Unlike Oliphant's case, little survives that reveals Grant's own views on his writing. But in his later years, he felt obliged to call on the resources of the Royal Literary Fund to supplement his income, and so commented on his career in his applications. The aim of such applications was to prove financial need despite demonstrable evidence of literary productivity: an applicant was required to supply evidence of his or her publishing activity and a declaration of income. But even allowing for this necessary orientation, Grant's representation of the writing life is bleak. In each application, he stresses his lack of any financial recourse save literature, and his limited income from that. He has never been able to save anything, so that when unexpected circumstances intervene, such as failing eyesight (1874 and 1876), illness of his own (1879), or (in 1885) the protracted and fatal illness of his elder son, he has no funds to draw on. So he has to cover his needs by selling his copyrights, sometimes in advance of publication: his main publisher, Routledge, has given him a maximum of two hundred and fifty pounds for these, but it is more often one hundred pounds. His overall annual income averages about three hundred pounds. Because Grant can command only small sums, and sometimes relies on advances, he cannot, as he puts it in his first (1874) application, 'free [him]self or try a new market'. Therefore he has to work on in what he calls 'this literary and hopeless treadmill', and two years later, 'many years of unremitting literary labour'.[10] Grant was given four awards of eighty pounds in each of 1874, 1876, 1879, and 1885, while his widow Christian McDonell Grant received the same amount in 1887, the year of his death. She applied to the Fund because all he had been able to leave her was proceeds of about five hundred pounds from a small insurance policy. Grant's later years did however have a more positive dimension, and one related to his Scottishness, so I will return to this topic.

Margaret Oliphant, meanwhile, was very aware of how a writer whose prolific output was obvious evidence of his or her 'industry' could be slighted or patronised on this account, as Grant sometimes was. In her *Autobiography* (1899), written at various times over her life and published posthumously, Oliphant often reflected on her career, and especially on how her financial situation had impelled her to write prolifically and rapidly, accepting all opportunities for publication. She did this rather than harvest her energies to produce works that might gain more critical appreciation, and possibly more money per publication.

Oliphant had faced her first major financial crisis when she was unexpectedly widowed in October 1859, in debt, with two children to support and another on the way. Blackwood had been publishing articles of hers in *Blackwood's Edinburgh Magazine*, and had also brought out one of her novels with Scottish settings, *Katie Stewart* (1853, set during the Jacobite rebellion of 1745). The firm was to be a mainstay of Oliphant's publishing career, and part of the affinity she felt with its members, especially John Blackwood (1818–1879), arose from their shared Scottishness. By the end of 1860, however, Oliphant was desperate, as the Blackwood brothers had been declining her articles. This crisis was nevertheless the catalyst to her writing 'The Executor', the first in a series of fictions that became her most successful – later called the *Chronicles of Carlingford*. These novels, set in the fictional English town of Carlingford, explore with some comedy the local politics of both the Church of England and Dissenting groups. Following 'The Executor' (*Blackwood's*, May 1861) there were published in the magazine and in book-form between 1861 and 1866 'The Rector', *The Doctor's Family, Salem Chapel, The Perpetual Curate*, and *Miss Marjoribanks. Phoebe, Junior*, drawing on the same community, came out with Hurst & Blackett in 1876. A recurrent theme was the limited opportunity for gainful employment or meaningful activity for women, a topic that runs through much of Oliphant's fiction.

The most significant turning-point in Oliphant's fortunes came in 1870, when her brother failed in business and she became responsible for most of his family as well as her own. As Oliphant's biographer notes, the writer then had a pressing need for a regular annual income. But by the 1880s her outgoings always exceeded her revenue and (like James Grant's), her work was mortgaged in advance: she was in no position to drive hard bargains.[11] Oliphant comments on this predicament in her *Autobiography*: while her publishers 'were good and kind in the way' of giving her advances, 'they were never – probably because of these advances, and of [her] constant need and inability [...] to struggle over prices – very lavish in payment'.[12]

Although Oliphant's income from publication had contributed to the family during the lifetime of her husband (a stained-glass artist), his death, plus the ineffectuality of both her brothers, thrust her into the role of breadwinner. That is, she had to exercise the traditional maternal function of nurturing children while also financing their upbringing, education, and preparation for careers. The final outcome of all this was eventually a great source of anguish for Oliphant: she outlived all her children, with her daughter dying in childhood and her two sons succumbing at thirty-three and thirty-four respectively, neither having attained the successful and financially independent careers she had hoped for them. Her nephew, whom she had prepared for an engineer's career in India, died there in his twenties.

Before her sons' deaths, Oliphant had been induced to compare herself with Blackwood's most successful novelist, George Eliot (1819–1880), who had brought out novels far less frequently than Oliphant. The publication of Eliot's *Life and Letters* by her widower in 1885 gave Oliphant the impression that Eliot had been 'kept [...] in a mental greenhouse and taken care of', and she wondered how much her own career might have differed had she not had to publish so relentlessly for money.[13] Late in 1894, having lost both sons, Oliphant reflected on the long-dead but much respected woman novelist Charlotte Brontë. She acknowledged that Brontë's smaller output of fiction was superior to her own, but believed that her life had been fuller than Brontë's and she had gained more experience.[14] Even if that experience had now taken from her most of the people for whom she had striven, she at her 'most ambitious of times' would rather have been remembered by her children as their mother, and by her friends as a friend, than as a writer. Yet her 'industry' was not to be belittled – it often had been treated with 'delightful superiority' by people with neither hard work nor anything else to their credit.[15]

Oliphant also contends that her wider experience has induced her to 'take more a man's view of mortal affairs'. What she means here is the belief that 'the love between men and women, the marrying and giving in marriage, occupy in fact so small a portion of either existence or thought'.[16] She is judging what she sees as the emphasis of Brontë's novels, but a plot focused on courtship was also a convention of nineteenth-century fiction in general. This convention is one which many of Oliphant's novels followed – but not always in a conventional way. In as early a novel as *The Doctor's Family* (1863), the female protagonist agrees to marry so as to support her sister's children, while in *Miss Marjoribanks*, the eponymous heroine weds her cousin largely because her unexpected poverty following her father's death curtails her role as an arbiter of Carlingford social life. More cynically presented is the choice of clever Phoebe in *Phoebe, Junior* (1876) who espouses the less appealing of her suitors, the dull Clarence Copperhead, because through him she can exert vicarious political influence by managing his career. Then in *Hester*, published some years later in 1883, the treatment of marriage is darker: the impecunious heroine has suitors, but she would have been more fulfilled had she been empowered to exercise the business acumen that had been so prominent in the life of her wealthy aunt Catherine. As this brief outline suggests, Margaret Oliphant was sometimes able to adapt traditional motifs in order to hint at the inadequacy of women's options.

Throughout her career, Oliphant explored new outlets for her work – publishers and serialisation possibilities for her fiction, but also periodicals for her reviews and other commentaries. A case in point emerged not long after she took on the burden of her brother and his family. Oliphant serialised her 1872 novel, *At His Gates*, in the British religious monthly *Good Words*, and also in the up-and-coming New York-based publication *Scribner's Magazine*, with volume publication following on both sides of the Atlantic. *At His Gates* is of interest also because it thematises Oliphant's own predicament. The male protagonist is an artist who can rapidly turn out acceptable works for the market, but cannot – except in the extreme circumstances generated by an improbable plot – produce a work of genius.

Oliphant often spent time in Scotland, but did not live there for extended periods after the age of ten. Although she did produce novels with Scottish settings, these did not make up the bulk of her output. They are concentrated among her early publications, albeit not confined to these. The novel closest to James Grant's oeuvre in orientation is probably *Magdalen Hepburn: A Story of the Scottish Reformation* (1854), but its emulation of the dialogue used in Scott's novels set in the distant past is not convincing. In 1876 Alexander Innes Shand included several of

Oliphant's novels in a survey, 'Recent Scotch Novels'. He praises the impressive but 'quiet effects' of her first novel, *Passages in the Life of Mrs Margaret Maitland of Sunnyside* (1849), and the effective recreation in *Harry Muir: A Story of Scottish Life* (1853) of 'the poetical side of a hard-working and poverty-stricken life in a great manufacturing city'. Oliphant, declares Shand, 'has gone to nature for her men and women'. In addition, although Shand gestures to Scott's works as 'the alpha and omega of Scottish fiction', he does not comment on the inferiority or otherwise of Oliphant's fiction in that context. Rather, he contends that her work probes more deeply than the fiction of Scott's near-contemporary, John Galt (1779–1839).[17]

Scott was a crucial figure for Margaret Oliphant, and she wrote about him often: he was the novelist she admired most both as a writer and a human being. She especially respected and empathised with him as a man who, in his later years, desperately turned out as much publishable writing as he could so as to recoup for himself and his publisher partners the fortunes they had lost. When Scott's journal came out in 1890, Oliphant identified with his endurance of relentless work, loneliness, and bereavement, saying that she felt she knew him as well as she knew herself.[18]

Yet, however strong her felt affinity with Scott, Oliphant did not, by and large, model her novels on his. While her fiction is quite diverse, she deployed primarily contemporary settings and domestic life, and focused on characterisation – especially female characters. James Grant's writing possessed vitality and exciting plots, while in his latter works, he did locate his military protagonists in more contemporary arenas of conflict, such as the Crimea, India, Afghanistan, and Sudan. But characterisation, a quality increasingly valued in nineteenth-century criticism of fiction, was never Grant's strong suit, and thus he came to be seen as a dated writer, a weaker follower of Scott.

Neither James Grant nor Margaret Oliphant ever achieved financial security through literature. However much writing may have been their occupation of choice, the industrial-strength production in which they engaged carried risks, as I have suggested. The pair's lack of alternative resources weakened their bargaining power with publishers and thus forced them to ramp up their productivity, while this sheer productivity militated against their literary reputations. As far as the legacy of Scott was concerned, meanwhile, Oliphant was more successful than Grant in escaping from their forebear's shadow: a female novelist, after all, was not expected to emulate Scott's generally male-centred historical fictions.

Nonetheless, both writers, late in their careers, turned again to Scotland in writing if not in life, and this move catalysed some of their best work. James Grant, finding Cassell a more generous publisher than Routledge, produced for them the three-volume illustrated *Old and New Edinburgh* (1880–82). Here Grant harnessed all his deep and extensive knowledge of both history and geography to offer a street by street, sometimes building by building, account of the city. It was one of the best-received works of Grant's career, and was last reissued as recently as 2011. Meanwhile Margaret Oliphant published in 1890 one of her most impressive novels, *Kirsteen*, set partly in Scotland. Here the eponymous heroine actually must escape from Scotland to London, to evade a marriage imposed by her father – who is himself an acute study of a proudly Scottish but autocratic and misogynist man. While this plot-line hardly makes the novel autobiographical, what does evoke the author's own life is Kirsteen's professional career (as a dressmaker) devoted to supporting family members – plus her constant nostalgia for Scotland. Scotland, then, remained very much alive in the imaginations of both James Grant and Margaret Oliphant, long after they had moved to England.

CHAPTER SEVENTEEN

Scottish Travel Writing

Jennifer Hayward

Across the nineteenth century, Scottish travel writers were both central to the development of travel writing and virtually invisible. Early in the century, their national identity was generally ignored, if not actively concealed; by the 1890s, by contrast, they often made national character a central theme within their texts. This chapter will trace the evolution of Scots-specific travel across the century, establishing the factors that motivated Scots both to travel and to publish accounts of their experiences, exploring key tropes that connect the distinctive perspectives of Scots abroad, and identifying some of the central figures in the history of nineteenth-century Scottish travel.

Writing in 1857, the Scottish–Jamaican travel writer Mary Seacole (1805–1881) speaks to several of the factors that gave Scottish travel writers a distinctive perspective on empire. She explains that as a young adult she experienced

> [A] longing to travel which will never leave me while I have health and vigour. I was never weary of tracing upon an old map the route to England; and never followed with my gaze the stately ships homeward bound without longing to be in them, and see the blue hills of Jamaica fade into the distance.[1]

Seacole here expresses a nostalgia for 'home' that is shared by many travellers, but her own sense of 'home' would remain fluid throughout her life: as the child of a Jamaican healer of African descent and a Scottish soldier, she seems to have considered herself neither Jamaican, nor Scottish, nor English, although with connections to all three. Seacole thus captures an ambivalent relationship to a 'homeland' that often deliberately excluded its colonial subjects from citizenship, an ambivalence echoed by Scottish travel writers who felt similarly marginalised within an imperial culture generally normalised as 'English'. Seacole also foreshadows the geocultural curiosity, economic imperatives, and sheer wanderlust that drove many nineteenth-century Scots to share her 'longing to travel'.

Any overview of Scottish travel writing – here referring to travel writing by Scottish writers, rather than travel writing set in Scotland – must begin with the interrogation of national borders spurred by the dramatic changes in Scotland's position in the world at the beginning of the eighteenth century. With the Acts of Union of 1707, Scottish sailors, soldiers, scientists, and traders benefited from increased access to the fast-growing network of global trade and began to travel and to emigrate in numbers that increased rapidly over the next two centuries. Historian T. M. Devine's study of Scottish influence in the British Empire indicates the extent of the Scottish diaspora: roughly two million Scots emigrated during the nineteenth century, with annual numbers increasing from fewer than ten thousand per year before 1850 to between twenty thousand and thirty thousand from 1875 to 1900 – a higher proportion of the national population than for any country in Europe except Ireland and Norway.[2] Meanwhile, Scotland contributed disproportionately to the staffing of Empire: Nigel Leask notes that although Scotland's population was about one-tenth that of the British Isles as a whole, some ranks of the naval, military, and mercantile classes were anywhere from thirty to sixty per cent Scottish.[3]

In the late eighteenth and early nineteenth centuries, the legacy of the Scottish Enlightenment spurred development of a newly self-conscious Scottish identity that built on, but was distinct from, the project of British empire. Subsumed within and dependent upon Great Britain both politically and economically, Scots worked energetically to define an autonomous identity. Scottish writers shared a distinctive family of tropes throughout the nineteenth century, inspired by the influence of the Scottish Enlightenment; the Scots emphasis on education, including education for women and the working classes; and Scotland's unique history and identity within the British Isles.[4] For Scottish travel writers, a distinctive discourse of sympathy functioned both to strengthen ties with other wanderers in Empire, and to activate imaginative empathy for those Others encountered in the course of their travels. During the same period, too, Scotland developed a nationally inflected Romantic movement of its own.[5]

Travel literature as a genre

Scottish travellers were key contributors to the genre of travel literature right from the start. In the early years of nineteenth-century travel, from 1800 to 1832, the genre was still in an experimental phase – as was Scotland's relation to the larger project of the British Empire. For that reason, Scottish writers often 'passed' as English, whether to capitalise on the power of empire or to short-circuit prejudice against Scots; many writers therefore refer to themselves as 'English' or 'British' in print.[6] As this homogenising impulse implies, Scottish travel writers experienced marginalisation both in Britain and beyond, resulting in a unique perspective on the relationship between Britain and its colonies as well as a significant role in the development of the travel genre.

Early travel narratives established many of the central themes of later Scottish travel writing, including an emphasis on intellectual curiosity, a proto-ethnographic interest in the lives of local peoples, and a comparative consideration of human cultures. Indeed, there was a broad shift in travel writing from the scientific and 'objective' focus of the eighteenth century to a more 'literary' and introspective focus after the 1820s,[7] a transformation that paralleled the rise of the novel, and Scottish travellers played a central role in this shift. On a material level, these early narratives' extensive information 'about routes, resources, peoples, and languages served the agenda of European commercial and political expansion', Barbara Korte explains: 'Such texts are another reminder of how conflicted and contradictory relationships to non-Europeans were in a culture that took pride in its Enlightenment principles'.[8]

In the first years of the century, too, Scottish women writers began adapting the travel genre to create a space for themselves. Key figures include Anne Grant (1755–1838), who made crucial contributions to the rise of domestic tourism in works like *Letters from the Mountains* (1806) and *Essays on the Superstitions of the Highlanders* (1811); and Maria Graham (1785–1844), whose travel texts, including *Journal of a Residence in India* (1812), *Journal of a Voyage to Brazil,* and *Journal of a Residence in Chile* (both 1824) contributed to botanical and geological science as well as forging new paths for professional women writers.

In the works of these writers and many others, one powerful thread was the Scottish Enlightenment emphasis on sympathy, affect, and sensibility discussed above, which shaped many aspects of travel discourse, perhaps most notably Scottish travellers' perspective on abolition. Late eighteenth and early nineteenth-century travel writers including Graham,

John Gabriel Stedman (1744–1797) and Alison Stewart Carmichael (c. 1790–1885) set themselves apart from many travel writers of their time by actively intervening in the debate over slavery, with Graham advocating strongly for abolition. Of course, to be abolitionist did not necessarily imply anti-colonialist, as Carla Sassi and others have demonstrated.[9]

Equally influential were Adam Smith's (1723–1790) theories of free trade and *laissez-faire* economics, which would transform economic, trade, and imperial policy first in the New World and later throughout the British Empire and beyond. Smith's views on free trade are quoted either directly or implicitly by most Scottish travel texts of the first half of the nineteenth century, including Maria Graham's South American travels cited above as well as Thomas Cochrane's (1775–1860) *Narrative of Services to Chile and Brazil* (1859). As these two writers demonstrate, not only Britain's formal colonies but also what is sometimes termed its 'informal empire' were essential to Britain's continued development towards a 'commercial society'.

The development of sub-genres

As the travel and publishing industries moved full steam ahead, the travel genre continued to expand and to diversify in form and generic influences. Writers pursued a wide variety of sub-genres, innovating on traditions both old (exploration, scientific ventures, mores and manners-style texts, and so on) and new (tourism, adventure travels blurring the lines between fiction and nonfiction, imperial travel, and so on).

By the 1840s, Scottish travellers could be found on every continent and writing in every sub-genre. One influential but often overlooked development is the rise of women travel writers. Improved transportation technologies combined with cultural shifts to normalise women as travellers; they journeyed in increasing numbers, either independently or accompanying male relatives on imperial, commercial, or diplomatic assignments.[10] In addition to those already discussed, notable writers include Felicia Skene (1821–1899), Margaret Oliphant (1828–1897), Isabella Bird Bishop (1831–1904), Constance Frederica Gordon Cumming (1837–1924), and Flora Annie Steel (1847–1929). Oliphant's travel writings – although generally ignored in favour of her fiction – are particularly significant in illuminating the importance of travel in the Victorian periodical press.

With the increased popularity of travel literature came the development of new sub-genres. John MacGregor (1825–1892) contributed to the rise in tourism with a dozen or so travel texts ranging from *Three Days in the East* (1852) through *Our Brothers and Cousins: A Summer Tour in Canada and the States* (1859) to the Rob Roy canoe series for which he became most famous and which included *A Thousand Miles in the Rob Roy Canoe on Rivers and Lakes of Europe* (1866). MacGregor illustrates the tendency, even as late as mid-century, for Scots writers to 'pass' as English, albeit in a sometimes equivocal register; for example, while travelling in the Vermland region in *The Rob Roy on the Baltic* he notes, in what may be intended as a coded lesson in anti-nationalism, that 'desperate sticklers we may be for Old England and everything English; but repeated lessons abroad have at length forced me to confess that, in comparison with most of these "outlandish folks", we English are often very boorish'. He concludes that his travels have inspired him to 'behave in foreign lands with the modesty of one who feels his countrymen have much to learn'.[11]

The career of Frances Calderón de la Barca (1804–1882) illuminates the Scottish blurring of boundaries between politics, informal empire, and travel. Her influential *Life in Mexico during a Residence of Two Years in That Country* broke new ground in travel writing, helping to shift the genre's expectations and goals. The book caused a sensation when first published in 1843, first because its (initially) negative portrait of the newly independent country angered Mexicans, and later because the United States army relied on her detailed and accurate descriptions in shaping military strategy for the Mexican-American War. Indeed, Miguel Cabañas concludes, 'Calderón de la Barca's narrative opens up the possibility of United States intervention in Mexico, and foreshadows the Mexican-American War of 1846–48'.[12]

Calderón was born Frances Erskine Inglis in Edinburgh, but left Scotland in early adulthood. While living in the United States, she married Ángel Calderón de la Barca; after he was appointed as the first Spanish Ambassador to newly independent Mexico, the two lived in Mexico from 1839 to 1842. By the time Calderón wrote, the travel genre was well established as popular and profitable, and expectations for female versus male texts were clearly demarcated: women should focus on domestic life, mores and manners, avoiding masculine domains like politics, commerce, and violence. Calderón initially echoes many women travellers in the ways she diminishes her own authority. At the same time, however, she asserts an authoritative and privileged perspective, setting European civilisation against Mexican primitivism, which she depicts as a space both geographically and temporally removed from modernity; here again, Scottish Enlightenment ideas, and particularly stadial theory, inflect the world depicted by this Scottish travel writer.

But like many Scots travel writers, Calderón adopted an unusually hybrid subject position, dramatically altering her ideas on Mexico by the end of her residence there. She departs from the typical travel writer's perspective of authority and objectivity to acknowledge her own prejudice and chart a dramatic shift in perspective, ultimately refuting her inherited frameworks, including stadial theory, to challenge dominant representations of Mexicans as primitive. The result is an unusually complex and negotiated vision of Mexico and of national identity. As both a woman and a Scottish diasporic citizen all too conscious of the wages of nationalism and the costs of marginalisation, Calderón's powerfully conveyed transition from a position of imperial superiority to a more nuanced perspective on Mexican independence illuminates mid-century developments in both Scottish and Mexican national identity.

The mid-century blurring of travel writing's generic boundaries is also well illustrated in the works of Robert Michael Ballantyne (1825–1894), who capitalised on the slippage between travel and other narrative forms. In his early twenties Ballantyne was apprenticed to the Hudson's Bay Company. After returning to Scotland, he published *Hudson's Bay; or, every-day life in the wilds of North America* (1848). He then capitalised on the success of this fairly traditional travel text by publishing adventure fiction closely based on his travels. Popular titles include *The Young Fur-Traders* (1856), *The Coral Island* (1857), *Ungava: a Tale of Eskimo Land* (1857), *The Pirate City* (1874), and *The Settler and the Savage* (1877). Ballantyne was a strong influence on later Scottish writers; Robert Louis Stevenson (1850–1894) credited him with inspiring parts of *Treasure Island* (1883), paying homage to him as 'Ballantyne the brave' in the poem that introduces that novel. Virtually ignored for decades, Ballantyne's fiction gained new attention with the rise of postcolonial studies in the 1990s.[13]

Like most nineteenth-century travel writers, Scots explored the racial dynamics consequent on imperial expansion, with a perspective often inflected by their own marginalised position within the British Empire. A particularly interesting case is Seacole, whose equivocal relationship to England as 'home' opened this chapter. Seacole chose to open her *Wonderful Adventures of Mrs Seacole* (1857), by emphasising her Scottish heritage, asserting in her first paragraph, 'I am a Creole, and have good Scotch blood coursing in my veins', and adding that observers have 'traced to my Scotch blood that energy and activity which are not always found in the Creole race, and which have carried me to so many varied scenes; and perhaps they are right'.¹⁴ This passage sets the book's tone, articulating the complexities of double consciousness by simultaneously exposing and expressing racist stereotypes. Accepted as a Jamaican 'doctress' in some circles, rejected for her skin colour or her gender in others, Seacole lived the in-between state of constant navigation of differentially circumscribed identities.

Early in her text, Seacole describes her first encounter with North Americans in Panama, thus implicitly enforcing readers' awareness of differences in racist attitudes among whites. As she explains:

> Americans (even from the Northern States) are always uncomfortable in the company of coloured people, and very often show this feeling in stronger ways than by sour looks and rude words [...] I have a few shades of deeper brown upon my skin which shows me related – and I am proud of the relationship – to those poor mortals whom you once held enslaved, and whose bodies America still owns. And [...] knowing what slavery is; having seen with my eyes and heard with my ears proof positive enough of its horrors [...] is it surprising that I should be somewhat impatient of the airs of superiority which many Americans have endeavoured to assume over me?¹⁵

Writing just seven years before the Civil War began, Seacole implicates her reader by directly addressing us as 'you' and emphasising that the British were once as inhumane as 'our cousins across the Atlantic'.

Just as women travel writers had to conform to gendered expectations, so marginalised voices like Seacole's could intervene in the travel genre only by speaking in a specific register: sensational, docile, and coded as safe rather than subversive. Nevertheless, Seacole manages to provide a uniquely Caribbean perspective on Scottish, English, and United States identity, exposing racial dynamics in the Atlantic in ways that counterbalance the dominant imperial perspective. Once virtually erased from both the scholarly and the professional record, Seacole has now been reclaimed as an active presence in the cultural memory of Jamaica.

Imperial and national identities

In the *fin de siècle*, Scottish travel writers played a key role in questioning imperial and national identities. Influential Scottish authors of this era include Constance Gordon-Cumming (1837–1924), who combined bohemian art and travel; John Muir (1838–1914), whose environmental writings blurred the boundaries between travel and memoir; and Lady Florence Caroline Dixie (1855–1905), who expanded possibilities for women writers by crafting an iconoclastic 'New Woman' persona blending traditionally gendered travel tropes with physical adventure. Moving towards the twentieth century, Robert Bontine Cunninghame Graham (1852–1936) depicted the pampas of Argentina through a Romantic lens while paralleling South America's and Scotland's struggles to preserve their 'wild' past in the process of moving towards an independent future.

Finally, and perhaps most significantly, Robert Louis Stevenson began his writing career with travel narratives whose border crossings anticipated the modernist experimentations that would reshape the genre. Wherever he wandered – through England, Europe, North America, or the Pacific – Stevenson developed metaphors to capture the uneasy coexistence of familiarity and alienation in the everyday life of the Scottish traveller: 'foreigner at home', 'stranger in my own house', 'strangers in the land of Egypt'.[16] After his early works, however, Stevenson departs from previous Scottish travel writers in that he does not conceal his national identity nor does he seek to 'pass' as English. In fact, the hybrid subject position of diasporic Scots becomes a crucial theme in his work. In *The Silverado Squatters*, his travel text on California, Stevenson echoes Seacole in musing about the 'longing' for a lost homeland – but he also anticipates a globalised future: 'indeed, I think we all belong to many countries. And perhaps this habit of much travel, and the engendering of scattered friendships, may prepare the euthanasia of ancient nations'.[17] We have much to learn from the Scottish travellers of the nineteenth century, who began by eliding their own identity in order to enter professional networks, but ended by thematising global interconnection. As Stevenson put it in his 1879 *Travels with a Donkey in the Cévennes*, 'we are all travellers in what John Bunyan calls the wilderness of this world'.[18]

CHAPTER EIGHTEEN

Travel Writing about the Highlands in the Nineteenth Century

Nigel Leask

In February 1809, Walter Scott (1771–1832) published a devastating review of Sir John Carr's *Caledonian Sketches*,[1] asking facetiously 'what news from the land of cakes and whiskey, from the region of mist and snow?'. Carr's 'hackneyed' travel account was 'neither remarkable for value [nor] accuracy [...] It would, perhaps, be somewhat difficult to bring us news from Scotland [...] the information which they seek in person may be found in a hundred volumes'. Scott listed some of the travel books – going back to Dr Johnson and Thomas Pennant – which he accused Carr of plundering.[2] Attributing the popularity of the Highland tour to the wartime closure of the continent, he speculated that recent overexposure had left the genre of travel writing about Scotland totally exhausted.[3]

Ironically, just as he rung the genre's death knell, Scott was busy inventing the literary conditions for the next wave of Highland tourism, based on the massive success of his verse romances *The Lady of the Lake* (1810) and *The Lord of the Isles* (1815), and his novels *Waverley* (1814) and *Rob Roy* (1817). Often building on the same authors scathingly dismissed in his review, Scott now portrayed the Highlands as 'the faery ground of romance and poetry'.[4] His own 1814 circumnavigation of Scotland's coasts on the lighthouse clipper *Pharos* provided an eye-witness supplement to his reading in travel literature: for example his visit to Loch Coruisk on Skye made such a profound impression that he would use it as the setting for a major episode in *The Lord of the Isles,* just as he had drawn on his holiday around the Trossachs in creating the picturesque setting of his best-selling verse romance *The Lady of the Lake.* Scott's romantic 'Highlandism' has been extensively studied by scholars,[5] especially his wrapping of Edinburgh in tartan for 'the King's Jaunt' (George IV's visit to Edinburgh in 1822). It would also powerfully influence the nineteenth century's understanding of Gaelic culture, from Queen Victoria to Marx and Engels.[6]

Despite the decline of published tours, the nineteenth-century Scottish tour continued to offer Britain's newly affluent middle classes the powerful associational *frisson* of literary and imaginative geographies that it had done in the previous century. The continuing taste for Macpherson's *Ossian* 'translations' was revealed in the attraction of sites like 'Ossian's Hall' at Dunkeld, or 'Fingal's Cave' on Staffa; the enormous popularity of the poems and songs of Robert Burns, who had made his own Highland Tour in 1787,[7] made visits to the birthplace cottage at Alloway or the 'Birks of Aberfeldy' compulsory; and above all, Scott's *The Lady of the Lake* had transformed the Trossachs into one of the premier tourists sites in Europe.[8] At least fifty thousand copies had been sold by 1836, and it anticipated the success of Scott's later poems and novels by being adapted for the popular theatre, opera, panoramic displays, and even wallpaper designs. Meanwhile, steam boats were opening up the Highlands and Western Isles, transforming the region and providing the basis for commercially organised mass tourism. Scott was an active sponsor of William Daniell's ambitious visual documentation of Scotland's coasts and islands, represented in over half of the 308 aquatint plates of his monumental eight-volume *Voyage Round Great Britain* (1814–25). It was a patriotic celebration of Britain's coasts, the defensive ramparts which had protected the nation from Napoleonic invasion.[9] Yet as the following discussion of nineteenth-century travel writing about Scotland will show, Scott did not hold a complete monopoly in representing the nation, as other voices and more critical perspectives challenged his mainstream 'Highlandism'.

Recent critics have demonstrated the extent to which Scott's masculine reinvention of Scottish tradition relied heavily on the novels and travel writings of female precursors, among them Anne Grant of Laggan's (1755–1838) *Essays from the Mountains* (1806). Born in North America of Scottish parents, and later settling with her military quartermaster father in the Highlands, Grant described herself as 'not absolutely a native, nor entirely a stranger'.[10] She proceded to learn Gaelic, championed the *Ossian* poems, and immersed herself in Highland culture, especially after her marriage in 1779 to the minister of the Badenoch parish of Laggan, where she enjoyed the patronage of both James Macpherson and the Duchess of Gordon. Partly a travel account, partly the epistolary autobiography of an aspiring romantic poet, Grant's *Letters from the Mountains* romanticised Gaeldom before Scott, idealising a traditional but dying culture somewhat insulated from the corruptions (and political radicalism) afflicting the modern world, and deeply vulnerable to the rapid effects of modernisation: 'a Highlander never sits at ease at a loom;

it is like putting a deer to the plough'.[11] Grant's defence of the Gaels, and her attacks on sheep clearance (although without blaming landowners), inspired Scott's friend David Stewart of Garth (1772–1829), Perthshire laird and Napoleonic war hero, whose *Sketches of the Character, Manners, and Present State of the Highlanders of Scotland* was published in March 1822, just a few months before the 'King's Jaunt', for which Garth supervised much of the tartan pageantry. Originally commissioned as a regimental history of the Black Watch, the book argued that the *dùthchas* (the Gaelic concept of hereditary trusteeship encompassing land and tradition) and military spirit of the tenant class was being destroyed by their transformation into a rural proletariat. This was creating an increasingly 'Irish' situation of class tension between tenants and landlords: 'can we expect high-spirited chivalrous soldiers', Garth demanded, 'preferring death to disgrace and defeat, from such a population, and such habits as these?'.[12]

It was in reaction to the romantic 'Highlandism' of Grant, Scott, and Garth that in 1825 the eminent geologist John Macculloch (1773–1835; despite his Scottish father, he identified himself as an Englishman) published his massive four-volume *The Highlands and Western Isles of Scotland [...] in Letters to Sir Walter Scott, Bart*.[13] Written in the facetious, De Quinceyan style of literary hyperbole that currently underpinned the huge commercial success of *Blackwood's Magazine*, Macculloch made satirical hay of both the Pennantian tradition of eighteenth-century travel writing and Scott's own version of the Highlands. Spanning a monumental 1924 pages, *Highlands and Western Isles* relentlessly traverses the whole encyclopedic range of topics listed in its long title. Above all, it underlined Scott's role in paradoxically destroying the old ways of the Highlands by means of the mass tourism that his works had inspired:

> [...] the mystic portal has been thrown open, and the mob has rushed in, dispersing all these fairy visions, and polluting everything with its unhallowed touch. Barouches and gigs, cocknies and fisherman poets, Glasgow weavers and travelling haberdashers, now swarm in every resting place, and meet us at every avenue.[14]

Claiming authority on the strength of a decade's worth of travel in the Highlands and Islands as a geological surveyor, Macculloch enlisted Scott's name in justifying landlord policies based on a racialised attack on the Gaels. 'The Gothic race', he thundered, 'was ordained [for the conquest of the Celts] [...] nothing short of extermination was applicable to the correction of a people who, even yet, are resisting the improvements that surround them'.[15] T. M. Devine has recently complained about the sidelining of the Lowland experience in his carefully titled *The Scottish Clearances* (2018), and the enduring modern appeal of histories of 'exile, victimhood and dispossession' in the Highlands.[16] Valid as his argument is, it overlooks the fact that apologists for the Lowland clearances never evoked the discourse of race as it was employed in the Highlands (and Ireland), an egregious feature of Macculloch's book. Despite being called to account by his critics, who demanded that Scott distance himself from the geologist's extreme views, 'The Great Unknown' insisted on maintaining a stolid silence.

Scott's 'romantic' Highlands may have triumphed over Macculloch's disturbing critique in the 'Balmoralisation' of the Victorian era, but *The Highlands and Western Isles* nonetheless anticipates the brutal era of clearance, famine, and emigration that followed in the decades immediately succeeding Scott's death in 1832. Katherine Haldane Grenier notes that 'the rhetoric of tourism increasingly froze Scotland in time in the nineteenth century, even though that country was fully a part of the economic, social and political transformations of the period'.[17] *Ossian* as well as Scott had romanticised the Highland deer-hunt, and in the Victorian era sporting tours of the Highlands became increasingly common, initially stimulated by Colonel Thomas Thornton's (1751/52–1823) *Sporting Tour through the Northern Parts of England and Great Part of the Highlands of Scotland* (1804), and later made fashionable by Prince Albert's obsession with deer stalking at Balmoral. As Christopher Smout indicates, the 'great age of slaughter' was really inaugurated by the invention of the copper percussion cap and the Game Act of 1831.[18] In contrast to the picturesque pilgrims mocked by Macculloch, 'hunting, fishing and shooting' tourists were often 'Philistines in search of their own particular brand of bloody fun', even if their sport later produced at least one literary classic in the shape of John Buchan's (1875–1940) novel *John Macnab* (1925).[19]

By mid-century, Highland 'holiday' narratives seem to have enjoyed more popularity than travel accounts proper, which always risked rehashing the information cheaply available in numerous tourist guide books like Black's *Picturesque Tourist of Scotland* (1840). They ranged across the whole social spectrum from the Edinburgh-based poet Alexander Smith's (1829?–1867) *A Summer in Skye* (1865), to Queen

Victoria's (1819–1901) *Leaves from the Journal of our Life in the Highlands* (1867). The fictional prototype seems again to have been Scott's *The Lady of the Lake*, where Ellen Douglas's island retreat on Loch Katrine permitted an escape from 'everyday duties and responsibilities' to 'a holiday house in which one's normal social identity can be cast aside, without forfeiting one's class privileges'.[20] Following the death of Albert in 1861, a broken-hearted Victoria prepared her Highland journals for publication, dedicated to 'the dear memory of him who made the life of the writer bright and happy'. The 'Highland Widow' remodelled a remote cottage at Glas Allt Shiel in 1868, and was 'rowed to the head of Loch Muick to enjoy a few days solitude with just a few attendants in what had been Prince Albert's favourite place'.[21] Balmoral became enshrined as the holiday home of Britain's monarchy, and the rich and famous emulated her example by purchasing 'Highland retreats', while Deeside became a mecca for tourists.[22] Not everyone was pleased: as the feisty Banffshire fisherwoman and diarist Christian Watt (1833–1923) wrote, 'after Royalty came Deeside was ruined'.[23]

On a more modest scale, Smith's *A Summer in Skye* is a classic of Victorian travel literature, describing his annual vacations on the island after his marriage to Flora Macdonald, daughter of Charles Macdonald of Ord. Smith portrays Skye as frozen in an Ossianic past, although his lively portrait of 'The Landlord' (Kenneth Macleod of Greshornish) does reveal the links between colonial rule in India and Highland land management in the mid-nineteenth century: 'The Landlord had spent the best part of his life in India, was more familiar with the huts of ryots, topes of palms [...] than with the houses of Skye cotters and the process of sheep-farming.'[24] Like the Queen, Smith retreated to the 'green solitude' of a remote bothy:

> My bed is the heather, my mirror the stream from the hills, my comb and brush the sea breeze, my watch the sun, my theatre the sunset and my evening service [...] watching the pinnacles of the hills of Cuchullin sharpening in intense purple against the pallid orange of the sky.[25]

Here he passed the time shooting at seagulls (a petit-bourgeois version of grouse shooting?) and composing his 'Poems written in a Skye Bothy', included in *A Summer in Skye*.[26] The clerk of Edinburgh University returned to the drudgery of urban employment a new man: 'soul and body were braced alike – into them had gone something of the peace of the hills, and the strength of the sea [...] I had covered the walls of my mind with a variety of new pictures.'[27]

Another popular form of later nineteenth-century writing about the Highlands which actually reversed the mobile perspective of travel writing was the parochial memoir, well exemplified by Norman Macleod's (1812–1872) bestselling *Reminiscences of a Highland Parish* (1867). Generically related to 'kailyard' literature discussed by Andrew Nash in the present volume, the genre's antecedents can be traced to Grant's *Letters from the Mountains*, John Galt's (1779–1839) fictionalised *Annals of the Parish* (1821), and the parochial reports contributed by Church of Scotland ministers to the *Statistical Accounts of Scotland* (1790s and 1834–1845). Macleod's *Reminscences* paints a detailed, somewhat whimsical, portrait of the old 'pre-improvement' Morvern of his boyhood, before the severe sheep-clearances of Patrick Sellar and other landlords. Reversing the usual 'tourist gaze', one chapter satirised 'Staffa tourists Forty Years Ago' from the local perspective, mocking a party of Cockney tourists who had 'brought red cloth, beads, and several articles of cutlery to barter with the natives', having read Captain Cook's Pacific voyages as a guide on 'how to deal with savages'.[28]

The book draws heavily on the Gaelic writings of the author's father (also Rev. Norman Macleod, celebrated as 'Caraid nan Gàidheal' or 'Friend of the Gael'), who as minister of St Columba's Kirk in Glasgow pioneered the first Gaelic periodical press in the late 1820s. Despite Macleod's untiring labours on behalf of his Glasgow parishioners (many of them Gaels recently arrived in the city), Sheila M. Kidd indicates that the advice offered to emigrants to America or Australia in his periodical *Cuairtear nan Gleann* 'encouraged passivity, offered spiritual comfort, and promoted emigrant destinations'.[29] One of the highlights of his son's *Reminiscences* is a translation of 'Caraid nan Gàidheal's' essay 'Long Mhòr nan Eilthireach' ('The Emigrant Ship') which rebukes one of the emigrants who is lamenting his departure for Canada:

> 'Silence', said the minister: 'Let me not hear such language. Are you going further from God than you were before? Is it not the same Lord that opened your eyelids today and raised you from the slumber of the night, who rules on the other side of the world?'[30]

A companion essay, 'The Story of Mary of Unnimore' (also based on one of Macleod senior's Gaelic pieces) captures the tragic plight of cleared villagers, becoming the most celebrated clearance narrative of the nineteenth century. Mary's voice is rendered in 'Gaelicised' English:

> The hissing of the fire on the flag of the hearth as they were drowning it, reached my heart [...] The bleat of the 'big sheep' was on the mountain. The whistle of the Lowland shepherd and the bark of his dogs was on the brae.[31]

Less often commented upon is the story's continuation: resettled in Glasgow, Mary's son John resists pressure to join a strike in the cotton-mill where he works, and patriotically enlists in a Highland regiment to serve his country instead.

The Clearances are central to another important parochial memoir of this period, Rev. Donald Sage's (1789–1869) *Memorabilia Domestica: or Parish Life in the North of Scotland* (1889), in which the minister of the Sutherland parish of Achness narrated the devastating effects of clearances on his parishioners in 1819 (edited and published by his son seventy years later). Although the book is more ready to criticise landlord policies than Macleod's *Reminiscences*, John Prebble notes 'there is no evidence that [Sage] spoke out against them *at the time*, and when his people expected him to follow where they went, he abandoned them'.[32] When the American abolitionist Harriet Beecher Stowe (1811–1896) whitewashed the clearances by her friend the Second Duchess of Sutherland as improvements in her travel book *Sunny Memories of Foreign Lands* (1854), it elicited an angry response from Donald Macleod (c. 1800–c. 1860?), a former Sutherland stonemason turned journalist who had emigrated to Canada. In his angry riposte *Gloomy Memories* (1857), Macleod provocatively compared the American slave system against which Stowe's abolitionist novel *Uncle Tom's Cabin* was pitched with Sutherland estate policies, declaiming 'there is not the least shadow of hope that ever the British aristocracy will think shame, or give up their system of slavery'.[33] Macleod's book was abridged and reprinted in Alexander Mackenzie's *History of the Highland Clearances* (1883), which had an important role to play in the retrospective inquiry into the injustice of the Clearances inaugurated by Gladstone's Liberal government in the era of the 'Crofters' War', namely the establishment of the Napier Commission (1883) and the Crofters' Act (1886). Alongside the impressive body of Gaelic poetry representing the reactions of ordinary Gaels to the cataclysmic changes affecting their lives, in some respects the body of evidence assembled by the Commission is the most detailed extant record of the nineteenth-century Highlands, going well beyond the investigations of earlier surveyors and travellers in recording their views, and countering many of the prejudices contained in Macculloch.[34]

If the Crofters' War represented the political crisis of the nineteenth-century Gàidhealtachd, its spiritual crisis was the 1843 Disruption, when 474 ministers left the Church of Scotland to form the Free Church in protest at the Tory violation of the Presbyterian principle of election of ministers. One of the leading intellectuals of the evangelical party was the Cromarty stonemason turned geologist Hugh Miller (1802–1856), a vehement critic of the Clearances, whose desperate struggle to reconcile his fundamentalist faith with the 'testimony of the rocks' contributed to his suicide in 1856. In the summer of 1844 Miller combined his two passions when he embarked on a three-month cruise of the West Highlands on the Free Church yacht *The Betsey*, narrating his experiences in serial form in his evangelical magazine *The Witness*, later published as *The Cruise of the Betsey: or, a Summer Ramble among the Fossiliferous Deposits of the Hebrides* (1857). Despite the book's title, the cruise was not so much a 'ramble' as a spiritual mission, accompanying Rev. Swanson, 'the minister of the Protestants of the Small Isles', on a preaching mission to the breakaway Free Church communities across the Hebrides. As they approached Rum,

> we could see the people wending their way, in threes and fours, through the dark moor, to the place of worship, – a black turf hovel [...] The appearance of the *Betsey* in the loch had been the gathering signal; and the Free Church islanders – three fourths of the entire population – had come out to meet their minister.[35]

Yet when not preaching, both men spent their time in geological 'ramblings', and the book contains a scientific account of the fossils deposited in the sedimentary rocks of the inner Hebrides. In some respects Miller's *Cruise of the Betsey* is an antidote to Macculloch's earlier 'geological' book of (anti-)travel, in which his precursor's racial critique of the Gaels is transformed into an overriding concern for their spiritual and material welfare in a period of profound social crisis. It serves as a reminder of the richness, variety, and depth of social concern demonstrated by nineteenth-century travel writing about the Highlands.

PART 3: EXPANSIONS

Sheila M. Kidd, Caroline McCracken-Flesher, and Kenneth McNeil

In many ways the distinctive feature of the Scottish publishing and book trade in the last third of the nineteenth century was that it became increasingly difficult to define it as distinctively Scottish. The period from 1870 to 1900 was an era of continued advancement in communication, distribution, and technology, and trends in Scottish printing and publishing followed trends taking place across the British Isles and beyond. Scots in the publishing trade continued to do what they had done in previous years, looking both inward and outward in the search for new and profitable arrangements and additional markets. So, on the one hand, *Chambers's Edinburgh Journal* by its thirteenth issue was simultaneously published in London and eventually dropped 'Edinburgh' in its name, as it began to feature more universal material to cater to its increasingly non-Scottish readership. On the other hand, 1886 saw the first issue of the *British Weekly, a Journal of Social and Christian Progress* published in London but edited by a Scot, William Robertson Nicoll (1851–1923). The Scottish edition of the *Weekly* proved key to its overall success, and in 1887 Nicoll recruited J. M. Barrie (1860–1937), who became a regular and popular contributor of Scottish character sketches. *Blackwood's*, like *Chambers's*, remained based in Edinburgh, although it managed to retain the 'Edinburgh' in its title for the rest of the century, but expansion of markets led to increased overlap and integration of London and Edinburgh publishing firms, as well as the establishment of overseas offices. Nelson, which became a leading publisher of textbook and education material, was the first British publisher to open a branch in the United States, in 1854, but by 1915 it had established further offices in Leeds, Manchester, Dublin, Paris, Leipzig, Toronto, and Bombay, with trading relations in Australia and South Africa.[1]

Gaelic publishing, by contrast, did not trend south. Glasgow remained central to Gaelic publishing with the family firm of Archibald Sinclair proving particularly productive. And importantly, the transnational dimension which had emerged in the middle decades of the century continued to flourish, connecting a global Gaelic readership. Angus Nicholson's monthly, *An Gaidheal*, established in Toronto in 1871, and transplanted within the year to Glasgow upon his appointment as Canadian government emigration agent for the Highlands, had contributors and readers in Australia and New Zealand as well as North America and Scotland. The final decade of the century would see *Mac-Talla* (*Echo*) appear in print in Sydney, Cape Breton, in 1892, the very first attempt at a weekly Gaelic newspaper – and the only sustained attempt to date – and which would run for twelve years before succumbing to the financial precarity which afflicted Gaelic publishing more generally.

An exception to the rule of internationalisation and expanding geographical markets was newspaper publishing. Taking advantage of increased literacy rates and the economies of scale in production, newspapers were at the centre of a mass circulation industry. John Leng's penny weekly *People's Journal*, with its largely working-class readership, reached its zenith of one hundred and thirty thousand in weekly circulation in the 1870s. Around the same time, the *Scotsman* installed machines capable of producing twelve thousand complete copies an hour to meet demand.[2] This expansion of the press was a boon for Gaelic writers, poets and readers as the language began to appear regularly in a small number of publications. This was in part due to an emerging language movement, galvanised by the failure of the Education (Scotland) Act (1872) to mention Gaelic and cross-fertilised by an increasingly vocal campaign for land rights in the Highlands. The radical Inverness newspaper the *Highlander* (1873–82) was the first to give a prominent position to a Gaelic column featuring a range of poetry and prose, and titles which would subsequently print regular Gaelic content included the *Oban Times*, *Northern Chronicle*, and *Highland News*, with the trend also represented in diaspora communities via columns in papers such as the *Toronto Daily Mail*.

The dynamic of looking inward and outward was echoed in Scottish writing. While much of Margaret Oliphant's (1828–1897) prodigious and sustained output was orientated around Scottish themes and settings, much of it was not, and her imagination roamed far and wide in both time and space in search of raw material. Nicoll fostered a popular strain of late-century sentimental fiction by publishing the writing of Barrie, joined by Ian Maclaren (pen-name of John Watson, 1850–1907) and S. R. Crockett (1859–1914). Catering to a mass readership, this strain proved immensely popular among reading publics internationally, as well as in Scotland, as part of a boom in reminiscence literature that recounted a proximate past in largely rural settings. While collectively dismissed in the early decades of the twentieth century under the reductive sign of 'Kailyard' as a retreat into the past and denial of the present, the diversity of this work is now recognised, and the unique contributions of writers once lumped together are seeing renewed appreciation. Reminiscence featured prominently in Gaelic literature too in the verse of Edinburgh-based Niall MacLeòid (Neil MacLeod, 1843–1913) and local colour in that of Glasgow-based Iain MacPhàidein (John MacFadyen, 1850–1935) with the work of both becoming a mainstay of entertainment for urban Gaelic speakers. And these new, regional communities of readers offered a new form of literary patronage. Not only was song and poetry, new and old, a feature of performance culture, but territorial organisations supported their publication with, for example, a revised edition of Iain MacLachlainn's (John MacLachlan, 1804–1874) work published posthumously under the auspices of the Ardnamurchan, Morven, and Suineart Association.

Scottish writers at the end of the century continued the exploration of past-in-present that a previous generation had initiated early in the century. While Gaelic literature acquired new forms of patronage in reading communities of urban Gaelic speakers, Anglophone writers such as Patrick Geddes (1854–1931) and William Sharp (1855–1905) – 'Fiona Macleod' – fomented a Celtic 'revival' that looked forward, too, as it looked backward to a pre-modern age. They offered the uses of myth for the foundation of a new indigenous cultural and social order, as a counter to middle-class complacency and the sterility of mass production. Scots at the end of the century gestured toward the future as they enlivened the past.

At the same time, Scottish writers, like many Scottish professionals, were borne on the global routes of empire and looked to far-flung locales to provide scope for their creative energy and livelihoods. Empire provided an arena for Scottish investigation in, if not Britain's right to rule, the ambivalence, ruptures, and dislocations that attended the colonial project. The embrace of far-flung locales guided the movements and imagination of the most well-known Scottish writer of the era, Robert Louis Stevenson (1850–1894), whose long sojourns in the South Seas and elsewhere prompted a body of 'travel' writing that blurred the lines between home and away. In perhaps a similar way but in a much different register, Stevenson offered an innovative mix of the improbable and the speculative in his fiction, revisiting and reinvigorating the historical romance while also crafting an incipient science fiction that, rather than being a flight from reality, instead took on the insistent social and scientific questions of the time.

In the same way that material scientists like James Clerk Maxwell (1831–1879) took imaginative leaps in their work to theorise a world that seemed increasingly abstract, Stevenson and others sought in their fiction to work out the implications of new ideas, particularly in anthropology and the human sciences. Such writing overlapped and often cross-pollinated with writing concerned with the relation between spirituality and science. George MacDonald's (1824–1905) faith prompted him to venture into the realm of the fantastic to argue for the ongoing value of religious belief in an age in which material science had seemed to cast doubt.

While centuries are strange narrative constructs, print, which had reached its apotheosis in nineteenth-century Scotland, was finally coming into question with the end of the era. The nineteenth century would be the last to see print dominate, particularly in book form, for the dissemination of information and entertainment. At century's end, newspapers, through their mass readership, maintained their hold on the average person's daily reading time, but the start of the new century also saw the dramatic rise of new and competing forms of media – moving pictures were shown for the first time in Scotland in 1896, in Edinburgh's Empire Palace Theatre.[3] Yet if film offered an alternative to books, new technologies also provided new possibilities for old literature. The collection of Gaelic song and poetry – ongoing throughout the nineteenth century – now rendered itself through voice. Whereas the beginning of the century brought the challenge to preserve oral culture in print without losing its mobility and changeability, the turn of the twentieth century captured Gaelic through new audio technology with Lucy Broadwood recording Dr Farquhar MacRae singing compositions by the eighteenth-century North Carolina emigrant, Iain mac Mhurchaidh (John MacRae, c. 1730–1780).[4] Oral tradition, manuscript, and print now met the opportunity and challenge of preservation in individual, and individually expressive, voice. And even as individual Gaelic voices spoke as audio, Scottish novels and plays translated into film. A full quarter of the films made in Scotland in the first two decades of the twentieth century were adaptions of the works of Barrie, Stevenson, or Scott. Before long, Hollywood would fully corporatise and internationalise texts from Barrie's *The Little Minister* (starring Katherine Hepburn) to *Peter Pan*.

The First World War and the post-war worldwide economic decline would prove a great shock to the book trade as for many other important industries. Yet if the uniquely Scottish element in a globalising trade became increasingly diluted, Scottish literature and culture would remain in circulation, continuing to thrive and expand, as it was exported for external consumption around the world.

CHAPTER NINETEEN

City Songs

Kirstie Blair

In studies of Scottish Victorian literature the consensus until recently was that industrialism and city life played little part in the literary cultures of the period; that writers deliberately chose to ignore the realities of life in the vital urban centres of Glasgow, Dundee, Edinburgh (not to mention the transformative presence of industry, in the form of factories and works, mines and railways, in smaller towns and villages across Scotland) in favour of nostalgic pastoral and 'Kailyard' literature.[1] Though there is some truth in these claims, it is inaccurate to state that Scottish literature lacked a 'literary expression' of industrialism and urban life.[2] What is true, however, is that it is difficult to unearth this expression, because it largely consists of popular works of fiction, prose, and poetry published in ephemeral sources – usually the local newspaper press – and often written anonymously or pseudonymously.[3]

This chapter highlights representative instances and seeks to show, through a primary focus on Glasgow writings, that Scottish poets were highly engaged with the 'nasty realities' of the industrial city. Although not dealt with here, there is a significant body of urban Gaelic song from the nineteenth century which has been discussed by both Michel Byrne and Donald Meek and touches on such realities.[4] I also note that the rapid growth of Scotland's cities fostered, enabled, and supported new literary cultures, particularly linked to working men and women as writers and readers. Lauren Weiss's research, for instance, has identified over two hundred 'literary' and mutual improvement societies in Victorian Glasgow, many of which also produced magazines for private circulation, and most of which were supported by aspiring young men located somewhere on the spectrum between manual labourer and respectable businessman.[5] James Myles wrote of Dundee, in 1850:

> Look at the great spinning-mills and workshops of such a town as Dundee, and think on the vast and complicated calculations, schemes and cares

> that are ever active in the mercantile management of such leviathan 'hives of industry;' and when you know that the regular motion of their engines and wheels gives employment and bread to thousands of our townsmen, are they not objects of interest more intense than the silent woods, sunny dells, and moss-covered ruins of the country? Look at the coffee-houses, reading rooms, hotels, lodging houses, mechanics' institutions, libraries, literary clubs, debating clubs, young men's societies, missionary societies, churches, chapels, in one word, all the intellectual, religious and social apparatus of a huge town.[6]

As Myles argues here, it is the spinning-mills and workshops of Dundee, and the consequent shift of population into the town, which led directly to the establishment of lively creative, cultural, and 'improving' industries. Dundee had one of Britain's first major public libraries, one of its earliest large public parks, an internationally known popular press, especially in the form of the *People's Journal* and *People's Friend*, and, as Erin Farley and Aileen Black have demonstrated, an extraordinarily active culture of local literature and song, much of it produced and disseminated by men and women working in Dundee's 'mills and workshops'.[7]

Such local 'city' literature tends to vacillate between nostalgia for a time before the growth of industry, and a celebration of the city's new status. In the pamphlet poem 'Address to the Spire of St Paul's Church, Castle Hill, Dundee' (1855), the church spire laments the changes it has presided over:

> The dwellings dense I see below
> Form, in their mass, a wretched show;
> Piled end on end, in patches wide,
> The grounds fill up on every side.
>
> In ancient places like Dundee
> Streets narrow and unshapely be;
> And, what is worse, the grounds behind
> Are now to dwellings dense consigned.
>
> How different this from days of yore,
> When gardens sprung from every door,
> And folks, in order to have air,
> Had only to step forward there.[8]

Like much of the poetry of the period, this poem is directed to a local audience and has activist intent: the author is criticising the authorities' failure to plan properly for the growth of the city. Since this sentiment is voiced by the old church spire, however, the reader is free to critique this perspective as behind the times: the main 'address' in this poem is spoken by the new factory chimneys, whose attitude towards industry is unsurprisingly positive.

It is this tension between a sense of self-congratulatory pride and investment in Scotland's industrial might, and a feeling of loss and sadness at the changes this industrialisation has wrought, which renders urban poetry of the period particularly interesting. Glasgow's *Citizen* newspaper, which played an important role in fostering the careers of several working-class writers, is one of the many sites in which this tension is evident. Many of its published poems deal positively with new developments. The unknown Thomas Dodds, for instance, in 'On Visiting the West-End Park' (1858), initially appears to lament the lost 'wild woods' of his childhood by the River Kelvin, now replaced by the mansions of Park Circus and Kelvingrove Park. But he concludes that the newly civilised landscape is positive:

> Haunt of my childhood! art and nature vie
> To make thee now a beautiful retreat
> To those who from the crowded city fly,
> From care and toil, to contemplation sweet.[9]

This deploys a common discourse about the new Victorian public spaces and what they offered to citizens, and indicates that the construction of housing and managed green spaces in what Dodds describes as 'a trackless, tangled wood' was a welcome sign of progress. Many *Citizen* poems take a similar line. But the poetry column also published verse which takes a darker view of city life, such as 'Richard's 'The Houseless' (1855):

> I've passed the long dim-lighted street,
>   And crowds that rose like thoughts around,
>   And o'er the paved unkindly ground
> I've borne my weary lingering feet.

[...]

> The red light from the windows streamed,
>   And wistful, weary eyes I raised;
>   Oh, often on these homes I've gazed,
> And wished that I were dead, or dreamed.
>
> I've knocked at doors, cold rayless eyes
>   Have met my own upturned glance,
>   And words, that wounded as a lance,
> Have pierced my heart's dark mysteries.[10]

Like much popular Victorian verse, this poem uses stereotypical language and setting: the outcast gazing in at happy family homes from a bleak city street, cut to the heart by the indifference produced by city life, is a recurring trope in both prose and poetry. As is the case here, the trope is designed to arouse the reader's sympathy and pity. There is a difference, however, when such scenes feature in a newspaper like the *Citizen*, as opposed to, say, Elizabeth Gaskell's (1810–1865) *Mary Barton*. Most of the poets published by the *Citizen* were working-class men. Many were in very precarious economic situations. Some of the best-known Glasgow working-class newspaper poets (for example, James Macfarlan, 1832–1862, John Young, 1825–1891, Thomas Elliot, 1820–1868, and Ellen Johnston, c. 1835–1874) experienced periods of unemployment, homelessness, and destitution, and newspapers tended to report on their circumstances to readers, to elicit sympathy and financial help. When 'Richard' writes 'The Houseless' in the first person, then, the reader could reasonably assume that it described personal experience. Using familiar tropes and language consciously renders the poem less innovative but also demonstrates that a writer representing himself (whether accurately or not) as homeless has the intelligence and learning to understand and work with generic norms.

The *Citizen* saw it as part of its mission to encourage Glasgow writers to take city life as their theme. In the early 1850s, it was particularly supportive of the careers of Macfarlan and Alexander Smith (1829–1867). Smith, a pattern-drawer and factory worker 'from our own western maze of manufactures', was one of few working-class writers who obtained some fame and success beyond his local context, as a leading light of 'spasmodic' poetry. His most famous poem, however, *A Life-Drama* (1853), is set in a fantasy world of upper-class English youth, far removed from his personal history. Though the *Citizen* admired it, it also implicitly criticised Smith – a *Citizen* contributor from the late 1840s – as part of a school of Glasgow writers who turned aside from the city's 'earnest life, its turmoil and bustle, and its din', failing to appreciate that: 'Large cities form an important element in the social economy of our day and generation; and he who would give utterance to the spirit of our age must learn to read aright the lessons which they teach'.[11] Smith seemed to take this to heart. His 1857 collection was titled *City Poems*, and besides his poem on 'Glasgow', it contained a semi-autobiographical narrative of his attitude towards his home city in 'A Boy's Life'. It starts with apparent regret for his failure to experience the happy rural Scottish childhood so beloved of popular literature:

> Ne'er by the rivulets I strayed,
> And ne'er upon my childhood weighed
> > The silence of the glens.
> Instead of shores where ocean beats,
> I hear the ebb and flow of streets.[12]

As the poem progresses, however, this statement begins to sound defiant rather than wistful. Smith recognises that the city has its own industrial sublime:

> In thee, O City! I discern
> Another beauty, sad and stern.
>
> Draw thy fierce streams of blinding ore,
> Smite on a thousand anvils, roar
> > Down to the harbour-bars;
> Smoulder in smoky sunsets, flare
> On rainy nights, while street and square
> > Lie empty to the stars.
> From terrace proud to alley base,
> I know thee as my mother's face.[13]

In common with other poets of industry, Smith employs strong opening verbs, enjambement, and alliteration to suggest the constant motion and activity of the industrial city, which is a monstrous site of noise and fire, yet also possesses its own strikingly modern beauty.

Smith's poems helped him to gain a foothold in the London literary world, and to move out of industrial labour. Macfarlan, in contrast, led a far more economically precarious and itinerant life; efforts by friends and patrons to find him work were repeatedly thwarted by his alcoholism. In a telling vignette of the operations of the literary economy in the Victorian city, George Eyre-Todd's biographical sketch represents Macfarlan writing his verse 'on the margins of old newspapers, amidst the distractions of a taproom' before hawking it to the newspapers (which did not explicitly pay contributors, but might informally tip a favoured author) or on the streets as a broadside, which he could get instantly printed by the Poet's Box shop on Gallowgate.[14] The *Citizen* championed Macfarlan and published his poems from the early 1850s. But though it welcomed his *City Songs* (1855) as part of 'a new school of poets' who 'pipe their lays from the midst of thronged thoroughfares', it regretted the tendency of *City Songs* (and implicitly Smith's *City Poems*) to focus on the negative aspects of city life, rather than 'the substantial comforts and conveniences of the city': 'Our modern bards see only sin-bloated faces, smoke, mammon-worship, and everything that is vile and hateful. Their heroines are wretched sempstresses, their heroes pale mechanics crushed under the wheels of commerce.'[15]

This is largely true of Smith's hero in 'A Boy's Life', and it is also an accurate depiction of Macfarlan's city poems. Like Smith, he emphasises his own subject-position as a city poet who has never known pastoral joys:

> I never nursed a poet's dream
>   Where raindrops dance upon the stream.
>
> My home o'erhung a narrow lane
>   Where woe and want were paired,
> Where vice o'erflowing ebb'd again;
>   And stealthy crime was laired;
> And from my window stretched for miles
> A dreary wilderness of tiles.[16]

His representations of city life uniformly emphasise darkness and despair, as in 'The Street':

> The engines thunder down the Street,
>   Sleep startles with a scream
> To hear the onward flood of feet,
>   And with that ghastly gleam,

> We see, through curtains wildly drawn,
> The midnight like a dismal dawn.
>
> Dark Street! I know thine inmost heart,
>   In thee my years were nurst;[17]

This language is again familiar (particularly reminiscent, in this instance, of Tennyson's famous stanzas on the 'dark unlovely street' from *In Memoriam*).[18] Like Smith, Macfarlan recognises a new characteristic of the mid-Victorian industrial city – that the fire and light of the works turn darkness into day – though his depiction of this development is unremittingly negative.

Reading such city poems as realist representations of Victorian Glasgow is problematic, and Eyre-Todd's description of Macfarlan's versatility shows us why: 'With equal promptitude he could invent a tale of distress or feign a family bereavement, to obtain sixpence'.[19] Working-class poets wrote what they thought would sell, and in the context of 'city poems' as a genre, misery was marketable. Unlike celebratory city poems or broadsides, which tend to invest in the naming of places and are very specific about what, where, and when they are celebrating – Baxter Park, Camperdown Dock, the Clydeside shipyards, the Singer sewing-machine works, the Loch Katrine water works, the Argyle Street arcade, Caird Hall – the city poem is designedly transferable to *any* city of the period. Macfarlan and Smith are therefore predecessors and influences on those later Scottish poets who wrote primarily about and from London, such as James [B. V.] Thomson (1834–1882) who, though born in Scotland, was brought up in a London orphanage, and whose well-known 'The City of Dreadful Night' (1874) is perhaps the bleakest of all city poems from this period, or John Davidson (1857–1909), who published *Fleet Street Eclogues* (1895, 1896). Davidson's *Eclogues*, written as verse conversations, feature London city journalists longing for the countryside amid the pains and pleasures of city life. His *Ballads and Songs* (1894), however, does contain a 'Glasgow' poem, recognisable as such because it highlights the commotion of shipbuilding:

> this grey town
> That pipes the morning up before the lark
> With shrieking steam, and from a hundred stalks
> Lacquers the sooty sky; where hammers clang

> On iron hulls, and cranes in harbours creak
> Rustle and swing, whole cargoes on their necks;
> Where men sweat gold that others hoard or spend,
> And lurk like vermin in the narrow streets.[20]

Davidson writes of industry as an outsider (he was a teacher, clerk, writer, and journalist), moving from a busy and potentially positive representation of Glasgow's impressive activities to a cynical view of the relationships and actions of both rich and poor within this industrial context.

While there are few Scottish women poets in this period who wrote city poems – though Janet Hamilton of Coatbridge (1795–1873) is a pre-eminent poet of industry – Marion Bernstein (1846–1906), also in Glasgow, was an important contributor to this genre. Bernstein, a music teacher, published in the *Glasgow Weekly Mail*, and was one of its better-known contributors. Her 'A Song of Glasgow Town' appeared on 10 October 1874, apparently in response to the editor's complaint that he was receiving too many poems about rural scenes: 'Has city life no phases worthy of poetic mention?' In her second verse, Bernstein writes:

> I'll sing a song of Glasgow town:
> On every side I see
> A crowd of giant chimney stalks
> As grim as grim can be.
> There's always smoke from some of them –
> Some black, some brown, some grey.
> Yet genius has invented means
> To burn the smoke away.
> Oh, when will Glasgow factories
> Cease to pollute the air;
> To spread dull clouds o'er sunny skies
> That should be bright and fair![21]

Her other verses lament the pollution of the Clyde, connecting this to the perceived corruption of the city's population through the failure to provide good education and food for the children of the poor. In responding to the editor's request, Bernstein has (typically) taken a defiant position: she will 'sing' the city, but her poem highlights very contemporary abuses and their possible resolutions. Rather than the horrified and awed descriptions of the smoke and din of Glasgow's built environment, supplied by Smith, Davidson, and hosts of other poems, Bernstein deploys simple and straightforward language to describe the 'grimness' of the industrial works, before moving on to a call for action. Like the 'Address to the Spire of St Paul's Church, Castle Hill, Dundee', this poem asks for the improvements seen in other areas of city life to expand to housing, environment, and the overall quality of life for the population.

In 1929, theatre manager Walter Freer suggested that such calls had been acted on:

> Optimist? Who could help being an optimist whose reminiscences stretch from the public well to Loch Katrine water; from the dirty cobbled streets and back courts of Saltmarket to electric cars, internal combustion engines, and bitumen roads; from slops and slush and a stinking Clyde to the cleanliness, purity, and precision of modern Glasgow?[22]

In Freer's terms, the poets and poems discussed here are located in precisely this period of transition, from early Victorian cities overwhelmed by rapid population growth and industrial development, and the problems these brought; to twentieth-century cities which had resolved at least some of these problems and moved into what Freer envisions as a new age of modernity. Scottish Victorian poets did not simply reflect new efforts, successful or unsuccessful, to 'improve' life in industrial cities, they sought to position themselves as *agents* of this change. All poems about city life are interventions in ongoing debates about how to manage new ways of living, mediated and continually transformed by the ongoing technological developments of this period and their reshaping of everyday life. The industrial city also gave the poets discussed here the means of production and dissemination: newspaper offices and the cheap printed press, as well as music-halls, theatres, and broadside printing shops, are outcomes of industrial development that enabled city writers to find a local audience. No less significantly in Glasgow, Edinburgh, Dundee, and Aberdeen than in London, New York, or Calcutta, poets constructed a new discourse of city life. Though Victorian city verse is not unique to Scotland, Scotland's combination of rapid industrial growth, a strong liberal or radical press with a commitment to working-class authors, and a body of such authors inspired by Scotland's tradition of 'peasant poets', created a distinctive set of poems through which working people negotiated the conditions in which they lived.

CHAPTER TWENTY

Gaelic Political Poetry 1870–1900

Priscilla Scott

Gaelic poetry historically has preserved valuable insights into the opinions and perspectives of Gaelic-speaking people on a range of political situations that, directly or indirectly, affected their lives. Without this rich seam of poetry preserved in the oral tradition and later collected we would have a limited understanding of how these situations were perceived and made sense of by those who experienced them. In the period between 1870 and 1900, Gaelic song poetry, for this was still a predominately oral culture and poetry was composed to be sung, remained an important vehicle for political comment and narrative, offering a channel of communication that was both accessible and easily disseminated. Newspapers and periodicals with a Highland focus were increasingly offering a new forum for debate and opinion on political matters impinging on the Highlands and, importantly, also printed Gaelic poems that might otherwise have disappeared. Although poets had long ceased to have a professional position in Gaelic society, many Gaelic poets embraced a public role, and within Gaelic-speaking communities there was an intuitive understanding of poetry as a conduit for vital opinion and comment.

The political issues that were particularly to the fore in the last three decades of a century of challenging social and economic upheaval in the Highlands reflected situations that had been developing throughout the century but were now beginning to be more robustly approached and addressed. None more so than the land question where the period saw a gradual movement towards protest and resistance, opposing landlord oppression and pushing for crofting rights. In tandem with this the Gaelic-speaking population was becoming more confident generally with its Gaelic identity, while remaining strongly loyal to Britain and the Empire. This more positive, more assured, more purposeful note resonates particularly in the poems of the Land Agitation but also more widely, although there were still poets around who recycled tired and elegiac perspectives.

Gaelic political poetry in the last quarter of the nineteenth century can be organised around four main topics – Land, Military Activity, Gaelic, and Church – none of which were new subjects for Gaelic poets, but they all had particular significance for the Highlands in the last three decades of the nineteenth century. The largest and most noteworthy corpus addresses the Land Agitation and provides a vivid and varied Gaelic narrative offering valuable insights into the politics of the land and the perspectives and attitudes of those involved.

Land

Although there were sporadic protests against evictions earlier in the century, an indication of an emerging spirit of organised resistance to the ruthless abuse of power on the part of some landowners and their factors surfaced in April 1874 in the Island of Great Bernera on the west coast of Lewis. In the Bernera Riot, as the protest became known, the angry response of the crofting population to notices of eviction led to the successful removal of the detested factor, Donald Munro, who had deployed his harsh, unfettered authority for two decades.[1] The significance of the events in Bernera prompted a number of poems including 'Spiorad a' Charthannais' ('*Spirit of Kindliness*'), composed by the Lewis poet, Iain Mac a' Ghobhainn (John Smith, 1848–1881).[2] This is one of the most polished and accomplished poems in the corpus of Gaelic poetry of the period, remarkable for the poet's intellectual vision in placing the exploitation of his own people in the wider context of class power, understood and referenced from a Christian perspective. It stands apart not just for its powerful imagery and richly expressive language, but particularly for the broad philosophical conversation it sets out. The poet delineates the persona of 'kindliness' in some detail, and then describes how the woes of the world reflect the absence of this generous spirit. He offers a scathing assessment of those who would wield their power without charity or compassion, making specific reference to Munro as well as those like him, reminding them that death is the great leveller and that under this particular 'landlord' their 'estate' would be reduced to a shroud and 'dà cheum de thalamh glas' ('*two paces of green grass*'). Although the antithesis at the heart of this poem is presented within a clear Christian framework, and from a personal faith, the message has a universality beyond a religious perspective and, as has been noted elsewhere, the poem 'has a wide and even timeless application'.[3] 'Spiorad a' Charthannais' in the breadth of its discussion, the clarity of its analysis, and the assured eloquence it exhibits, is an atypical example of the political poetry of the land protests, but it features aspects that are common across the corpus. These include referencing biblical teaching with a focus on a judgement to come, highlighting the contribution of Highland soldiers to British successes in the various imperial campaigns, and directing biting invective and satire against particular landlords or factors for their abuse of power.

One of the most prominent Gaelic poets of the period, and of the Land Agitation in particular, was Màiri Nic a' Phearsain (Mary MacPherson, 1821–1898), better known as Màiri Mhòr nan Òran (Big Mary of the Songs), whose poems vividly and passionately articulate the sentiments of the people in their struggle for the land. They also reflect her personal perspective on the land as vital to the communal way of life she had known in her youth, and which in turn maintained the Gaelic language and the wider culture it supported. Her own searing experience of injustice as a widow facing a court of law in 1872 and her subsequent brief imprisonment,[4] together with her skilful working of words and imagery, gave her poetry a resonance and relevance that people responded to. Màiri Nic a' Phearsain was actively involved in the public face of the land protests, particularly in the 1880s in her native island of Skye, and her poems have an immediacy that reflects this proximity to the events and the people involved. When protests in Skye escalated in April 1882 and a contingent of policemen was brought from Glasgow to deal with the unrest in the Braes district, national newspapers reporting on the confrontation often portrayed those involved in negative terms, particularly the women who were in the front line. Màiri Nic a' Phearsain's response in 'Òran Beinn Lì' ('*Song on Ben Lee*'), some verses of which were composed very soon after the events in Braes and publicly performed,[5] makes clear the good character of the people:

> 'S na diùlnaich a b'uaisle
> 'S nach robh riamh ann an tuasaid
> Chaidh na ruighich a shuaineadh
>   Gu cruaidh air an dùirn.
>   […]
>   'S na mnathan bu shuairce
>   'S bu mhodhaile gluasad,

> Chaidh an claiginn a spuaiceadh
> Ann am bruachan Beinn Lì.

Those heroes most noble / Who were never in a fracas / Had their wrists put in handcuffs, wrapped hard around their fists. [...] And the kindliest women, / Of conduct most mannerly, / Their skulls were broken / On the braes of Beinn Lì.[6]

Verses would later be added to celebrate the victory of the restored grazing rights, but the immediate purpose of the song was to encourage and reassure those who had dared to oppose the rule of authority.

Màiri Nic a' Phearsain's earliest poems were political, composed in support of the Liberal MP Charles Fraser Mackintosh when he first won the seat for the Inverness Burghs in 1874. Here, she harnesses the strong seam of poetic eulogy present in Gaelic poetry. This transference of traditional modes to new socio-political circumstances came naturally to poets composing within a strong oral culture; likewise, a powerful legacy of dispraise or satire, the converse of bardic and clan panegyric, utilised to great effect in eighteenth-century Gaelic political poetry, also found ready targets in the events of the land protests. Màiri Nic a' Phearsain's satirical elegy for Sheriff Ivory, whose heavy-handed approach to protests in Skye over some six years made him a reviled figure in the eyes of the crofters, is a fairly robust example:

> Saighdear, mas fhìor,
> Chan fhacas a ghnìomh
> Ach air siteig no liath òtraichean.

A soldier, supposedly, / He was to be seen in action / Only on a dung-hill or on grey muck-heaps.[7]

In similar vein, 'Bodach Isgein',[8] a poem composed by Dòmhnall MacCaluim (Rev. Donald MacCallum, 1849–1929) targets Joseph Platt who leased the deer forest of Park in Lewis as a sporting estate thus depriving the local people of access to desperately needed land, a situation that was challenged in the 'Park Deer Raid' of November 1887.[9] The narrative of the poem is in the voice of Platt and thus he condemns himself as a conceited and mercenary landlord, with the repeated phrase 'Tha mise rìoghachadh / Cho fad 's a chì mi' (*'My rule extends / Over all that I see*') suggesting a possible parody of William Cowper's 'I am monarch of all I survey, / My right there is none to dispute'.[10] MacCaluim, a minister in the Established Church, was vocal and active in supporting the crofters, and was himself eulogised in a number of poems for his willingness to stand with the people and face the possible consequences.[11] The Gaelic poets did not shy away from discussing, and criticising if necessary, the role of ministers and the Church in the Land Agitation, commentaries that in general support the view that the Church's response varied according to local situations and the perspectives of individual ministers.[12]

Military Activity

The poems addressing the politics of the land frequently refer to the fact that Highland regiments were fighting with the British army in the various war arenas of the period and warn that the continuing depletion of the population of the Highlands would drastically reduce recruits for the army, and therefore be a threat to British safety. Some poets are occasionally more explicit. Màiri Nic a' Phearsain, for example, advises those who have not emigrated and are still on the land not to accept the 'king's shilling':

> Ach sibhs' 'tha fuireachd anns an tir
> Bithibh dileas do chach
> Tha mi an duil nach tog sibh arm
> 'Chur air falbh luchd a' mhail.[13]

> *But you who remain on the land, / Be loyal to each other / I hope you will not take up arms / to send away the rent collectors.*

However, the same poet is not always consistent in her views and is more likely to celebrate 'luchd-breacan', the tartan-clad soldiers of the Highland regiments, and in one example declares that from her native island of Skye, 'Bha còrr agus deich mìle / fon Rìgh a ghabh an t-òr' ('*There were more than ten thousand / who took the king's gold coin*').[14]

Possibly the most powerful commentary on the subject comes from Iain Mac a' Ghobhainn in 'Spiorad a' Charthannais' (already mentioned) in which he refers in particular to the contribution of the Gaels to the British victory on the 'bloody plains of Waterloo'. He describes the Highland soldiers returning to find the land turned into sporting estates and contrasts the 'gaisgich' ('*heroes*') of Waterloo with the 'stròdhailich' ('*squanderers*') who abuse the land for their pleasure. The contribution of the kilted Highland regiments to the British army in the nineteenth century earned them a reputation for military prowess and fearlessness, a view that was encapsulated in the iconic image of the kilted Highland soldier – a remarkable rehabilitation to official respectability of the 'fierce' tartan-clad Highlanders who had supported the Prince in the previous century. Individual Highland regiments were raised by clan chiefs and strongly identified with particular localities, and therefore deep, traditional loyalties existed that were readily harnessed and transferred to the British cause. The Gaelic poetry on military engagements for the most part reflects this discourse of loyalty and valour, easily adapting traditional modes of praise to address individual leaders and regiments. A poem in praise of the Gordon Highlanders[15] by Iain MacPhàidein (John MacFadyen, 1850–1935) uses traditional praise conventions throughout the text in, for example, the terms of address and the reciting of victories:

> 'S lionar blàr 'san d' fhuair sibh cliù ann;
> 'S gann mo chainnt an rannt' g' an cùnntas;
> 'Fontenoy', 'Peninsula',
> 'Waterloo', 's 'Victoria'.[16]

Plentiful the battles where you earned respect; / I scarcely have the vocabulary to list the range; / 'Fontenoy', 'Peninsula', / 'Waterloo', and 'Victoria'.

The war poetry, however, is notable for an absence of overt political discussion or statement and is mostly celebratory in tone,[17] eulogising victories, bravery, and loyalty to Britain and the Empire in such phrases as 'Na leoghainn chalm 'san earb an Rìoghachd' ('*The brave lions in which the Kingdom trusts*').[18] Even when reflecting on defeat and heavy losses there is little to suggest criticism of the campaign or the leadership,[19] and neither is there any concern expressed for those on the receiving end of the Imperial onslaught. One military issue that did provoke a critical response was the proposal by the War Office in 1881 to abolish the distinctive regimental tartans. Taking the lead in challenging the issue was the Gaelic Society of Inverness, a scholarly society formed in 1871 and an important public forum in this period, with a spectrum of political opinions represented within its membership. A poem by the Lochaber poet, Màiri NicEalair (Mary MacKellar, 1834–1890), who was Bard to the Society, reflected the general opinion on the matter in emphasising the empowering, symbolic, and historical associations the tartan carried for Highland soldiers,[20] and Màiri Nic a' Phearsain was also passionate in expressing similar perspectives.[21] At a time when feelings on the land question were running high, the issue of the regimental tartans united landlord and tenant in protest, and while there were some in the land movement who voiced the contradictions involved, this was not reflected to any great extent in the poetry.

Gaelic

The Gaelic Society of Inverness, although primarily antiquarian in purpose was not, as just noted, averse to campaigning on Gaelic-related matters, and was quick to voice concern at the neglect of Gaelic in the 1872 Education (Scotland) Act. In the same period, the Society was championing the efforts of Professor John Stuart Blackie to establish a Chair of Celtic at Edinburgh University. The poets of the period give a lot of space to praising Blackie who was also, significantly, very vocal in support of the crofters in their struggle for the land. While numerous poets celebrated the successful endowment of the Celtic Chair in 1882, making much of the fact that Queen Victoria had been a subscriber, poems addressing the marginalisation of Gaelic in the education system are less prominent, often taking as their target the hard-line attitudes of the schoolmasters:

> Tha ri'r cànain iad cur cùl
> Agus diùlt' bhith 'ga teagaisg
> Chum 's gum fògair às an dùthaich
> Chainnt is rùnaich do'r n-anam.

They have turned away from our language / And are refusing to teach it / In order to expel from the land / The language most beloved to our soul.[22]

In similar vein but from a more overtly religious perspective, another poet, Gilleasbuig Farcharson (Archibald Farquharson, 1801–1878), satirises the methods used to enforce English in the schools, stating that he had made 'tamhuis ceithir-mheurach' (*'a four-fingered tawse'*) to be used to punish and shame the schoolmaster for the contempt he has shown for Gaelic.[23] In contrast to those poems concerned with the lack of support for Gaelic in the education system, a more prominent and effusive stream of poetry celebrated the language with an overly buoyant optimism, taking encouragement from the success of the Celtic Chair, from census figures for Gaelic speakers that were on the surface positive enough, and from the establishment of such high-profile groups as An Comunn Gàidhealach, formed in 1891. The well-known Skye poet Niall MacLeòid (Neil MacLeod,1843–1913), who was extremely popular with the Gaelic diaspora in the Lowlands, composed a poem that posed as its title the question 'Am Faigh a' Ghàidhlig Bàs?' ('*Will Gaelic die?*'),[24] and answered it in the final line with a defiant phrase that became something of a slogan: ''S chan fhaigh a' Ghàidhlig Bàs' ('*And Gaelic will not die*'). However, this type of inflated rhetoric, while encouraging positivity towards the language, possibly served to conceal the reality of the considerable challenges facing Gaelic going into the twentieth century.

Church

Doctrinal debates between the different denominations of the Presbyterian churches in Scotland featured in the second half of the nineteenth century, and in the Highlands in particular inter-denominational politics were heated.[25] Murchadh MacLeòid / Murchadh a' Cheisdeir (Murdo MacLeod / Murdo, son of the Catechist, 1837–1914), a Temperance agent, lay-preacher and evangelist, articulates strong opinions on a range of issues in his poetry,[26] and in addressing church politics he anticipates the Union of 1900 between the Free Church and the United Presbyterian Church.[27] Originally from Lewis, he moved to the Lowlands as a young man, which possibly influenced his stance in favour of the Union when the majority in the Highlands opted to remain with the Free Church. The somewhat strident rhetoric of 'Oran an Aonaidh' ('*Song of the Union*')[28] probably reflected the reality of the bitter tensions that surfaced in the Union debate and, significantly, the poem was omitted from the second edition of his poetry collection, leaving the more moderate 'Eaglais an Aonaidh' ('*The Church of the Union*').[29] MacLeòid's sharp words on denominational schism can be compared to the responses found in women's evangelical poetry, a rich corpus of intense and personal spiritual verse, that contains ample comment on socio-political issues of the day.[30] Here the tone is of profound sorrow in seeing discord replacing the harmony that previously existed between people who looked upon each other as brothers and sisters, sentiments condensed in one example in the refrain: 'O nach robh na laithean fagaisg / Anns nach cluinnte leinn mu sgaradh!' ('*Oh were not the days close / when we would hear nothing of division!*').[31] Notable also in shunning the denominational wrangling and doctrinal point-scoring is the judicious perspective of Iain Mac a' Ghobhainn in 'Spiorad a Charthannais':

> An duine caomh a dhèireas suas
> Gu nèamh air sgiath a' ghràidh,
> Cha deasbair dian mu chreudan e,
> 'S cha bhi e beumadh chàich.

The gentle man who will ascend / To heaven on love's wing / Is no contender about creeds, / Nor will others feel his sting. [32]

Biblical imagery and references abound across the range of socio-political subjects addressed by the Gaelic poets of the period, as has been noted already in the poetry of the land struggle, reflecting the fact that for most people at this time in Gaelic-speaking communities, the spiritual and the secular were not experienced as polarities. It was therefore perfectly natural to draw on biblical teaching to make incisive political comment, knowing that those who heard the poem would understand both the reference and the point being made.[33]

Conclusion

In a well-crafted and expressive Gaelic poem from a slightly earlier period than the specific time-frame of this chapter, the poet Uilleam MacDhunlèibhe (William Livingston, 1808–1870), describing the post-Clearance landscape in Islay, uses the refrain, 'Thoir am fios seo chun a' Bhàird' (*'Take this message to the Poet'*).[34] Although there were personal reasons for MacDhunlèibhe choosing this particular phrase, it also carries a traditional sense of community expectation that Gaelic poets should bear witness in their verse to significant events. The poets discussed in this chapter would have an implicit awareness of this responsibility when addressing the socio-political issues of the period, while still retaining the autonomy of their poetic voice.

In the last three decades of the nineteenth century, the voice of Gaelic poets is at its most communal and vital in the poetry of the Land Agitation, reflecting the extent of political engagement by the Gaelic-speaking population in direct protest and resistance, and an acute awareness of the power and class structures involved. There is a strong sense in much of this poetry of the poets speaking with the people, as seen particularly in the poems of Màiri Nic a' Phearsain and Dòmhnall MacCaluim.

Beyond the land issue, however, very few poets successfully unpick the complexities involved in military, church, and language politics and their impact on Gaelic-speaking communities.

The Gaelic poetry of the nineteenth century frequently suffers in being compared with the work of the poets who came before and after, and this is a particularly stark comparison in the case of political poetry, but it is a corpus that should be understood in the context of the particular circumstances in which it was composed. The nostalgic, retrospective poetry of the first half of the century that tends to over-eulogise the pre-clearance Highlands was prompted by the abject despair of the Clearances and the changes they brought about, but a more confident and forward-looking note can increasingly be discerned as the century progresses. The poetic skill and rhetorical force of 'Fios chun a Bhàird' (mentioned above) can perhaps be seen as representing this mid-century change of tone. Although few poems in the three decades that followed can match Iain Mac a' Ghobhainn's eloquently expressed alternative to the oppressive power of the land-owning class, other poems on political issues are compelling in the force and immediacy of their narrative. This is particularly true of Màiri Nic a' Phearsain, whose perspectives on place, community, and Gaelic culture underpinned her passionate support for the crofters in their struggle for the land, and this, combined with her personal experience of injustice, gives her best poems a striking vitality.

CHAPTER TWENTY-ONE

The Kailyard Novelists

Andrew Nash

The term 'Kailyard' was first used by J. H. Millar in 1895 to describe a style of fiction that had become popular both within and beyond Scotland. The 'Kailyard School', as it came to be known, was not, however, a literary movement, and the writers identified with it were not motivated by shared artistic intentions. In the twentieth century, the term came to stand for apparently regressive characteristics of Scottish literature in the nineteenth century: a nostalgic preoccupation with the past; a parochial outlook; a focus on rural or small-town Scottish life; an emphasis on religious piety; and above all a tendency to ignore social and political realities, especially the effects of industrialisation and urbanisation.[1] This chapter does not address these issues, which in any case are a misrepresentation of the range of Scottish writing produced in the period.[2] Instead it offers an introduction to the work of the three writers most closely associated with the term: J. M. Barrie (1860–1937), S. R. Crockett (1859–1914), and 'Ian Maclaren' (Rev. John Watson) (1850–1907).

Maclaren is of interest partly as a publishing phenomenon. His sketches of life in 'Drumtochty', based on his early experiences as a Free Church of Scotland minister in Logiealmond, Perthshire, and collected as *Beside the Bonnie Brier Bush* (1894) and *The Days of Auld Lang Syne* (1895), were among the best-selling works of the 1890s. His literary career owed much to the influence of William Robertson Nicoll, Scottish editor of the *British Weekly*, where the earliest sketches appeared. With their nostalgic tone and nonconformist religious message, Maclaren's books proved especially popular in North America. In 1896 he toured the United States giving lectures, sermons, and readings from his work. He became as much a literary celebrity in America as Oscar Wilde, and died there in 1907 while on another speaking tour. Although this part of his career has received some attention,[3] the astute marketing of his work and personality, and his status as a media celebrity, remains under-researched.[4]

Much of Maclaren's ministerial life was spent in Liverpool, and the Drumtochty sketches have often been dismissed as the distorted vision of an émigré. Yet the opening of *Brier Bush* clearly signals that we are entering a fictional realm set firmly in the past. Drumtochty is presented as an isolated world resistant to the influence of towns and cities, and its customs are marked out as those of a simpler, slower age. The present school-house, which is 'treeless and comfortless [...] all very neat and symmetrical, and well-regulated', is contrasted with the 'auld schule house' in the sweet pine-woods. The talk is about 'Domsie', the local schoolteacher, and his 'gleg' laddies who carried the Drumtochty name at university. Within a page, several characteristics of Maclaren's writing have been established: the use of natural images to express an organic order; the interplay between Scots and English (the 'present school-house' contrasting with the 'auld schule'); the expression of local pride; above all the nostalgic pull towards an idealised past. Before the story has even started Domsie has 'slippit awa', and with his passing not just the physical landscape but a whole world has disappeared.[5]

Nostalgia for the past is one component of Maclaren's sentimental aesthetic. His stories are designed to arouse an emotional response in the reader, and his many death-bed scenes reportedly did induce tears in the eyes of many. It is difficult for a modern audience, less attuned to the sentimental mode in literature, to appreciate the appeal and effects of this artistic technique. In the protracted account of Doctor Maclure's death in the final *Brier Bush* story, the doctor hovers between life and death, his sleep interrupted by dreams of his visits to the sick and memories of his childhood prayers. The scene is reminiscent of the death of Paul Dombey in Dickens's *Dombey and Son* (serialised 1846–48), and while the sentimental mode was becoming old-fashioned by the 1890s (less so in America where a lengthier tradition persisted), it still held popular appeal.

Although Maclaren's sentimentalism can make his fiction seem far removed from late nineteenth-century Scotland, his work repays reading against a historical context. As one critic has noted, the Drumtochty sketches deal in part with 'the social consequences of agrarian capitalism' in the 1860s.[6] The opening stories in *The Days of Auld Lang Syne* concern the relations between landowner, factor, and tenant farmer, and turn on a dispute over the renewal of a farm lease. Maclaren's evocation of an agrarian world based not on accumulation of capital but on shared community values may seem contrived, but it explores similar themes as William Alexander's (1826–1894) more gritty *Johnny Gibb of Gushetneuk* (1871).

The religious dimension of Maclaren's writing also demands careful historicising. His stories are an important index to religious life in late Victorian Scotland. He was writing during a period of turmoil in the Scottish churches, with fierce debates over Biblical scholarship and the relationship between church and state. As John Carmichael, Free Church minister of Drumtochty, observes: 'we were living in an age of transition'.[7] In his sketches, as in his ministerial work, Maclaren sought a consensus between different religious types, and his stories dramatise the power of sentiment to beat upon creeds, heal personal conflicts, and resolve points of dissension. His Free Church principles were not dogmatic, and while he saw theology as 'an absolute intellectual necessity', his faith and teaching were avowedly Christological.[8] When one Drumtochty minister, 'being still young, expounded a new theory of the atonement of German manufacture', he is sorely judged by the glen for his 'blindness of heart'.[9] For Maclaren, theology based upon intellect alone was inadequate. In another story a young minister's intention to 'state the present position of theological thought' is brought into conflict with the memory of his dead mother, whose only parting hope was that her son should, in his first sermon, 'speak a gude word for Jesus Christ'.[10] Like several other novelists of his generation John Watson wrote his own life of Christ, *The Life of the Master* (1901).

Although Maclaren wrote fiction in other modes, including a children's book, *Young Barbarians* (1901), and a covenanting tale, *Graham of Claverhouse* (1908), he is remembered only for Drumtochty. S. R. Crockett's *oeuvre* is much more wide-ranging, both in form and setting. Even restricting the scope to the Victorian period (he continued writing up to his death in 1914), his settings include Germany, Italy, and Spain as well as Scotland. The early sketches collected in *The Stickit Minister and Some Common Men* (1893) are less representative of his prodigious output than the adventure romance *The Raiders* (1894), arguably his best work. Scottish history was an irresistible source for Crockett and he wrote several covenanting tales. Adventure romance was only one of his many modes, however. Published in the same year as *The Raiders*, *The Lilac Sunbonnet* (1894) weaves a rustic comedy and an attack on doctrinal religion around a highly sensuous evocation of the Galloway countryside.

Unlike Maclaren, Crockett was a writer by vocation. Shortly after the success of *The Raiders* he left his position as Free Church minister in Penicuik. The significance of his religious and ministerial background has been misunderstood by critics like George Blake – who claimed that he always wrote about 'life as seen through the manse window'.[11] The early sketches published in the Glasgow penny weekly *The Christian Leader*, later collected in *The Stickit Minister*, are strikingly ambivalent, exposing the hypocrisy and sycophancy among ministers, elders, and parishioners alike. The author's covenanting heritage is more important to understanding his writing than his Free Church ministry. In an interview Crockett explained: 'Our people were strict Cameronians, Covenanters, and I was brought up in the faith.' *The Men of the Moss-Hags* (1895) was 'written from a Covenanter's standpoint as fairly as Scott's *Old Mortality* was written from the other standpoint'.[12] But it was not just a matter of sympathy for 'the faith of my fathers' that led Crockett to the Covenanters. Because 'most books are forbidden to the Cameronians', he explained, the only books he knew as a child 'were books about the Covenant', and these fuelled his imagination: 'I was a hunted Covenanter, and hid myself – a quaking little lad of five – whilst any stirring thing, a black bull, or a pine shaken by the wind, or a mere shadow on the brae was Claverhouse.'[13] In locating the inspiration for storytelling in the childish imagination, Crockett's words embody Robert Louis Stevenson's (1850–1894) theorisation of adventure romance in 'A Gossip on Romance' (1882). Crockett was no hackneyed follower of Stevenson; he embodied his artistic spirit.

Crockett's plotlines may seem derivative and repetitive, but his depiction of the Galloway landscape is distinctively his own. In *The Raiders*, that landscape becomes a world of fear and terror, charged with supernatural and apocalyptic overtones:

> I saw a weird wide world, new and strange, not yet out of chaos – nor yet approvan of God [...] a huge, conical hill in front, the Hills of the Star, glimmering snow-sprinkled, as it rose above the desolations of Loch Enoch and the depths of Buchan's Dungeon. To the right the great steeps of the Merrick, bounding upward to heaven like the lowers steps of Jacob's ladder.[14]

This depiction of a natural world under threat of dissolution is characteristic of Crockett's writing (it pervades *The Lilac Sunbonnet* in a different way). Though different in tone and style than the feminised Celtic Twilight of Fiona Macleod/William Sharp (1855–1905), it is equally evocative of the *fin de siècle*.

Crockett's fiction set in urban or working environments is another under-researched area. *Cleg Kelly: Arab of the City*, serialised simultaneously in the prestigious *Cornhill Magazine* and the religious periodical the *Sunday School*, was judged by one reviewer as 'out of sight the ablest and richest story of gamin, or street urchin, life that has appeared in our time – the story that recalls most readily *Oliver Twist* and *The Hunchback of Notre Dame*'.[15] Consistent with the gamin genre, the plot is episodic, and the story is comprised not of chapters but a sequence of 'adventures'. It begins arrestingly with Cleg's defiant statement: 'It's all a dumb lie – God's dead'.[16] In the early chapters Crockett draws on his student experiences to expose the failings and hypocrisy of the work of the missionaries in the Edinburgh Pleasance of the 1870s, and his depictions of the brutalising effects of tenement life and Cleg's home environment are unsparing. Environment is important too in a later novel, *Vida, or the Iron Lord of Kirktown* (1907), serialised in the *People's Friend*. The narrative is again romantic and melodramatic, but the portrayal of the working lives of a mining community is sharply delineated, as in this description of the predestined life-journey of the community's young:

> The wide airy world is not for them – except that straight piece of dusty road between two dustier hedges which conducts them from the little red kitchen in Block C, to the hole in the ground down which a great cage of iron dives incessantly.[17]

Cleg Kelly was dedicated to J. M. Barrie who, before he became the most successful playwright of his generation, was considered a major writer of prose fiction. Barrie's two most important novels, *Sentimental Tommy* (1896) and *Tommy and Grizel* (1900), which deal with the artistic sensibility, cannot be adequately addressed here.[18] His association with 'Kailyard' rests on *Auld Licht Idylls* (1888) and *A Window in Thrums* (1889). Set in a fictionalised version of his native Kirriemuir, and drawn in part from his mother's childhood memories, these novels are not to be read as social history. More than anything, they are concerned with the process of storytelling. The narrator is the local dominie who conjures up a picture of the small town of Thrums from the seclusion of his snowed-up schoolhouse. Significantly, the customs of the town and its inhabitants are presented to us only after the striking opening chapter which lays emphasis on the dominie's solitude. Confronted by his isolated life in the glen, where the 'road to Thrums has lost itself miles down the valley' and the 'shutter bars the outer world from the schoolhouse', his visualisation of the town is presented as an act of imagination.[19] He sees Thrums literally and metaphorically through a mist:

> I like to linger over the square, for it was from an upper window in it that I got to know Thrums [...] In my schoolhouse, however, I seem to see the square most readily in the Scotch mist which so often filled it, loosening the stones and choking the drains.[20]

In Barrie's writing, narrative is never a transparent 'window' onto life.

Although *Auld Licht Idylls* is not documentary in style, it still contains a sharp and ironic commentary on aspects of early nineteenth-century Scottish life. As Eric Anderson observes, 'Barrie goes out of his way to remind the reader that the world being described is past'.[21] This applies both to the religious traditions – 'There are few Auld Licht communities in Scotland nowadays' – and to the depiction of the handloom industry which shapes the life of the community: 'Until twenty years ago' a handloom filled 'every other room' in Thrums, but though its 'clatter can still be heard', the industry and its way of life have gradually been displaced by 'the two factories in the town'.[22] Barrie's choice of name for his fictional town was not arbitrary. Thrums are the fringes of the warp threads left on the loom after the cloth has been removed, and the stories are about the fringes and remnants of past ways of life which are left hanging in the present. The lengthy account of the farm bothy is typical of the way Barrie contrasts past and present. The narrator enters 'a bothy of to-day' which encourages him to look back on a pre-mechanical past when 'hands' were 'huddled together [...] in squalid barns more like cattle than men and women'.[23] The description of the old 'bothy system at its worst' is unflinching in its realism, and there is nothing idyllic about Thrums or about the author's manner of presentation: his account of the meal mob riots and the bloodthirsty battles with the neighbouring town, which leave the street littered with 'prostrate lumps of humanity from which all shape had departed', are unsparing.[24]

In *Auld Licht Idylls* the dominant mode is humour, especially in the portrayal of the puritanical Auld Lichts (part of the body that seceded from the Established Church in 1733). In *A Window in Thrums* there is a new element of pathos which involves a shift in the presentation of the past. In the opening chapter the narrator leads the reader into the world of the story by underlining the process of imaginative reconstruction:

> I speak of the chairs, but if we go together into the 'room' they will not be visible to you. [...] Worn boards and ragged walls, and the rusty ribs fallen from the fireplace, are all that meet your eyes, but I see a round, unsteady, waxcloth-covered table, with four books lying at equal distances on it.[25]

The text turns everywhere on this play between the timeless and the here and now which entails an emphasis on the fictionality of the picture, as only memory and imagination can effect a balance between the temporal and the eternal. The literary method in *A Window in Thrums* is both sentimental – in the way the narrator establishes a relationship with his audience and charges objects with emotional content – and elegiac in the way he imagines his readers at the end of their lives, and encourages them to pick up the remembered scenes and images of the past:

> We have all found the brae long and steep in the spring of life. Do you remember, how the child you once were sat at the foot of it and wondered if a new world began at the top? [...] Yet are we no longer the child; we look now for no new world at the top, only for a little garden and a tiny house, and a hand-loom in the house.[26]

It was this elegiac mood which led Robert Louis Stevenson to tell Barrie he had 'the glamour of twilight on his pen'.[27] The word glamour derives from the Scots 'gramarye', and is defined by the *OED* as 'a magical or fictitious beauty'.[28] The fictitious twilight of *A Window in Thrums* is painted with a highly self-conscious pen. The story of Jess and her son Jamie, who returns to Thrums from London too late to see his dying mother, is concerned principally with the process of storytelling and the construction of emotion through art. The narrator hints in the opening chapter at the 'awful ordeal' Jamie will go through, and throughout the text uses prolepsis to anticipate the 'dire day of which I shall have to tell'.[29]

As a storyteller he is conscious of his power to manipulate our view of the tale through the window of the narrative. In the closing chapters he draws attention to the different ways in which his story might be told, contrasting 'play-acting' with 'real life'[30] as he imagines a happy ending for the scene. It is this creative interest in the interaction between storytelling and reality that lifts Barrie's early writing beyond the narrow confines of the Kailyard (as it has been understood) and links it to his mature prose and drama wherein lies his real achievement.

CHAPTER TWENTY-TWO

The International Author: Stevenson

Lesley Graham

Robert Louis Stevenson's (1850–1894) itinerant life has left traces of many sorts scattered across the various international sites with which he is associated. His boots are in the Writers' Museum in Edinburgh, his baby cap at Saranac Cottage in the state of New York, while some furniture and books can be seen in the Stevenson Museum at Vailima in Samoa. His wedding ring and his toy soldiers are in the Stevenson Museum in Saint Helena and his flageolet sheet music at Stevenson House in Monterey, both in California. Plaques on the façades of dozens of buildings in Europe, North America, and Oceania commemorate his residence there. People come from afar to climb to his grave on Mount Vaea or to walk in his footsteps along officially sanctioned hiking trails in Scotland, England, France, and America. The virtual universe is similarly strewn with traces of Stevenson. His online reach can be measured by the number of times aphorisms from his work – authentic and otherwise – are shared and re-shared across social media every day. In a fitting reflection of his engagement with the world and with moving through it, many of these quotations are themselves related to the practice of travel: 'we are all travellers in […] the wilderness of this world'; 'There are no foreign lands, it is the traveller only who is foreign'; 'For my part, I travel not to go anywhere, but to go. I travel for travel's sake. The great affair is to move.'[1]

The global spread of Stevenson's footprint through the publication, distribution, adaptation, and translation of his work outside Britain began in earnest with the French translations of *Treasure Island* in 1885.[2] Translations into Danish, Dutch, Finnish, German, Hungarian, Polish, Russian, Spanish, and Swedish also appeared rapidly.[3] In Japan, an abridged and heavily adapted translation of *Treasure Island* was serialised in four parts in a monthly journal titled *Bungei Kurabu* as early as 1895,[4] and the novel appeared in Chinese in 1904.[5] The ways in which the texts initially circulated internationally were not always straightforward: translations were sometimes translations of other translations while others were so free as to be adaptations rather than translations. The first Russian version of *Treasure Island* published in Moscow in 1886 as an appendix to the magazine *Вокруг Света*, for example, was based on a French edition while Oshikawa Shunrō gave characters in the *New Arabian Nights* Japanese names but kept the British backdrop. The international transmutations occasionally ricocheted back to augment the original as when, for instance, plates by George Roux originally produced for the first illustrated French translation were used in the first illustrated edition in English imparting a Gallic touch to the reading experience of the British public.

Stevenson is now the twenty-sixth most translated author in the world[6] and is generally considered to be Scotland's most translated author. He has, as Paul Barnaby and Tom Hubbard note, 'now appeared in eighty-nine languages, and is the only Scot translated into a significant number of non-European languages'.[7] Meanwhile *Strange Case of Dr Jekyll and Mr Hyde* is not only the most frequently adapted work of Scottish literature in world cinema but, according to Richard Butt, probably the third most adapted of any work of literature, falling just behind *Macbeth* and *Hamlet*.[8] Indeed, Stevenson's most famous works – *Treasure Island* and *Jekyll and Hyde* – are members of that exclusive club of international popular culture phenomena that have broken free of the literary works that engendered them. Their titles, characters, plots, and tropes have seeped into the subjective experience of people of most nationalities through reading, viewing, and even video-gaming.

The world caught the reading bug in the nineteenth century and made Stevenson one of its first truly international celebrities so that when, in 1887, he disembarked in America for the second time the event was front page news. Journalists descended on his hotel and theatre-goers rushed to see one of the first adaptations of *Jekyll and Hyde*, the novella they had recently discovered and the main driver behind Stevenson's sudden notoriety. He used the interviews he gave in New York to draw attention to the question of international copyright, a problem that had exercised him for some time and that worked both for and against his transatlantic literary career. Stevenson's fame was a direct consequence of the cheapness and availability of his books overseas, notably in America, but he was not gaining financially from those sales. Soon after disembarking in New York on his first visit to America in 1879, Stevenson had purchased a pirated copy of *Travels with a Donkey in the Cévennes* which surprisingly had been released there in the very same month as in Great Britain. Some years later, he claimed in an interview that just a week after the publication of *Kidnapped* (1886) in Great Britain, there were twenty-five different editions for sale in America. Occasionally, the British publisher was involved in the subterfuge as Stevenson pointed out in an unpublished essay:

> I have known this same system of calling operations by other names to lead a respectable publisher into an act that was certainly illegal; I have known him (that is) to hold a book subject to a royalty, to sell the advance sheets in America, and not to account for the proceeds of the sale.[9]

Foreign authors received no copyright protection in the United States: the accepted practice for American publishers was simply to reprint their works without paying the author. Stevenson's situation was symptomatic of a changing global book market, and clearly already thinking in terms of an imagined international professional community of writers, he framed the piracy as a threat not only to his own livelihood but also to that of American writers who simply could not compete with cheap reproductions of foreign novels. He repeatedly drew attention to the issue in interviews, essays, and letters, actively lobbying for international copyright law. In an unpublished letter to Robert Underwood Johnson, secretary of the American Copyright League, Stevenson declared that:

> As one of the sufferers, it is hardly necessary for me to express my sympathy for the movement; and as one who has in some way suffered least, it would be difficult to do so gracefully. The question is one which lies before the American people; and in the solution of that, and in all parts of its National affairs, I trust it may be guided well.[10]

A particularly indignant letter written in 1887 to the New York publishers Harper & Brothers, denouncing their 'act of piracy' was published in *The Times* under the heading 'International Copyright'.[11] Shortly afterwards, an article by Stevenson's main publisher in America, Charles Scribner, appeared in the *Publishers' Weekly* confirming the author's extraordinary popularity and supporting his analysis of the situation:

> Stevenson's works are now the most popular here of all living novelists. And this very popularity is assisted in large measure by the cheapness of his works, for the want of an international copyright law makes possible the

publication of four of Stevenson's novels in one volume, all for twenty cents. You can readily perceive that a sale thus rendered large through the want of statutory protection tends to shut out home products through the very cheapness of the article, thus not only depriving the British author of his dues but interfering with the sale of American novels.[12]

Through collaboration with his stepson Lloyd Osbourne, an American citizen protected by American copyright laws, Stevenson was able to safeguard his financial interests in America to some extent. Although he denied that this was the sole objective of their collaboration, he did admit that 'the result is certainly attained by it'.[13] In July 1891 the United States Congress eventually passed the Chace Act, the first American International Copyright Law affording foreign authors some protection if the books were manufactured in the United States. By then, Stevenson's earnings had begun to reflect his popularity worldwide. He was, as Bill Bell notes, the first bankable Scottish writer to capitalise on the burgeoning international market, along with J. M. Barrie (1860–1937), Arthur Conan Doyle (1859–1930), and John Buchan (1875–1940), 'making their marks on the metropolitan book trade and reaping the rewards of international success'.[14]

Stevenson initially messed up his business dealings in America, leaving himself open to accusations of duplicity after a mix-up concerning incompatible engagements he entered into with both Scribner's and McClure, and this made him wary of future contracts. He had grown up in a city that was, in his own words, part of the 'world of everyday reality, connected by railway and telegraph-wire with all of the capitals of Europe'.[15] Later, however, geographical distance from these means of rapid communication meant that he relied heavily on a network of friends at home to negotiate deals for him and to look after his literary interests. Charles Baxter and Sidney Colvin were the main elements in this network along with W. E. Henley. They often dealt with publishers and contracts, not to mention editing. Stevenson worked hard at creating then maintaining this network of social and professional relationships that would promote and distribute his work while he was geographically distant from the centres of the literary world. Transatlantic dealings were managed in a more efficient way when in 1924, thirty years after Stevenson's death and just before his work passed out of unrestricted copyright, his four main publishers swiftly agreed to bring out a uniform edition of the complete works at two different prices (the Tusitala and Skerryvore editions) on either side of the Atlantic.[16]

As a traveller and expatriate Stevenson was not satisfied with simply dwelling in other parts of the world but made a conscious effort to engage with them in purposeful ways, often drawing inspiration from their literatures and cultures. Much of his travel writing was inspired by his geographical position on the globe, but also his essays, and his political writing from the Pacific. There, rather than being an instrument of colonialism, he became a particularly notable example of what Michelle Keown identifies as typical Scots radicalism in action, so that while *A Footnote to History* (1892) may stop short of 'outright condemnation of European colonialism *per se*, the text criticizes the wrangling for power amongst British, German, and US settlers and colonial forces in Samoa'.[17]

Stevenson was influenced by writers from elsewhere – he repeatedly cited Montaigne, Dumas, Whitman, and Thoreau – and he in turn influenced generations of writers and critics working in other parts of the world and in other languages. Notable admirers abroad have included Alain-Fournier, Atushi Nakajima, Borges, Calvino, Gide, Nabokov, Le Clézio, Lev Lunts, Malraux, Proust, Jacques Rivière, Schwob, and Sôseki Natsume – many reacting enthusiastically to his work at the same time as it was being side-lined by the gatekeepers of the English literary canon. The process was one of transculturation, as his work was read and accommodated in new cultural environments, modifying the literary output and altering the structures of feeling, literary trends, and popular culture in diverse elsewheres.[18] Authors recognised Stevenson's influence both as a writer and as a theorist, variously citing his work as having been significant in the development and evolution of Latin American magic realism,[19] French symbolism, the European Gothic, a compromise between the realist and the psychological novel,[20] and the adventure novel. Given Stevenson's place and standing in world literature at the end of his life, it is little wonder that his obituarist in *Le Temps* declared that his death was a loss not only for English literature but for universal literature and indeed for humanity.[21]

The process of literary globalisation is certainly more complicated than the reciprocal trading of texts and influences between geographical spaces. To paraphrase Pascale Casanova, there is a struggle at play between competing forces in the global literary field, in which those who emerge as international rather than national writers obtain greater freedom for their work.[22] Accordingly, it is no coincidence that as Stevenson's international reputation grew, the perception of his national identity receded. In the process of internationalisation, as Ian Brown has argued, Stevenson's Scottishness was effaced:

> If one accepts that world literature may be defined in terms of its commodification in production, publication, appropriation and circulation, then the global promulgation of Stevenson's novel, not to mention its many adaptations for – besides film – stage, television, radio and comics, marks it not only as a key text of 'English' literature, but also a key text of world literature [...] Jekyll and Hyde are entities in the global imaginative mindscape and have been evacuated of their Scottish genesis.[23]

But although Stevenson's audience may now be unaware of his Scottishness, he himself, without ever over-sentimentalising his connection to an increasingly unattainable home, never forgot where he was from. Despite his active presence elsewhere and his growing awareness of the globalisation of experience, he continued to engage with Scotland, calling on his familiarity with Scottish history, particularly that of the Highlands, not only to create new fiction but also to better apprehend Pacific cultures.

Stevenson was what Henry James famously called 'a Scotchman of the world'.[24] This Scot was, in fact, a resolutely *glocal* writer. He was cosmopolitan in lifestyle and world view but able to hold and promote a simultaneously international and local perspective in his work, consciously writing for a worldwide readership while upholding his subjective Scottish experience – combining his knowledge of the world with a feeling for the indigenous. However, instead of making a global product fit the local market as is usual in current commercial strategies, he made texts anchored in local realities and real localities speak to a global market. The Scribner's essays, written initially for an American readership but drawing on much Scottish subject matter, are a good example of this syncretism. In the series of twelve essays, although he wrote about universal moral topics, he also riffed on personal reminiscences of places and experiences rooted in his homeland and unfamiliar to the majority of his readers. He wrote about places like Anstruther and Wick and unselfconsciously used expressions like 'well kent', 'links' and 'land' with specific meanings in Scots, trusting his American readers to shift their fields of reference accordingly. This was an international writer who expected his readers to be international readers. In creating key texts in world literature that held both the universal and the local in focus, Stevenson proved that one could be simultaneously a Scottish and a world writer.[25]

CHAPTER TWENTY-THREE

Celticists and Anthropologists

Michael Shaw

In a letter to his cousin Bob, written in Samoa in September 1894, Robert Louis Stevenson (1850–1894) discusses one of his other cousins, Graham Balfour, who would go on to write an early biography of Stevenson. In the letter, the 'wizard of Samoa' responds to Bob Stevenson's implication that Balfour, born in London, was not a Celt:

> 'Imagine Graham Balfour a Celt?' say you. But that is just what he is; his name bewrays him. Balfour = cold croft. Get the Anglo-Saxon heresy out of your head; they superimposed their language, they scarce modified the race; only in Berwickshire and Roxburgh, have they very largely affected the place names. The Scandinavians did much more to Scotland, than the Angles. The Saxons didn't come.[1]

Echoing an early letter to J. M. Barrie (1860–1937) from 1892 – where he explains to Barrie that he consciously gave the protagonist of *Kidnapped*, David Balfour, a 'Gaelic' name – Stevenson here asserts the Celtic derivation of his cousin's surname and Scotland's nationwide Celtic inheritance.[2] Although he subtly acknowledges that the Scots are defined by racial intermixture, Stevenson nevertheless highlights here that the Scottish Celts, and Scotland's Celtic legacy, are not limited to the Highlands.

Stevenson's impassioned language in the above quotation reflects his concerted interest in dispersing or diluting Lowland Scotland's identification with Saxonism to foster a more cohesive Scottish nationality in an era when Scotland was still characterised by some as sharply divided between two races – Highland Celts and Lowland Saxons. But the above quotation also speaks to the rising identification with, and enthusiasm for, Celticism in *fin-de-siècle* Scotland and beyond. The end of the nineteenth century witnessed the proliferation of loosely connected Celtic Revival movements in various nations, especially in Ireland, Scotland,

Wales, and Brittany. Some Celtic revivalists were focused on reviving the Celtic languages of these nations, but many were enthused by Celtic myths, literatures, music, and the supposed racial traits of the Celts, showing limited interest in the Celtic languages themselves, thus often occluding existing Gaelic culture in Scotland. What is striking about the rise of the Celtic Revival is that it owed debts to two very different, at times opposing, aspects of *fin-de-siècle* cultural politics. On the one hand, the rise of Celtic revivalism in the United Kingdom was a consequence of growing political and constitutional tensions, especially over the issues of land reform and home rule, which is most clearly evidenced in Scotland with Ruaraidh Erskine of Mar's magazine *Guth na Bliadhna* that focused on Gaelic Revival efforts and Scottish nationalism, as well as featuring contributions by Irish nationalists and Celtic revivalists, including Patrick Pearse. For some, Celtic revivalism became a means of defining and distinguishing the 'Celtic nations' or Celtic peoples against their 'Saxon' neighbours, offering a counter-hegemonic site for collaboration between these nations. But, on the other hand, many *fin-de-siècle* Celticists were deeply indebted to the work of Matthew Arnold, especially his treatise *On the Study of Celtic Literature*, which characterised the Celt as feminine, irrational, and superstitious, and argued for greater cultural intermixture between the Celts and Saxons to temper the excesses of Celtic intuition and Saxon rationality and to yield a more moderate, advanced culture. This duality, of *fin-de-siècle* Celticism – underpinned by discourses that hoped to distinguish the 'Celtic peoples' and also to absorb them – is neatly distilled in the following quotation from Daniel G. Williams:

> From one perspective Celticism is a product of English epistemological mastery and political domination, an internal form of Orientalism in which the feminine, superstitious, and poetic Celt could be easily accommodated as a junior partner in the British Imperial adventure. From another, Celticism offers a radical reconceptualization of national identities within the British Isles, fostering new avenues of dialogue and artistic and political collaboration.[3]

It is this polyvocal, complex and, at times, contradictory nature of *fin-de-siècle* Celticism that this chapter attends to. Scotland's Celtic Revival, like Celticism more widely, was deeply complex. And this complexity was reflective of a contested period in Scottish history where cultural and political paradigms were shifting. While several Scottish revivalists were indebted to Arnold and themselves constructed caricatures of the Celts that were derided by contemporaries for their lack of authenticity – an aspect of *fin-de-siècle* Scottish Celticism that literary criticism has tended to foreground – many Scots (including those inspired by Arnoldian Celticism) were using the Celtic Revival as a means of distinguishing and invigorating Scottish nationality. They were also looking to the latest studies in anthropology to inspire their movement and lend it greater authenticity.

The Arnoldian strain of Celticism was undoubtedly evident in *fin-de-siècle* Scotland, and it is most clearly voiced in the works of William Sharp (1855–1905), who is best known for his fictional writings set in and around the Hebrides, written under the heteronym of 'Fiona Macleod'. Sharp was drawn to the image of the melancholic, nature-loving, feminine Celt that Arnold constructs, and he uses some of his writings to advance that construction and herald the rise of an assimilated Anglo-Celtic people. This Arnoldian Celticism is explicitly articulated in Sharp's introductory essay to Elizabeth Sharp's (1856–1932) volume of poetry *Lyra Celtica: An Anthology of Representative Celtic Poetry* (1896), published as part of Patrick Geddes and Colleagues' Celtic Library. Sharp describes Arnold as the most 'sympathetic and penetrating critic of the Celtic imagination', and defines the Celt in terms that are strikingly akin to Arnold's.[4] In Sharp's hands, the Celts are 'sweet', 'feminine', 'haunting', 'indefinable', 'sombre' 'dreamers', defined by their 'love of nature', 'melancholy', 'hyperbole', 'passion' and 'sentiment'.[5] Taken together, these words dissociate the Celts from the realms of rationality, science, and political aptitude, mirroring Arnold's project. Sharp's paradigm of the Celt further resembles Arnold's in its implicit cultural unionism: Sharp approvingly quotes from a lecture by the former Anglican chaplain Stopford Brooke, 'On the Need and Use of Getting Irish Literature into the English Tongue' (1893), in which Brooke argues that, with more Irish literature available in English, 'we may bring England and [Celtdom] into a union which never can suffer separation'.[6] Sharp makes a concerted effort to use Celticism to integrate the 'Celtic nations' into Britain, enacting what Murray Pittock terms 'the Arnoldian landscape of Britishness'.[7] Moreover, the essay reveals Sharp's interest in assimilating the Celts into the Saxon race. Through his proleptic eulogy of the Celts, a race that has 'reached its horizon', and his heralding the absorption of Celtic attributes 'into the hearts of the mightier conquering people',[8] Sharp deploys Celticism to advance both the absorption of the Celts and the ascendancy of a fundamentally Saxon race, albeit one with 'Celtic' inflections.

It was Sharp's attempts to further British unity that led to his rejection by several Irish revivalists, such as George Russell (Æ) and W. B. Yeats, despite the fact that both were initially enraptured by the Fiona Macleod writings. In response to Macleod's essay 'Celtic' (1900), in which she defines the Saxon as the 'greater race' and asserts pride in Britishness,[9] Russell stridently rebukes her as an 'English writer' who should not speak on behalf of the Gaels,

> for the Gael in Ireland, in addition to his traditions, which are shared to some extent by the Scottish Celt, has the aspiration to a distinct and self-governed nationality, and no one can claim to represent him who does not share this national aspiration.[10]

Russell defines what he perceives to be the difference between the Scottish and Irish Revivals: the Irish Celts have concerns beyond focusing on Celtic myths and cultural inheritance, principally distinguishing themselves from Britain and the Saxon and achieving political autonomy. Certainly, the Irish revivalists were far more concerned with the question of political self-governance than the Scottish revivalists, but that did not mean they never used Celticism to further a 'distinct [...] nationality' for Scotland, or even to appeal for Scottish self-government. Although it was more muted and contested, Celticism informed cultural and political nationalism in Scotland too.

One figure who tried to further a 'distinct [...] nationality' for Scotland through Celticism was Sharp's colleague and collaborator, the polymath Patrick Geddes (1854–1932). Geddes was a town planner, sociologist, and botanist (among various other professions), who also became one of the leading figures of Celtic revivalism in Edinburgh. Geddes published Celtic Revival writings, commissioned murals inspired by Celtic mythology, and wrote essays in defence of Celtic culture and identity. Like Sharp, Geddes did not seek to defy British constitutional unity, but he was deeply critical of the processes of centralisation and cultural absorption in the United Kingdom, which underpinned his enthusiasm for Celticism. Geddes believed that Celticism could help reinvigorate Scottish nationality: in his essay 'The Scots Renascence' (1895), in which he calls for greater national feeling and awareness of cultural history in Scotland, he explicitly associates the 'Scots Renascence' with 'our Celtic Renascence'.[11] This association of Scotland with Celticism, Gerard Carruthers writes, was 'a rather undiscriminating homogenization of Scotland's self-image',[12] but it reflected Geddes's interest in reanimating Lowland Scotland's Celtic inheritance – developed through his friendship with the folklorist John Stuart-Glennie, who argued that much Lowland Scottish topography was indebted to the Celtic Arthurian myth – and in resisting the marginalisation of the Celts. Challenging centralisation and the belittling of the Celts, Geddes argued that Celtic culture should lead the way, declaring 'it is not for London to educate Iona; it is for Iona to educate London'.[13]

Like several other *fin-de-siècle* Celticists, including John Stuart Blackie (1809–1895), who is applauded in the opening of 'The Scots Renascence', Geddes's circle was not as removed from the concern with 'self-governed nationality' as Russell suggests. Although he declined an invitation to join the recently formed Scottish Home Rule Association (of which Blackie had been chairman), Geddes revealed his tacit support for the principle of Scottish Home Rule, writing a letter in response that he wanted to build up the health of Scotland's literature, art, and industries, which would, in turn, advance the case for Home Rule. He wrote: 'I believe I can do my best service to the cause by working at the realities of the Scots Renascence'.[14] Geddes was deeply disenchanted with parliamentary politics, but this letter reveals that there were links between Celtic revivalism and the growing concerns with Home Rule in Scotland, although fewer and less marked than in Ireland.

Celticism also helped develop a 'distinct [...] nationality' for Scotland via the international partnerships and dialogues it fostered with the 'Celtic nations' and beyond. This phenomenon was evident in the more radical work of Ruaraidh Erskine (1869–1960), but it also underpins several developments in Geddes's circle. Geddes and Colleagues' Celtic Library published *The Fiddler of Carne* by the Welsh revivalist Ernest Rhys, *The Shadow of Arvor* – a collection of Breton folktales – by Edith Rinder, and contributions by Irish revivalists in *The Evergreen*, including Douglas Hyde, Standish O'Grady, and Katharine Tynan. Despite his Arnoldian Celticism, Sharp did at times voice a cultural nationalism and he was among those who believed international dialogues could help develop and distinguish Scottish literature. He drew comparisons between the Scottish Revival and both the Belgian Revival and Finnish cultural nationalism, referencing the Finnish national epic *Kalevala* in the Macleod poetry collection, *From the Hills of Dream*. These international ambitions were furthered through Geddes's efforts to circulate *The Evergreen* widely, and the international imprint of Scotland's Celtic Revival writers is still evident today: in Japan, several of Fiona Macleod's writings remain in print, enjoying a longevity they have not experienced in Scotland.[15]

As it was criticised for authenticating the Arnoldian image of the Celt and for promoting cultural absorption, so was Celticism – especially the Celticism found in Edinburgh – criticised for its lack of authenticity. The anthropologist, poet, folklorist, and author Andrew Lang (1844–1912) led this critique in an 1897 essay published in *Blackwood's*, mounting a scathing attack on 'the conquering legions who now march under Mr William Sharp, Miss Fiona Macleod [...] Professor Geddes, and other leaders'.[16] Lang identifies the Arnoldian Celticism of 'Fiona Macleod', amongst others, and disputes their association of the love of style, melancholy, and natural magic with the Celtic race. He argues these traits are found amongst many other races and are not embodied in all Highland writers. Lang also challenges Arnold and Sharp's attempts to attribute 'Celtic blood' to major English and Lowland authors, on account of their works embodying 'the Celtic element'. Lang cautions that 'when we bring race into literary criticism, we dally with that unlovely fluent enchantress, Popular Science'. As a remedy to this form of Celticism, Lang calls for more writings in the vein of Neil Munro's (1864–1930) more 'knowledge[able]' tales of Highland life, which make it 'live again'.[17] Here, the author of *Myth, Ritual and Religion* (1887) casts Edinburgh's Celtic revivalists as taking liberties with history, folklore, and anthropology, demanding 'proof' throughout.

While the Celtic revivalists that circled around Geddes in Edinburgh certainly appropriated Highland legends and literature, several revivalists, including Sharp, were nevertheless looking to the most current anthropological studies to inform and inspire their works. Written by the Glaswegian social anthropologist J. G. Frazer (1854–1941), *The Golden Bough* (originally published in 1890, but expanded over a course of twenty-five years) proved to be one of the most influential pieces of *fin-de-siècle* anthropology globally. Inspired by the work of other Scottish anthropologists, including his friend William Robertson Smith, Frazer's detailed, cross-cultural depictions of ritual, myth, and magic were revelatory to contemporary readerships and are now known for inspiring various Modernist writings, including T. S. Eliot's *The Waste Land*. As Cairns Craig notes, it was Frazer's 'negation of progressive history, [his] awareness of the fact that even the "light" of modern science is rooted in the "dark" truths of the primitive, that made [him] the prophet of the modern consciousness'.[18] What is less well known is that *The Golden Bough* also likely inspired Celtic revivalists in the 1890s.

Sharp's writings post-1890, especially those written under the guise of Fiona Macleod, feature various myths and concepts that are delineated in *The Golden Bough*. Although Frazer believed that 'the curtain must soon descend on savagery for ever',[19] he nevertheless identified various continuing pagan rituals across Scotland that would have appealed to Sharp, who at times asserted his concern with defending and reviving 'the old barbaric emotion' of the Celts.[20] One of Macleod's best-known collections, *The Sin-Eater and other Tales* (1895), draws on the ostensibly Welsh custom of 'sin-eating' that Frazer outlines in *The Golden Bough*; the custom involves the 'transference of evil from one person to another' by the symbolic act of eating bread over their corpse. Frazer notes that, in some circumstances, the poor were hired to perform this custom, pawning their own soul.[21] Alongside sin-eating, Frazer's assessments of 'tree-worship', and the 'savage' belief that trees are 'animate', are also reflected in Sharp's works.[22] In 'The Annir-Choille' from Macleod's *The Washer of the Ford*, the protagonist, Cathal, experiences the fluidity of spirits between humans and trees, which Sharp himself was familiar with: Lady Gregory reminisced that Sharp once hugged a tree and felt his soul flow through its sap.[23] Allusions to the myths that Frazer outlines in the opening of *The Golden Bough* regarding the worship of Diana at Lake Nemi, situated in the Alban Hills of Italy, feature in Sharp's writings: his poem, 'The Swimmer of Nemi', depicts a male figure who swims across the lake with a branch from a tree, resembling the bough that features in Frazer's analysis of Lake Nemi's mythologies. Similarly, Sharp's short prose drama, 'The Black Madonna', which represents sacrifices to a female God, resembles Frazer's note that the Nemi rituals descended from the ritual of the Tauric Diana, where 'every stranger who landed on the shore was sacrificed on her altar'.[24]

Lake Nemi has further significance for Sharp, and for the Scottish Revival, because it was whilst visiting Lake Nemi on 3 January 1891, in the company of his muse Edith Rinder, that 'Fiona Macleod' was born. Along with Rinder, whom Sharp at times associated with Macleod and to whom he dedicated his first Macleod volume, *Pharais*, Frazer may well have played a role in the formation of the Fiona Macleod identity. Much like Diana, who Frazer writes 'might still linger by this lonely shore, still haunt these woodlands wild',[25] Fiona Macleod as a spirit or faery first appeared to Sharp

> on the banks of Lake Nemi, when she was enjoying a sun-bath in what she deemed was a virgin solitude, after swimming the lake. 'That moment began', [Sharp] declared, 'my spiritual regeneration. I was a New Man, a

mystic, where before I had been only a mechanic-in-art. Carried away by my passion, my pen wrote as if dipped in fire'.[26]

In this recounting to Ernest Rhys, Sharp believed that Rhys, who had a touch of the 'sight', would understand that Macleod was 'seen by very few'. In this context, it is noteworthy that several of the Fiona Macleod writings are concerned with woodland realms and the green life, as it provides a further connection to Diana of the Wood.

Beyond Sharp, Celtic Revival painters were also looking to anthropological literature for inspiration. In *The Golden Bough*, Frazer presents a quotation from Pliny the Elder, the Roman natural philosopher, which describes the rites of Celts in Ancient Gaul. Pliny's account clearly forms the subject matter of Scotland's most iconic Celtic Revival painting, George Henry and E. A. Hornel's *The Druids Bringing in the Mistletoe* (1890), painted the same year Frazer's text was released. Frazer quotes Pliny as follows:

> The Druids, for so they call their wizards, esteem nothing more sacred than the mistletoe and the tree on which it grows, provided only that the tree is an oak. [...] After due preparations have been made for a sacrifice and a feast under the tree, they hail it as the universal healer and bring to the spot two white bulls, whose horns have never been bound before. A priest clad in a white robe climbs the tree and with golden sickle cuts the mistletoe, which is caught in white cloth.[27]

Hornel and Henry's painting, featuring druids, mistletoe, the moon, a golden sickle, two bulls carrying the mistletoe, and a solemn ceremony, owes a clear debt to Pliny and demonstrates the fact that Celtic revivalists were turning to anthropological literature – modern and classical – to give authenticity to their works.[28]

In his introductory note to his edition of James Macpherson's *Ossian*, Sharp notes that Macpherson's text was a 'self-contradictory, and sometimes grotesquely impossible rendering of disconnected, fugitive' lore.[29] He could have almost been writing about his own works, and *fin-de-siècle* Celtic revivalism more widely. The Celtic Revival in Scotland, as in other nations, was ultimately a deeply complex, fragmented, and at times contradictory phenomenon, which appealed to different individuals at different times for different reasons, and drew from various sources. Celticism could both defend and eulogise Celtic culture, and its promoters could shamelessly romanticise the Celts while also drawing from anthropological studies to inform their work. This short chapter has only touched on a few of the complexities of *fin-de-siècle* Celticism, but they are reflective of the ironies and inconsistencies of the Revival and the shifting cultural and political ground in 1890s Scotland.

CHAPTER TWENTY-FOUR

Science and Speculation

Julia Reid

Genealogies of nineteenth-century science fiction usually chart a path through English writers, from Mary Shelley (1797–1851) to H. G. Wells (1866–1946), with detours through the US and French traditions exemplified by Edgar Allan Poe (1809–1849) and Jules Verne (1828–1905). The only Scottish writers to receive regular attention are Robert Louis Stevenson (1850–1894) and Arthur Conan Doyle (1859–1930).[1] Gavin Miller observes that, with the exception of *Strange Case of Dr Jekyll and Mr Hyde*, science fiction was 'largely absent from the Scottish canon', as nineteenth-century Scottish writers were 'far less willing or able to explore this new literary possibility' than their English or French counterparts.[2] Some genre-centred criticism excludes even *Jekyll and Hyde* from the science fiction canon: for Darko Suvin, the novel's 'unclear oscillation between science and fantasy' situates it in the 'misshapen subgenre' of 'science-fantasy'.[3] This relative neglect is striking given the prominence of science-fiction writers – from Naomi Mitchison (1897–1999) to Iain M. Banks (1954–2013) and Ken MacLeod (b. 1954) – in twentieth- and twenty-first-century Scotland. Broadening the focus from science fiction to a more loosely defined speculative fiction, however, reveals a rich tradition in nineteenth-century Scottish culture. As Caroline McCracken-Flesher has argued, Scottish authors have a 'long tradition of writing at the margin of worlds'.[4] 'Speculative fiction' includes not only science fiction but also fantasy, the Gothic, utopias and dystopias, and other forms of non-mimetic fiction whose imagined worlds depart in some significant way from the world of our experience. Nineteenth-century Scottish culture proved a hospitable environment for speculative writing, which manifested itself in both fictional and scientific texts.

Recent studies have demonstrated that intellectual life in Victorian Scotland, long seen as being in marked decline from its pre-eminence during the Scottish Enlightenment, remained vibrant.[5] Scottish scientists were critical in opening up new disciplinary domains including energy physics and anthropology. Both of these domains were shaped by an interest in the relationship between science and the creative imagination, and by a recognition that there was no epistemological discontinuity between science and literature. In the anthropologist J. G. Frazer's (1854–1941) words, 'imagination, the power of inward vision, is as necessary to science as to poetry'.[6] Both, too, created space for scientific speculation, whether about the future or past. Andrew Lang (1844–1912) recognised the conjectural nature of scholarly constructions of the past, referring drily to 'that branch of hypothetics which is known as prehistoric science'.[7] Scientific speculations were taken up and spun further by literary writers. Scottish writers including Florence Dixie (1855–1905) and Catherine Spence (1825–1910), for example, drew on and challenged anthropological and ethnological work by J. F. McLennan (1827–1881) and others on gender and marriage, creating feminist utopian worlds in their novels.[8] This chapter will confine itself to energy physics, which Cairns Craig has suggested provided inspiration for important works of Scottish fantasy from Stevenson's *Jekyll and Hyde* and George MacDonald's (1824–1905) *Phantastes* to J. M. Barrie's (1860–1937) *Peter Pan*.[9] I will investigate some speculative patterns that connect the new physics of energy with literary work by Stevenson, Conan Doyle, Robert Duncan Milne (1844–1899), and MacDonald.

The new energy physics of the mid-nineteenth century was a markedly Scottish enterprise. Scottish physicists, notably William Thomson (later Lord Kelvin; 1824–1907), P. G. Tait (1831–1901), and James Clerk Maxwell (1831–1879), developed the sciences of thermodynamics and electromagnetism, replacing an older language of mechanical 'forces' with an interest in energy. Maxwell was alive to the power of language in this paradigm shift, observing in one of his serio-comic poems that

> Force becomes of Energy a mere
> Space-variation.
>
> Force, then, is Force, but mark you! not a thing,
> Only a Vector

and concluding jubilantly: 'Thy reign, O Force! is over'.[10] The first law of thermodynamics (the conservation of energy), formulated in the 1840s, described a world in which energy could be neither created nor destroyed.

The second law (the dissipation of energy) proposed a bleaker – and often apocalyptic – vision of entropy and waste, involving the eventual death of the sun. Thomson warned in 1862 that 'inhabitants of the earth cannot continue to enjoy the light and heat essential to their life, for many million years longer, unless sources now unknown to us are prepared in the great storehouse of creation'.[11] Here, Thomson's ominous prediction of the death of the sun is offset by the tantalising possibility of a get-out clause: that 'sources now unknown' may avert this disaster.

Responses to the dissipation of energy displayed a decidedly speculative bent, as scientists used conjecture, extrapolation, and fictional techniques such as analogies and metaphors to probe future possibilities. Maxwell offered his famous thought experiment featuring a 'sorting demon' who might theoretically evade the workings of entropy.[12] The most intriguing scientific response was the revealingly titled *The Unseen Universe or Physical Speculations on a Future State* (1875) by the Scottish physicists P. G. Tait and Balfour Stewart (1828–1887). In *The Unseen Universe*, Tait and Stewart accept the death of the sun and of the 'visible universe', but propose that 'nature's apparent prodigality' is deceptive, as the energy and motion lost to entropy will be stored in the ether for use in the 'unseen universe'.[13] *The Unseen Universe* offers a consolatory fiction to evade entropy's apocalyptic ending; it is, as Tamara Ketabgian notes, a 'thermodynamic fantasy'.[14] It is pervaded by fictional techniques, whose use in science Stewart elsewhere defended ('parables and proverbs are or ought to be not fictions but truths').[15] Countering scientific materialism, Tait and Stewart provide arguments for the immortality of soul and its transcendence of the material world.[16] They explain that thought is a mode of motion, and thus thoughts will not be lost in 'empty space' but conveyed by the ether to be preserved in the 'spiritual body'.[17] A work of Christian apologetics, the book also offered encouragement to spiritualists. Indeed, Stewart was an active member of the Society for Psychical Research, which advocated the scientific study of occult phenomena.[18] *The Unseen Universe*'s representation of the ether most obviously connects the book with spiritualism, psychical research, and occultism. Spiritualists and occultists drew on Maxwell's electromagnetic field theory – with its model of invisible energies radiating through the ether – to understand the transmission of spiritual energies, from telepathy to 'psychic force'.[19] In later editions, Tait and Stewart also deployed higher-dimensional mathematics to underwrite their invisible world, as did other religious and occultist thinkers. By 1876, in the sixth edition, they imagined 'our (essentially three-dimensional) matter to be the mere skin or boundary of an Unseen whose matter has *four* dimensions' and posited 'the ultimate conception of an infinite series of Universes'.[20]

Literary writers including Stevenson, Conan Doyle, Milne, and MacDonald took up the speculative challenge offered by energy physics. They created fictional worlds that explored questions which were still undecided in this new science: questions about the reversibility of entropy, the continuity and unity of physical laws, the relations of spirit and matter, the boundaries between science and the occult, the future possibilities of electromagnetic science, the unintended consequences of scientific and technological discoveries, and the existence of higher dimensions.

Stevenson's *Jekyll and Hyde* engages with a range of different scientific discourses, from psychology to degeneration theory, but for present purposes its investment in energy physics is particularly interesting. Stevenson enjoyed close family connections with Scottish energy physics, was taught by Tait at Edinburgh University, and was familiar with *The Unseen Universe*.[21] Dr Jekyll's speculative excesses align him with the anti-materialist Tait and Stewart. Frequently 'speak[ing] by theory alone', 'too fanciful' and 'unscientific' for his peers, Jekyll champions 'the mystic and the transcendental' over the 'narrow and material'.[22] Jekyll's experimental unleashing of Hyde from his 'fortress of identity' notably turns on the relationship between the seen and unseen.[23] He describes 'this seemingly so solid body in which we walk attired' as but a 'fleshly vestment', a 'mere aura and effulgence' of his 'spirit'.[24] Jekyll's language chimes with Tait and Stewart's claim that 'it is a glorious garment this visible universe, but not an immortal one'.[25] Yet where Tait and Stewart use the notion of the 'unseen universe' to evade the workings of entropy, Stevenson's narrative is less consolatory in its handling of thermodynamical tropes. The novella's depiction of Jekyll's identity transformations, as Allen MacDuffie cogently argues, rejects the thermodynamic 'fantasy' of 'reversibility': Jekyll's growing loss of control over Hyde underlines instead the 'irreversible depletion of resources' and the inevitably entropic movement of personal identity from 'order' to 'disorder'.[26]

Conan Doyle's speculative fiction was wide-ranging in its preoccupations, from aeronautical experimentation to the discovery of surviving prehistoric forms in the classic *The Lost World* (1912). Energy and the relationship between spirit and matter, however, are at the heart of much of his nineteenth-century output. 'The Los Amigos Fiasco' (1892) explicitly scrutinises the mysterious possibilities of new electromagnetic science. In this wryly narrated tale, scientific 'experts' devise an experimental electrocution, only to find they have 'increased the man's vitality' instead of killing him: as the 'harmless crank' whose warnings they dismissed explains, 'Electricity is life, and you have charged him with it to the utmost'.[27] Conan Doyle's work persistently investigated the borderland between science and the occult. He became interested in spiritualism and Theosophy in the mid-1880s and joined the Society for Psychical Research in 1893.[28] His awareness of the shifting nature of the boundary between 'respectable' science and heterodoxy acts as an affirmation of speculation and conjecture. The occult scholar in 'The Leather Funnel' (1902) parries the allegation that the 'psychology of dreams' is a 'science of charlatans': 'The charlatan is always the pioneer. From the astrologer came the astronomer, from the [...] mesmerist the experimental psychologist'.[29] Conan Doyle's Egyptian romance fiction also blurs the line between science and the occult. In 'The Ring of Thoth' (1890), echoing the Theosophist interpretation of occult knowledge, the Egyptian priest claims his creation of a life-prolonging elixir involves 'nothing of mystery or magic [...]. It was simply a chemical discovery'.[30] *The Parasite* (1894) investigates what Conan Doyle elsewhere describes as 'the ill-defined relations between mind and matter'.[31] In this Gothic novel, mesmeric experimentation vanquishes scepticism and scientific materialism. The protagonist, Gilroy, initially dismisses psychological research as 'nebulous semi-science', and regards the 'spirit' as a mere 'product of matter. The brain, I thought, secreted the mind, as the liver does the bile'.[32] Falling under Miss Penelosa's mesmeric influence, however, Gilroy accepts that the 'body' is 'rather the rough instrument by which the spirit manifests itself'.[33] He eventually realises that mesmeric power is 'a natural force', 'subject to physical laws'.[34] The novella endorses psychology as a 'science of the future', welcoming the disruption of scientific orthodoxies.[35] But the racialised, sexualised, and demonic figure of Miss Penelosa shows that, for Conan Doyle, the affiliation of the occult with female power was deeply threatening.

Robert Duncan Milne, a now largely forgotten Scottish writer, emigrated to the States and published science fiction tales in the San Francisco journal *The Argonaut* in the 1880s and 1890s, covering topics from cryogenics to aerial warfare. His speculative inventiveness and narrative style recall Wells. (Indeed, readers of the Hungarian translation of his cryogenics tale, 'Ten Thousand Years in Ice', were unsure whether it was fact or fiction, prefiguring the well-known response to the radio dramatisation of *The War of the Worlds*.)[36] Many of his stories explore the borderland between science and the occult, explaining spectacular psychical phenomena by reference to energy, the ether, and electromagnetic field theory. Fictional extrapolations of the new physics, they probe what Tait and Stewart called the 'mysteries' that 'persistently hover around the border' of 'the illuminated sphere of scientific thought'.[37] Such tales are often sanguine, affirming electrical energy as an underlying principle of unity across the physical and spiritual worlds. In 'A New Palingenesis' (1883), a doctor captures his dying wife's 'vital force' (explained as a 'mysterious electrical agency') and enables it to rematerialise in a new body.[38] The denial that death annihilates individual identity ('Nature does not deal in such wanton waste of energy') is framed in terms that recall Tait and Stewart's assertion of a continuing spiritual world.[39] In 'Professor Vehr's Electrical Experiment' (1885), psychic communication travels through an invisible 'medium' that sounds like the ether.[40] The tale scientises spiritual energies, explaining that apparently 'supernatural' psychical phenomena are just 'beyond the present scope of applied science', and that the 'mesmeric trance' follows the 'accepted laws of electrical science'.[41] But Milne's tales sometimes warned against scientific and technological hubris, and here the Professor's transmission through space of two individuals (their bodies 'etherealized' as electromagnetic waves) ends in their electrical combustion.[42] Most uplifting in its treatment of occult energies is 'The Palæoscopic Camera' (1881), which draws in detail on the German Karl von Reichenbach's theory of 'Odic Force' (a supposed life-force, introduced to British audiences by the Scottish chemist William Gregory in the 1840s).[43] In this story, a photographer captures moving images from the past: the walls of a ruined cathedral, 'charged' with light rays from past scenes, cause 'vibrations of the luminous ether'; these are converted into 'that mysterious odic force' and imprinted on the photographic plate.[44] A reassuring affirmation of the conservation of energy and the 'unity of all natural law', the tale also staves off entropy and apocalypse, noting that 'nothing is lost' and that, even if the planet dies, its 'records' will be preserved: 'The luminous ether-waves' will go on rolling, and 'each one of them will yet be read'.[45]

George MacDonald draws on physics to much more ambiguous effect in his visionary fantasy *Lilith: A Romance* (1895). His narrator, Mr Vane, stumbles through a mirror in his attic – an 'aërial portal' – into 'the region of the seven dimensions', a strange realm where he finds that 'the material and psychical relations of our world had ceased to hold' and where he must undertake a spiritual and literal journey.[46] Among many influences on MacDonald's 'seven dimensions', higher-dimensional physics and mathematics stand out. MacDonald had studied Chemistry and Natural

Philosophy at King's College, Aberdeen; he may also have been familiar with Edwin Abbott's (1838–1926) higher-dimensional fiction *Flatland* (1884).[47] Vane introduces himself as a student of 'the physical sciences' and mentions Maxwell, who was interested in dimensionality.[48] Wells praised MacDonald's exploration of higher-dimensional worlds: 'I have wanted to get into such kindred worlds for the purposes of romance for several years, but I've been bothered by the way. Your polarization and mirror business struck me as quite neat in the extreme.'[49] Wells clearly sees *Lilith*'s 'aërial portal' as a functional plot device, but MacDonald's use of higher-dimensional theories is freighted with spiritual significance. Just as Vane draws 'strange analogies' between 'physical hypotheses' and 'suggestions glimmering out of [...] metaphysical dreams', MacDonald uses geometrical hypotheses to divine spiritual truths.[50] Vane's journey into higher dimensions involves moving from the limited plane of human existence to a heightened spiritual awareness. MacDonald, then, like Tait and Stewart and other religious and occult thinkers, spiritualises the fourth dimension. For Colin Manlove, *Lilith* goes beyond this; its vision of paradox and indeterminacy anticipates twentieth-century quantum physics.[51] Indeed, the narrative refutes Vane's common-sense assumption that '[t]wo objects cannot exist in the same place at the same time', revealing instead that the three- and seven-dimensional worlds exist simultaneously: both are 'real, interpenetrating yet unmingling'.[52]

Speculative fiction was not a new development in Victorian Scotland – Thomas Erskine's (1750–1823) satirical fantasy *Armata* appeared in 1817, for example – but it was certainly reinvigorated by scientific advances. Nineteenth-century Scottish scientists speculated, hypothesised, and constructed imaginary pasts and futures, as they sketched out new disciplinary domains. In Maxwell's words, 'Science lifts her pinions / In Speculation's wild dominions'.[53] Nowhere was this truer than in energy physics, where, as Roger Luckhurst notes, hypotheses were 'developed in advance of empirical proofs', and the new science accordingly remained in a 'suspensive state'.[54] This state of suspension invited literary writers – many of them trained in science in Scottish universities – to join the debate. In time-travel tales or Gothic romances, these writers imagined the relations of the material and the transcendental, weighed continuity and unity against entropy and disorder, plotted the future direction of scientific developments, and entertained the possibility of other worlds.

CHAPTER TWENTY-FIVE

Scotland's New Women

Juliet Shields

The Woman Question – the question of what kinds of work women were naturally suited for and what social roles they might occupy – occupied the British press for much of the Victorian era, becoming more urgent towards the end of the century as women began to claim their rights to own property, attend university, and vote. The New Woman, a figure who emerged in *fin-de-siècle* journalism and fiction, constituted a discursive response to the Woman Question.[1] Detractors represented the New Woman as a cigarette-smoking, bicycle-riding, freethinking adulterer. But sympathetic representations were more nuanced, depicting the New Woman's struggle for economic and moral independence – the right to earn a living, make her own decisions, and find fulfilment in multiple roles, including but not limited to those of wife and mother.

Scottish women writers were as active in posing answers to the Woman Question as their counterparts elsewhere in Britain. I have chosen to focus here on Mona Caird (1854–1932), Flora Annie Steel (1847–1929), and Annie S. Swan (1859–1943), because they not only addressed the Woman Question in their writing, but also were visibly active in politics and the suffrage movement. Caird joined the National Society for Women's Suffrage in 1878 and participated in a number of other suffrage organisations. Her essay 'Why Women Want the Franchise' was read at the Women's Emancipation Union Conference in 1892. Steel joined the National Union of Women's Suffrage Societies in 1907 and became president of the Women Writer's Suffrage League in 1912–13. It is unclear whether Swan belonged to any suffrage societies, but she was a founding member of the Scottish National Party and described 'Self-Government for Scotland' as 'pre-eminently a woman's question' on the grounds that Scots were 'only asking leave to manage our own household'.[2]

Late nineteenth-century Scotswomen's writings illustrate a range of responses to the Woman Question that cannot be neatly categorised as feminist or anti-feminist, progressive or conservative. Nor do the opinions women expressed in writing always reflect their own choices and actions: for instance, Swan, seemingly the most conservative of the three, ran for Parliament in 1922, and Caird, although highly critical of the institution of marriage, was herself married. In addition to illustrating a spectrum of responses to the Woman Question, these three writers remind us that gender identities are bound inextricably with class and racial identities. The journals and newspapers in which they published their polemical pieces suggest that when they argued for the full legal and political personhood of women, they had middle-class white women in mind. Thus, Swan doled out different advice to her working-class and middle-class women readers and Steel saw British women's enfranchisement as necessary to the perpetuation of the nation's imperial power in India and elsewhere.

The figure of the New Woman was inspired by the writings of a woman whose claims to Scottishness were oblique. Ironically, given her criticisms of the institution of marriage, little is known about the life of Mona Alison before her marriage to James Henryson-Caird, owner of the large estate of Cassencary, in western Kirkcudbrightshire. Mona Caird achieved literary notoriety almost overnight in August 1888 when *The Westminster Review* published her polemical essay 'Marriage', which traced women's devaluation back to the Reformation and the teachings of that 'thick-skinned, coarse-fibred monk of the sixteenth century', Martin Luther.[3] By historicising marriage, Caird called into question its inevitability and its utility as a social institution. 'Marriage' initiated a debate carried out in the pages of the *Daily Telegraph*, which invited readers to respond to Caird's contentions that the institution of marriage had outlasted its historical utility and that it stifled any possibility of individual liberty. Roughly twenty-seven thousand people responded in writing to the question 'Is Marriage a Failure?', and the debate only ceased when the *Daily Telegraph* refused to accept any more letters.

Given her renown in her own time, it is fitting that over the past two decades, feminist critics have rescued Caird from obscurity, with Sally Ledger arguing persuasively that she 'should be regarded as the most significant foremother of modern feminism at the *fin de siècle*'.[4] Despite the increasing attention paid to Caird's works, however, critics have overlooked the thematic importance of Scotland to *The Daughters of Danaus* (1894), her best known New Woman novel. *Daughters of Danaus* is self-consciously polemical: its characters represent recognisable positions in the debates surrounding the New Woman, and they often engage in abstract conversations concerning the rights and obligations of the individual in society that reflect the influence of John Stuart Mill's philosophy on Caird's work. The novel's title alludes to a Greek myth in which Danaus forced his fifty daughters into marriage; when they proceeded to kill their husbands, they were 'condemned to the idiot's labour of eternally drawing water in sieves from fathomless wells'.[5] Caird's protagonist Hadria shares the sense of futility that Danaus's daughters must have felt, as an endless round of socially sanctioned domestic duties prevents her from cultivating her remarkable talents as a musician.

Daughters of Danaus is not just the story of any late Victorian woman's futile struggle to develop her musical talents; it is specifically the story of a Scotswoman's struggle. Hadria's Scottishness is an integral part of her identity as a musician. For Hadria, the 'bleak and solitary' regions of northern Scotland where she grows up both inspire and inhibit her creativity.[6] Throughout the novel, Hadria's musical genius is consistently associated with the Highland landscape and her 'Celtic blood'.[7] Hadria 'seemed to have absorbed the spirit of the northern twilights', so that her compositions are haunted by a 'spectral loneliness' and evoke images of 'a sudden storm among the mountains', 'the wind-swept heavens at midnight', and 'the lonely sea'.[8] But if the Scottish landscape inspires Hadria's compositions, parochial Scottish society censors her originality. Her musical compositions – described by one of her neighbours as 'things without any tune that bore one to death' and by a renowned French composer as 'rebel music, offensive to the orthodox' – are viewed askance.[9] For 'in this out-of-the-way district, society smiled upon conformity, and glared vindictively at the faintest sign of spontaneous thinking'.[10] The repressive conventions of rural Scottish society prevent Hadria from cultivating her talents and attaining the independence she desires. Several decades before Willa Muir (1890–1970) would write *Mrs Grundy in Scotland* (1936), Caird recognised that middle-class censoriousness made it very difficult for a New Woman to flourish north of the Tweed.

Perhaps Flora Annie Steel recognised this too. Her New Women tend to find scope for their ambitions in India, as did Steel herself during her twenty-two years in the Punjab, where her husband, an engineer with the Indian Civil Service, was stationed. By no means one of the 'memsahibs' whom she mocks in her novels – bored white women who spent their days drinking tea, gossiping, and flirting with soldiers – Steel occupied herself learning Hindi, inquiring into local customs and, after she was appointed Inspectress of Schools, monitoring women's and children's education across the Punjab. After returning to Britain in 1889, she began to experiment with the conventionally masculine genre of the adventure story or imperial romance developed by her contemporaries Rudyard Kipling (1865–1936) and H. Rider Haggard (1856–1925).

Steel's adventure stories were set in India and drew on the conventions of the New Woman novel to foreground women's participation in the work of empire-building. In contrast to female characters in works by other so-called Raj writers, such as Maud Diver (1867–1945), Bithia Mary Croker (1849–1920), and Alice Perrin (1867–1934), Steel's heroines become participants in, rather than spectators or victims of, imperial adventures. In *The Hosts of the Lord* (1900) Erda, a Scotswoman who has arrived at missionary work in Eshwara by way of East London's slums, has a much deeper understanding of Hindu and Muslim culture than do the British soldiers stationed in the city because her work takes her among its native inhabitants. From Am-ma, whose wife she assisted in childbirth, Erda learns that the followers of a discontented yogi plan to take control of the sluices regulating the city's waterways. Erda undertakes a perilous voyage down the rising river on Am-ma's raft to warn those stationed at the army's headquarters of the plot, thereby preventing widespread chaos among the thousands of pilgrims passing through the city on their way to the Cradle of the Gods. Although Steel critiqued the masculine exclusivity of adventure fiction, she did not entirely reject the imperial ideologies it propagated, for Erda aims above all to preserve British rule in the region.[11]

Despite her active and daring heroines, Steel believed that women's highest calling was to be found in marriage and motherhood, through which they might help perpetuate British imperial power across generations. In an article on 'the marriage market' published in the *Lady's Realm* in 1897, Steel sought to deromanticise marriage, critiquing the ideal of a union founded in exalted passion or spiritualised sentiment. In contrast to Caird's suggestion that marriage had outlived its usefulness, Steel regarded marriage as a valuable but entirely pragmatic relationship founded in duty – the duty of husband and wife to each other and to their children, but also to what she might have conceptualised as Western civilisation or, in the eugenicist terms of her day, the Anglo-Saxon race.

Steel's belief in duty as the foundation of marriage informs *Miss Stuart's Legacy* (1893), which traces the development of its Scottish protagonist, Belle Stuart, into a New Woman. Shortly after her arrival in Faizapore, Belle is manipulated into marriage with crooked military officer John Raby, who knows what Belle does not – that she is about to receive a legacy of thirty thousand pounds from a cousin who had loved her deeply. Belle's boorish husband squashes her laudable desire to learn more about 'what the people we govern think, and say, and do', encouraging her to confine her interests to ballgowns and babies.[12] As she gradually comes to detest her husband, Belle struggles against her feelings, failing to realise that 'what they call Love is the bribe held out by Nature to induce her thoughtless children to undertake a difficult duty'.[13] When she learns that Raby married her for her inheritance, Belle continues to feel that it is her duty to love her husband, rather than approach marriage as a pragmatic relationship to which love is incidental.

Although Belle believes that her own marriage ought to be founded in romantic sentiment, she does not apply this standard to Indian marriages, observing around her numerous marital relationships – arranged, polygamous, informal – all of which appear equally functional. Steel here uses Indian customs to critique the Western institution of marriage that many New Woman novels denounced. Steel suggests that if women understood marriage pragmatically, as a social relationship founded in mutual duties or obligations, rather than idealising it as an exalted state founded in romantic love, they might not only be happier with their lot, but also find fulfilment in pursuits beyond the home. As she reconciles herself to her loveless marriage, Belle, who has learned Hindustani, begins to take an interest in 'the tragic, poverty-stricken, yet contented lives of the poor around her', and to administer basic medical treatment to women and children in purdah, as did Steel herself.[14]

The serial fiction on which Annie S. Swan's reputation rested seems in many ways the antithesis of novels by Caird and Steel. While the female protagonists in the many serials she wrote for *The People's Friend* do question their socially sanctioned roles as wives and mothers, they usually end up reconciling themselves to the ideals of middle-class feminine domesticity. It is important to remember, though, that for the working-class women who comprised the majority of the *Friend*'s readership, staying at home to raise their children rather than going out to work in a jute mill or cleaning another woman's house might well have seemed like a highly desirable luxury. In the articles and stories that she wrote for *The Woman at Home* – a magazine with a middle-class readership comparable, in economic terms, at least, with Caird's and Steel's readerships – Swan expresses her support for women's suffrage in no uncertain terms.[15] The 'day when the enfranchisement of women becomes law will be welcomed by me as a new era in our social history', she asserted.[16]

However, Swan's feelings about middle-class women undertaking paid work outside the home were more ambivalent. Swan, as a wife, mother, and literary celebrity was, in Kate Krueger's words, an 'ideal role model for readers who were attempting to bridge the gap between women's domestic and professional roles'.[17] Swan responded directly to her readers' concerns about marriage, motherhood, and work in her advice column 'Over the Teacups', which featured regularly in the magazine. Margaret Beetham observes that the 'most persistent' problem that Swan was called upon to solve for her correspondents was 'how to earn a living as a middle-class woman' without engaging in work that was degrading or improper.[18] Swan emphasised that women should not be ashamed to work outside the home in order to support themselves and their families if they needed to, pointing out that many of them were already accustomed to the substantial labour involved in running a household. Indeed, she argued that the '"woman at home" should be put on a satisfactory pecuniary basis, and that however small may be the remuneration, she should have an equivalent in money for domestic service rendered'.[19]

The Woman at Home also ran serial fiction by Swan that depicted professional women in a positive and occasionally even heroic light. Nonetheless, in the very first paragraph of the first instalment of *Elizabeth Glen, M.B., the Experiences of a Lady Doctor* (1893–94), Swan's narrator hastens to assure readers that Elizabeth is 'a woman of so large a heart and so wide an experience that I have often said wifehood and motherhood could scarcely improve her in that respect'.[20] Swan's middle-class working women belong to what we would now call the 'helping professions', and their deep capacity for sympathy suits them for their vocations. Moreover, Swan makes it clear that these professional women have sacrificed their longings for the domestic affections other women enjoy. Ironically, this emotional self-sacrifice, arguably a particularly feminine characteristic, allows them to retain their claims to womanliness in conditions that might otherwise undermine them. Only in the last instalment of Elizabeth's story do we learn that her 'desire to be a doctor, and to live a more useful and a fuller life' than she thought she could as a wife and mother put an end to a youthful courtship.[21] Her suitor, Keith Hamilton, 'pooh-poohed' her ambitions, declaring that medical work 'will rob you of that exquisite womanliness which makes everybody love you'.[22] Swan's account of how her profession has nurtured Elizabeth's most womanly qualities prepares us to recognise Keith's objection as mistaken. Indeed, the spirited Elizabeth replied, 'If my womanliness is to be so easily damaged, Keith Hamilton, it is a quality not worth possessing'. But twelve years later she regrets her choice deeply, and when Keith, now an MP, proposes again, she is only too happy to 'settle down into a member's wife' and renounce her career.[23]

While Caird, Steel, and Swan's works begin to illustrate the complexity of Scottish responses to the Woman Question, much work remains to be done on late nineteenth-century Scottish writers' representations of women's rights and roles. For instance, J. M. Barrie's (1860–1937) sketches of village life in *A Window in Thrums* (1889) enshrine women such as the ailing mother Jess and her industrious daughter Leeby in the heart of the home, while the co-authored novels of Mary (1865–1963) and Jane (1866–1946) Findlater, *Crossriggs* (1908) and *Penny Monypenny* (1911), explore the stultifying boredom and frustration experienced by women who occupy this position.[24] A wealth of local and regional newspapers and periodicals also remains to be explored. It would be instructive to compare the discussion of women's suffrage in the *Dundee Courier* and the *Edinburgh Evening News*, for example. While Edinburgh, as a more cosmopolitan city, was a hub for the suffrage movement, many women in Dundee were the primary breadwinners in their households thanks to the jute industry. Scottish literary feminism did not, after all, begin with Catherine Carswell (1898–1946) and Willa Muir, nor was its expression limited to a London-based print marketplace. To appreciate its twentieth-century manifestations, we must look to its nineteenth-century antecedents.

Endnotes

Introduction

1 Edwin Muir, *Scott and Scotland: The Predicament of the Scottish Writer* (London: Routledge, 1936), pp. 11–12.
2 Donald E. Meek, 'Gaelic Literature in the Nineteenth Century', in Ian Brown, Thomas Owen Clancy, Susan Manning, and Murray Pittock (eds), *The Edinburgh History of Scottish Literature, Vol. 2: Enlightenment, Britain and Empire (1707–1918)* (Edinburgh: Edinburgh University Press, 2007), pp. 253–66 (p. 266).
3 Somhairle Mac Gill-eain, 'The Poetry of the Clearances', in William Gillies (ed.), *Ris a' Bhruthaich. The Criticism and Prose Writings of Sorley MacLean* (Stornoway: Acair, 1985), pp. 48–74 (p. 57).
4 Cairns Craig, *Out of History* (Edinburgh: Polygon, 1996), p. 221.
5 Susan Oliver, *Walter Scott and the Greening of Scotland: Emergent Ecologies of a Nation* (Cambridge: Cambridge University Press, 2021); Michael Morris, *Scotland and the Caribbean, c. 1740–1833* (Abingdon: Routledge, 2018); Andrew Nash, *Kailyard and Scottish Literature* (Amsterdam: Rodopi, 2007); Michael Newton (ed.), *Seanchaidh na Coille: The Memory-keeper of the Forest. Anthology of Scottish Gaelic Literature of Canada* (Sydney, NS: Cape Breton University Press, 2015); Cairns Craig, 'Scotland's Fantastic Physics: Energy Transformation in MacDonald, Stevenson, Barrie, and Spark', in Caroline McCracken-Flesher (ed.) *Scotland as Science Fiction* (Lewisburg, PA: Bucknell University Press, 2012), pp. 15–28.

PART 1: EXPERIMENTS

1 Henry Cockburn, *Memorials of His Time* (Edinburgh: Adam and Charles Black, 1856), p. 281.
2 Paruig Mac-an-Tuairneir (ed.), *Comhchruinneacha do Dh' Orain Taghta Ghaidhealach nach robh riamh roimhe clo-bhuailte gus a nis* (Duneidionn: T. Stiubhard, 1813).

3. See Michael Fry, *The Dundas Despotism* (Edinburgh: Edinburgh University Press, 1992).
4. Henry Cockburn, *Life of Lord Jeffrey*, 2 vols (Edinburgh: Adam and Charles Black, 1853) II, p. 134; p. 153.
5. *An Teachdaire Gae'lach* 1 (1829), p. 3.
6. Bill Bell, 'The Scottish Book Trade at Home and Abroad, 1707-1918', in Susan Manning (ed.), *The Edinburgh History of Scottish Literature, Volume 2: Enlightenment, Britain and Empire (1707-1918)* (Edinburgh: Edinburgh University Press, 2007), pp. 221-27 (p. 224).
7. Jon P. Klancher, *The Making of English Reading Audiences, 1790-1832* (Madison, WI: University of Wisconsin Press, 1987), p. 50.
8. Peter Garside, 'Publishing', in Bill Bell (ed.), *The Edinburgh History of the Book in Scotland, Volume 3: Ambition and Industry 1800-1880* (Edinburgh: Edinburgh University Press, 2007), pp. 79-122 (p. 85).

1. Gaelic Poets and New Patterns of Patronage

1. See, for instance: Robert A. Dodgshon, *From Chiefs to Landlords: Social and Economic Change in the Western Highlands and Islands, c. 1493-1820* (Edinburgh: Edinburgh University Press, 1998); T. M. Devine, *Clanship to Crofters' War: The Social Transformation of the Highland Region* (Manchester: Manchester University Press, 1994); Allan I. Macinnes, *Clanship, Commerce and the House of Stuart* (East Linton: Tuckwell Press, 1996).
2. See, for instance: Andrew Mackillop, *More Fruitful Than the Soil* (East Linton: Tuckwell Press, 2001); Matthew P. Dziennik, *The Fatal Land: War, Empire, and the Highland Soldier in British America* (New Haven, CT: Yale University Press, 2015).
3. Derick Thomson, *An Introduction to Gaelic Poetry* (London: Victor Gollancz, 1974), p. 157.
4. For more on the panegyric code in Gaelic poetry, see: John Macinnes, 'The Panegyric Code in Gaelic Poetry and its Historical Background', *Transactions of the Gaelic Society of Inverness* 50 (1976-1978), pp. 435-98; *An Lasair: Anthology of 18th Century Scottish Gaelic Verse*, ed. Ronald Black (Edinburgh: Birlinn, 2001).
5. Ronald Black, 'The Gaelic Book', in Stephen Brown and Warren McDougall (eds), *The Edinburgh History of the Book in Scotland, Volume 2: Enlightenment and Expansion 1707-1800* (Edinburgh: Edinburgh University Press, 2012), pp. 177-87; Ronald Black, 'Gaelic Secular Publishing', in *Edinburgh History of the Book in Scotland, Volume 2*, pp. 595-612; Donald E. Meek, 'Gaelic Printing and Publishing',

in Bill Bell (ed.), *The Edinburgh History of the Book in Scotland, Volume 3: Ambition and Industry 1800–1880* (Edinburgh: Edinburgh University Press, 2010), pp. 107–22.

6   For mac Mhaighstir Alasdair's influence, see: Ronald Black, 'Alasdair mac Mhaighstir Alasdair and the New Gaelic Poetry', in Susan Manning (ed.), *The Edinburgh History of Scottish Literature, Volume 2: Enlightenment, Britain and Empire (1707–1918)* (Edinburgh: Edinburgh University Press, 2007), pp. 110–24.

7   Thomson, Introduction, p. 183.

8   Duncan Macintyre, *Òrain Dhonnchaidh Bhàin*, ed. Angus MacLeod (Edinburgh: Scottish Gaelic Texts Society, 1952), p. xv.

9   Donald Meek, 'The Pulpit and the Pen: Clergy, Orality and Print in the Scottish Gaelic World', in Adam Fox and Daniel Woolf (eds), *The Spoken Word: Oral Culture in Britain, 1500–1850* (Manchester: Manchester University Press, 2002), pp. 84–118.

10 Macintyre, *Òrain*, p. xxxi.

11 Ibid.

12 Mac an t-Saoir lost out to Donald Shaw (fl. 1789) in a competition to compose a poem on 'the warlike exploits of the 42nd Regiment', Macintyre, *Òrain*, p. xxxi. For the influence of the Royal Highland Society, see Ronald Black, 'The Gaelic Academy: The Cultural Commitment of the Highland Society of Scotland', *Scottish Gaelic Studies* 14 (1986), pp. 1–38.

13 Black, 'The Gaelic Book', p. 179.

14 Michel Byrne and Sheila M. Kidd, '"Vintners and Criminal Officers": Fo-sgrìobhaichean Leabhraichean Earra-Ghàidhealach san Naoidheamh Linn Deug', in Wilson McLeod et al. (eds), *Bile Ós Chrannaibh: A Festschrift for William Gillies* (Ceann Drochaid: Clann Tuirc, 2010), pp. 29–44.

15 Ibid., p. 30.

16 Black, 'The Gaelic Book', p. 177.

17 Anja Gunderloch, 'Donnchadh Bàn Mac an t-Saoir and his Subscribers', in Michel Byrne and Sheila M. Kidd (eds), *Lìontan Lìonmhor: Local, National and Global Gaelic Networks from the 18th to the 20th Century* (Glasgow: Celtic and Gaelic, University of Glasgow, 2019), pp. 35–84.

18 Ibid., p. 41.

19 112 of the subscribers to this collection have a military rank. For Gaelic poetry and the British military, see Wilson McLeod, 'Gaelic Poetry and the British Military Enterprise, 1756–1945', in Carla Sassi and Theo van Heijnsbergen (eds), *Within and Without Empire: Scotland*

Across the (Post)colonial Borderline (Newcastle: Cambridge Scholars Publishing, 2013), pp. 61–76; Ruairidh Maciver, 'The Gaelic Poet and the British Military Experience, 1756–1856' (unpublished doctoral thesis, University of Glasgow, 2018).

20 Gunderloch, 'Donnchadh Bàn Mac an t-Saoir and his Subscribers', p. 41.
21 Ibid., p. 39.
22 Macintyre, *Òrain*, p. viii.
23 Dùghallach was a tailor and his blindness, according to John Mackenzie, is said to have been caused by an injury he sustained after aiming a barb at a fellow apprentice, who then attacked him with a needle. John Mackenzie (ed.), *Sar-Obair nam Bard Gaelach: or The Beauties of Gaelic Poetry* (Glasgow: Macgregor, Polson & Co., 1841), p. 298.
24 See Brian D. Osborne, *The Last of the Chiefs: Alasdair Ranaldson Macdonell of Glengarry 1773–1828* (Glasgow: Argyll Publishing, 2001).
25 This volume 'soon became exceedingly popular – especially in that part of the country: to say that it possessed merit is saying too little.' John Mackenzie, *Sar-obair*, p. 299.
26 An earlier exception was the Uist poet, Iain mac Fhearchair, hired as a poet to the MacDonalds of Sleat in 1763. See William Matheson (ed.), *Òrain Iain Mhic Fhearchair* (Edinburgh: Scottish Gaelic Texts Society, 1938).
27 Mackenzie, *Sar-Obair*, p. 299.
28 Ibid.
29 Ibid.
30 The Glengarry Highlanders were active at garrisons in Jersey and Guernsey until they were reduced in 1802. Many then emigrated to Canada, where, along with other emigrants, they raised the 'Glengarry Fencibles' during the American War (1812–14). Michael Brander, *The Scottish Highlanders and their Regiments* (East Lothian: The Gleneil Press, 1971), p. 211; Marianne McLean, *The People of Glengarry: Highlanders in Transition, 1745–1820* (Montreal: McGill-Queen's Press, 1991), pp. 131–33; pp. 146–47.
31 Ailean Dùghallach, *Orain, Marbhrannan agus Duanagan, Ghaidhelach* (Inbheirneis: Alastair Mac-an-Toisich, 1829), p. 10.
32 *Tuath is Tighearna: Tenants and Landlords*, ed. Donald E. Meek (Edinburgh: Scottish Gaelic Texts Society, 1995), p. 91.
33 Ronald Black, 'The Poetry of Ailean Dall', in Christopher MacLachlan and Ronald W. Renton (eds), *Gael and Lowlander in Scottish Literature* (Glasgow: Scottish Literature International, 2015), p. 33. John Cameron

was a celebrated military commander. He became Lieutenant Colonel of the Gordon Highlanders and was killed in a skirmish at Quatre Bras, during the Waterloo campaign of June 1815.

34 Mackenzie, *Sar-Obair*, p. 300.
35 Black considers MacLachlainn to have been Dùghallach's '*real* friend and his *real* patron'. Black, 'The Poetry of Ailean Dall', p. 24.
36 Dùghallach, *Orain*, p. iii.
37 MacGilleain trained as a shoemaker in Tiree and Glasgow, and was also a merchant on a small scale in Tiree.
38 Robert D. Dunbar, 'The Secular Poetry of John MacLean, "Bàrd Thighearna Chola", "Am Bàrd MacGilleain"' (unpublished doctoral thesis, University of Edinburgh, 2006), p. 111.
39 *Tiree Bards and their Bàrdachd*, ed. Eric Cregeen and Donald W. Mackenzie (Isle of Coll: Society of West Highland and Island Historical Research, 1978), p. 8.
40 Dunbar, 'The Secular Poetry of John MacLean', pp. 5-6.
41 Ibid., p. 112.
42 Iain MacIlleain, *Orain Nuadh Ghaedhlach* (Duneudainn: R. Meinnearach, 1818), p. 14; Dunbar, 'The Secular Poetry of John MacLean', appendix 1.
43 Dunbar, 'The Secular Poetry of John MacLean', p. 41.
44 A number of individuals, mostly ministers, were engaged in the collection of Gaelic verse in the eighteenth and early nineteenth century. The Skye poet, Dòmhnall MacLeòid/Dòmhnall nan Òran (Donald Macleod/Donald of the Songs, 1787–1873), was also a collector-poet, while the Rev. James McLagan (Seumas MacLagain, 1728–1805), who gathered arguably the most significant collection of Gaelic poetry in the eighteenth century, also composed verse.
45 MacIlleain, p. 84.
46 Dunbar, 'The Secular Poetry of John MacLean', appendix 1.
47 Ibid., p. 44.
48 Dunbar, 'Am Bàrd MacGilleain', in Kenneth E. Nilsen (ed.), *Rannsachadh na Gàidhlig 5* (Sydney, NS: Cape Breton University Press, 2010), pp. 42–66 (p. 56).

2. Inspiring Songs: The Rise of Ballad Culture

1 Allan Ramsay, *The Ever Green* (Edinburgh: Thomas Ruddiman, 1724), pp. vii–viii.
2 Walter Scott, *Minstrelsy of the Scottish Border*, 2nd edition, 3 vols (Edinburgh: Longman and Rees, 1803), I, pp. cxvi–cxvii.

3   William Donaldson, 'Herd, David (bap. 1732, d. 1810)', *Oxford Dictionary of National Biography.*
4   David Buchan, *The Ballad and The Folk* (London: Routledge and Kegan Paul, 1972), p. 6.
5   See Walter Scott, *Minstrelsy of the Scottish Border*, 3rd edition, 3 vols (Edinburgh: Longman, Hurst, Rees and Orme, 1806), I, especially pp. i, xlxv–xlxvii, cxvii–cxviii, cxxii.
6   See, for instance, Valentina Bold, '"An Irish Boy he may well be but he spak braid Scots when he coortit me": Song Connections between Ireland and South West Scotland', *Traditiones* 38.1 (2009), pp. 131–40; Valentina Bold, 'The David Murray Collection: From Scrapbook to Website', *Scottish Studies Review* 5.1 (Spring 2004), pp. 33–39.
7   I am grateful to Ted Cowan for helping me to come to this conclusion.
8   Valentina Bold, 'Collection as Colonization', in Thomas A. McKean (ed.), *The Flowering Thorn: International Ballad Studies* (Logan, UT: Utah State University Press, 2003), pp. 353–62.
9   See Valentina Bold, '"Nouther right spelled nor right setten down": Scott, Child and the Hogg Family Ballads', in Edward J. Cowan (ed.), *The Ballad in Scottish History* (East Linton: Tuckwell Press, 2000), pp. 116–41.
10 Ibid., p. 52.
11 David Atkinson, *The Anglo-Scottish Ballad and its Imaginary Contexts* (Cambridge: Open Book Publishing, 2014), p. 16.
12 Ibid., p. 17.
13 Ibid., p. 19.
14 See William Montgomerie, 'A Bibliography of the Scottish Ballad Manuscripts 1730–1825: Part V', *Studies in Scottish Literature* 6.2 (2013), pp. 91–104 (p. 92).
15 The manuscript of 'A Collection of Old Songs Written from the Memory of Mrs Creighton By her Daughter Agnes Thorburn Creighton January 31st 1818' is held in the Ewart Library, Dumfries.
16 Charles Kirkpatrick Sharpe (ed.), *A Ballad Book* 1823, reprinted ed. David Laing (Edinburgh: Blackwood, 1880), pp. v–vi.
17 Ibid., pp. 1–9, 12–16, 37–38, 45–54, 71–80.
18 *Letters From and To Charles Kirkpatrick Sharpe Esq.*, ed. Alexander Allardyce, 2 vols (Edinburgh: Blackwood, 1888), II, p. 326; Sharpe 1880, p. 156. There is also a version of 'Captain Glen' in the National Library of Scotland: L.C.Fol.70 (46a).

19 John Leyden, 'The Mermaid', *Minstrelsy*, III, pp. 297–320, including notes; see Allan Cunningham, 'Biographical and Critical History of the Literature of the Last Fifty Years', *The Athenaeum* 33 (26 October 1833), p. 769; John Leyden, 'The Cout of Keeldar', *Minstrelsy*, III, pp. 389–408.
20 See, for instance, the discussion of the characteristics of ballad in M. J. C. Hodgart's classic study, *The Ballads* (London: Hutchison, 1950).
21 'Lord William', *Minstrelsy*, III, pp. 264–68.
22 'Proud Lady Margaret', *Minstrelsy*, III, pp. 275–79.
23 'The Water Kelpie', *Minstrelsy*, III, pp. 355–66.

3. The Novel: Romance and History

1 This oversimplifies a complex historical theory. For how 'four-stage' theories fit within the larger discourse of conjectural history, see Mark Salber Phillips, *Society and Sentiment: Genres of Historical Writing in Britain 1740–1820* (Princeton, NJ: Princeton University Press, 2000), pp. 171–96.
2 Jane Porter, *Thaddeus of Warsaw*, 3rd ed., 4 vols (London: Longman, Hurst, Rees, and Orme, 1805), I, p. 2.
3 Porter, *Thaddeus* I, p. 80.
4 Sir Walter Scott, *The Pirate* in *The Waverley Novels*, vols 24–25 (Edinburgh: Cadell, 1831), XXIV, p. viii.
5 Review of *The Pirate*, *Quarterly Review* 26 (January 1822), pp. 454–74 (p. 456).
6 James Hogg, 'The Surpassing Adventures of Allan Gordon', in Gillian Hughes (ed.), *Altrive Chapbooks* 2.1 (1987), pp. 1–57 (p. 3).
7 Ann Rigney, *Imperfect Histories: The Elusive Past and the Legacy of Romantic Historicism* (Ithaca, NY: Cornell University Press, 2001), p. 28.
8 John Galt, *Bogle Corbet; or, The Emigrants*, 3 vols (London: Henry Colburn and Richard Bentley, 1831), III, p. 282.
9 Galt, *Bogle Corbet*, I, pp. iii–iv.

4. Slavery, Kinship, and Capital

1 Kirsten E. Wood, 'Gender and Slavery', in Mark M. Smith and Robert L. Paquette (eds), *The Oxford Handbook of Slavery in the Americas* (Oxford: Oxford University Press, 2012), pp. 513–34.
2 Jennifer L. Morgan, *Reckoning With Slavery: Gender, Kinship, and Capitalism in the Early Black Atlantic* (Durham, NC: Duke University Press, 2021), p. 4.
3 Ibid., p. 5.

4 Douglas Hamilton, *Scotland, the Caribbean and the Atlantic World 1750–1820* (Manchester: Manchester University Press, 2005); T. M. Devine, *Scotland's Empire 1600–1815* (London: Allen Lane, 2003).
5 Morgan, p. 6.
6 Caroline McCracken-Flesher, 'Mary Prince "At Home" in Blackwood's: Maga's Origins and the End of Slavery', in Nicholas Mason and Tom Mole (eds), *Romantic Periodicals in the Twenty-First Century: Eleven Case Studies from Blackwood's Edinburgh Magazine* (Edinburgh: Edinburgh University Press, 2020), pp. 183–206.
7 Robert Wedderburn, *The Horrors of Slavery and other writings by Robert Wedderburn*, ed. Iain McCalman (Princeton: Markus Wiener, 1991), p. 18.
8 Robert Wedderburn, *The Horrors of Slavery; exemplified in the Life and History of the Rev. Robert Wedderburn V.D.M Son of the late James Wedderburn Esq, of Inveresk, Slave-Dealer, by one of his Slaves in the island of Jamaica* (London: R. Wedderburn, 1824), pp. 5–6. The original is available at www.archive.org/details/horrors_of_slavery/mode/2up. References are to this edition.
9 Geoff Palmer, *The Enlightenment Abolished: Citizens of Britishness* (Penicuik: Henry Publishing, 2007), pp. 39–40.
10 Wedderburn, *The Horrors of Slavery*, p. 15.
11 Ibid., p. 21.
12 Ibid., p. 23.
13 Ibid., p. 6.
14 Ibid., p. 7.
15 Ibid., p. 18.
16 Ibid., p. 22.
17 Elizabeth A. Bohls, *Romantic Literature and Postcolonial Studies* (Edinburgh: Edinburgh University Press, 2013), p. 77.
18 Wedderburn, *The Horrors of Slavery*, p. 24.
19 Anon., *Marly; or A Planter's Life in Jamaica* (Glasgow: Richard Griffin, 1828), 2nd edition, ed. Karina Williamson (London: Macmillan Caribbean Classics, 2005), p. xiv.
20 Ibid., p. 17.
21 Ibid.
22 Ibid., p. 19.
23 Ibid.
24 Ibid., p. 29.
25 Ibid., p. 7.
26 Ibid., p. 318.

27 Ibid., p. 43.
28 Ibid., p. 43.
29 Ibid., p. 50.
30 Ibid., p. 157.
31 Ibid., p. 185.
32 *The History of Mary Prince*, ed. Sara Salih (London: Penguin Classics, 2004), p. 21.
33 Ibid., p. 8.
34 Ibid.
35 Ibid., p. 9.
36 Ibid., p. 10.
37 For an excellent discussion, see Juliet Shields, *Mary Prince, Slavery, and Print Culture in the Anglophone Atlantic World* (Cambridge: Cambridge University Press, 2021).
38 Thomas Pringle's Supplement, in *History of Mary Prince*, p. 57.
39 Paul Henderson Scott, 'John Galt', in H. C. G. Matthew and Brian Harrison (eds), *Oxford Dictionary of National Biography* (Oxford: Oxford University Press, 2004).
40 Galt's three 'Letters on West Indian Slavery' are reproduced in *Fraser's Magazine for Town and Country* 2 (August 1830–January 1831). Letter 1, pp. 440–49; Letter 2, pp. 556–71 (p. 563); Letter 3, pp. 706–13; Letter 2, p. 571.
41 Letter 3, p. 708.
42 Letter 3, p. 707.
43 Letter 1, p. 442 and Letter 2, p. 556.
44 John Galt, *Bogle Corbet or the Emigrants*, 3 vols (London: Henry Colburn and Richard Bentley, 1831), I, p. 217.
45 Kenneth McNeil, *Scottish Romanticism and Collective Memory in the British Atlantic* (Edinburgh: Edinburgh University Press, 2020), pp. 269–333.
46 McNeil, p. 301.
47 Galt, *Bogle Corbet*, I, pp. 3–4.
48 Kimberly Wallace-Sanders, *Mammy: a Century of Race, Gender, and Southern Memory* (Ann Arbor, MI: University of Michigan Press, 2008), p. 13.
49 Galt, *Bogle Corbet*, I, p. 4.
50 Ibid., p. 295.
51 Galt, Letter 1, p. 442.
52 Galt, *Bogle Corbet*, I, p. 73.
53 Galt, Letter 1, p. 444.

54 Galt, *Bogle Corbet*, I, p. 281.
55 Letter to Birmingham Ladies' Society for Relief of Negro Slaves by Margaret Pringle, supplement to *History of Mary Prince*, p. 64. Mary revealed her scars by way of bearing witness to Margaret Pringle, Susanna Strickland, Susan Brown, and Martha A. Brown.
56 Galt, *Bogle Corbet*, II, p. 20.
57 Galt, *Bogle Corbet*, I, p. 299.
58 *Memoirs and anecdotes of Philip Thicknesse, late Lieutenant Governor of Land Guard Fort, and unfortunately father to George Touchet, Baron Audley* (Dublin: William Jones, 1790), p. 74.
59 Galt, *Bogle Corbet*, I, p. 298.
60 Ibid.
61 Ibid., p. 300.
62 Ibid., pp. 292, 298.
63 Ibid., p. 299.
64 Galt, Letter 2, p. 564.
65 *Bogle Corbet*, II, pp. 19, 21. See chapter on 'Negro Children', pp. 17–23.

5. Private Thoughts and Public Display: Gender, Genre, and Lives

1 'Life-writing' in this chapter includes autobiography, memoirs, journals, and letters, along with fiction and poetry where those forms are the main narrative vehicle.
2 William St Clair, *The Reading Nation in the Romantic Period* (Cambridge: Cambridge University Press, 2004). Scott's novels were published anonymously until he admitted authorship in 1826. However, he was widely understood to be the 'Author of *Waverley*' long before then and had become a household name because of his long narrative poems and ballad collection *Minstrelsy of the Scottish Border*.
3 Walter Scott, *The Journal of Walter Scott*, ed. and intro. W. E. K. Anderson (Oxford: Oxford University Press, 1972), p. 132.
4 Ibid., p. 141.
5 Ibid., pp. 80–81.
6 Ibid., pp. 166–67.
7 Ibid., p. 166.
8 Ibid., p. 174.
9 See Doris Langley Moore, *The Late Lord Byron: Posthumous Dramas* (London: John Murray, 1961), pp. 46–47.
10 George Gordon Byron, *Byron's Letters and Journals: a New Selection*, ed. Richard Lansdowne (Oxford: Oxford University Press, 2015), p. xi. For Byron and poetic form, see Susan Wolfson, *Formal Charges*:

The Shaping of Poetry in British Romanticism (Stanford: Stanford University Press, 1997), pp. 133–63; Matthew Bevis, 'Byron's Feet', in Jason Hall (ed.), *Meter Matters: Verse Cultures of The Long Nineteenth Century* (Athens, OH: Ohio University Press, 2011), pp. 78–104.

11 For Scott's and Byron's interconnectedness, see Susan Oliver, *Scott, Byron and the Poetics of Cultural Encounter* (Basingstoke: Palgrave Macmillan, 2005), and 'Crossing "Dark Barriers": Intertextuality and Dialogue between Lord Byron and Sir Walter Scott', *Studies in Romanticism* 47.1 (2008), pp. 15–35.

12 George Gordon Byron, *Letters and Journals*, ed. Leslie A. Marchand, 11 vols (London: John Murray, 1973–1981; 1978), VIII, p. 13.

13 Ibid., p. 23.

14 Susan Edmonstone Ferrier, *Memoir and Correspondence of Susan Ferrier, 1782–1854*, ed. J. A. Doyle (London: John Murray, 1898), p. 131.

15 Ferrier, *Memoir and Correspondence*, p. 178.

16 Scott, *Journal*, p. 734.

17 Ferrier, *Marriage, a Novel* (Edinburgh: William Blackwood, 1818), p. 242. Ferrier was first named as author in Richard Bentley's *Standard Novels* edition, 1841.

18 Ibid., p. 192.

19 Ibid., p. 189.

20 Lisa Wood, *Modes of Discipline: Women, Conservatism, and the Novel after the French Revolution* (Lewisburg, PA: Bucknell University Press, 2003), p. 28.

21 For Ferrier and Scott, see Caroline McCracken-Flesher, 'Where We Never Were: Women at Walter Scott's Abbotsford', in Caroline McCracken-Flesher and Matthew Wickman (eds), *Walter Scott at 250: Looking Forward* (Edinburgh: Edinburgh University Press, 2021), pp. 142–60; and 'Six Degrees from Walter Scott: Separation, Connection and the Abbotsford Visitor Books', *The Yearbook of English Studies* 47 (2017), pp. 19–35 (p. 28). For Ferrier, Brunton and Scott, see Andrew Monnickendam, *The Novels of Walter Scott and his Literary Relations: Mary Brunton, Susan Ferrier and Christian Johnstone* (New York, NY: Palgrave Macmillan, 2013).

22 Walter Scott, *The Letters of Sir Walter Scott*, ed. H. J. C. Grierson, 12 vols (London: Constable, 1932–37), III, p. 2.

23 Mary Brunton, *Emmeline, with Some Other Pieces*, ed. Caroline Franklin (London: Routledge Thoemmes, 1992), p. lxxii.

24 Ibid., pp. 106–07.

25 Elizabeth Grant, *Memoirs of a Highland Lady, 1797–1827*, ed. Angus Davidson (London: John Murray, 1950), p. 2.
26 Ibid., p. 16. 'Duchus' and its definition as 'domain' are included in all editions. For a fuller explanation of the Gaelic word, see John MacInnes, 'The panegyric code in Gaelic poetry and its historical background,' *Transactions of the Gaelic Society of Inverness* 50 (1976–1978), pp. 435–98 (p. 452).
27 Ibid., pp. 2–4.
28 Ibid., p. 15.
29 See Susan Oliver, *Walter Scott and the Greening of Scotland: Emergent Ecologies of a Nation* (Cambridge: Cambridge University Press, 2021).
30 Grant, *Memoirs*, p. 143.

6. The Gothic, Supernatural and Religious

1 Ian Duncan, 'Walter Scott, James Hogg and Scottish Gothic', in David Punter (ed.), *A Companion to the Gothic* (Oxford: Blackwell, 2000), pp. 70–80 (p. 73). On the phenomenon more broadly, see Carol Margaret Davison and Monica Germanà (eds), *Scottish Gothic: An Edinburgh Companion* (Edinburgh: Edinburgh University Press, 2017). Duncan's *Modern Romance and Transformations of the Novel: The Gothic, Scott, Dickens* (Cambridge: Cambridge University Press, 1992) remains fundamental.
2 A useful history covering the present period of concern is Andrew L. Drummond and James Bulloch, *The Scottish Church 1688–1843: The Age of the Moderates* (Edinburgh: Saint Andrew Press, 1973).
3 For an intriguing overview of how religion figures in Scottish literature of this era, see Crawford Gribben, 'Religion and Scottish Romanticism', in Murray Pittock (ed.), *The Edinburgh Companion to Scottish Romanticism* (Edinburgh: Edinburgh University Press, 2011), pp. 112–23. In such studies as *Evangelical Millennialism in the Trans-Atlantic World, 1500–2000* (New York, NY: Palgrave, 2011), meanwhile, Gribben explores the global situation of Scottish Protestantism and related religious traditions.
4 On the Romantic-period beginnings of cultic modernism, see Robert Crawford, *The Modern Poet: Poetry, Academia, and Knowledge since 1750* (Oxford: Oxford University Press, 2001).
5 'The Ayrshire Legatees, Or the Correspondence of the Pringle Family', *Blackwood's Edinburgh Magazine* 7.39 (June 1820), pp. 262–71 (p. 262).
6 Perhaps uncoincidentally, the surname is also that of *Blackwood's* founding editor Thomas Pringle.

7   John Galt, *Annals of the Parish, The Ayrshire Legatees, and The Provost* (Edinburgh: Saltire Society, 2002), pp. 193–94.
8   Walter Scott, *Waverley*, ed. P. D. Garside (Edinburgh: Edinburgh University Press, 2007), p. 19.
9   Ibid., p. 345.
10 E. M. Forster, *Aspects of the Novel* (New York, NY: Harcourt, Brace & World, 1954 (1927)), p. 36.
11 William Hazlitt, *The Spirit of the Age: Or Contemporary Portraits* (London: Henry Colburn, 1825), p. 136.
12 See also Fiona Robertson, *Legitimate Histories: Scott, Gothic, and the Authorities of Fiction* (Oxford: Clarendon Press, 1994), pp. 203–05.
13 Walter Scott, *The Black Dwarf*, ed. P. D. Garside (Edinburgh: Edinburgh University Press, 1993), p. 1.
14 Ibid., p. 6.
15 Ibid., p. 9.
16 Fiona Robertson, 'Gothic Scott', in Carol Margaret Davison and Monica Germanà (eds), *Scottish Gothic*, pp. 102–14 (p. 108).
17 Scott, *The Black Dwarf*, p. 8.
18 Duncan, 'Walter Scott, James Hogg, and Scottish Gothic', p. 76.
19 Ian Duncan, *Scott's Shadow: The Novel in Romantic Edinburgh* (Princeton, NJ: Princeton University Press, 2007), p. 249.
20 Ian Duncan, 'Altered States: Galt, Serial Fiction, and the Romantic Miscellany', in Regina Hewitt (ed.), *John Galt: Observations and Conjectures on Literature, History, and Society* (Lewisburg, PA: Bucknell University Press, 2012), pp. 53–72 (p. 56).
21 Crawford Gribben, 'James Hogg, Scottish Calvinism and Literary Theory', *Scottish Studies Review* 5.2 (2004), pp. 9–26 (p. 21).
22 Joseph Conrad, 'The Heart of Darkness', *Blackwood's Edinburgh Magazine* 165.1000 (February 1899), pp. 165–460; continued in nos 1001 (March 1899), pp. 461–620; and 1002 (April 1899), pp. 621–780. For an argument placing Conrad's opus in *Blackwood's* imperialist tradition, see William Atkinson, '"Bound in "Blackwood's": The Imperialism of "The Heart of Darkness" in Its Immediate Context', *Twentieth Century Literature* 50.4 (2004), pp. 368–93.

7. Drama and Adaptation

1   See Barbara Bell, 'The Scottish theatrical landscape leading into the emergence of the National Drama', *International Journal of Scottish Theatre and Screen* 8.1 (2015), pp. 27–53.
2   See Barbara Bell, 'Nineteenth-Century Stage Adaptations of the Works

of Sir Walter Scott on the Scottish Stage: 1810–1900' (unpublished doctoral thesis, University of Glasgow, 1991).
3   See *The Monthly Mirror* and *The Courant* quoted in James C. Dibdin, *The Annals of the Edinburgh Stage with an Account of the Rise and Progress of Dramatic Writing in Scotland* (Edinburgh: R. Cameron, 1888), p. 259.
4   See Bell, 'The Scottish theatrical landscape', pp. 19–21.
5   Walter Scott to Joanna Baillie, '15 August 1809', *Letters of Sir Walter Scott*, 12 vols (London: Constable, 1932–37), II, p. 218.
6   Joanna Baillie, 'The Family Legend', Abbotsford MS, 1810, v.1.18.
7   Henry Siddons, letter to Walter Scott, says he is returning the MS with 'some few curtailments and very slight alterations'. Royal College of Surgeons MS HB.IX.52, quoted in Judith Bailey Slagle, *Joanna Baillie, a Literary Life* (Madison, NJ: Fairleigh Dickinson University Press, 2002), p. 130.
8   See Baillie, 'The Family Legend', the end of Act III, Scene 3 (MS, p. 70) where Siddons cuts the last ten lines describing something that the audience will have seen.
9   Ibid., p. 71.
10 Ibid., p, 8.
11 See for example, Scott, '27 October 1809', *Letters*, II, p. 257.
12 Scott, '30 January 1810', *Letters*, II, p. 291.
13 See *Caledonian Mercury*, 3 February 1810, p. 3, col. 4.
14 Scott, p.s. to '27 October 1809', *Letters*, II, p. 260.
15 Scott, '31 January 1810', *Letters*, II, p. 293.
16 Scott, '6 February 1810', *Letters*, II, p. 296.
17 Scott, '22 January 1810', *Letters*, II, p. 288.
18 Scott, '30 January 1810', *Letters*, II, p. 291.
19 Scott, '31 January 1810', *Letters*, II, p. 294.
20 Scott, '6 February 1910', *Letters*, II, p. 295.
21 Henry Siddons had translated/adapted a treatise on physicality in performance, published as *Illustrations of Gesture and Action* (London: Richard Phillips, 1807), and Scott deplored his mannered style of movement – see letter to Joanna Baillie, '15 August 1809', *Letters*, II, p. 220.
22 Joanna Baillie, *The Family Legend*, 2nd edn (Edinburgh: James Ballantyne for John Ballantyne, 1810).
23 Barbara Bell, '"… arranged in a fanciful manner and in an ancient style": The First Scenic Realisations of Scott's Work and the Desire for a New "Realism" on Scottish Stages', *Studies in Scottish Literature* 44.2 (2019), pp. 23–38.

24 See MS, pp. 25, 37.
25 See *Sir Walter's Post-Bag*, ed. Wilfred Partington (London: John Murray, 1932), p. 50, December 1809.
26 Folger Shakespeare Library, Henderson Scottish Collection, playbill no. Sc3:56.
27 See *The Scots Magazine* 72 (1810), p. 116; *Glasgow Herald*, 2 February 1810, p. 4, cols. 3–4.
28 Edmund John Eyre, *The Lady of the Lake: a Melo-dramatic Romance, in Three Acts* (New York, NY: D. Longworth, 1811).
29 'Didascalia – The Lady of the Lake at London and Edinburgh', *The Literary Panorama and Annual Register* (London: C. Taylor, 1811), pp. 307–08, says that 'this piece has at least the merit of not wandering from its model'.
30 See Bell, '"… arranged in a fanciful manner"', pp. 37–38.
31 The Theatres Royal were slow to take up the new *Waverley* dramas when they were introduced by the Minor houses and more likely to describe adaptations as 'melo-dramatic'.
32 See Folger Shakespeare Library, Henderson Waverley playbills no. W15:9.
33 Isabella Alexander, '"Neither Bolt nor Chain, Iron Safe nor Private Watchman, Can Prevent the Theft of Words": The Birth of the Performing Right in Britain', in Ronan Deazley, Martin Kretschmer, and Lionel Bently (eds), *Privilege and Property: Essays on the History of Copyright* (Cambridge: Open Book Publishers, 2010), pp. 321–46.
34 Scott wrote to Baillie that there would be 'pirated copies to a certainty if we do not print soon': '20 February 1810', *Letters*, II, p. 303. The introduction to the printed edition is bound into the front of the manuscript, dated 'Hampstead/March 19th 1810'.
35 See letters to/from Joanna Baillie and Henry Siddons, 6 and 16 February 1815, Claremont College Digital Library, Philbrick Library Collection of Theater Letters, www.ccdl.claremont.edu/digital/collection/phl/id/1419/rec/3.

8. The Short Story to 1832

1 James Hogg, *The Collected Letters of James Hogg, Volume 1: 1800–1819*, ed. Gillian Hughes et al. (Edinburgh: Edinburgh University Press, 2004), p. 145.
2 Ibid.
3 Hogg's brother, William, describes their mother's storytelling and singing to them as young boys and concludes, 'These songs and tales,

which were sung & told in a melancholy, plaintive air, had an influence on James's mind altogether unperceived at the time, and perhaps undescribable even now' (James Hogg Collection, Beinecke Rare Book and Manuscript Library. GEN MSS 61, Box 1, Folder 19).

4 James Hogg, *The Spy: A Periodical Paper of Amusement and Instruction*, ed. Gillian Hughes (Edinburgh: Edinburgh University Press, 2000), p. xli. *The Spy* was published in fifty-two weekly numbers from 1 September 1810 until 24 August 1811. The paper was a miscellany of essays, poetry, and stories by various writers, but Hogg himself was the author of most of the paper's contributions.

5 *Collected Letters of Hogg Volume 1*, p. 136.

6 James Hogg to Bernard Barton, *Collected Letters of Hogg Volume 1*, p. 151.

7 Ibid., p. 136.

8 Ibid., p. 151.

9 Robert Crawford, 'Bad Shepherd', *London Review of Books* 23 (5 April 2001), pp. 28–29 (p. 29).

10 For discussion of the influence of *Blackwood's* on the growth of the magazine press, see Tim Killick, *British Short Fiction in the Early Nineteenth Century: The Rise of the Tale* (Aldershot: Ashgate, 2008).

11 *Tales of Terror from Blackwood's Magazine*, ed. Robert Morrison and Chris Baldick (Oxford: Oxford University Press, 1995), p. xviii.

12 Ibid., p. xiii.

13 John Galt, *Selected Short Stories*, ed. Ian A. Gordon (Edinburgh: Scottish Academic Press, 1978), p. vii. For a more detailed assessment of *The Steam-Boat* and Galt's stories, see Caroline McCracken-Flesher, 'The Sense of No Ending: John Galt and the Travels of Commoners and Kings in "The Steam-Boat" and "The Gathering of the West"', in Regina Hewitt (ed.), *John Galt: Observations and Conjectures on Literature, History, and Society* (Lewisburg, PA: Bucknell University Press, 2012), pp. 73–92.

14 Galt, *Selected Stories*, p. vii.

15 *Tales of Terror*, p. xviii.

16 Hogg, *The Spy*, p. xli.

17 Ibid.

18 James Hogg, *Contributions to Blackwood's Edinburgh Magazine Volume 2, 1829–1835*, ed. Thomas C. Richardson (Edinburgh: Edinburgh University Press, 2012), p. 5.

19 Ibid., p. 4.

20 Ibid., p. 13.
21 Ibid., p. 23.
22 James Hogg, *Contributions to Blackwood's Edinburgh Magazine Volume 1, 1817–1828*, ed. Thomas C. Richardson (Edinburgh: Edinburgh University Press, 2008), p. 263.
23 Ibid., p. 139.
24 Ibid., p. 143.
25 *Blackwood's Edinburgh Magazine* 21 (May 1827), pp. 549–62 (pp. 549–50). See also James Hogg, *The Shepherd's Calendar*, ed. Douglas S. Mack (Edinburgh: Edinburgh University Press, 1995), pp. 118–19.
26 Hogg, *Contributions to Blackwood's Volume 2*, pp. 112–21.
27 Ibid., p. 155.
28 'The Hunt of Eildon', *The Brownie of Bodsbeck; and Other Tales*, 2 vols (Edinburgh: William Blackwood, 1818), II, pp. 229–346.
29 Hogg, *Contributions to Blackwood's Volume 1*, p. 30.
30 Hogg, *Contributions to Blackwood's Volume 2*, p. 79.
31 Hogg, *Contributions to Blackwood's Volume 1*, p. 29.
32 See Ian Duncan, 'Introduction', James Hogg, *Winter Evening Tales, Collected Among the Cottagers in the South of Scotland*, ed. Ian Duncan (Edinburgh: Edinburgh University Press, 2002), pp. xi–xli.

PART 2: CONSOLIDATIONS

1 Walter Scott, *The Betrothed*, 1825, ed. J. B. Ellis et al. (Edinburgh: Edinburgh University Press, 2009), p. 5.
2 *Cuairtear nan Gleann* 12 (February 1841), p. 284.
3 Charles Lyell, *Principles of Geology*, 3 vols (London: John Murray, 1830–1833).
4 [Robert Chambers], *Vestiges of the Natural History of Creation* (London: John Churchill, 1844).
5 Mrs [Margaret] Oliphant, *Annals of a Publishing House: William Blackwood and his Sons, their Magazine and Friends*, 2 vols (Edinburgh: William Blackwood, 1897).
6 J. G. Lockhart, *Memoirs of the Life of Sir Walter Scott, Bart.*, 7 vols (Edinburgh: Cadell, 1837–1838).
7 Thomas Carlyle, Review, 'Memoirs of the Life of Sir Walter Scott, Baronet. Vols. I–VI. Cadell. Edinburgh, 1837', *London and Westminster Review* 6/28.2 (1838), pp. 293–345.
8 Thomas Carlyle, *Past and Present* (London: Chapman and Hall, 1843), p. 244.

9. Diaries and Letters

1. Ian Duncan, *Modern Romance and Transformations of the Novel: The Gothic, Scott, Dickens* (Cambridge: Cambridge University Press, 1992), pp. 180–85; *Scott's Shadow: The Novel in Romantic Edinburgh* (Princeton, NJ: Princeton University Press, 2007), p. 275.
2. Ann Rigney, *The Afterlives of Walter Scott: Memory on the Move* (Oxford: Oxford University Press, 2012), p. 163.
3. John Gibson Lockhart, *Memoirs of the Life of Sir Walter Scott, Bart.*, 7 vols (Edinburgh: Robert Cadell, 1837–38), see V, p. 178. Subsequent references to this edition.
4. Lockhart, VII, p. 398.
5. Thomas Carlyle, 'Sir Walter Scott', in *Critical and Miscellaneous Essays*, 5 vols (London: Chapman and Hall, 1899), IV, pp. 22–87 (p. 29); Hesketh Pearson, *Walter Scott: His Life and Personality* (London: Methuen, 1954), p. 285.
6. Francis Russell Hart, *Lockhart as Romantic Biographer* (Edinburgh: Edinburgh University Press, 1971), pp. 164–252.
7. See Davidson Cook, 'Lockhart's Treatment of Scott's Letters', *The Nineteenth Century* 102 (1927), pp. 382–98; H. J. C. Grierson, *Lang, Lockhart, and Biography* (London: Oxford University Press, 1934); Ian Jack, 'Two Biographers: Lockhart and Boswell', in M. M. Lascelles (ed.), *Johnson, Boswell, and Their Circle* (Oxford: Clarendon Press, 1965), pp. 268–85.
8. See Hart, p. 210, and Gerald P. Mulderig, 'Writer, Reader, and Rhetoric in John Gibson Lockhart's *Memoirs of Sir Walter Scott, Bart.*', *Studies in Scottish Literature* 38.1 (2012), pp. 119–38 (p. 137).
9. Hart, p. 188.
10. Mulderig, pp. 121–25.
11. Duncan, *Modern Romance*, pp. 186–87.
12. Gerard Carruthers, 'Remaking Romantic Scotland: Lockhart's Biographies of Burns and Scott', in Arthur Bradley and Alan Rawes (eds), *Romantic Biography* (Aldershot: Ashgate, 2003), pp. 93–108 (esp. pp. 106–07).
13. Duncan, *Scott's Shadow*, p. 153.
14. Henry Cockburn, *Memorials of his Time* (Edinburgh: Adam and Charles Black, 1856), p. 181; also Cockburn's *Life of Lord Jeffrey* (1852) and *Journal* (posthumous, 1874).
15. Karl Miller, *Cockburn's Millennium* (London: Duckworth, 1975), p. 306.
16. Cockburn, *Memorials*, p. [iii].

17 Ibid., p. 80.
18 Ibid., p. 28.
19 Mark Salber Phillips, *Society and Sentiment: Genres of Historical Writing in Britain, 1740–1820* (Princeton, NJ: Princeton University Press, 2000), pp. 309–20.
20 *Journal of Henry Cockburn: Being a Continuation of the Memorials of his Time, 1831–1854*, 2 vols (Edinburgh: Edmonston and Douglas, 1874), II, p. 198.
21 Cockburn, *Memorials*, p. 174.
22 Ibid., pp. 291, 427.
23 Ibid., p. 42.
24 Julian North, 'Portraying Presence: Thomas Carlyle, Portraiture, and Biography', *Victorian Literature and Culture* 43 (2015), pp. 465–88.
25 Thomas Carlyle, *Reminiscences*, 1881, ed. Ian Campbell and K. J. Fielding (1997; Glasgow: Kennedy & Boyd, 2009), p. 3.
26 Ibid., p. 216.
27 Ibid., p. 385.
28 Ibid., p. 365.
29 Ian Campbell, '"More about myself than him": Carlyle's *Reminiscences*', *Carlyle Studies Annual* 18 (1998), pp. 175–83 (esp. pp. 181–82); '"True to the life": Thomas Carlyle's *Reminiscences*', *Carlyle Studies Annual* 25 (2009), pp. 83–100 (esp. p. 95); 'Introduction' to Carlyle, *Reminiscences*, eds. Campbell and Fielding, pp. xi–xxii (esp. p. xv).
30 Edwin Morgan, *Crossing the Border: Essays on Scottish Literature* (Manchester: Carcanet, 1990), p. 133.
31 Norma Clarke, *Ambitious Heights: Writing, Friendship, Love: The Jewsbury Sisters, Felicia Hemans and Jane Carlyle* (London: Routledge, 1990), p. 144; 'Jane Welsh Carlyle: Letters, the Self, and the Literary', *Carlyle Studies Annual* 16 (1996), pp. 7–14 (p. 7). On silence, see Andrew Rennick, 'Silence and Masculinity in Carlyle's *Reminiscences*', *Nineteenth Century Prose* 26.2 (1999), pp. 53–62.
32 Campbell, '"True to the Life"', pp. 88–89.
33 Albert J. LaValley, *Carlyle and the Idea of the Modern: Studies in Carlyle's Prophetic Literature and its Relation to Blake, Nietzsche, Marx, and Others* (New Haven, CT: Yale University Press, 1968), p. 332; Campbell, '"True to the Life"', p. 93; Rennick, p. 55. Also David Amigoni, 'Displacing the Autobiographical Impulse: A Bakhtinian Reading of Thomas Carlyle's *Reminiscences*', in Philip Shaw and Vincent Newey (eds), *Mortal Pages, Literary Lives: Studies in Nineteenth-Century Autobiography* (Aldershot: Scolar Press, 1996), pp. 120–39.

34 Chene Heady, 'Carlyle "versus *the Devil and All Men*": The Ironic Rhetorical Success of Carlyle's *Reminiscences*', *Carlyle Studies Annual* 28 (2012), pp. 107–20.
35 Aileen Christianson, 'Rewriting Herself: Jane Welsh Carlyle's Letters', *Scotlands* 2 (1994), pp. 47–52; 'Constructing Reality: Jane Welsh Carlyle's Epistolary Narratives', *Carlyle Studies* 16 (1996), pp. 15–24; 'Jane Welsh Carlyle's Private Writing Career', in Douglas Gifford and Dorothy McMillan (eds), *A History of Scottish Women's Writing* (Edinburgh: Edinburgh University Press, 1997), pp. 232–45; 'Jane Welsh Carlyle: Imaginary Letters and Ghost Publications', *Women's Writing* 10 (2003), pp. 469–83. Also Norma Clarke, *Ambitious Heights*; 'Jane Welsh Carlyle: Letters, the Self, and the Literary', *Carlyle Studies* 16 (1996), pp. 7–14. Overview in Abigail Burnham Bloom, 'Jane Welsh Carlyle: A Review of Recent Research, 2004–2013', *Carlyle Studies Annual* 30 (2014), pp. 133–46. J. A. Froude's *Letters and Memorials* featured annotations from Carlyle.
36 Letter to Mrs Aitken, Dumfries, April 1850, in *Letters and Memorials of Jane Welsh Carlyle*, ed. James Anthony Froude, 3 vols (London: Longmans, Green, 1883), II, p. 105.
37 Clarke, 'Jane Welsh Carlyle', p. 13; Christianson, 'Jane Welsh Carlyle's Private Writing Career', p. 236.
38 See *I Too Am Here: Selections from the Letters of Jane Welsh Carlyle*, ed. Alan Simpson and Mary McQueen Simpson (Cambridge: Cambridge University Press, 1977), where the contrast between bleak and comic selections seems particularly stark, and *Newly Selected Letters*, ed. Kenneth J. Fielding and David R. Sorensen (Aldershot: Ashgate, 2004).
39 Clarke, *Ambitious Heights*, p. 39.
40 Letter to Jeannie Welsh, 19 May 1846, in *I Too Am Here*, pp. 72–73.
41 Clarke, 'Jane Welsh Carlyle', p. 8, suggests Welsh Carlyle envisaged her letters being published posthumously.
42 See Christianson, 'Rewriting Herself', p. 51.
43 Kenneth McNeil, *Scotland, Britain, Empire: Writing the Highlands, 1760–1860* (Columbus, OH: Ohio State University Press, 2007), pp. 146–78.
44 Adrienne Munich, *Queen Victoria's Secrets* (New York, NY: Columbia University Press, 1996), p. 40.
45 Margaret Homans, *Royal Representations: Queen Victoria and British Culture, 1837–1876* (Chicago: University of Chicago Press, 1998),

pp. 131–46; and Cynthia Huff, 'Scripting the Materimperium: The Queen's Highland Journals, Colonial Women's Diaries, and the Victorian Imagined Community', *Prose Studies* 24 (2001), pp. 41–62.
46 Margaret Oliphant, 'The Queen of the Highlands', *Blackwood's Edinburgh Magazine* 103 (1868), pp. 242–50 (p. 247).
47 Queen Victoria, *More Leaves from the Journal of a Life in the Highlands, from 1862 to 1882* (London: Smith, Elder, 1884), p. 271.
48 Ibid., p. 255.
49 Ibid., p. 282.

10. Public Education, Science, and Metaphor

1 Anthony Cooke, *From Popular Enlightenment to Lifelong Learning: A History of Adult Education in Scotland 1707–2005* (Leicester: NIACE, 2006), p. 45.
2 Douglas Sutherland, 'Adult Education, c. 1750–1950: A Distinctive Mission?', in Robert Anderson, Mark Freeman, and Lindsay Paterson (eds), *The Edinburgh History of Education in Scotland* (Edinburgh: Edinburgh University Press, 2015), pp. 246–64 (p. 250).
3 John Stevenson, 'Scottish Schooling in the Denominational Era', in Robert Anderson et al., *Edinburgh History of Education in Scotland*, pp. 133–52 (p. 143).
4 Hugh Miller, *My Schools and Schoolmasters, or, The Story of My Education* (Edinburgh: Johnstone and Hunter, 1854), p. iv.
5 Ibid., p. 147.
6 Ibid., p. 148.
7 See James C. Livingston, 'Natural Science and Theology', in David Fergusson (ed.), *The Blackwell Companion to Nineteenth-Century Theology* (Chichester: Wiley-Blackwell, 2010), pp. 141–64 (p. 141).
8 Thomas Dick, *The Christian Philosopher* (Edinburgh: Longman, Hurst, Rees and Orme, 1823), p. 21.
9 Robert Chambers, *Vestiges of the Natural History of Creation*, 3rd edn (London: John Churchill, 1845), p. 170.
10 Quoted from *Scottish Christian Herald* 3 (1838), p. 766, in Hugh Miller, *The Testimony of the Rocks* (Edinburgh: Thomas Constable, 1857), pp. 416–17.
11 Ibid., p. 216.
12 Charles Lyell, *Principles of Geology*, 2 vols (London: John Murray, 1830), I, pp. 82–83.
13 Miller, *My Schools and Schoolmasters*, pp. 302–03.

11. Religion and Popular Literature in Scotland: The Literary Imagination as Inspiration

1. George MacDonald, *The Portent: A Story of the Inner Vision of the Highlanders, Commonly Called the Second Sight* (London: Smith, Elder, 1864), pp. 82–84.
2. Angus Calder, 'The Disruption in Fiction', in Stewart J. Brown and Michael Fry (eds), *Scotland in the Age of the Disruption* (Edinburgh: Edinburgh University Press, 1993), pp. 113–34 (p. 114).
3. Stewart J. Brown, *Thomas Chalmers and the Godly Commonwealth in Scotland* (Oxford: Oxford University Press, 1982).
4. William Hazlitt, *The Spirit of the Age* (London: Henry Colburn, 1825), p. 97.
5. Brown, *Thomas Chalmers*, p. 109.
6. Mrs [Margaret] Oliphant, *The Life of Edward Irving*, 3rd edn (London: Hurst and Blackett, 1864), p. 79.
7. Oliphant quotes Thomas Chalmers: '[Irving] is drawing prodigious crowds. We attempted this morning to force our way into St Andrew's Church; but it was all in vain' (p. 229).
8. Hazlitt comments that Irving 'merely makes use of the stronghold of religion as a resting place, from which he sallies forth, armed with modern topics and with penal fire, like Achilles of old rushing from the Grecian tents, against the adversaries of God and man' (*Spirit of the Age*, p. 91).
9. 'Catholic' used here to denote the 'universal' nature of the denomination.
10. George MacDonald, *Robert Falconer* (Boston, MA: Loring, 1868), p. 304.
11. George MacDonald, Letter to his Father, in Greville MacDonald, *George MacDonald and His Wife* (New York, NY: Dial, 1924), p. 108.
12. Kerry Dearborn, *The Baptised Imagination: The Theology of George MacDonald* (Aldershot: Ashgate, 2006), p. 19.
13. George MacDonald, *Thomas Wingfold*, 3 vols (London: Hurst and Blackett, 1876), III, p. 135.
14. George MacDonald, *Phantastes: A Faerie Romance for Men and Women* (London: Smith, Elder, 1858).
15. Ibid., p. 212.
16. Anonymous Review of George MacDonald's *Poems* (London: Longman, Brown, Green, Longmans, and Roberts, 1857), *Scotsman*, 12 August 1857.

17 Robert Lee Wolff (ed.), *1837–1900, The Victorian Age* (New York, NY: Stonehill, 1985) p. 4, quoted in A. Robin Hoffman, '*Holiday House*, childhood, and the end(s) of time', *Children's Literature* 41 (2013), pp. 115–39 (p. 133).
18 Catherine Sinclair, Preface to *Holiday House: A Book for the Young* (Edinburgh: William Whyte and Co., 1839), pp. iv–v.
19 See Hoffman, '*Holiday House*'.
20 Sinclair, Preface to *Holiday House*, pp. iv, vi.
21 Catherine Sinclair, *Modern Accomplishments; or The March of Intellect* (Edinburgh: Waugh and Innes, 1836).
22 Ibid., p. 315.
23 Catherine Sinclair, *Modern Society: or, The March of Intellect. The Conclusion of Modern Society* (Edinburgh: Waugh and Innes, 1837).
24 Ibid., p. 118.
25 Timothy C. Baker, 'Catherine Sinclair, Domestic Community, and the Catholic Imagination', *Studies in the Novel* 45.2 (Summer 2013), pp. 143–60 (p. 148).
26 Catherine Sinclair, *Beatrice; Or, The Unknown Relatives*, 3 vols (London: Richard Bentley, 1852).
27 Catherine Sinclair, Expanded Preface to *Beatrice*, published as *Modern Superstition* (London: Simpkin, Marshall, 1857), p. 3.
28 Sinclair, *Beatrice*, I, p. 292.
29 Baker, p. 158.
30 George MacDonald, *David Elginbrod* (London: Hurst and Blackett, 1863), p. 36.
31 George MacDonald, *A Dish of Orts: Chiefly Papers on the Imagination, and Shakespeare*, enl. ed. (London: Sampson, Low, Marston, 1893), p. 15.
32 MacDonald, *Phantastes*, p. 211.

12. Social Comment

1 For periodicals in the context of Scottish publishing, see Ian Duncan, *Scott's Shadow: The Novel in Romantic Edinburgh* (Princeton, NJ: Princeton University Press, 2007), pp. 298–302.
2 See Robert Anderson, Mark Freeman, and Lindsay Paterson (eds), *The Edinburgh History of Education in Scotland*, (Edinburgh: Edinburgh University Press, 2015), especially Ewen A. Cameron, 'Education in Rural Scotland, 1696–1872', pp. 153–70; Douglas Sutherland, 'Adult Education, c. 1750–1950: A Distinctive Mission?', pp. 246–64; Robert Anderson and Stuart Wallace, 'The Universities and National Identity in the Long Nineteenth Century, c. 1830–1914', pp. 265–85.

3   Thomas Carlyle, 'Signs of the Times', in *A Carlyle Reader: Selections from the Writings of Thomas Carlyle*, ed. G. B. Tennyson (Cambridge: Cambridge University Press, 1984), pp. 30–54.
4   Samuel Smiles, 'Railway Travelling', *Eliza Cook's Journal* 1.7 (June 16, 1849), pp. 97–99.
5   Social commentary in Gaelic literature, in the form of the còmhradh (*conversation* or *prose dialogue*), is discussed by Sheila M. Kidd (ed.), *Còmhraidhean nan Cnoc: The Nineteenth-Century Gaelic Prose Dialogue* (Glasgow Scottish Gaelic Texts Society, 2016).
6   Janet Hamilton, *Poems, Essays and Sketches*, ed. James Hamilton (Glasgow: James Maclehose, 1880), p. 402.
7   Florence S. Boos, 'Janet Hamilton: Working-class Memoirist and Commentator', in Glenda Norquay (ed.), *The Edinburgh Companion to Scottish Women's Writing* (Edinburgh: Edinburgh University Press, 2012), pp. 63–74 (p. 72).
8   Hamilton, *Poems*, pp. 213–14.
9   Thomas Carlyle, *On Heroes, Hero-Worship, and the Heroic in History*, ed. Michael K. Goldberg, Joel J. Brattin, and Mark Engel (Berkeley: University of California Press, 1993), p. 169; *Past and Present*, ed. Chris R. Vanden Bossche, Joel J. Brattin, and D. J. Trela (Berkeley: University of California Press, 2005), p. 281.
10 *On Heroes*, pp. 153, 163, 134.
11 *Past and Present*, pp. 266–67.
12 *On Heroes*, pp. 169–70; *Past and Present*, pp. 269–70.
13 *On Heroes*, p. 175; cf. *Past and Present*, pp. 203–05.
14 *Past and Present*, p. 203.
15 Chris R. Vanden Bossche, 'Chartism, Class Discourse, and the Captain of Industry: Social Agency in *Past and Present*', in Paul E. Kerry and Marylu Hill (eds), *Thomas Carlyle Resartus: Reappraising Carlyle's Contribution to the Philosophy of History, Political Theory, and Cultural Criticism* (Madison, NJ: Fairleigh Dickinson University Press, 2010), pp. 30–48.
16 Samuel Smiles, *Self-Help: With Illustrations of Character, Conduct and Perseverance*, ed. with an Introduction, Peter W. Sinnema (Oxford: Oxford University Press, 2002), p. 242.
17 Smiles's misgivings about educational systems and Chartism are detailed in John Hunter, *The Spirit of Self-Help: A Life of Samuel Smiles* (London: Shepheard-Walwyn, 2017), pp. 102–10 and 86–91.
18 *Self-Help*, pp. 3, 18.
19 *Self-Help*, p. 21. For Smiles's support of libraries, see Alistair Black,

'From Voluntary to State Action: Samuel Smiles, James Silk Buckingham and the Rise of the Public Library Movement in Britain', in Kyle B. Roberts and Mark Towsey (eds), *Before the Public Library: Reading, Community, and Identity in the Atlantic World, 1650–1850* (Leiden: Brill, 2017), pp. 349–69 (pp. 358–63).

20 Smiles, 'Thomas Carlyle', in *Brief Biographies* (Philadelphia, PA: Ticknor and Fields, 1861), pp. 270–85.
21 Smiles, 'Harriet Martineau', in *Brief Biographies*, pp. 499–510 (p. 499).
22 *Self-Help*, p. 297.
23 Hunter, pp. 170, 181–82; cf. Black, pp. 359–63.
24 For details about Hamilton and working-class periodicals, see Boos, 'Memoirist', pp. 67–68.
25 Cameron, p. 160; Hamilton, 'Social Science Essay on Self-Education', in *Poems*, pp. 369–81 (p. 380).
26 Boos, 'Memoirist', pp. 64–67; see also *The New Biographical Dictionary of Scottish Women*, ed. Elizabeth Ewan et al. (Edinburgh: Edinburgh University Press, 2018), p. 186.
27 Hamilton, 'Self-Education', p. 369.
28 Ibid., pp. 370–72, 376–77.
29 'Address to Working-Women', pp. 395–96.
30 Ibid., p. 390.
31 Ibid., p. 394.
32 Ibid., p. 392; 'Self-Education', p. 380.
33 'Self-Education', pp. 380, 379.
34 'Address', p. 395.
35 For the program, see George W. Hastings (ed.), *Transactions of the National Association for the Promotion of Social Science, 1860* (London: John W. Parker, Son, and Bourne, 1861).
36 Hamilton, 'Rhymes for the Times – II', in *Poems*, pp. 70–73 (p. 73); 'On the Meeting', in *Poems*, pp. 103–04 (p. 104).
37 Hamilton, 'Reminiscences of the Radical Time in 1819–20', in *Poems*, pp. 456–64 (p. 456, 464).
38 Ibid., p. 464.
39 Ibid.

13. 'Urban Folk': Scottish Victorian Adaptations and Transmutations of Earlier Verse Traditions

1 Michael Lynch, *Scotland, a New History* (London: Century, 1991), pp. 411–12.
2 The notion of a pristine rural oral tradition was a fiction resulting

from the prejudices of middle-class collectors. Dave Harker, *Fakesong* (Milton Keynes: Open University Press, 1985), pp. 101–40; David Buchan, *The Ballad and the Folk* (London: Routledge, 1972), p. 199; Steve Roud, 'Introduction', in David Atkinson and Steve Roud (eds), *Street-ballads in Nineteenth-century Britain, Ireland, and North America* (London: Routledge, 2014), pp. 1–18.

3. Dave Harker, 'The Making of the Tyneside Concert Hall', *Popular Music* 1 (1981), pp. 27–56, (pp. 27, 54); J. S. Bratton, *The Victorian Popular Ballad* (Lanham: Rowman and Littlefield, 1975), pp. 30–33.
4. An increasing nineteenth-century practice (Bratton, p. 91).
5. First edition 1832, with bookseller David Robertson as primary editor; further editions up to 1890 ('Robertson, David, 1795–1854', *DNB*). Second edition used here (1838). For the definition of the title, see 'Dissertation' in 1832 and 1842 editions or the *DNB* entry cited.
6. Gerard Carruthers, *Scottish Literature* (Edinburgh: Edinburgh University Press, 2009), pp. 109–10.
7. *Whistle-binkie*, pp. 63–64.
8. Ibid., pp. 18–20.
9. Ibid., pp. 15–16.
10. Ibid., pp. 71–74 (p. 74).
11. Generic imagery; see C. M. Jackson-Houlston, 'The Cheek of the Young Person: Sexualized Popular Discourse as Subtext in Dickens', *Leeds Working Papers in Victorian Studies* 4 (2001), pp. 31–45.
12. *Whistle-binkie*, pp. 77–80 (p. 80).
13. Ibid., pp. 29–32.
14. Ibid., pp. 100–02.
15. Ibid., pp. 63–64.
16. Ibid., p. 62.
17. Ibid.
18. *The Red, White and Blue Monster Song Book* (London: Berger, [1865?]) contains forty-nine patter songs.
19. Ibid., pp. 7–13.
20. See G. R. Potter, *Macaulay* (London: Longman, 1959), p. 19. Via classical education in British private schools, lines of 'Horatius' (notably 'even the ranks of Tuscany / Could scarce forbear to cheer') acted as a cultural shibboleth up through the twentieth century. Thomas Babington Macaulay, *Lays of Ancient Rome, Essays and Poems*, intro. by G. M. Trevelyan (London: Dent, 1910), p. 432. For Aytoun's popularity with 'generations of British schoolboys', see W. L. Renwick

in *W. E. Aytoun: Stories and Verse*, ed. W. L. Renwick (Edinburgh: Edinburgh University Press, 1964), p. x.
21 Macaulay, *Lays*, pp. 407–12.
22 Thomas Percy, 'An Essay on the Ancient English Minstrels', *Reliques of Ancient English Poetry*, 3 vols (London: Dodsley, 1765), I, pp. xv–xxiii; Macaulay, pp. 405–06, 416–19; Aytoun analyses the high sums paid to their singers, musicians, and composers in *The Ballads of Scotland*, 2 vols (Edinburgh: Blackwood, 1858), I, pp. lxxx–lxxxvi.
23 Macaulay, p. 426.
24 Ibid., pp. 424, 444.
25 Ibid., p. 432.
26 Ibid., p. 430.
27 *Ballads of Scotland*, I, p. xxii–xxiv.
28 See *American Notes* (1842) and *Martin Chuzzlewit* (1844).
29 *Lays of the Scottish Cavaliers, with Notes for Junior Classes*, 4 parts (London: Blackwood, [1889–90]). Each pamphlet cost 2d.
30 'The ruthless spoiler' shall not 'Lay his hot insulting hand / On the sisters of our heroes', 'Edinburgh After Flodden', in *Lays of the Scottish Cavaliers and Other Poems* (Edinburgh: Blackwood, 1849), p. 26.
31 Ibid., p. 95.
32 For birth date, see Norman Watson, *Poet McGonagall: A Biography* (Edinburgh: Birlinn, 2010), pp. 15–16. He was not, as suggested by Hugh MacDiarmid, illiterate (Watson, pp. 234, 92–94).
33 Cf. Robert Tannahill (1774–1810), William Thom (c. 1798–1848), John Robertson (1767–1810), and his contemporary, the mill worker Ellen Johnson. She moved to McGonagall's adopted hometown, Dundee, in 1861, publishing a volume of poems in 1867 (Watson, p. 67). McGonagall complained that working-class genius is 'sure to be disregarded' (Watson, p. 71).
34 For the economics, see Watson pp. 100–02, 199–200, 175–76, and William McGonagall, *Collected Poems*, intro. Chris Hunt (Edinburgh: Birlinn, 2006), pp. xiv–xv.
35 Watson, pp. 211–12.
36 Even the sympathetic Thomas M. Disch admits 'McGonagall was surely innocent of all prosody', 'Inverse Genius: On the Greatness of William McGonagall', *Parnassus* 24 (1999), pp. 198–211 (p. 207). For extreme negative comments, see Kurt Wittig, *The Scottish Tradition in Literature* (Edinburgh: Oliver and Boyd, 1958), p. 253; Alan Bold, *Modern Scottish Literature* (London: Longman, 1983), p. 18.

37 McGonagall, *Collected Poems*, pp. 109–11, 279–82, 503–05; 310–11; 489–91, 551–53.
38 Ibid., p. 557.
39 Ibid., p. 470.
40 Ibid., pp. 169–72.
41 For a London broadside in prose and verse, see David Cornforth, 'The Theatre Royal Fire – 1887', 'Events 1887', *Exeter Memories*.
42 McGonagall, *Collected Poems*, p. 34.
43 Hamish Henderson, 'McGonagall and the Irish Question', *New Edinburgh Review* 14 (1971), pp. 38–44 (pp. 39, 42–44).
44 www.digital.nls.uk/broadsides/view/?id=16409. Based on 'The Miner's Dream of Home' (1891), it struggles to achieve syllabic counts that fit the tune.
45 Watson, p. 168.
46 Ibid., pp. 70–73, 95–96.
47 See the cover of McGonagall's 1878 collection of four poems (Watson, illustration 11).
48 *Allan's Illustrated Edition of Tyneside Songs and Readings*, ed. Thomas and George Allan (Newcastle: Allan, 1891), pp. 422–26.
49 Shamus O. D. Wade, 'Who Was the Better Poet? Kipling or William McGonagall?' *Kipling Journal* 82 (2008), pp. 40–49, www.mcgonagall-online.org.uk/articles.
50 *The Jupiter Book of Ballads*, Isla Cameron et al. (Folkways Records, 1962) www.youtube.com/watch?v=LIsHaSI5IkQ.
51 McGonagall, *Collected Poems*, p. 29.
52 Watson, illustration 24. Partly misled by the poet, Watson miscounts (pp. 89, 165).
53 Watson, p. 214.
54 Watson, pp. 233, 261–64.
55 Ibid., pp. 39, 73, 109.

14. Gaelic Literature of the Diaspora

1 *An Teachdaire Gae'lach* 1 (1829), p. 3.
2 'Comhradh eadar Cuairtear nan Gleann agus Eachann Tirisdeach', *Cuairtear nan Gleann* 4 (June 1840), p. 82.
3 Iain Mac-Lachain, *Dain agus Orain* (Glasgow: G. Mac-na-Ceardadh, 1869), p. 17.
4 Ibid., p. 27.
5 Ibid., p. 29.

6   Iain MacDhughaill, *Dain agus Orain* (Edinburgh: MacLachlan & Stewart, 1862), pp. 45–46.
7   Ibid., pp. 57, 24, 32.
8   Iain Mac-Dhughaill, *Gaisge nan Gaidheal: Orain agus Dain* (Sandbank: J. E. & R Inglis, 1870), p. 30.
9   Uilleam Mac Dhunleibhe, *Duain agus Orain* (Glasgow: A. Sinclair, 1882), p. 174.
10 Eobhan MacColla, *Clàrsach nam Beann*, 3rd ed. (Glasgow: Archibald Sinclair, 1886), pp. 51–52.
11 Robert MacDougall, *Ceann-Iùil an Fhir-Imrich do dh'America mu Thuath* (Glasgow: J. & P. Campbell, 1841), pp. 51, 124.
12 Rob Mac-Dhughaill, *Tomas Seannsair* (Glasgow: E. Khull, 1840), p. 45.
13 Ibid., p. 47.
14 *Teachdaire nan Gaidheal*, 7 (1845), p. 55.
15 *The Emigrant Experience*, ed. Margaret MacDonell (Toronto, ON: University of Toronto Press, 1982), p. 82. The translation given here is MacDonell's. For discussion of this song, see Michael Kennedy, '"Lochaber no more": A critical examination of Highland emigration', in Marjory Harper and Michael E. Vance (eds), *Myth, Migration and the Making of Memory: Scotia and Nova Scotia, c. 1700–1990* (Halifax, NS: Fernwood, 1999), pp. 267–97 (pp. 286–88); Robert Dunbar, 'The poetry of the emigrant generation', *Transactions of the Gaelic Society of Inverness* 64 (2004–06), pp. 22–125 (pp. 38–40).
16 Allan MacDonald, *As a' Bhràighe. The Gaelic Songs of Allan the Ridge MacDonald 1794–1868*, ed. Effie Rankin (Sydney, NS: Cape Breton University Press, 2005), pp. 78–79. The translations given here are Rankin's.
17 MacDonell, pp. 84–85.
18 Rankin, pp. 78–81.
19 Iain Mac Gillios, *Tuireadh airson Cruaidh-Chas nan Gaidheal: Agus airson Fasachadh Tir nam Beann, nan Gleann, 's nan Gaisgeach* (Glasgow: n.p., 1854), p. 3.
20 Ibid., p. 4
21 *Litir bho Iain Mac-Gil'-Ios' á New Zealand* (Glasgow: N. Campbell, [1858]), p. 3.
22 Iain MacGilleain 'Oran do'n Chuairtear', in A. MacGilleain Sinclair (ed.), *Filidh na Coille: Dain agus Orain leis a bhard Mac-Gilleain agus le Feadhainn Eile* (Charlottetown, PEI: Examiner, 1901), pp. 104–07 (p. 107).

15. David Pae, the Newspaper Novel, and the Imagined Community of North Britain

1 Benedict Anderson, *Imagined Communities*, rev. ed. (London: Verso, 1991), pp. 24–25.
2 Ibid., p. 36.
3 For 'transtrentane' see 'trans-, *prefix* 7. A' (*OED*).
4 William Donaldson, *Popular Literature in Victorian Scotland* (Aberdeen: Aberdeen University Press, 1986), p. 154, n. 31.
5 Ibid., p. 14.
6 See A. H. Millar, 'Robert Scott Fittis', in Robert Scott Fittis, *The Mosstrooper* (Perth: Wood & Son, 1906), pp. v–xv.
7 Donaldson, p. 103.
8 'Death of a Scottish Novelist', (Dundee) *Evening Telegraph*, 9 March 1885, p. 3.
9 *List of Serial Stories, Written by David Pae for Publication in Newspapers* (Ardrossan: *Ayrshire Evening News* Office, [1870]).
10 Graham Law, *Serializing Fiction in the Victorian Press* (New York, NY: Palgrave, 2000).
11 Updates list in David Pae, *Lucy, the Factory Girl*, ed. Graham Law (Hastings: Sensation Press, 2001), pp. 345–48. Available at: www.f.waseda.jp/glaw/ASLS/Pae_Serials.pdf.
12 These include: *Helen Armstrong* ('A Tale of the Borders') written for the *Berwick Journal*; and *Grace Darling* as an early offering to the *Northeastern Daily Gazette*.
13 Examples are *The Heir of Douglas* in Ardrossan (1865), after appearing in the *Ayrshire Weekly News*, and *Hard Times* in Ashton-under-Lyne (1886), following its run in the *Cotton Factory Times*.
14 As recorded in descriptive sub-titles like 'A Tale of Highland Eviction', 'A Tale of the Great Glasgow Bank Robbery', etc.
15 These include Clanranald, Deacon Brodie, and again Grace Darling.
16 Serial first issued in the weekly (Dundee) *People's Journal*, 21 August 1880–7 May 1881, and reprinted, among other locations, in the *North-Eastern Daily Gazette*, 24 September–30 December 1881. Also in yellowback form in Dundee (John Leng, 1888), after Pae's death.
17 *Grace Darling, the Maid of the Isles* (Newcastle-on-Tyne: W. & T. Fordyce, 1839), unsigned but evidently by Jerrold Vernon.
18 Ibid., pp. 116–17, 314; 209–18.
19 Cited in Constance Smedley, *Grace Darling and Her Times* (London: Hurst & Blackett, 1932), p. 218.

20 See Thomas Arthur, *The Life of Grace Darling, the Heroine of the Farne Isles* (London: Adam, 1875), and 'Eva Hope' (Marianne Farningham), *Grace Darling: Heroine of the Farne Islands* (London: Adam, [1876]).

21 See [Thomasin Darling], *Grace Darling, her True Story* (London: Hamilton, Adams, 1880), and *The Journal of William Darling* (London: Hamilton, Adams, 1887).

22 David Pae, *Grace Darling* (Dundee: John Leng, 1888), p. 378.

23 Ibid., p. 377.

24 Ibid., p. 426.

16. Industrial-Strength Fiction: Margaret Oliphant and James Grant

1 'Our London Correspondence', *Liverpool Mercury*, 7 May 1887 (and widely syndicated).

2 7 May 1887.

3 'James Grant 1827 [sic.]–1887', letter of James Grant to the Fund, 8 November 1879, f. 36, Archives of the Royal Literary Fund 1790–1918.

4 Ibid., f. 36.

5 Trevor Royle, 'The Military Kailyard: The Iconography of the Nineteenth-Century Soldier', *Scottish Cultural Review of Language and Literature* 18 (2012), pp. 119–35 (pp. 130–31).

6 Ibid., p. 131.

7 *Athenaeum* 2076 (10 August 1867), p. 173.

8 *Literary Gazette* 1730 (16 March 1850), pp. 197–98.

9 Stewart M. Ellis, *Mainly Victorian* (London: Hutchinson,1925), p. 110, quoted in Royle, 'The Military Kailyard', p. 131.

10 'James Grant 1827–1887', letters of James Grant to the Fund, 6 April 1874, and 1 March 1876, ff. 11, 21, Archives of the Royal Literary Fund 1790–1918.

11 Elisabeth Jay, *Margaret Oliphant: 'A Fiction to Herself'* (Oxford: Oxford University Press, 1995), pp. 21, 281–88.

12 *The Autobiography and Letters of Mrs M. O. W. Oliphant* (1899), ed. Linda H. Peterson, in *The Selected Works of Margaret Oliphant*, ed. Joanne Shattock and Elisabeth Jay, 25 vols (London: Pickering & Chatto, 2012), VI, p. 95.

13 Ibid., pp. 16–18.

14 Ibid., p. 55.

15 Ibid., pp. 95–96.

16 Ibid., p. 55.

17 [Alexander Innes Shand], 'Recent Scotch Novels', *Edinburgh Review* 143 (April 1876), pp. 317–52 (pp. 323–28).
18 *Autobiography and Letters*, pp. 397–98.

17. Scottish Travel Writing

1 Mary Seacole, *Wonderful Adventures of Mrs. Seacole in Many Lands*, ed. W. J. S. (London: James Blackwood, 1857). For page reference, see *Wonderful Adventures of Mrs Seacole in Many Lands*, ed. Sarah Salih (London: Penguin, 2005), p. 13.
2 T. M. Devine, *The Scottish Nation: A History 1700–2000* (New York: Viking, 1999), pp. 468–69.
3 Nigel Leask, 'Imperial Scots' (Review), *History Workshop Journal* 59 (Spring 2005), pp. 262–270 (p. 267).
4 Evan Gottlieb, *Feeling British: Sympathy and National Identity in Scottish and English Writing, 1707–1832* (Lewisburgh, PA: Bucknell, 2007).
5 See Katie Trumpener, *Bardic Nationalism* (Princeton, NJ: Princeton University Press, 1997) for a specifically Scottish Romanticism, now well established. For a synthesis of the debate and recent work on Scottish Romanticism's roots in the Scottish Enlightenment, see Murray Pittock (ed.), *The Edinburgh Companion to Scottish Romanticism* (Edinburgh: Edinburgh University Press, 2011), pp. 1–5.
6 An alternate explanation is that Scots considered themselves 'North British' during this period. See David Cordingly, *Cochrane: The Real Master and Commander* (London: Bloomsbury, 2007), p. 315; Gertrude Himmelfarb, *Roads to Modernity* (New York, NY: Random House, 2004), p. 13. The private documents left by mobile Scots belie this interpretation.
7 Nigel Leask, *Curiosity and the Aesthetics of Travel Writing, 1770–1840* (Oxford: Oxford University Press, 2002). Leask complicates the dichotomy between enlightenment objectivity and romantic subjectivity, pp. 4–14.
8 Barbara Korte, 'Western Travel Writing, 1750–1950', *Routledge Companion to Travel Writing* (Abingdon: Routledge, 2015), pp. 173–84 (p. 175).
9 Carla Sassi, *Why Scottish Literature Matters* (Edinburgh: The Saltire Society, 2005), p. 87.
10 Benjamin Colbert, *Women's Travel Writing, 1780–1840*, btw.wlv.ac.uk
11 John MacGregor, *The Rob Roy on the Baltic*, 3rd ed. (London: Sampson Low, Marston, Low, and Searle, 1872), p. 49.

12 Miguel A. Cabañas, 'North of Eden: Romance and Conquest in Fanny Calderón de La Barca's *Life in Mexico*', *Studies in Travel Writing* 9 (2005), pp. 1–19 (p. 17).
13 For recent studies, see for example Jochen Petzold, 'Anti-Slavery Discourse in Three Stories by R. M. Ballantyne', in Carla Sassi (ed.), *Empires and Revolutions: Cunninghame Graham and his Contemporaries* (Glasgow: Scottish Literature International, 2017), pp. 32–46; Nilay Erdem Ayyildiz, *British Children's Adventure Novels in the Web of Colonialism* (Newcastle: Cambridge Scholars, 2018); David Agruss, 'Boys gone wild: island stranding, cross-racial identification, and metropolitan masculinity in R. M. Ballantyne's The Coral Island', *The Victorian* 1.1 (2013), pp. 1–19.
14 *Wonderful Adventures of Mrs. Seacole in Many Lands*, p. 11.
15 Ibid., pp. 20–21.
16 Robert Louis Stevenson, 'The Foreigner at Home', *Cornhill Magazine* 45 (1882), pp. 534–41; *Strange Case of Dr Jekyll and Mr Hyde* (London: Longmans, Green & Co, 1886), p. 113; 'The Scot Abroad', in *From Scotland to Silverado*, ed. James D. Hart (Cambridge, MA: Belknap Press, 1966), p. 213.
17 Robert Louis Stevenson, *The Silverado Squatters*, in *From Scotland to Silverado*, ed. James D. Hart (Cambridge, MA: Belknap Press, 1966), p. 203.
18 Robert Louis Stevenson, 'Dedication to Sidney Colvin', *Travels with a Donkey in the Cévennes*, ed. Trevor Royle (London: J. M. Dent, 1993), p. 108.

18. Travel Writing about the Highlands in the Nineteenth Century

1 [Walter Scott], 'Carr's *Caledonian Sketches*', *Quarterly Review* 1.1 (February 1809), pp. 178–93 (p. 193).
2 Ibid., p. 182.
3 Ibid., p. 183. For other reviews of Carr, see Ina Ferris, 'Mobile Words: Romantic Travel Writing and Print Anxiety', *Modern Language Quarterly* 60.4 (December 1999), pp. 451–468 (p. 454).
4 He employed the phrase in his anonymous review of the Culloden Papers, *Quarterly Review* 14.28 (January 1816), pp. 283–333 (p. 333). See Nigel Leask, *Stepping Westward: Writing the Highland Tour, c. 1720–1830* (Oxford University Press, 2020), pp. 218–260.
5 See for example T. M. Devine, *Clanship to Crofters' War* (Manchester: Manchester University Press, 1994), pp. 84–99; Silke Stroh, *Gaelic Scotland in the Colonial Imagination: Anglophone Writing*

from 1600–1900 (Evanston: Northwestern University Press, 2017), pp. 132–36.

6 Kenneth McNeil, *Scotland, Britain, Empire: Writing the Highlands, 1760–1860* (Columbus, OH: Ohio State University Press, 2007), p. 206; Neil Davidson, 'Marx and Engels on the Scottish Highlands', *Science and Society* 64.3 (Fall 2001), pp. 286–326 (p. 312).

7 For Burns's Highland and Borders Tours, see Nigel Leask, *Oxford Edition of the Works of Robert Burns, Vol.1, Commonplace Books, Tour Journals and Miscellaneous Prose* (Oxford: Oxford University Press, 2014), pp. 110–59.

8 Ian Brown (ed.), *Literary Tourism: The Trossachs and Walter Scott* (Glasgow: Scottish Literature International, 2012).

9 See *Daniell's Scotland: A Voyage Round the Coast of Scotland and the Adjacent Isles, 1815–22*, 2 vols (Edinburgh: Birlinn and National Library of Scotland, 2006), I, p. xxii.

10 Anne Grant, *Essays on the Superstitions of the Highlands of Scotland*, 2 vols. (London: Longman, Hurst, Rees, and Brown, 1811), I, p. 9.

11 Anne Grant, *Letters from the Mountains*, ed. with notes by J. P. Grant, 6th ed. 2 vols (London: Longman, Brown, Green, and Longmans, 1845), I, p. 215.

12 Major-General David Stewart, *Sketches of the Character, Manners, and Present State of the Highlanders of Scotland*, 3rd ed., 2 vols (Edinburgh: Constable, 1825), I, pp. 217, 134.

13 John Macculloch, *The Highlands and Western Isles of Scotland [...] in Letters to Sir Walter Scott, Bart*, 4 vols (London: Longman, Hurst, Rees, Orme, Brown, and Green, 1824).

14 *Ibid*, I, p. 196.

15 *Ibid.*, IV, p. 298. See Stroh, pp. 185–211.

16 T. M. Devine, *The Scottish Clearances* (Harmondsworth: Penguin, 2019), pp. 10–11.

17 Katherine Haldane Grenier, '"Scottishness", "Britishness", and Scottish Tourism, 1770–1914', *History Compass* 4.6 (2006), pp. 1000–23 (p. 1006).

18 Col Thomas Thornton, *A Sporting Tour through the Northern Parts of England and Great Part of the Highlands of Scotland* (London: Vernon and Hood, 1804); Smout, 'Tours in the Highlands of Scotland from the 18th to the 20th Century', *Northern Scotland* 5.2 (1983), pp. 99–121 (p. 111); Peter Womack, *Improvement and Romance: Constructing the Myth of the Highlands* (Basingstoke: Macmillan, 1988), pp. 149–65 (pp. 158–62); Mary Miers, *Highland Retreats: The*

Architecture and Interiors of Scotland's Romantic North (New York: Rizzoli, 2017), pp. 44–75.
19 Smout, p. 111.
20 Nicola Watson, *The Literary Tourist* (Basingstoke: Palgrave Macmillan, 2006), p. 157; Womack, pp. 149–65.
21 Miers, p. 113.
22 David Duff (ed.), *Queen Victoria's Highland Journals* (Exeter: Webb & Bower, 1980), p. 11; McNeil, pp. 16–67.
23 Quoted by Miers, p. 115.
24 Alexander Smith, *A Summer in Skye*, ed. William F. Laughlan (1965; Hawick: Byway Books, 1983), p. 124.
25 Ibid., p. 105.
26 Ibid., p. 110.
27 Ibid., p. 184.
28 Ibid., p. 159.
29 Sheila M. Kidd, 'Caraid nan Gaidheal and "Friend of Emigration": Gaelic Emigration Literature of the 1840s', *Scottish Historical Review* 82.211, Pt. 1 (April 2002), pp. 52–69 (p. 61).
30 Norman Macleod, *Morvern: A Highland Parish* (1867), ed. Iain Thornber (Edinburgh: Birlinn, 2002).
31 Ibid., p. 178. The original was titled 'Sgeul mu Mhàiri nighean Eoghainn bhàin; air aithris leatha fein'.
32 John Prebble, *The Highland Clearances* (London: Secker and Warburg, 1963), p. 105. For a more contemporary attack on the Clearances, see Robert Somers, *Letters from the Highlands on the Famine of 1846* (1848), (rpt. Inverness: Melven Press, 1977).
33 Donald Macleod, 'Gloomy Memories', in Alexander Mackenzie, *History of the Highland Clearances* (1883), (rpt. Inverness: Melven Press, 1979), p. 118.
34 See for example the poems collected in *Tuath Is Tighearna: Tenants and Landlords*, ed. Donald E. Meek (Edinburgh: Scottish Academic Press, 1995); *Report of the Commissioners of Inquiry into the Condition of the Crofters and Cottars in the Highlands and Islands of Scotland* (London, 1884).
35 Quoted in Elizabeth Bray, *The Discovery of the Hebrides: Voyages to the Western Isles, 1745–1883* (Edinburgh: Birlinn, 1996), p. 231.

PART 3: EXPANSIONS

1 David Finkelstein and Alistair McCleery, 'Introduction', in David Finkelstein and Alistair McCleery (eds), *The Edinburgh History of*

the Book in Scotland, Volume 4: Professionalism and Diversity 1880–2000 (Edinburgh: Edinburgh University Press, 2007), p. 6.
2. Bill Bell, 'Introduction', in Bill Bell, (ed.), *The Edinburgh History of the Book in Scotland, Volume 3: Ambition and Industry 1800–1880* (Edinburgh: Edinburgh University Press, 2007), p. 2.
3. Richard Butt, 'The Competitors', in David Finkelstein and Alistair McCleery (eds), *The Edinburgh History of the Book in Scotland, Volume 4* (Edinburgh: Edinburgh University Press, 2007), p. 17.
4. www.bl.uk/World-and-traditional-music/Ethnographic-wax-cylinders/025M-C0037X1537XX-0100V0 (accessed 13 August 2021).

19. City Songs

1. See, for example, Michael Fry, *A New Race of Men: Scotland 1815–1914* (Edinburgh: Birlinn, 2013), p. 364; Douglas Gifford and Alan Riach (eds), *Scotlands: Poets and the Nation* (Manchester: Carcanet, 2004), p. xxv.
2. For a fuller discussion, see Kirstie Blair, *Working Verse in Victorian Scotland: Poetry, Press, Community* (Oxford: Oxford University Press, 2019), pp. 137–73.
3. The seminal study of popular prose literature in the Scottish press remains William Donaldson's *Popular Literature in Victorian Scotland: Language, Fiction and the Press* (Aberdeen: Aberdeen University Press, 1986).
4. Michel Byrne, '"Chan e chleachd bhith an cabhsair chlach": Am bàrd Gàidhlig 's am baile mòr bhon 17mh linn chun an 20mh linn', in Sheila M. Kidd (ed.), *Glasgow: Baile Mòr nan Gàidheal /City of the Gaels* (Glasgow: Celtic Dept, University of Glasgow, 2007), pp. 55–88; Donald E. Meek, 'Sitirich an Eich Iarainn ('The Neighing of the Iron Horse'): Gaelic perspectives on steam power, railways and shipbuilding in the nineteenth century' in Wilson McLeod, Abigail Burnyeat, Domhnall Uilleam Stiùbhart, Thomas Owen Clancy and Roibeard Ó Maolalaigh (eds), *Bile ós Chrannaibh. A Festschrift for William Gillies* (Ceann Drochaid: Clann Tuirc, 2010), pp. 271–92.
5. Lauren Weiss, 'The Literary Clubs and Societies of Glasgow during the Long Nineteenth Century' (unpublished doctoral thesis, University of Stirling, 2017). See also Weiss, 'Glasgow's Literary Bonds', www.glasgowsliterarybonds.org.
6. James Myles, *Rambles in Forfarshire; or Sketches in Town and Country* (Dundee: James Myles, 1850), p. 18. Myles was a factory worker, Chartist speaker, and later bookseller and literary man.

7   Erin Farley, 'The Place of Poetry in Victorian Dundee' (unpublished doctoral thesis, University of Strathclyde, 2018); Aileen Black, *Gilfillan of Dundee, 1813–1878* (Dundee: Dundee University Press, 2006).
8   James or William Brown, 'Address to the Spire of St Paul's Church, Castle Hill, Dundee' (Dundee: C. D. Chalmers, 1855).
9   Thos. Dodds, 'On Visiting the West-End Park', *Glasgow Citizen*, 28 August 1858.
10 'Richard', 'The Houseless', *Glasgow Citizen*, 7 April 1855.
11 'Another Local Aspirant to Poetic Honours', *Glasgow Citizen*, 2 July 1853.
12 Alexander Smith, *City Poems* (London: Macmillan, 1857), p. 41.
13 Ibid., p. 43.
14 George Eyre-Todd, *The Glasgow Poets, Their Lives and Poems* (Glasgow: William Hodge, 1903), pp. 377, 380.
15 'City Songs and Other Poetical Pieces by James Macfarlan', *Glasgow Citizen*, 14 July 1855.
16 James Macfarlan, *The Poetical Works of James Macfarlan*, with memoir by Colin Rae-Brown (Glasgow: Robert Forrester, 1882), p. 27.
17 Ibid., p. 21.
18 Alfred Tennyson, *In Memoriam* VII, in *Tennyson: A Selected Edition*, ed. Christopher Ricks (Harlow: Longman, 1989), pp. 351–52.
19 Eyre-Todd, p. 377.
20 John Davidson, 'A Ballad in Blank Verse', in *Ballads and Songs* (London: John Lane, 1894), pp. 8–9.
21 Marion Bernstein, *A Song of Glasgow Town: The Collected Poems of Marion Bernstein*, ed. Edward H. Cohen, Anne R. Fertig and Linda Fleming (Glasgow: ASLS, 2013), p. 24. See p. 227 for a note on this poem's original composition and the newspaper's comments on city verse.
22 Walter Freer, *My Life and Memories* (Glasgow: Civic Press, 1929), p. 93. Freer was a power-loom tenter who later moved into theatre management.

20. Gaelic Political Poetry 1870–1900

1   See Joni Buchanan, *The Lewis Land Struggle* (Stornoway: Acair, 1996), pp. 25–36; *Tuath is Tighearna: Tenants and Landlords*, ed. Donald E. Meek (Edinburgh: Scottish Gaelic Texts Society, 1995), pp. 88–89.
2   For text, translation and contextual discussion see Meek, *Tuath is Tighearna*, pp. 90–97, 213–20. Also Donald MacAulay, 'The Poetry of Seonaidh Phàdraig (John Smith), The Earshader Bàrd', *Transactions*

of the Gaelic Society of Inverness 60 (1997–98), pp. 1–16; Somhairle Mac Gill-eain, 'The Poetry of the Clearances', in William Gillies (ed.), *Ris a' Bhruthaich* (Stornoway: Acair, 1985), pp. 48–74 (p. 61).
3 Meek, *Tuath is Tighearna*, p. 97.
4 See *Màiri Mhòr nan Òran*, ed. Domhnall Eachann Meek (Edinburgh: Scottish Gaelic Texts Society, 1998), pp. 23–27.
5 'The Crofters Agitation in Skye', *Scotsman*, 27 April 1882.
6 Text and translation in Meek, *Tuath is Tighearna*, pp. 163–65, 264–66.
7 Ibid., pp. 167–68, 267–68.
8 Ibid., pp. 180–83, 275–78.
9 See Buchanan, *Lewis Land Struggle*, pp. 39–47.
10 William Cowper (1731–1800), poet and hymnwriter.
11 See James Hunter, *The Making of the Crofting Community* (Edinburgh: Birlinn, 2000), pp. 216–17; Meek, *Tuath is Tighearna*, p. 322.
12 For the role of the churches in the land politics of the Highlands, see Allan W. MacColl, *Land, Faith and the Crofting Community* (Edinburgh: Edinburgh University Press, 2006), including 'The poetry of the land agitation', pp. 147–54. See also Meek, *Tuath is Tighearna*, pp. 178–79.
13 'Òran Loch-Iall', in Mary MacPherson, *Poems and Songs* (Inverness: A. & U. Mac-Coinnich, 1891), pp. 267–69 (p. 268).
14 'Eilean a' Cheò': Text and translation in *Caran an t-Saoghail: The Wiles of the World. Anthology of 19th Century Scottish Gaelic Verse*, ed. Donald E. Meek (Edinburgh: Birlinn, 2003), pp. 366–75. See also 'Breacan Màiri Uisdein', in Mary MacPherson, *Poems and Songs*, pp. 31–34.
15 'Reiseamaid nan Gordonach', in John MacFadyen, *An t-Eileanach* (Glasgow: MacLaren, 1921), pp. 110–11.
16 MacFadyen, *An t-Eileanach*, p. 111.
17 See Wilson McLeod, 'Gaelic Poetry and the British Military Enterprise, 1756–1945', in Carla Sassi and Theo van Heijnsbergen (eds), *Within and Without Empire: Scotland across the (Post)colonial Borderline* (Newcastle: Cambridge Scholars Publishing, 2013), pp. 61–76.
18 MacFadyen, *An t-Eileanach*, p. 111.
19 See, for example, poems on the British defeat at the Battle of Magersfontein in 1899 during the second Boer War in which the Highland regiments, and the Black Watch in particular, sustained large losses.
20 Mary MacKellar, 'Fleasgach an Fhuilt Chraobhach, Chais' ('*Handsome young man of flowing tresses*') in *Transactions of the Gaelic Society of Inverness* 10 (1881–83), pp. 72–73.

21 'Caoidh nam Ban Gàidhealach', Mary MacPherson, *Poems and Songs*, pp. 77–84.
22 Gilleasbuig Mac Iain, 'Cuiribh glùn air na Bodaich', *Highlander*, 28 October 1876. Text and translation in Michael Newton, *Warriors of the Word* (Edinburgh: Birlinn, 2009), pp. 359–61.
23 Archibald Farquharson, *Christ's Forerunner in the Highlands* (Glasgow: Archibald Sinclair, 1870).
24 Text and translation in *Bàird Ghleann Dail*, ed. Meg Bateman (Edinburgh: Birlinn, 2014), pp. 47–51.
25 For this aspect of the Church in the Highlands see Douglas Ansdell, *The People of the Great Faith: The Highland Church 1690–1900* (Stornoway: Acair, 1998).
26 Including poems on the Land Struggle, Temperance, the Budget, and the Gaelic language. See Murdo MacLeod, *Bardachd Mhurchaidh a' Cheisdeir* (Edinburgh: Darien Press, 1962 and 1965).
27 For the Union of 1900 in the Highlands see Ansdell, *People of the Great Faith*, pp. 187–99.
28 MacLeod, *Bardachd Mhurchaidh a' Cheisdeir* (1962), p. 62.
29 MacLeod, *Bardachd Mhurchaidh a' Cheisdeir* (1965), pp. 60–61.
30 This corpus has been compiled and explored in depth in Anne Macleod Hill, 'The Pelican in the Wilderness: Symbolism and allegory in women's evangelical songs of the Gàidhealtachd' (unpublished doctoral thesis, University of Edinburgh, 2016). I am indebted to Anne Macleod Hill for suggesting and referencing a number of relevant texts.
31 'Mo Thuras gu Mangersta': Text in *Òrain le Bean Iain Dòmhnullaich a Breanish, Uig, Leòdhas, a tha 'n diugh An Sgìre Shlèite anns an Eilean Sgìtheanach*, a photocopy in Leabharlannan nan Eilean Siar, G783, pp. 11–16.
32 Text and translation from Meek, *Tuath is Tighearna*, pp. 93, 216.
33 Donald E. Meek has published widely on this subject; see for example 'The Bible and Social Change in the Nineteenth-Century Highlands', in David. F. Wright (ed.), *The Bible in Scottish Life and Literature* (Edinburgh: St Andrews Press, 1988), pp. 9–23. See also MacColl.
34 'Fios chun a' Bhàird': Text and translation in Meek, *Caran an t-Saoghail*, pp. 42–49.

21. The Kailyard Novelists

1 Ian Campbell, *Kailyard* (Edinburgh: Ramsay Head Press, 1981).
2 Andrew Nash, *Kailyard and Scottish Literature* (Amsterdam and New York: Rodopi, 2007).

3 Thomas D. Knowles, *Ideology, Art and Commerce: Aspects of Literary Sociology in the late Victorian Scottish Kailyard* (Goteburg: Acta Universitatis Gothoburgensis, 1983).
4 Andrew Nash, 'A. P. Watt and the Marketing of Ian Maclaren', *Journal of the Edinburgh Bibliographical Society* 4 (2009), pp. 49–59.
5 Ian Maclaren, *Beside the Bonnie Brier Bush* (London: Hodder & Stoughton, 1894), pp. 3–4.
6 Ian Carter, 'Kailyard: The Literature of Decline in Nineteenth-Century Scotland', *Scottish Journal of Sociology* 1.1 (1976), pp. 1–13 (p. 2).
7 Maclaren, *Brier Bush*, p. 59.
8 Ian Maclaren, *The Cure of Souls* (London: Hodder & Stoughton, 1896), p. 87.
9 Maclaren, *Brier Bush*, p. 30.
10 Ibid., p. 45.
11 George Blake, *Barrie and the Kailyard School* (London: Arthur Barker, 1951), p. 45.
12 Robert Harborough Sherard, 'S. R. Crockett at Home', *Idler* 7 (July 1895), pp. 797–817 (p. 801).
13 Ibid., p. 802.
14 S. R. Crockett, *The Raiders* (London: T. Fisher Unwin, 1894), pp. 352–53.
15 William Wallace, 'Two Scottish Novels', *The Academy*, 9 May 1896.
16 S. R. Crockett, *Cleg Kelly: Arab of the City* (London: Smith, Elder, 1896), p. 1.
17 S. R. Crockett, *Vida, or: The Iron Lord of Kirktown* (London: James Clarke, 1907), p. 192.
18 See Sarah Green, 'The Problem of Sex in J. M. Barrie's Fiction', *English Literature in Transition* 60.2 (2017), pp. 185–209; Andrew Nash, 'Barrie, Sentimentality and Modernity', in Valentina Bold and Andrew Nash (eds), *Gateway to the Modern: Resituating J. M. Barrie* (Glasgow: Scottish Literature International, 2014), pp. 103–20.
19 J. M. Barrie, *Auld Licht Idylls* (London: Hodder & Stoughton, 1888), p. 8.
20 Ibid.
21 Eric Anderson, 'The Kailyard Revisited', in Ian Campbell (ed.), *Nineteenth-Century Scottish Fiction: Critical Essays* (Manchester: Carcanet, 1979), pp. 130–47 (p. 132).
22 Barrie, *Auld Licht Idylls*, pp. 11–12.
23 Ibid., p. 48.

24 Ibid., p. 121.
25 J. M. Barrie, *A Window in Thrums* (London: Hodder & Stoughton, 1889), p. 2.
26 Ibid., p. 4–5.
27 *The Letters of Robert Louis Stevenson*, ed. Bradford A. Booth and Ernest Mehew, 8 vols (New Haven and London, Yale University Press), VII, p. 447.
28 See also the *Dictionary of the Scots Language* entry at www.dsl.ac.uk/entry/snd/glamour.
29 Barrie, *A Window in Thrums*, pp. 9, 4.
30 Ibid., p. 181.

22. The International Author: Stevenson

1 From the prefatory letter to *Travels with a Donkey in the Cévennes*, *The Silverado Squatters*, and *Travels with a Donkey in the Cévennes* respectively. Robert Louis Stevenson, *Travels with a Donkey, An Inland Voyage, The Silverado Squatters* (London: Dent, 1984), pp. 94, 231, 130.
2 André Laurie (tr.), *L'Île au trésor*, serialised in *Le Temps* (from 25 September 1884) then published as *L'Île au trésor* (Paris: J. Hetzel, 1885); Louis Despréaux (tr.), *L'Île au trésor* (Paris: Calman-Lévy, 1885).
3 For Stevenson in translation see Paul Barnaby and Tom Hubbard, 'The International Reception and Literary Impact of Scottish Literature of the Period 1707–1918', in Susan Manning (ed.), *The Edinburgh History of Scottish Literature, Volume 2: Enlightenment, Britain and Empire 1707–1918* (Edinburgh: Edinburgh University Press, 2007), pp. 33–44; Tom Hubbard, 'Dva brata: Robert Louis Stevenson in translation before 1900', *Scottish Studies Review* 8.1 (2007), pp. 17–26; Richard Dury, 'Stevenson in Italy and Italian', *Scottish Studies Review* 9.1 (2008), pp. 61–78. For Stevenson's reception in France, see Mark Fitzpatrick, '"Tout à fait un grand écrivain", Stevenson's place in French literary history', in Richard Hill (ed.), *Robert Louis Stevenson and the Great Affair: Movement, Memory and Modernity* (London: Routledge, 2017), pp. 202–18.
4 Translated as *Shin Takarajima*. See Yukinobe Tanabe, *Robert Louis Stevenson's View of the Japanese*, no date, no place of publication.
5 Translations of *New Arabian Nights* (1908) and *Strange Case of Dr Jekyll and Mr Hyde* (1917) followed. I am grateful to Dr Kang-yen Chiu for information about translations into Chinese.

6 See the UNESCO Index Translationum *World Bibliography of Translation 1978–Present* (UNESCO, 2019): www.unesco.org/xtrans/bsstatexp.aspx?crit1L=5&nTyp=min&topN=50. The only other author with significant Scottish connections in the top fifty is Arthur Conan Doyle at number fourteen.
7 Barnaby and Hubbard, 'The International Reception', p. 41.
8 Richard Butt, 'Literature and the Screen Media since 1908', in Ian Brown (ed.), *The Edinburgh History of Scottish Literature, Volume 3: Modern Transformations, New Identities (from 1918)* (Edinburgh: Edinburgh University Press, 2007), pp. 53–63 (pp. 53–54).
9 See Robert Louis Stevenson, *The Lantern Bearers and Other Essays*, ed. Jeremy Treglown (New York, NY: Cooper Square, 1988), pp. 259–64 (p. 262).
10 See 'Bibliography: New Letters', The RLS Website, www.robert-louis-stevenson.org/richard-dury-archive/new%20letters.htm.
11 *The Letters of Robert Louis Stevenson*, ed. Bradford A. Booth, and Ernest Mehew, 8 vols (New Haven, CT: Yale University Press, 1994), V, p. 375.
12 *Publishers' Weekly* 31 (2 April 1887), pp. 489–90.
13 R. C. Terry, *Robert Louis Stevenson: Interviews and Recollections* (Basingstoke: Macmillan, 1995), p. 154.
14 Bill Bell, 'The Scottish Book Trade at Home and Abroad, 1707–1918', in *The Edinburgh History of Scottish Literature, Volume 2* (Edinburgh: Edinburgh University Press, 2007), pp. 221–27 (p. 226). After the success of *Dr Jekyll and Mr Hyde*, Stevenson was regularly earning somewhere between four thousand and five thousand pounds a year (Patrick Leary and Andrew Nash, 'Authorship', in David McKitterick (ed.), *The Cambridge History of the Book in Britain, Volume 6: 1830–1914* (Cambridge: Cambridge University Press, 2009), pp. 172–213 (p. 212).
15 Robert Louis Stevenson, *Edinburgh, Picturesque Notes* (London: Seely, Jackson & Halliday, 1879), p. 3.
16 See Andrew Nash, *The Culture of Collected Editions* (Basingstoke: Palgrave Macmillan, 2003), p. 122. Stevenson's works became public domain in December 1944, until when a ten per cent royalty was payable to his stepson, Lloyd Osbourne.
17 Michelle Keown, 'Isles of Voices: Scotland in the Indigenous Pacific Literary Imaginary', *International Journal of Scottish Literature* 9 (Autumn/Winter 2013), pp. 51–67 (p. 52).
18 The term 'transculturation' was coined by the Cuban anthropologist Fernando Ortiz. See Regenia Gagnier, *Literatures of Liberalization*,

Global Circulation and the Long Nineteenth Century (Basingstoke: Palgrave Macmillan, 2018), p. 4.
19 See Barnaby and Hubbard, 'The International Reception', p. 42.
20 'Marcel Schwob bolstered his own reputation with perceptive readings of Stevenson – notably finding in him the middle-road between the realist and the psychological novel' (Fitzpatrick, p. 206).
21 'La mort de Robert-Louis Stevenson est un deuil et pour les lettres universelles et pour l'humanité', *Le Temps*, 18 December 1894.
22 Pascale Casanova, *The World Republic of Letters*, trans. Malcolm DeBevoise (Cambridge, MA: Harvard University Press, 2004), pp. 108–10.
23 Ian Brown, *Our Multiform, Our Infinite Scotland: Scottish Literature as 'Scottish', 'English' and 'World' Literature* (Glasgow: Association for Scottish Literary Studies, 2012), p. 1.
24 Henry James, 'Robert Louis Stevenson', *The Century Magazine* 35 (April 1888), pp. 869–79 (p. 874).
25 Stevenson is further discussed in this series in Penny Fielding (ed.), *The Edinburgh Companion to Robert Louis Stevenson* (Edinburgh: Edinburgh University Press, 2010).

23. Celticists and Anthropologists

1 *The Letters of Robert Louis Stevenson*, ed. Bradford A. Booth and Ernest Mehew, 8 vols (New Haven: Yale University Press, 1995), VIII, pp. 363–64. (The etymology presented here is not quite correct, see Simon Taylor with Gilbert Márkus, *The Place-Names of Fife*, vol 2, www.fife-placenames.glasgow.ac.uk/placename/?id=1460).
2 Ibid., VII, pp. 238–39.
3 Daniel G. Williams, 'Celticism', in Laura Marcus, Michele Mendelssohn and Kirsten E. Shepherd-Barr (eds), *Late-Victorian into Modern* (Oxford: Oxford University Press, 2016), pp. 67–82 (pp. 81–82).
4 William Sharp, 'Introduction', in Elizabeth A. Sharp (ed.), *Lyra Celtica: An Anthology of Representative Celtic Poetry* (Edinburgh: Patrick Geddes and Colleagues, 1896), pp. xix–li (p. xliii).
5 Ibid., pp. xxxi, xxxv, xli, xlii, xlvii–xlix.
6 Ibid., p. xxxv. Sharp replaces 'Ireland' with 'Celtdom'.
7 Murray Pittock, *Celtic Identity and the British Image* (Manchester: Manchester University Press, 1999), p. 72.
8 Sharp, 'Introduction', p. li. Sharp quotes from Fiona Macleod here.
9 William Sharp, *The Winged Destiny: Studies in the Spiritual History of the Gael* (London: Chapman and Hall, 1904), pp. 195–96.

10 Æ, 'Irish Ideals and Fiona Macleod', *All Ireland Review* 1.33 (1900), p. 1.
11 Patrick Geddes, 'The Scots Renascence', *The Evergreen* 1 (1895), pp. 131–39 (p. 139).
12 Gerard Carruthers, *Scottish Literature* (Edinburgh: Edinburgh University Press, 2009), p. 9.
13 Patrick Geddes, 'Keltic Art' (26 July 1899), p. 8, Archives and Special Collections, University of Strathclyde: T-GED 5/2/7.
14 Letter from Patrick Geddes to Mr Campbell, 1 November 1895, National Library of Scotland, MS 10508A.
15 For more on Fiona Macleod and Japan, see Masaya Shimokusu, 'True poetic comrades: Mineko Matsumura and the Reception of Fiona Macleod in Japan', in Willy Maley and Alison O'Malley-Younger (eds), *Celtic Connections: Irish-Scottish Relations and the Politics of Culture* (Bern: Peter Lang, 2012), pp. 115–32.
16 Andrew Lang, 'The Celtic Renascence', *Blackwood's Magazine* 161 (1897), pp. 181–91 (p. 181).
17 Ibid., p. 191.
18 Cairns Craig, 'Introduction', in J. G. Frazer, *The Golden Bough: A Study in Comparative Religion* (Edinburgh: Canongate, 2004), pp. vii–xxvi (p. xi).
19 J. G. Frazer, *The Golden Bough: A Study in Comparative Religion* (Edinburgh: Canongate, 2004), p. 694.
20 William Sharp, *The Washer of the Ford: and other Legendary Moralities* (Edinburgh: Patrick Geddes and Colleagues, 1896), p. 4. For Frazer on Scottish rituals, see Frazer, pp. 24, 482, 476.
21 Frazer, pp. 483–84.
22 Ibid., p. 51.
23 William F. Halloran, 'W. B. Yeats, William Sharp and Fiona Macleod: A Celtic Drama, 1897', *Yeats Annual* 14 (2001), pp. 159–208 (p. 185).
24 Frazer, p. 3.
25 Ibid., p. 1.
26 Ernest Rhys, *Everyman Remembers* (New York, NY: Cosmopolitan Book Corporation, 1931), pp. 79–80.
27 Frazer, pp. 597–98.
28 For the Pliny connection, see Frances Fowle, 'Celticism, Internationalism and Scottish Identity: Three Key Images in Focus', in Anna-Maria von Bonsdorff and Riitta Ojanperä (eds), *European Revivals: from Dreams of a Nation to Places of International Exchange* (Helsinki: Finnish National Gallery, 2020), pp. 49–64 (pp. 53–54).

29 William Sharp, 'Introductory Note', in *Ossian* (Edinburgh: Patrick Geddes and Colleagues, 1896), pp. ix–xxiv (pp. xxiii–xxiv).

24. Science and Speculation

1   See Brian Stableford, 'Science Fiction before the Genre', in Edward James and Farah Mendlesohn (eds), *The Cambridge Companion to Science Fiction* (Cambridge: Cambridge University Press, 2003), pp. 15–31; Adam Roberts, *The History of Science Fiction* (Basingstoke: Palgrave Macmillan, 2006).
2   Gavin Miller, 'Scottish Science Fiction: Writing Scottish Literature Back into History', *Etudes écossaises* 12 (2009) www.journals.openedition.org/etudesecossaises/197.
3   Darko Suvin, *Metamorphoses of Science Fiction: On the Poetics and History of a Literary Genre*, new ed. (Oxford: Oxford University Press, 2016), pp. 86, 84.
4   Caroline McCracken-Flesher, 'Introduction', in Caroline McCracken-Flesher (ed.), *Scotland as Science Fiction* (Lewisburg, PA: Bucknell University Press, 2012), p. 1.
5   See Cairns Craig, 'Nineteenth-Century Scottish Thought', in Susan Manning (ed.), *The Edinburgh History of Scottish Literature, Volume 2: Enlightenment, Britain and Empire (1707–1918)* (Edinburgh: Edinburgh University Press, 2007), pp. 267–76.
6   J. G. Frazer, 'Fison and Howitt' (1909), in *The Gorgon's Head and Other Literary Pieces* (London: Macmillan, 1927), pp. 291–331 (p. 302).
7   Andrew Lang, 'The Romance of the First Radical' (1880), in *In the Wrong Paradise and Other Stories* (London: Kegan, Paul, Trench, 1886), pp. 179–209 (pp. 179–80).
8   Florence Dixie, *Gloriana; Or, The Revolution of 1900* (London: Henry, 1890); Catherine Spence, *Handfasted* (1879), ed. Helen Thomson (Ringwood, Australia: Penguin, 1984).
9   See Cairns Craig, 'Scotland's Fantastic Physics: Energy Transformation in MacDonald, Stevenson, Barrie, and Spark', in McCracken-Flesher (ed.), *Scotland as Science Fiction*, pp. 15–28.
10 J. C. Maxwell, 'Report on Tait's Lecture on Force: – B. A., 1876', in Lewis Campbell and William Garnett, *The Life of James Clerk Maxwell: With a Selection from his Correspondence and Occasional Writings and A Sketch of his Contributions to Science* (London: Macmillan, 1882), pp. 646–48 (p. 647).
11 William Thomson, 'On the Age of the Sun's Heat', *Macmillan's Magazine* 5 (1862), pp. 388–93 (p. 393).

12 See Allen MacDuffie, *Victorian Literature, Energy, and the Ecological Imagination* (Cambridge: Cambridge University Press, 2014), p. 170.
13 [Balfour Stewart and Peter Guthrie Tait], *The Unseen Universe or Physical Speculations on a Future State* (London: Macmillan, 1875), pp. 157, 118.
14 Tamara Ketabgian, 'The Energy of Belief: *The Unseen Universe* and the Spirit of Thermodynamics', in Lara Karpenko and Shalyn Claggett (eds), *Strange Science: Investigating the Limits of Knowledge in the Victorian Age* (Ann Arbor, MI: University of Michigan Press, 2016), pp. 254–78 (p. 255).
15 Balfour Stewart and Norman Lockyer, 'The Sun as a Type of the Material Universe: Part II', *Macmillan's Magazine* 18 (1868), pp. 319–27 (p. 319).
16 See MacDuffie, p. 75.
17 [Stewart and Tait], *Unseen Universe* (1875), pp. 155, 159.
18 Janet Oppenheim, *The Other World: Spiritualism and Psychical Research in England, 1850–1914* (Cambridge: Cambridge University Press, 1985), pp. 330, 135.
19 See Roger Luckhurst, *The Invention of Telepathy, 1870–1901* (Oxford: Oxford University Press, 2002), p. 88.
20 Balfour Stewart and P. G. Tait, *The Unseen Universe: Or Physical Speculations on a Future State*, 6th ed. (London: Macmillan, 1876), pp. 220–21.
21 See Julia Reid, *Robert Louis Stevenson, Science, and the* Fin de Siècle (Basingstoke: Palgrave Macmillan, 2006), pp. 112–14.
22 Robert Louis Stevenson, *The Strange Case of Dr Jekyll and Mr Hyde and Other Stories*, ed. Jenni Calder (London: Penguin, 1979), pp. 84, 36, 80–81.
23 Ibid., p. 83.
24 Ibid., pp. 82–83.
25 [Stewart and Tait], *Unseen Universe* (1875), p. 155.
26 MacDuffie, pp. 191, 178.
27 Arthur Conan Doyle, *The Conan Doyle Stories* (Leicester: Blitz Editions, 1990), pp. 803, 810, 804, 810.
28 Arthur Conan Doyle, *Memories and Adventures* (Cambridge: Cambridge University Press, 2012 [1924]), pp. 84–87, 116–17.
29 Conan Doyle, *Conan Doyle Stories*, p. 468.
30 Ibid., p. 794.
31 Conan Doyle, 'The Great Keinplatz Experiment' (1894), in *Conan Doyle Stories*, pp. 728–46 (p. 728).

32 Arthur Conan Doyle, *The Parasite* (London: A. Constable, 1894), pp. 6, 30–31.
33 Ibid., p. 31.
34 Ibid., p. 70.
35 Ibid., p. 3.
36 Robert Duncan Milne, *Into the Sun and Other Stories*, ed. Sam Moskowitz (West Kingston, RI: Donald M. Grant, 1980), pp. 179–84.
37 [Stewart and Tait], *Unseen Universe* (1875), p. 183.
38 Milne, *Into the Sun*, p. 68.
39 Ibid., p. 76.
40 Ibid., p. 83.
41 Ibid., pp. 83, 89.
42 Ibid., p. 93.
43 Robert Duncan Milne, 'The Palæoscopic Camera', *The Argonaut* 9.26 (24 December 1881), pp. 14–16 (p. 15); Oppenheim, *The Other World*, pp. 445–46.
44 Ibid., p. 15.
45 Ibid., pp. 15, 16.
46 George MacDonald, *Lilith: A Romance* (1895; Mineola, NY: Dover, 2008), pp. 15, 20, 11.
47 Greville MacDonald, *George MacDonald and his Wife* (New York, NY: L. MacVeagh, 1924), p. 68; see Jeffrey Bilbro, '"Yet more spacious Space": Higher-Dimensional Imagination from *Flatland* to *Lilith*', *North Wind* 28 (2009), pp. 1–12.
48 MacDonald, *Lilith*, pp. 5–6; see Maxwell, 'A Paradoxical Ode', in Campbell and Garnett, *Life*, p. 650.
49 Wells, in Greville MacDonald, *Reminiscences of a Specialist* (London: G. Allen & Unwin, 1932), p. 323.
50 MacDonald, *Lilith*, p. 5.
51 Colin Manlove, 'The Electromagnetic World of George MacDonald's Visionary Romances', *North Wind* 36 (2017), pp. 54–70 (p. 66).
52 MacDonald, *Lilith*, pp. 22, 35.
53 Maxwell, 'A Paradoxical Ode', in Campbell and Garnett, *Life*, p. 649.
54 Luckhurst, *Invention*, p. 82.

25. Scotland's New Women

1 For an overview of the Woman Question, see Nicola Diane Thompson (ed.), *Victorian Women Writers and the Woman Question* (Cambridge: Cambridge University Press, 2012). On the New Woman, see Sally

Ledger, *The New Woman: Fiction and Feminism at the fin de siècle* (Manchester: Manchester University Press, 1997).

2   Annie S. Swan, 'A Message to the Women of Scotland', *Motherwell Times*, 23 November 1934, p. 2. I am indebted to Charlotte Lauder for this reference. On Scottish participation in the suffrage movement more generally, see Leah Leneman, *A Guid Cause: the Women's Suffrage Movement in Scotland*, rev. ed. (Edinburgh: Mercat Press, 1995).

3   Mona Caird, 'Marriage', *The Westminster Review* 130 (1888), pp. 186–201 (p. 191).

4   Ledger, p. 22.

5   Mona Caird, *The Daughters of Danaus* (New York, NY: The Feminist Press, 1989), p. 467.

6   Ibid., p. 16.

7   Ibid., p. 17.

8   Ibid., p. 266.

9   Ibid., pp. 66, 321.

10 Ibid., p. 12.

11 For trenchant critiques of Steel's imperial attitudes, see Nancy Paxton, 'Feminism under the Raj: Complicity and Resistance in the Writings of Flora Annie Steel and Annie Besant', *Women's Studies International Forum* 13.4 (1990), pp. 333–46; Benita Parry, *Delusions and Discoveries: India and the British Imagination, 1880–1930*, new ed. (London: Verso, 1998), pp. 103–26.

12 Flora Annie Steel, *Miss Stuart's Legacy* (London: Macmillan, 1897), p. 210.

13 Ibid., p. 223.

14 Ibid., p. 231.

15 On the demographics of the *Woman at Home*'s readership, see Margaret Beetham, *A Magazine of her Own? Domesticity and Desire in the Woman's Magazine, 1800–1914* (London: Routledge, 1996), pp. 158, 170–71.

16 Annie S. Swan, 'Over the Teacups', *The Woman at Home* 1 (1894), p. 303.

17 Kate Krueger, '*The Woman at Home* in the World: Annie Swan's Lady Doctor and the Problem of the Fin de Siècle Working Woman', *Victorian Periodicals Review* 50.3 (2017), pp. 517–33 (p. 517).

18 Beetham, p. 169.

19 Swan, 'Teacups', p. 304.

20 Annie S. Swan, *Elizabeth Glen, M.B., the Experiences of a Lady Doctor* (London: Hutchinson, 1895), pp. 10, 11.

21 Ibid., p. 202.
22 Ibid., p. 299.
23 Ibid.
24 On Barrie's and other 'Kailyard' writers' representations of women, see Samantha Walton, 'Scottish Modernism, Kailyard Fiction, and the Woman at Home', in Kate MacDonald and Christoph Singer (eds), *Transitions in Middlebrow Writing, 1880–1930* (London: Palgrave Macmillan, 2015), pp. 141–60. On the Findlaters' feminism, see Juliet Shields, 'The Unknown and the Unknowns: Naturalism in Scottish Domestic Fiction', *The Bottle Imp*, Supplement 2 (2015), www.thebottleimp.org.uk/2015/04/the-unknown-and-the-unknowns-naturalism-in-scottish-domestic-fiction/.

Further Reading

Bell, Bill (ed.), *The History of the Book in Scotland, Volume 3: Ambition and Industry 1800–1880* (Edinburgh: Edinburgh University Press, 2007).

Carruthers, Gerard, David Goldie, and Alastair Renfrew, *Scotland and the Nineteenth-Century World* (Amsterdam: Rodopi, 2012).

Crawford, Robert, *Scotland's Books* (Harmondsworth: Penguin, 2007).

Dictionary of the Scottish Language, www.dsl.ac.uk.

Donaldson, William, *Popular Literature in Victorian Scotland* (Aberdeen: Aberdeen University Press, 1986).

Duncan, Ian, *Scott's Shadow: The Novel in Romantic Edinburgh* (Princeton, NJ: Princeton University Press, 2007).

Dwelly, Edward, *The Illustrated Gaelic-English Dictionary* (Glasgow: Akerbeltz, 2011).

Gifford, Douglas (ed.), *The History of Scottish Literature Volume 3: Nineteenth Century* (Aberdeen: Aberdeen University Press, 1988).

Grenier, Katherine Haldane, *Tourism and Identity in Scotland, 1770–1914* (Aldershot: Ashgate, 2006).

Kidd, Sheila M. (ed.), *Còmhraidhean nan Cnoc: The Nineteenth-Century Gaelic Prose Dialogue* (Glasgow: Scottish Gaelic Texts Society, 2016).

Manning, Susan (ed.), *The Edinburgh History of Scottish Literature, Volume 2: Enlightenment, Britain and Empire (1707–1918)* (Edinburgh: Edinburgh University Press, 2007).

Meek, Donald E. (ed.), *Caran an t-Saoghail: The Wiles of the World: Anthology of 19th Century Scottish Gaelic Verse* (Edinburgh: Birlinn, 2003).

Meek, Donald E. (ed.), *Tuath is Tighearna: Tenants and Landlords* (Edinburgh: Scottish Gaelic Texts Society, 1995).

Newton, Michael (ed.), *Seanchaidh na Coille: The Memory-keeper of the Forest: Anthology of Scottish Gaelic Literature of Canada* (Sydney, NS: Cape Breton University Press, 2015).

Sassi, Carla, et al., *Caribbean-Scottish Relations: Colonial and Contemporary Inscriptions in History, Language and Literature* (London: Mango, 2007).

Shields, Juliet, *Scottish Women's Writing in the Long Nineteenth Century: The Romance of Everyday Life* (Cambridge: Cambridge University Press, 2021).

Notes on Contributors

Samuel Baker is Associate Professor of English at the University of Texas at Austin. He has published *Written on the Water: British Romanticism and the Maritime Empire of Culture* (2010), and essays on Ann Radcliffe, William Wordsworth, and Walter Scott, among others. His current research includes media theory, artificial intelligence, and Scottish Gothic.

Paul Barnaby is Scottish Literary Collections Curator at Edinburgh University Library, where he also edits the Walter Scott Digital Archive. He has published widely on the European reception of Scott and of twentieth-century Scottish writing. He has also written on nineteenth-century Italian literature and its links to French Naturalism.

Barbara Bell pioneered the digital deconstruction of the nineteenth-century theatre repertoire to reveal hidden patterns of production and reception. She has written widely on nineteenth-century Scottish theatre with a particular interest in the relationship between audiences, performers and the material, publishing recently on the Gothic and on scene painting.

Kirstie Blair is Professor of English at the University of Strathclyde. Her books include *Working Verse in Victorian Scotland: Poetry, Press, Community* (2019) and *The Poets of the People's Journal: Newspaper Poetry in Victorian Scotland* (2016).

Valentina Bold is Heritage Officer with the Crichton Trust, having previously spent many years in academia. Her books include *James Hogg: A Bard of Nature's Making* (2007), *Robert Burns' Merry Muses of Caledonia* (2016) and, with Andrew Nash, *Gateway to the Modern: Resituating J. M. Barrie* (2014).

Cairns Craig is Glucksman Professor of Irish and Scottish Studies at the University of Aberdeen. He has written extensively on the history of ideas, and on Scottish, Irish and American literature. His most recent books are *The Wealth of the Nation: Scotland, Culture and Independence* (2018) and *Muriel Spark, Existentialism and the Art of Death* (2019).

Lesley Graham is senior lecturer at the University of Bordeaux. Her research interests centre on nineteenth-century Scottish literature, in particular travel writing and other non-fiction genres. She is the editor of the New Edinburgh Edition of *Robert Louis Stevenson's Uncollected Essays 1880–94* (2018) and president of the French Society for Scottish Studies.

Jennifer Hayward is Virginia Myers Professor of English and Global Media and Digital Studies at the College of Wooster. She publishes on nineteenth-century British travellers in Latin America, focusing on Scottish authors including Maria Graham and Robert Louis Stevenson. She co-directs the Anglophone Chile project, a digital archive of the newspapers published by the nineteenth-century British colony in Chile.

Regina Hewitt is Professor of English at the University of South Florida. Her publications include *John Galt: Observations and Conjectures on Literature, History, and Society* (2012). She is editing John Galt's *Lawrie Todd*, and is a Consulting Editor for the *European Romantic Review*.

Alison Jack is Professor in Bible and Literature at the School of Divinity, University of Edinburgh. She has published widely on the intertextual relationships between the Bible and English, Scottish and American literature, most recently focusing on the parable of the Prodigal Son. She is currently Director of the Scottish Network for Religion and Literature.

Caroline M. Jackson-Houlston is recently retired from a Senior Research Fellowship at Oxford Brookes University. Her books include *Ballads, Songs and Snatches: The Appropriation of Folk Song and Popular Culture in British Nineteenth-century Realist Prose* (1999) and *Gendering Walter Scott: Sex, Violence and Romantic Period Writing* (2016).

Sheila M. Kidd is Senior Lecturer in Celtic and Gaelic at the University of Glasgow. Her research has dealt with Gaelic literature from the eighteenth to the early twentieth century and her edition of nineteenth-century *còmhraidhean* (prose dialogues) was published by the Scottish Gaelic Texts Society in 2016.

Graham Law is Professor in Culture and Media at Waseda University, Tokyo. He is a specialist in book history, with a particular focus on nineteenth-century newspapers and periodicals. He has published widely on Victorian literature and media, including *Serializing Fiction in the Victorian Press* (2000).

Nigel Leask is Regius Professor of English Language and Literature at the University of Glasgow. He publishes on romanticism, particularly Scottish literature, orientalism and travel, most recently publishing *Stepping Westward: Writing the Highland Tour c. 1720–1830* (2020). He is a Fellow of the British Academy and the Royal Society of Edinburgh, and a Vice-President of the Association for Scottish Literature.

Ruairidh Maciver is a Senior Journalist with BBC Gaelic news in Inverness. He received his doctorate from the University of Glasgow in 2018 and his research has focused on Gaelic poetry and the military in the eighteenth and nineteenth centuries.

Caroline McCracken-Flesher is Professor of English at the University of Wyoming, and Director of UW's Center for Global Studies. Her publications include *Possible Scotlands: Walter Scott and the Story of Tomorrow* (2005), *The Doctor Dissected: A Cultural Autopsy of the Burke and Hare Murders* (2012), and the co-edited *Walter Scott at 250: Looking Forward* (with Matthew Wickman, 2021).

Kenneth McNeil is Professor of English at Eastern Connecticut State University. His publications include *Scotland, Britain, Empire: Writing the Highlands, 1760–1860* (2007) and *Scottish Romanticism and Collective Memory in the British Atlantic* (2020).

Michael Morris is Senior Lecturer in the School of Humanities at the University of Dundee. His research focuses on Scottish connections with the Caribbean and Atlantic slavery more broadly, and includes *Scotland and the Caribbean, c. 1740–1833: Atlantic Archipelagos* (2015).

Andrew Nash is Reader in Book History and Director of the London Rare Books School at the Institute of English Studies, University of

London. In addition to books and articles on Scottish and Victorian literature, he co-edited volume 7 of *The Cambridge History of the Book in Britain* (2019).

Susan Oliver is Professor of Literature and Faculty Dean of Research at the University of Essex. Her books include *Scott, Byron and the Poetics of Cultural Encounter* (2005) and *Walter Scott and the Greening of Scotland: Emergent Ecologies of a Nation* (2021). She edited the 2017 Yearbook of English Studies (vol 47) titled *Walter Scott: New Interpretations.*

Pam Perkins is Professor of English at the University of Manitoba. Her publications include editions of fiction by Elizabeth Hamilton and (with Kirsteen McCue) travel writing by Anne Grant and Isabella Elizabeth Spence. She is researching late eighteenth- and early nineteenth-century British travels around the North Atlantic rim, ranging from the northern islands of Scotland to Newfoundland and Labrador.

Julia Reid is Lecturer in Victorian Literature at the University of Leeds. Her books include *Robert Louis Stevenson, Science, and the Fin de Siècle* (2006), and a scholarly edition of Stevenson's *The Amateur Emigrant* (2018). She is editing Stevenson's *The Silverado Squatters*, and working on *'She Who Must be Obeyed': Matriarchy in Victorian Anthropology and Fiction.*

Thomas C. Richardson is Professor of English and Eudora Welty Chair at Mississippi University for Women. He edited *Contributions to Blackwood's Edinburgh Magazine* for the Stirling/South Carolina Research Edition of the Collected Works of James Hogg (2 volumes, 2012), and is Series Editor for the Edinburgh Critical Edition of the Works of John Gibson Lockhart for Edinburgh University Press.

Priscilla Scott received her doctorate from the University of Edinburgh in 2014. Her research interests are in the social history and literature of the Gaelic-speaking people in the late nineteenth and early twentieth century, and particularly in the lives and perspectives of women who were active in cultural forums promoting Gaelic.

Michael Shaw is Lecturer in Scottish Literature at the University of Stirling. He researches late Victorian and Edwardian Scottish literature and art, and the relationships between Scottish culture and wider European developments. His publications include *The Fin-de-Siècle Scottish Revival: Romance, Decadence and Celtic Identity* (2020).

Juliet Shields is Professor of English at the University of Washington. She researches the intersections of gender, race, and nationality in the Anglophone Atlantic world, with a particular focus on women writers and diasporic literatures. Her most recent book is *Scottish Women's Writing in the Long Nineteenth Century: The Romance of Everyday Life* (2021).

Joanne Wilkes is Professor of English and Postgraduate Director for the School of Humanities at the University of Auckland. Her publications include *Women Reviewing Women in Nineteenth-Century Britain: the Critical Reception of Jane Austen, Charlotte Brontë and George Eliot* (2010), and volumes of essays and literary criticism in *The Selected Works of Margaret Oliphant* (2013, 2012, 2011).

Index

abolitionism, 8, 34, 142–43, 154
adaptations
   films, 159
   Stevenson's works, 188–89, 190
   theatrical, 59, 62–63
   Whistle-binkie, 76, 108–10
adventure fiction, 145, 147, 213
Æ. *see* Russell, George
Aitchison, Alexander, 86
Alexander, William, 127
   Johnny Gibb of Gushetneuk, 94, 182
Anderson, Benedict, 125
anthropology, 92, 159, 196, 199, 201, 204
antiquarianism, 5, 8, 20, 53, 126
Arnold, Matthew, 195–96
Atkinson, David, 21
Aytoun, William Edmondstoune
   Book of Ballads, 111
   Lays of the Scottish Cavaliers, 110–12

Baillie, Joanna
   The Family Legend, 59–62, 63
   Gothic style, 50
   Orra, 24
Baldick, Chris, *Tales of Terror*, 66, 67

Balfour, Graham, 194
ballad culture, 18–19, 20–23, 25
   see also Scott, Walter
ballads
   imitation and experimentation, 19, 23–25, 111
   supernatural, 56
   Whistle-binkie, 76, 108–10
Ballantine, James, 109
Ballantyne, Robert Michael, 145
Am Bard MacGilleain. *see* MacGilleain, Iain
Bàrd Thighearna Chola. *see* MacGilleain, Iain
Barrie, J. M., 156, 157
   Auld Licht Idylls and *A Window in Thrums*, 184–87, 216
   correspondence, 194
   film adaptations, 159
   international market and, 191
   Peter Pan, 204
Bernstein, Marion, 168–69
biographies, 75–78, 101, 129–30, 194
   see also life writing; memoirs
Black, William, 127, 151
Blackie, John Stuart, 176, 198
Blackwood, William, 6, 65

276 INDEX

Blackwood stories. *see* Hogg, James
Blackwood's Edinburgh Magazine, 6, 34, 38, 50, 156, 199
   Aytoun's writings, 111
   George III, funeral account, 51–52
   Oliphant's writings, 135
   pro-slavery arguments, 8
   short stories, 65–66, 67–71
   social commentary, 100
   as Tory, 73
   travel writing, 52
Blair, Hugh, 51
Blind Aleck, 110
Bochanan, Dùghall (Dugald Buchanan), 9
Bogle, Robert, 39
border ballad, notion of the, 20, 23
Brewster, David, 86
British Empire, Scots and, 141, 145
Brougham, Henry, 86
Brown, Ian, 192–93
Brown, Samuel, 'Itinerating Library', 86
Brown, Stewart J., 94
Brunton, Mary, 42–43
   background, 46
   Discipline, 47
   Emmeline, 47
   Self-Control, 46
   travel writing, 47
Buchan, David, 20, 21
Buchan, John, 191
   John Macnab, 151
Burke, Edmund, 52
Burns, Robert, 19–20, 50
Byron, Lord
   as celebrity author, 42

Childe Harold's Pilgrimage, 44
Don Juan, 24, 42
Gothic style, 52
life writing, 44–45

Caird, Edward, 89
Caird, Mona
   New Woman writings, 211–12
   women's suffrage, 210
Calder, Angus, 93, 94
Calderón de la Barca, Frances, 144–45
Campbell, John, fourth Earl of Breadalbane, 12
'Captain Glen', 23
Carlyle, Thomas, 76
   Irving and, 95
   Letters and Memorials of Jane Welsh Carlyle, 81–82
   Reminiscences, 80–81
   social commentary, 100, 101, 102–03
Carmichael, Alison Stewart, 143
Carrick, John Donald, 109
Carruthers, Gerard, 78, 108, 197
Celtic Revival/Celticism, 193–202
   and Scottish nationalism, 197, 198
censorship, 58
Chalmers, Thomas, *Discourses on the Christian Revelation*, 94
Chambers, Robert
   Chambers's Edinburgh Journal, 89, 156
   Chambers's Encyclopaedia, 89
   Vestiges of the Natural History of Creation, 74, 88, 89
Chambers, William, *Chambers's Edinburgh Journal*, 74
Church of Scotland, 50

Citizen newspaper, 163–65
city poems, 162–69
Clan Campbells, 10
clanship, decline of, 9
Clarke, Norma, 82
Clearances, 150, 151
 narratives, 153–54
 and nostalgic poetry, 179
Cochrane, Thomas, 143
Cockburn, Henry, *Memorials*, 8, 78–80
Collins, Wilkie, 128
colonial romance, 36–37, 39
colonialism, 158, 192
comic songs, 20
Conan Doyle, Arthur, 191, 203, 206–07
Constable, Archibald, 64, 65, 73
copyright laws, and piracy, 189–91
Covenanters, 56, 183
Craig, Cairns, 2, 199, 204
Creighton, Mrs, 'A Collection of Old Songs', 22
Crockett, S. R.
 Cleg Kelly, 184
 The Raiders, 183–84
 Scots vernacular, 127
 serialisations, 184
 The Stickit Minister, 183, 184
crofters and crofting, 154, 174, 179
Cuairtear nan Gleann (*Traveller of the Glens*), 73, 74
Cunningham, Allan, *Sir Marmaduke Maxwell*, 24

Darwin, Charles, *On the Origins of Species*, 88
Davidson, John
 Ballads and Songs, 167–68
 Eclogues, 167

Devine, T. M., *The Scottish Clearances*, 141, 151
diaspora, Scottish
 extent of, 141
 and Gaelic literature, 115–24
 newspapers, 157
Dick, Thomas, *The Christian Philosopher*, 88
Dickens, Charles, 114, 181
Disruption of the Scottish Church (1843), 88, 93–94, 155
Dixie, Florence Caroline, 147, 204
Dodds, Thomas, 163–64
Donaldson, William, 19, 126
dramatisations, 58–63
Dughallach, Ailean (Allan MacDougall), 12–15
 elegy for Cameron of Fassiefern, 14
 Orain Ghaidhealacha, 13
 'Oran do na Ciobairibh Gallda' ('*Song to the Lowland Shepherds*'), 14
 panegyric code, 13–14
 subscriptions, 14–15
Duncan, Ian, 50, 56
Dundee People's Journal, 74, 76, 127, 157, 162

Edinburgh
 Celticism, 197, 199
 New Town, 48
 School of Arts, 86–87
 Theatre Royal, 58, 62–63
Edinburgh Encyclopaedia, 86
Edinburgh Review, 6, 8, 65, 73, 86, 100, 101
education
 Gaelic and, 157, 176–77
 Gaelic schools, 7

education (*cont.*)
   parish schools, 87, 100
   self-education, 85–87, 104–06
   of women, 105–06
electromagnetic science, 206–07, 208
Eliot, George, 136
Eliot, T. S., 199
Ellis, Stewart M., 134
emigration, 32, 141
   see also diaspora
Encyclopaedia Britannica, 85–86
Encyclopaedia Perthensis, 86
energy physics, 206, 209
   see also physics
Enlightenment, Scottish, 26, 142, 203–04
epic, 19, 20
Episcopal Church schools, 87
ether, 205, 208
Evangelicalism, 94
evolutionary biology, 88, 89
Eyre, E. J., Scott adaptation, 59, 62–63
Eyre-Todd, George, 166, 167

fantasy fiction, 96, 127
Farcharson, Gilleasbuig (Archibald Farquharson), 176
feminism
   in fiction writing, 204
   New Woman writings, 211
   proto-feminism, 74
Ferrier, Susan, 42–43
   Destiny: or, the Chief's Daughter, 45
   The Inheritance, 8, 45
   Marriage, 45–46
films, adaptations, 159
Fraser's Magazine, 39

Frazer, J. G., 85, 204
   The Golden Bough, 199, 200, 201
Free Church
   formation, 88, 93, 155
   General Assembly, 85
   popular literature and, 94
   schools and colleges, 85, 87
   Union and, 177
Free Church College, Aberdeen, 85
free trade, 143
Freer, Walter, 169

Gaelic (language), education system, 157, 176–77
Gaelic critics, 1
Gaelic journals, 7, 73–75, 120
   Glasgow, 73–74, 119, 123–24, 156–57
   transnationalism, 157
Gaelic Society of Inverness, 175
Galt, John, 8–9, 75, 101
   Annals of the Parish, 31, 153
   The Ayrshire Legatees, 52, 56
   Bogle Corbet, 31–32, 39–41
   The Covenanters, 56
   pro-slavery, 39
   Scottish Gothic, 56
   short stories, 66
Garth, David, Stewart of, 150
Geddes, Patrick, 158, 197–98
geology, 88, 89, 90–91, 150
George III, funeral, account of, 51–52
George IV, 'the King's Jaunt', 148
Gladstone, William, 154
Glasgow
   Citizen newspaper, 163–65

Gaelic journals, 73
Glasgow Weekly Mail, 168
newspaper novels, 127
periodical press, 7
Glengarry, Alexander Ranaldson Macdonell, 12–14
Good Works, 88
Gordon Cumming, Constance Frederica, 146–47
Gothic, 50, 51–55, 57, 209
Grace Darling, 128–31
Graham, Maria, 142–43
Grant, Anne, 142
Grant, Elizabeth, *Memoirs of a Highland Lady*, 43, 47–49
Grant, James
  diverse genre-writing, 132
  historical fiction, 133–34, 138
  Old and New Edinburgh, 139
  representation of the writing life, 134–35
Gray, Alasdair, 70
Gribben, Crawford, 57

Hamilton, Janet
  city poet, 168
  Sketches of Village Life and Character, 101
  social and political commentary, 101, 105–06
Harper & Brothers (publishers), 190
Hazlitt, William, 53–54, 55
Herd, David, *Ancient and Modern Songs*, 19–20
Herder, Johann Gottfried, 19
heroic ballads, 20
Highland culture
  idealisation of, 83
  see also travel writing
Highland 'holiday' narratives, 151–52
Highland regiments, 174–76
Highland societies, 118–19
Highland Society of Scotland, 11, 16
Highlandism, romantic, 149, 150
Highlands
  myths, and revivalism, 199, 200
  travel writing, 148–55
  see also Clearances
historical fiction, 26–29, 31–32, 57
historical progress, stadial history and, 30–31
Hogg, James
  Blackwood stories, 67–71
  Jacobite Songs, 23
  'Lord William, 24
  persona as the Ettrick Shepherd, 70
  Private Memoirs and Confessions of a Justified Sinner, 29, 57, 72
  A Queer Book, 24
  Romantic cult of the author, 51
  romanticised history, 26
  Scottish Gothic, 50
  Spy stories, 64–65, 67
  'Surpassing Adventures of Allan Gordon', 29–30, 31
Hudson Bay company, 35
Hughes, Gillian, 64, 67
Hume, David, 51
Hutton, James, *Theory of the Earth*, 88

imperialism, 31–32
  see also British Empire

industrial novels and biographies, 101
see also city poems
Irish Revival, 197
Irving, Edward, 93, 98–99
  The Coming of Messiah (translation), 95

Jacobites and Jacobite songs, 9, 20, 23, 34
Jamieson, Robert, 'Water Kelpie', 24
Jeffrey, Francis, 6, 8, 73, 78
Johnson, James, *Scots Musical Museum*, 19, 108
Johnstone, Christian Isobel, 74
journals
  Gaelic, 7, 73–75, 119, 120
  see also Gaelic journals; periodicals; *individual names of journals and periodicals*

'Kailyard' literature, 158, 161, 180, 184
Krueger, Kate, 215

land protests
  poetry of, 171–74
  see also Clearances; crofters and crofting
Lang, Andrew, 199, 204
language movement, 157, 176–77
Laurie, John, 114
Leask, Nigel, 141
Leng, John, 74, 76, 127, 157
letters. *see* life writing
Leyden, John, 'The Mermaid', 23–24
libraries, 86, 93, 98, 162

life writing, 42, 43–45, 75–76, 77–84
literacy rates, 86
Livingston, William (Uilleam MacDhunleibhe), 118–19, 178
Lockhart, J. G., biography of Scott, 75–76, 77–78
Lowlands, 115, 151, 198
  see also Glasgow
Lyell, Charles, 74, 89, 90–91
  Principles of Geology, 88
lyric, in Scottish song culture, 19

Mac a' Ghobhainn, Iain (John Smith), 'Spiorad a Charthannais', 171–72, 174–75, 178
Mac an t-Saoir, Donnchadh Ban, 10–12, 17
mac Fhearchair, Iain (John MacCodrum), 9
mac Mhaighstir Alasdair, Alasdair, 10
mac Mhurchaidh, Iain (John MacRae), 159
MacAoidh, Rob Donn (Rob Donn MacKay), 9
Macaulay, Thomas Babington, *Lays of Ancient Rome*, 110–11
MacCaluim, Dòmhnall (Rev. Donald MacCallum), 173–74
MacCoinnich, Iain, 13
MacColla, Eòghann
  The Mountain Minstrel, 75
  Song in praise, 119
Macculloch, John, *Highlands and Western Isles*, 150–51, 155
MacDhòmhnaill, Ailean (Allan MacDonald/Allan the Ridge), 120

'Moladh Albainn Nuaidh' ('*In Praise of Nova Scotia*'), 121
MacDhòmhnaill, Iain (Iain Sealgair), 'Oran do dh'America' ('*Song to America*'), 121, 122
MacDhùghaill, Iain (John MacDougall), 117–18
MacDhùghaill, Raibeart (Robert MacDougall)
  Gaelic emigrant guide, 119
  Tomas Seannsair (*Tam o' Shanter*), 119–20
MacDhunlèibhe, Uilleam (William Livingston), 118–19, 178
MacDonald, George, 98–99, 127
  fiction with a theological function, 96–97, 159
  Lilith: A Romance, 208–09
  Phantastes, 96, 204
  The Portent, 93
  Robert Falconer, 95
  Thomas Wingfold, 96
MacDonalds of Sleat, 6
Macfarlan, James, 164, 165–67
MacGilleain, Iain (John MacLean), 15–17, 123–24
  'Do Thighearna Chola' ('*To the Laird of Coll*'), 16–17
  Nova Scotian verse, 17
  Orain Nuadh Ghaedhlach, 16
  'Oran do dh'Alasdair MacGilleain' ('*Song to Alexander Maclean*'), 16
MacGillÌosa, Iain (John Gillies), *Lament for the Adversity of the Gaels*, 122–23
MacGregor, John
  Rob Roy canoe series, 144
  travel writing, 143–44
MacGregor, Rev. Alexander, 75
Macintyre, Joseph, Rev., 11
Mackenzie, Alexander, 154
Mackenzie, John (Iain MacCoinnich), 13
MacLachlainn, Dr Iain (John MacLachlan), 117, 158
  'Dan do'n Chubhaig' (Song to the Cuckoo), 75
MacLachlainn, Eòghann (Ewen MacLachlan), 15
Maclaren, Ian (Rev. John Watson)
  Drumtochty sketches, 180–82
  other fictional modes, 182
Maclean, Alexander, 15th Laird of Coll, 15–16
Macleod, Donald, 154
Macleod, Fiona (William Sharp), 197, 198, 199, 200–01
MacLeòid, Murchadh (Murdo, son of the Catechist), 177
MacLeòid, Niall, 158, 177
MacLeòid, Tormod (Rev. Dr Norman MacLeod), 7, 116
  Reminiscences, 153–54
MacPhaidein, Iain (John MacFadyen), 158, 175
'Macphail of Colonsay', 23–24
Macpherson, James, 5, 19, 50, 201
MacPherson, Mary. *see* Nic a' Phearsain, Màiri
MacQueen, James, 34, 38
magazines, and short stories, 70
  see also journals; periodicals
magic realism, 69
Màiri Mhòr nan Òran (Big Mary of the Songs). *see* Nic a' Phearsain, Màiri
Manlove, Colin, 209

Marly; or a Planter's Life in Jamaica, 34, 36–37
marriage
    in Ferrier's storylines, 45–46
    New Woman writings, 211, 213–16
Martin, Sir Theodore, 111
Maxwell, James Clerk, 204, 205, 209
    'Maxwell's demon', 91, 92
McGonagall, William
    critique and reviews of, 113–14
    Poetic Gems, 112
    'The Rattling Boy from Dublin', 113
    'The Tay Bridge Disaster', 114
McLennan, 204
McNeil, Kenneth, 39, 83
McQueen, William, 127
Mechanics Institutes, 86–87
Meek, Donald, 1, 161
Melgun, Lord, 87
memoirs, 42–43
    Highlands, 153
    posthumous, 78–82
    Queen Victoria's, 82–84
    see also life writing; *individual names of authors*
Menzies, Robert, 17
military, 16, 17, 174–76
Miller, Hugh
    Cruise of the Betsey, 155
    Footprints of the Creator, 87, 90
    imaginative literature and, 91
    My Schools and Schoolmasters, 87
    The Old Red Sandstone, 87
    reconciliation of science and religion, 90
    and *Witness* newspaper, 87–88
Miller, Lydia, *Passages in the Life of an English Heiress*, 94
Milne, Robert Duncan, 207–08
Morgan, Jennifer L., 33
Morrison, Robert, *Tales of Terror*, 66, 67
Motherwell, William, 109, 110
Muir, Edwin, 1
Muir, John, 147
Munroe, Donald, 171
Murray, John, 44, 45
Murray, W. H., 63
mutual improvement societies, 161
Myles, James, 161–62
myths, and Celtic revivalism, 197, 198–200

Nairne, Lady, 24
Napier Commission (1883), 154–55
narrative ballads, 19
narrative verse, 64
National Drama, 58
national identity, 125, 141, 145, 146–47, 192–93
nationalism, Scottish, 197, 198, 210
    origins of, 125
    religious/cultural, 50, 56–57, 198
    Scottish Gothic and, 50
New Woman writings, 210–16
Newcastle Chronicle, 129–30
newspapers
    Citizen newspaper, 163–65
    Dundee, newspaper hub, 74
    Gaelic, 157
    mass circulation, 157, 159
    New Woman writings, 211

serials, 125–31
  on women's suffrage, 216
Nic a' Phearsain, Màiri (Mary MacPherson), 174, 176, 179
  'Oran Beinn Li', 172–73
  satirical elegy, 173
NicEalair, Màiri (Mary MacKellar), 175–76
Nicholson, Angus, *An Gaidheal*, 157
Nicoll, William Robertson
  British Weekly, 156
  reminiscence literature, 157–58
nostalgia, 117, 180, 181
Nova Scotia, 17
novels, newspaper. *see* newspapers, serials

occultism. *see* spiritualism and occultism
Oliphant, Margaret, 70, 75, 95, 128, 143
  Autobiography, 135, 136
  Blackwood's articles, 135
  diverse genre-writing, 132, 157
  fiction-writing, 135, 137–39
Ossian poems, 5, 151, 201

Pae, David, newspaper serials, 125–31
  Grace Darling, 128–31
panegyric code, 9–10, 16, 123–24, 175
pastoral literature, 20, 161
Patent houses, 63
patronage, 6, 12–14
  Gaelic societies and, 118–19
  new networks of, 10, 11
  traditional, 15, 17

patter song, 110
penny weekly magazines, 126
People's Friend, 184, 214
People's Journal. *see Dundee People's Journal*
periodicals, 6, 7, 8, 66, 115–16, 143, 153, 184
  see also Gaelic journals; individual names of journals
physics, 87, 204–05, 209
  see also electromagnetic science; thermodynamics
Pinkerton, James, 109
Pliny the Elder, 201
Poe, Edgar Allan, 71, 203
Porter, Jane
  The Scottish Chiefs, 27
  Thaddeus of Warsaw, 26–27
Prebble, John, 154
Presbyterianism, 50, 56, 177
  see also religious themes
Prince, Mary, 37–38, 40
Pringle, Thomas
  Gothic style, 52
  History of Mary Prince, 34, 37–38
prose dialogue (còmhradh), 116
psychology, 207
public education. *see* education; individual names of schools and colleges
publication, industrious, Oliphant and Grant, 133, 134–35, 138

Quarterly Review, 6, 28

Radcliffe, Ann, 52
Ramsay, Allan, 19
re-composition, 21

religion. *see* Free Church; Presbyterianism; Roman Catholic Church; scriptural literalists
religious themes
   denominational schism, 177–78
   in *Jekyll and Hyde*, 206
   MacDonald's fiction, 96–97, 159
   Maclaren's fiction, 182
   Pae's serial, 130–31
   popular religion and literature, 94–99
   Scottish Gothic, 50, 54, 55
reminiscence literature, 157–58
   see also 'Kailyard' literature
Rhys, Ernest, 198, 201
Riddell, Robert, *Collection of Scottish Antiquities*, 22
Ritson, Joseph, 20
Robertson, Fiona, 55
Robertson, John, 109
Robertson, Rev. William, 51
Rodger, Alexander, 109
Roman Catholic Church, 87, 94
romance, critique of, 29–30
romantic historical novels, 26–29, 31–32
Romanticism, 51, 78
Ros, Uilleam (William Ross), 9
An Rosroine (*The Rose of the Field*), 7
Russell, George, 197

Sage, Rev. Donald, 154
Sassi, Carla, 143
science fiction, 68, 159, 203, 206–08
Scots language, 24, 58

Scott, Walter, 48
   The Antiquary, 28, 53–54, 72
   ballad collecting, 5
   biography of, 75–76
   as celebrity author, 42
   correspondence, 43, 46–47, 60, 61
   death of, 76
   as editor, 22, 61
   on Ferrier, 45
   Glengarry and, 12
   Guy Mannering, 53
   The Heart of Mid-Lothian, 55
   on Highland society, 26
   on Highland tourism, 148
   Highlandism of, 149, 150, 151
   Ivanhoe, 52–53
   Journal, 43–44
   The Lady of the Lake, 59, 62–63, 64, 148, 149, 152
   Lay of the Last Minstrel, 24
   legacy and influence, 133, 134, 138
   Marmion, 7, 24, 64
   mass tourism and, 150
   Minstrelsy of the Scottish Border (ballads), 18–19, 20–23, 24, 64
   The Pirate, 28–29, 30
   short stories, 66–67
   St Ronan's Well, 28
   Tales, 54–55, 56
   Waverley, 5, 7–8, 26, 27–28, 53, 66
   Waverley, theatre adaptations, 58
Scottish Revival, 197
Scribner, Charles, 190–91
scriptural literalists, 89, 90
Seacole, Mary, 140–41

Wonderful Adventures of Mrs Seacole, 145–46
secularisation, 51
self-education, 85–87, 104–06
serialisation, 94, 137
    New Woman, 214–16
    newspaper, 125–31
    periodicals/journals, 52, 74, 184
Shand, Alexander Innes, 137–38
Sharp, William, 158, 196, 198, 200–01
    see also Macleod, Fiona
Sharpe, Charles Kirkpatrick
    Ballad Book, 22–23
    correspondence with Scott, 23
Shelley, Mary, 203
short stories, 64–71
Siddons, Henry, 58–59, 60, 63
Simms, William Gilmore, 71
Sinclair, Archibald, 115
Sinclair, Catherine, 93, 98–99
    Beatrice, 98
    Holiday House: A Book for the Young, 97
    Modern Accomplishments, 97–98
    Modern Society, 98
sin-eating, 200
slaves, slavery
    and abolitionism, 34, 142–43, 154
    kinship networks, 33, 38
    slave-capital and kinship, 35, 40, 41
    West India lobby, 38–39
Smiles, Samuel
    industrial biographies, 101
    Self-Help, 86, 103–04
Smith, Adam, 143
Smith, Alexander, 167
    City Poems, 164–65
    A Summer in Skye, 151, 152–53
Smith, William Robertson, 85, 88, 92
social class
    Hamilton's perspective, 105–06
    land protests, 171
    New Woman writings and, 211, 215
    see also working class
social commentary
    Carlyle, 102–03
    Hamilton, 105–06
    role of poet in, 115
    Smiles, 103–04
Society for Psychical Research, 207
Society for the Diffusion of Useful Knowledge (SDUK)
    Library of Useful Knowledge, 86
    Penny Cyclopedia, 86
speculative fiction, 203, 206–08, 209
Spence, Catherine, 204
Spence, Thomas, 34
spiritualism and occultism, 205–06, 207, 209
Spy, The (periodical), 64–65, 67
Statistical Accounts of Scotland, 153
Steel, Flora Annie
    New Woman writings, 212–14
    women's suffrage, 210, 211
Stevenson, Robert Louis, 70, 186
    biographies of, 194
    essays, 190, 193
    fiction-writing, 159

Stevenson, Robert Louis (*cont.*)
   Footnote to History, 192
   influences, 192
   Kidnapped, 190, 194
   national identity, 192–93
   New Arabian Nights, 189
   Strange Case of Dr Jekyll and Mr Hyde, 189, 203, 204, 206
   travel writing, 147, 189–90, 192
   Travels with a Donkey in the Cévennes, 189–90
   Treasure Island, 145, 188–89
Stewart, Balfour, *The Unseen Universe*, 91–92, 205–06, 208
Stowe, Harriet Beecher, 154
subscriptions, 11–12, 14–15
suffragette movement, 210, 214, 216
supernatural, 51, 56
Swan, Annie S., 210, 211
   New Woman writings, 214–16

Tait, Peter Guthrie, 88
   The Unseen Universe, 91–92, 205–06, 208
Tait's Edinburgh Magazine, 74
'Tale of the Wreck of the Forfarshire', Pae's retelling, 128–31
tartan, regimental, 175–76
An Teachdaire Gae'lach (*The Highland Messenger*), 7
An Teachdaire Ur Gaidhealach (*The New Highland Messenger*), 75
theatre adaptations, 58–63
thermodynamics, 88, 91, 204–05
Thomson, Derick, 10
Thomson, William (Lord Kelvin), 88, 91, 204–05

Thornton, Colonel Thomas, 151
tourism, 144, 148, 149, 150, 151
travel writing/writers, 43, 44, 47, 56, 140–55
   genre and sub-genres, 142–46
   Highlands, 148–55
   imperial and national identities, 146–47
   marginalisation, 142, 145
Turner, Patrick, Gaelic song collection, 6

Union, Acts of (1707), 141
union of the crowns (1603), 125
universities, Scottish, 100

Verne, Jules, 203
Vernon, Jerrold, 129–30
Victoria, Queen, Highland Journals, 82–84, 152

W. & R. Chambers, 89
Wallace-Sanders, Kimberly, 40
Walpole, Horace, 52
Ward, James, 85
Waterloo, Battle of, 14, 174–75
Watson, John (*pen-name* Ian Maclaren), 157
Watson, Norman, 114
Watt, Christian, 152
Watt, James, 87
Waverley. see Scott, Walter
Wedderburn, James, 34, 37
Wedderburn, Robert
   Horrors of Slavery, 34, 35–36
   portrayal of his enslaved mother, 37
Wedderburn, Sir John, 34
Wedderburn-Colville, Andrew, 35
Welsh Carlyle, Jane, 81–82

West India lobby, 38–39
Whigs, 8, 79
Whistle-binkie (folk-song collection), 76, 108–10
Williams, Daniel G., 195
Wilson, John, 66
Witness newspaper, 87–88, 155
women
    city poets, 168–69
    evangelical poetry, 177
    New Woman writings, 210–16
    political protests, 172–73
    social commentary, 104, 105–06
    travel writers, 140–43, 145–46
    see also individual names of women writers
work, and women. *see* New Woman writings
working class
    newspaper poets, 163–65
    periodicals and newspapers, 74, 75, 100, 157, 162
    protest and resistance, 36, 109
    self-help, and self-education, 102–06
    writers and collectors, 109, 112
    see also social class

www.ingramcontent.com/pod-product-compliance
Lightning Source LLC
Chambersburg PA
CBHW052103230426
43671CB00011B/1916